Praise for *Cortés and the Downfall of the Aztec Empire*:

"White brings a pleasing style and psychological insight to the re-creation of a brilliant, cruel, kind and just man." —*American Library Association Booklist*

"The author contends that Cortés has been reviled in Mexico and neglected in Spain . . . Excellent writing."—*Library Journal*

"The great merit of this book is that it clears away a large number of misconceptions . . . and preserves a proper sense of proportion."—*Illustrated London News*

CORTÉS
AND THE DOWNFALL
OF THE AZTEC EMPIRE

Jon Manchip White

Carroll & Graf Publishers, Inc.
New York

To
Robert and Teresa
Ricketts

First Carroll & Graf edition 1989

Carroll & Graf Publishers, Inc.
260 Fifth Avenue
New York, NY 10001

ISBN: 0-88184-461-6

Manufactured in the United States of America

Contents

Illustrations

The illustrations are grouped in a center section of the book.

Figures

INTRODUCTION

How can one follow W. H. Prescott? The question is bound to haunt anyone who is bidden to write an account of the Conquest of Mexico. Prescott's famous work appeared as long ago as 1843: and to re-read it is to be struck anew by the stature of Prescott's achievement. His book is a true and authentic classic, in the full sense of that abused word. He had all the gifts of the historian. One does not know whether to admire more his learning, industry, insight, or the breadth of his understanding and compassion; but more important, one must admire a super-added ability not given to many historians, yet necessary if their work is to survive as long as *The Conquest of Mexico*: I mean the ability to write lively and sinewy prose. The directness and energy of Prescott's mind have remained undiminished by the years. He had the ability to rise to the occasion, to describe with rare force the scenes of action which were the high-points of his narrative. His book, except in details, has not really been superseded. One marvels the more when one realizes that he not only never visited Mexico, but was almost totally blind when he wrote it; he employed readers in order to undertake his research, and the actual writing was done with the aid of a machine called a noctograph. This handicap did not prevent him from writing biographies of Ferdinand and Isabella, and of Philip II, in addition to his accounts of the Conquests of Mexico and Peru.

There are, of course, other excellent histories of the Conquest of Mexico beside Prescott's. Many of them are glanced at in the following pages. The biographies of Cortés by F. A. McNutt and by the Mexican historian Carlos Peyrera are valuable, also the majestic biography of Salvador de Madariaga; while a standard work on the period is R. B. Merriman's *The Rise of the Spanish Empire in the Old World and the New*. Also to be recommended as fair-minded and readable is Sir Arthur Helps' *The Spanish Conquests in America*. Published in 1855–61, this useful work was reissued in 1966. Other books of a similar character are listed in the bibliography.

Neither Prescott nor the earlier writers could have known of the major developments in pre-Columbian archaeology or Mexican anthropology

that have taken place during the past half-century. Prescott and his con-
temporaries were virtually ignorant of Mexican history prior to the
Aztecs, and were therefore unable to see Aztec civilization in a true
historical perspective. They knew nothing, for example, of the Mayas, for
Stephens and Catherwood and Lord Kingsborough had hardly begun to
publish their researches; Stephens' *Incidents of Travel in Yucatán* only
appeared in the year that *The Conquest of Mexico* was published. It is
possible, then, for a modern writer, if he cannot add a great deal to
Prescott's account of the Conquest itself, to view the Conquest from the
greatly enlarged viewpoint which has resulted from later studies. The
Aztecs have also been subjected, since Prescott's time, to a prolonged
scrutiny of which the modern historian can avail himself.

The modern writer, then, can be permitted to step back a little from
the literal facts and consider his subject in a general light. One is regarding
the issues raised by the Conquest in the larger context of world history.
In this book the dramatic events of the Conquest are described with a close
attention to detail, but where the account may perhaps claim to possess a
certain originality is that it tries to embrace and to balance both the
Spanish and Mexican elements in the Conquest. The majority of books on
conquistadores or Aztecs are predominantly studies of one or the other,
often dealing with the opposing side almost as an afterthought.

The British historian Maitland remarked that historians ought to
remember that 'events which are now in the past were once in the future'.
It is not possible to tease the reader about the outcome of the story; he
will know that the Spaniards won and the Aztecs lost. But I have tried to
remind him that the Conquest was not a walk-over, or in some way pre-
ordained; Cortés and his lieutenants were faced with continuous and
agonizing choices, as were the leaders of the Aztecs. To me, the fascina-
tion of great historical events lies very largely in one's ability to put oneself
in the shoes of the men involved in them. To do this is to appreciate more
keenly their cleverness and courage. The key-word of the present book is
'motivation': the motivation of Cortés, the motivation of Moctezuma or
Cuauhtémoc. To try to fathom a man's motivation is to try to comprehend
his individual character and the character of his culture, country and
century. I take it that one of the principal tasks of the historian is to
describe the interaction of the individual and the flux of events, without
concentrating too much on the one to the detriment of the other. Furthermore, one must risk discussing it in psychological and even philosophical
terms. With many previous factual accounts available, the justification of
one more study of the Conquest is the willingness to break, in modest
measure, a certain amount of fresh ground.

Prescott, a Bostonian gentleman of means, was widely criticized because he was sympathetic to Spain at a time when it was not fashionable to be so. Dedicated democrats like Emerson and the Transcendentalists frowned on his admiration for Cortés, a representative of a nation which was supposed to have been cruel and reactionary. It is still not permissible in some quarters to admire *las cosas de España*, largely because of the Nationalist victory in the Civil War; but such attitudes have become increasingly untenable. The present writer has sought to be objective, but—perhaps as a result of having lived for some years in Spain—he must confess to a partiality for the figure of Hernán Cortés. Prescott was right to eschew a 'democratic' and 'progressive' view of history. As Henry Bamford Parkes has written, in his introduction to an edition of *The Conquest of Mexico*: 'In the long run Prescott's lack of a democratic philosophy has contributed to the enduring value of his works. They have survived far better than those whose works were pervaded with an almost religious faith in the inevitable triumph of democracy.' To view the achievements and aspirations of such men as Cortés through democratic spectacles is to distort them ludicrously. Cortés has suffered severely in the past century at the hands of hostile propagandists, and it seems time to redress the balance. This can be done by trying to place *conquistadores* and Amerindians more accurately within the context of their time. Again, it is a question of motivations, the writer's preoccupation with which will, I hope, become clear in the pages that ensue.

I have drawn on a wide variety of sources, both Spanish and Mexican; but the reader will notice that I have used three more frequently than the rest. These are the *Historia verdadera* of Bernal Díaz del Castillo, the *Historia de la Conquista* of Francisco López de Gómara, and the Despatches of Cortés. I have featured them prominently because they are exceptionally earthy and compelling and are based on the testimony of actual eye-witnesses. Few outstanding events in history can have been so graphically covered as the Conquest. Bernal Díaz's veracity has never been questioned, and the fact that the blunt old veteran was disgruntled with Cortés yet revered him nonetheless only adds flavour to his wonderful narrative. Francisco López de Gómara has been unduly disparaged because he pretended to write a history of the Conquest which was really a laudatory biography of Cortés, whose secretary he was. His latest editor and translator wisely calls his edition 'The Life of the Conqueror by his Secretary', which puts it in better perspective. Its style is graceful, lively, and has a nice touch of irony—the marks of the style of Cortés himself, as revealed in his Despatches. Nor was Gómara above criticizing and even castigating his employer when occasion demanded; the Spaniards of that time were not much given to self-deception and Victorian-type humbug, a trait which makes their Golden Age so absorbing and entertaining to read about. One should use the testimony of Gómara and Cortés with circumspection, but their evidence on most major issues rings true. Together, these three books provide a splendidly vigorous portrayal of the events in question.

It seems unnecessary to re-translate these and other works of which first-rate modern translations exist. I have used Lesley Byrd Simpson's translation of Gómara, J. M. Cohen's of the major portion of Bernal Díaz, and Blacker and Rosen's version of the Despatches. For the minor authorities, I have made my own translations from the Spanish, or from Spanish renderings of prose and poetry in Náhuatl. In particular I have made extensive use of Sánchez-Barba's definitive edition of Cortés' Despatches and letters. At times I have taken the liberty of touching up a word or two here and there in the existing translations, in the interests of the flow of my own narrative; I am sure the translators concerned will not take this occasional rearrangement as a reflection on their own excellent editions.

In the interests of my narrative, I have also eliminated individual notes and references. I have incorporated in the text the name and author of the work referred to, and listed these works in the bibliography, which is comprehensive. Similarly, I have simplified and standardized where necessary the names of Mexican gods and Mexican towns, and the names of such persons as Moctezuma and Cuauhtémoc, most of which have been rendered over the years in a dozen ways. I have used the forms which seem authoritative and easily identifiable. In the case of Moctezuma and Cuauhtémoc, these are the forms currently used in Mexico itself. I have also employed *Hernán* for the first name of Cortés, as having a better claim than *Hernando* or *Fernando*. For the sake of consistency, I have adhered thereafter to the chosen form throughout the book, quotations included. Having adopted the form *Huitzilopochtli*, for example, I believe it would only confuse the reader if he were to meet it at other points as *Uitzilopochtli*, *Huichilobos*, or in such eccentric guises as Madariaga's *Witchywolves*. Nor is there any point, having settled on *Moctezuma* and *Cuauhtémoc*, in reverting later to *Montezuma* or *Motecuzohma, Guatemoczin* or *Guatemozin*. Finally, it is perhaps worth mentioning that when the *conquistadores* and early historians spoke of Mexico, they meant not the present country of Mexico but the territory ruled by the Mexica-Aztecs, or sometimes Mexico City. 'The march to Mexico' signified 'the march to Mexico City'. Later, by extension, the word came to possess its modern connotation; but originally its meaning was restricted. I have used the name Tenochtitlán for Mexico City until the latter part of the book, when Tenochtitlán was destroyed by desperate siege and the new capital of Mexico City rose on its ruins.

By chance, this book, commissioned in Europe, came to be written in a house on the Mexican-American border, a mile from the Río Grande. When I was engaged on it, I had only to lift my head to see, towering above the river, the mountains of Mexico, one of them surmounted by a glittering silver Cross. It would be impossible for me to list all the many friends in Texas and Mexico who have rendered my task easier. In Texas, I must mention my colleagues at the University of Texas at El Paso and Mrs. Virginia Lawrence Ehmann, who typed a long and difficult manuscript; and in Mexico, Don Pablo Romero Bush, the noted Mexican archaeological organizer, and Mr. Fergus Dempster, Counsellor at the British Embassy in Mexico City. Mr. and Mrs. Dempster, old friends from Madrid days, were the hosts of my wife and me in Mexico City while I was engaged on this work. I also owe a special debt of gratitude to the Conde Tomás Jesús Bolé de Paduca. To Mr. Christopher Sinclair-Stevenson, of my London publishers, I must extend, once again, my profound thanks for his help and for his altogether exceptional patience and good humour.

PART ONE

HERNÁN CORTÉS

> *'A man resembles the time he lives in more closely than he resembles his own father.'*
>
> *Arab Proverb*

I

i tan buen dia por la cristiandad
ca fuyen los moros della e della part!

What a great day for Christendom when the
Moors are driven out from every part!

Poema del Cid

HERNÁN CORTÉS, foremost of the line of Spanish *conquistadores* and
fundadores, was born in 1485 in the small and obscure town of Medellín
in the province of Extremadura. When he was born Columbus had not yet
planted the banner of the Catholic Kings on the soil of the Caribbean
islands. When he died, sixty-two years later, the Spanish flag flew over six
thousand miles of American territory from the Río Grande in the north
to the Río de la Plata in the south.

The story of Spain's seizure and subjugation of such vast regions within
a single generation is one of the most vivid and remarkable in history.
In view of its deep and lasting influence on the life and culture of a major
portion of the globe, it is also one of the most important. The Spanish
conquest would have taken place in any case, with or without the participation of Cortés; but his extraordinary character lends a distinctive
colouring to the unfolding of that dramatic event. The destinies of many
millions of people, on two huge continents, over the course of four and a
half centuries, have been profoundly affected not only by the mistakes and
miscalculations he made but also by his courage, compassion, independence and individuality, and by the workings of his clear and brilliant
intelligence. In the last analysis, as Treitschke pointed out, history is
made by men. Hernán Cortés was very much a man. Indeed, he was more
than a man—he was a hero: one of those inspired and inspiring beings
who, as André Malraux puts it in his *Les Voix du Silence*, expresses our
highest values and represents our highest form of defence: 'Each hero,
saint or sage stands for a victory over the human situation.' If the
conveying of the Western and Christian presence to the New World
was a turning point in human affairs, then the forces that shape human

ends found, for once, a noble and worthy instrument to bring it about.

*   *   *

The circumstances of his birth were not at first glance conducive to a heroic career. Medellín was a little insignificant walled town, situated in a distant, sparsely inhabited and largely infertile corner of New Castile. His parents were of respectable lineage without belonging to the true aristocracy. Fray Bartolomé de Las Casas, the Dominican reformer who admired Cortés personally while detesting what he thought Cortés stood for, would grant him no more than that 'he was the son of a squire of my acquaintance, a man who was impoverished and of modest station, but a good Christian and reputed to be of noble blood'. His secretary and chaplain, Francisco López de Gómara, spoke out more positively. 'His father and mother were both noble, for the four lines of Cortés, Monroy, Pizarro and Altamirano are very ancient, noble and honourable. They had little wealth but much honour, and their neighbours respected them for their goodness and piety.'

His father, Martín Cortés de Monroy, could adequately be described as a somewhat penurious country gentleman. He was a stranger to Medellín, for his family came from Salamanca, but he was stubbornly loyal to the cause of his adoptive Extremadura. Thus he actually had the temerity to take up arms against Queen Isabella on behalf of the order of Alcántara, which owned approximately half of Extremadura, and whose right to appoint its own Master had been removed from it by royal edict. Martin Cortés was the leader of a troop of horse in this episode, so he was accustomed to command. He must also have possessed intelligence, for in later years he often acted as his son's surrogate and agent at the court of Charles V. However, as Salvador de Madariaga has noted, it is interesting that Gómara does not bestow on him the prefix of 'Don', although his wife is referred to as *Doña* Catalina Pizarro Altamirano. It was therefore Hernán's mother, daughter of the majordomo of the countess of Medellín, who would appear to have possessed the more elevated ancestry. It also appears likely that it was Doña Catalina who brought her husband the meagre income they derived from a few properties, together with the proceeds from the sale of a little wine, wheat and honey. Poor though they were, there is no doubt that parents and son were devoted to each other, and that this devotion survived the inevitable discords of adolescence. After his father's death, Cortés prevailed upon his mother to sell her home in Medellín and join him in America.

The future *conquistador*, then, was brought up in somewhat spartan surroundings, and spent his boyhood in simple country pursuits. Gómara tells us that as a child 'he was so frail that many times he was on the point of dying'; but eventually he grew into a hale and virile youngster and developed the constitution needed to survive the inhuman hardships of the campaigns in Central America. Except for a little information given us by Gómara, cautiously fed to him by his employer, we know little about the early years in Medellín. This was not only because Gómara was anxious to plunge straight into the part of his narrative he knew would most interest contemporary readers, the conquest of the Aztecs: it was also because Cortés was an exceedingly prudent and reticent man. He lived in an age when to open one's mouth too wide was to invite trouble. He was a born diplomat, and though he was by no means taciturn or uncommunicative, it was his nature to be discreet. For a man who became one of the most prominent men of his age, a man about whom all Europe was immensely curious, we possess very few personal details. He succeeded at an early age in perfecting a bland and urbane but extremely private persona. Indeed, his complete control of his emotions, under every condition of stress and provocation, was largely responsible for his success. Some of the details we do possess are highly entertaining—scandalous and mildly scabrous. They whet our appetite for more. They reveal clearly that Cortés, for all his self-control, was anything but a cold fish; on the contrary, in his own individual way he was warm-blooded and richly humorous, passionately involved with every aspect of human existence. A curious mixture: a man compounded of fire and ice. But he was no self-confessor. In spite of their great air of frankness and honesty, his magnificent dispatches from the New World are as interesting for what he leaves out as for what he puts in. 'The truth about a man,' Malraux has written in his *Antimemoirs*, 'lies first and foremost in what he hides.' Unfortunately, Cortés concealed himself so capably that we will never know much of the inner truth about him. However, Malraux goes on to observe: 'We know how Stendhal loved minor details about the great: but why not major ones too? To re-create the Napoleon of Austerlitz is at least as worthwhile as to reveal his habit of smearing his son's face with jam.' So it is with Cortés. It would be interesting to be better informed about his personal proclivities and peccadilloes, to be able to be sly and patronizing about him, to cut him down to size, to explain, emasculate and democratize him. But as Hegel insisted, nations and men are what their deeds are: and the deed of Spain at the epoch of which we speak was to conquer the New World, and the deed of Hernán Cortés was to conquer it for Spain. It is also possible that, if he had lacked that element of the enigmatic, that touch of secretiveness and *diablerie*, the story of the defeat of the Aztecs would lose some of its savour. Their cousins the Incas were unfortunate, in more ways than one, in that they were crushed by a freebooter as brutal and obvious as Pizarro.

*   *   *

If Cortés was an unusual man, it was because he entered the world at an unusual time. Nothing that happens in Spain is ever humdrum: but the last quarter of the fifteenth century was a prodigious period even for Spain. Ortega y Gasset, in his *Man and Crisis*, asserts that 'the fifteenth is the most complicated and enigmatic century in all European history, up to our own day', and adds that 'he who does not understand the fifteenth century well, understands nothing of what has happened since'. He continues: 'The fifteenth century is the period of *the* historic crisis, the only true crisis thus far suffered by the new peoples of the west, those who surged out of another crisis, much older and graver, much more catastrophic, the crisis in which the culture of the ancient world succumbed. The peculiar complexity of the fifteenth century comes from two causes. The first cause is that life within it, like life in all its crises, is at its very root a dual existence. On the one hand is the persistence of medieval life, which still lives, or we may better say, survives. On the other hand is the obscure germination of new life. Two contradictory movements meet and collide in every one of those *quattrocento* men; medieval man falls like a skyrocket consumed and already ash. But out from this falling and inert ash there breaks forth a new rocket recently fired and mounting, pure heavenly vigour, pure fire, the energetic though confused beginning of a new type of living, of modern living. The shock between the dead and living which is produced in mid air results in the most varied combinations.'

Because of its isolated geographical situation and the obstinate individuality of its character, Spain has often been tardy in experiencing great cultural movements which have already become well advanced elsewhere in Europe. The Middle Ages lingered on in the Iberian peninsula when the countries beyond the Pyrenees were enjoying the full flowering of the Renaissance. Nevertheless the date of the accession of Isabella I to the throne of Castile in 1474 can be taken to mark the watershed in Spain between medieval and modern times. We shall not understand Cortés or the ethos of the men with whom he associated, or the monarchs whom they served, unless we can visualize them as straddling not only an Old and a New World but also an old and a new ordering of human affairs. Cortés was a *quattrocento* man, a skyrocket man, a man of intense and deliberately cultivated individuality. This was the age of the *uomo universale*, the age of which Alberti proclaimed: 'Men can do all things if they will.' On the other hand, Cortés was also imbued with the outlook imparted to the Spanish nobility and squirearchy by an eight-hundred-year continuous struggle against a foreign invader, against the infidel. The psychological effects of so many centuries of virtually unbroken warfare were not lightly shaken off. The invasion of Central America by Cortés and his comrades not only represents the first step towards the growth of the modern colonial empires: it has also been called the last of the Crusades.

So bitter and obsessive a struggle, occupying the whole span of the Middle Ages, was bound to make a permanent imprint on the Iberian consciousness. Neither side, of course, waged the contest at full pitch all the time; there were lulls, periods of accommodation, even periods of fraternization and mutual admiration. Islamic Spain produced great courts and great kings, great philosophers and physicians, great poets and mathematicians. For a time it was fashionable for Christian Spaniards to emulate them and even copy their manners and their modes of dress. But between Spaniard and Arab, between Christian and Moslem, there could be no permanent understanding. There was also the shock and lasting feeling of shame that the original defeat had inflicted on Spanish pride. In Roman times, Hispania had been the most important province of the Empire; there were occasions when Hispania outshone Rome itself, or came to Rome's rescue. Spaniards had provided Rome with fighting men and sinews of war, and furnished Emperors of the quality of Trajan, Hadrian, Marcus Aurelius, Constantine, and Theodosius, last Emperor to rule over a united Roman world. It was to Spain that Rome owed the principal writers of the Silver Age: the two Senecas, Lucan, Martial, Columella, Quintilian, Pomponius Mela.

During the later Roman era, Spain had also played a leading part in the conduct of the affairs of the Church. It was at ecclesiastical councils held in Spain that the Church had received the name of Catholic; had endorsed the Nicene Creed; had enunciated the doctrines of celibacy and prohibition against marriage with non-Christians; and had made major pronouncements concerning heresy. A Spaniard, St. Damasus, had been a notable Pope. Nor was the eminent position of Spain in secular and religious affairs affected by the collapse of the Empire, or by the barbarian invasions in the early part of the fifth century. The Visigoths, who were themselves Christians, quickly brushed the barbarians aside, and introduced into Spain the cardinal institution of the monarchy. Later generations of Spaniards looked back to the era of the Visigothic kings, who reigned for three centuries, with as much pride as they looked back to the Romans. The leaders of the Visigoths learned how to become good rulers, good Christians and good Spaniards; one of them, Hermenegildo, even became a martyr and a saint. Arts and letters flourished. St. Isidore of Seville wrote his *Etymologiae*, and the period saw the activities of such celebrated poets as the great Prudentius—'the Virgil and Horace of the Christians'—Orentius and Eugenius, a Visigoth who became Archbishop of Toledo.

Then the Visigoths were swept aside as ruthlessly as they themselves had disposed of the barbarian Vandals, Alans and Suevi. In 710, eighty years after the death of Mohammed, a force of twelve thousand Arabs and Berbers led by a general called Tariq crossed the narrow straits from Africa and landed at Gibraltar (*Jebel-Tariq*, the Rock of Tariq). The following year Tariq was joined by another force under the governor of Mauretania, and in six years the two commanders overran four-fifths of the peninsula, except for its extreme north-western corner. Nor did the armies of Berbers, Moors and Syrians, directed by an able Arab hierarchy, halt at the Pyrenees. In the next fourteen years they subdued half of France, and were only prevented from reaching Paris and the English Channel by Charles Martel, who stopped them and turned them back when they reached the Loire at Tours.

They were expelled from France in double-quick time. Not so from Spain. There the Ommeyad dynasty consolidated its gains under the supremacy of the Emirs of Córdoba, whose firman extended throughout Iberia with the exception of the minuscule kingdoms of Galicia and Asturias. The internal quarrels of the Visigothic nobles and princes had contributed to their extinction; but a much larger factor in the *débâcle* was the fanatical Muslim faith of their opponents. This faith would make them impossible to dislodge until it could be matched by a faith as fanatical as their own—a fact which explains the peculiarly nationalistic and warlike character of the Catholicism which Cortés would carry with him to Mexico City. Moreover, it was an easier matter for the Arab caliphs to reinforce their co-religionists in Spain than it would have been to send reinforcements to France. They had only a narrow strait to negotiate, and the Mediterranean was their preserve. They therefore proceeded to organize the new realm which had fallen into their lap in a thoroughgoing fashion. Pushing them out would be a protracted business. Furthermore, the Spaniards would have to do it on their own. The other emerging nations of Europe, absorbed with the problems of forging their own identities after the crash of the classical world, would leave this unfortunate part of the continent to its own devices.

At the death of Charlemagne, a full hundred years after the initial invasion, Christian Spain had made no headway whatever with the task of liberation. It was only three centuries later, on the eve of the First Crusade, that the Spaniards were able to show a little more progress. The kingdoms of Castile, León, Navarre and Aragon, together with the country of Portugal, had now come into existence, and the southernmost tip of Castile extended across the River Tagus, embracing Toledo; but the amount of territory controlled by the Moors, as they had come to be called, still amounted to three-quarters of the area of Iberia. However, by this time the Moors themselves had fallen victims of the same divisive rivalries that had afflicted their enemies. Their possessions had been carved up into separate emirates or *taifas*—Saragossa, Valencia, Albarracín, Toledo, Badajoz, Córdoba, Seville, Granada—and during the course of the twelfth and thirteenth centuries they began to succumb one after another to the growing might of Castile and Aragon. The northern emirates were subdued in the early part of the twelfth century, and then, after a short lull, the south was conquered in the first half of the thirteenth. Badajoz fell in 1229, Valencia in 1238, Córdoba in 1246, Seville in 1248; and in 1250 the Spaniards were at Cádiz. Much of the Reconquest was the work of two great Alfonsos, Alfonso VII of León and Castile (1104–1157), and Alfonso VIII of Castile (1155–1214). There were setbacks, occasioned by the quarrels and rivalries of the Christian kingdoms and by humiliating reverses on the battlefield; and three hundred years after the first Moorish invasion under Tariq a second wave of invaders, the fierce Berber tribesmen known as the Almorávides, crossed to the peninsula in 1086 and had to be contained. Nevertheless, after 1257, with the exception of the emirate of Granada in the extreme south, the soil of Iberia had been cleared of the Moors and the kingdom of Portugal had assumed the classic shape it has retained ever since. The Spanish monarchs were therefore free to devote the next century and a half to internal campaigns or alliances that reduced the original territories of Castile, León, Aragon, Navarre and Barcelona to the powerful twin-kingdoms of Castile and Aragon, with the insignificant appendage of Navarre.

The task of reducing Granada was not in fact undertaken until three years before Hernán Cortés was born, and was only concluded when he was a boy of seven; his birth therefore occurred on the cusp, as it were, of the old Spain and the new. Furthermore, the fighting proved unexpectedly sharp and memorable. Granada turned out to be a tough nut to crack; indeed, the cracking took ten full years to accomplish. The famous and beautiful city withstood a determined siege and did not capitulate until 1492. Cortés, growing up only two hundred miles to the west of the theatre of war, must have heard and remembered vivid tales of the swaying fortunes of the campaign and the heroic deeds of individual participants on both sides. He was thus nurtured in a country that had girded itself for the ultimate stages of a centuries-old conflict, and was old enough to take part in the fiestas and *Te Deums* which celebrated the entry of Ferdinand and Isabella into the Alhambra and the final cleansing of the soil of his home-land. He was cradled and reared to the accompaniment of the clash of arms.

Queen Isabella was present in person at the reduction of Granada. She was not a woman to delegate such tasks to others, and like Cortés she had been inured to battle from her youngest years. While still in her teens she had had to fight for her throne. At one time she and her husband, whom she had insisted on marrying against all advice, had been excommunicated and driven as rebels from Castile. Nominally she ascended the throne of Castile in 1474, but it took five years of warfare to defeat the partisans of her cousin Joanna and make her position secure.

In 1479, on the death of her husband's father, she became joint ruler of Aragon as well as of Castile. Her husband, Ferdinand of Aragon, was himself of Castilian blood, and together they embarked immediately on a series of startling reforms and innovations. Their aim was to yoke their two kingdoms indissolubly together, and to raise them to a position of power and glory which they had never known individually. To this end, for the twin purposes of discipline and centralization, they challenged and succeeded in drastically reducing the quasi-independent privileges of the aristocracy, the church and the towns. The nobles they took by the scruff of the neck, dismantled their fortresses, made them disgorge the crown lands they had seized in times of unrest, and forbade them to indulge in the time-honoured luxury of fighting local wars with one another. They also established crown law in place of feudal law, and set up a royal police force called the Holy Brotherhood. Next they curbed the authority of the provincial and frontier governors, and seized control of the Masterships of the Military Orders. As for the Church, it was reformed and reor-ganized by the formidable Francisco Ximénez de Cisneros, Cardinal Archbishop of Toledo, one of the most forceful figures in Spanish history. The Spanish Inquisition was established in 1480 and held its first *auto da fé* in the following year. Torquemada was appointed the first Inquisitor General, presiding over a *Suprema*, or Council of the Supreme and General Inquisition. Like Cardinal Ximénes, he was a most efficient and thorough-going administrator, and the lax organization of the feudal church received a rude shaking-up. Finally it was necessary to deal with the swollen and self-assertive power of the towns. To this end, they were brought under close central supervision by means of the newly-established *corregidores*, a team of royal investigators or assessors travelling from one part of the country to the other on a permanent tour of inspection. Civic officials were appointed only with royal approval, and the collection of taxes, particularly the hated *alcabala* or value-added tax on commercial transactions, was put on a ruthlessly businesslike basis.

These high-handed policies were not carried through without spirited opposition. We have already seen that interference with the affairs of the Military Orders had caused uprisings, in one of which Martin Cortés took up arms against his sovereign. It would actually be wrong to exaggerate the degree of homogeneity that Isabella and Ferdinand managed to impose on their subjects. Spaniards are by nature unruly and fiercely jealous of their ancient civic and personal rights. The union of Castile and Aragon was destined to be neither as strong nor as permanent as its rulers desired. The history of Spain, from the earliest times to the Carlist Wars and the Civil War, is the history of regional rivalries. In Spain a man's *patria chica*—his province—tends to exact a more passionate loyalty than *la patria* itself. Nevertheless the achievement of Ferdinand and Isabella, especially when one bears in mind the inadequate power-base from which they began, was by any standards extraordinary. What they effected was the creation of modern Spain, Spain as we recognize it today. At a time when Italy and Central Europe were still balkanized, only Spain, Portugal, France and England had been consolidated into distinct and vigorous entities, a fact which would be bound to have a bearing on the founding of overseas empires that was soon to follow. Ferdinand and Isabella forged Spain into a secular and religious totality, one aspect of life subsuming the other. Their domain was not only politically unified, but from north to south, from east to west, it was inhabited only by adherents of the True Faith. The remaining Moors, whether in Granada or in the rest of Spain, were baptized or expelled, while the Jews became either *conversos* or victims of the Inquisition. Spain was Catholic, and her rulers well merited the title of *los reyes católicos* bestowed upon them, by an admiring Spanish Pope, in 1494.

Ferdinand of Aragon was not a likeable man. He was foxy, deceitful and untrustworthy. But he was also an exceptionally shrewd and farsighted politician—much too farsighted, as it happened, for towards the end of his reign he involved Spain in the first of those trans-Pyrenean dynastic entanglements that would ultimately prove fatal to her. His marriage with Isabella could not be described as a love-match. Precocious and ambitious beyond her years, she had married him, instead of the elderly King of Portugal, for strategic and not personal reasons. She was far from beautiful, and her husband was keenly interested in other women. But from the beginning, as queen of emergent Castile, she was the predominant partner: and Ferdinand was content to have it so. As bare and sombre Aragon had once attached itself to exuberant Catalonia, so now it attached itself to irresistible Castile, this time bringing Catalonia with her into the alliance. Ferdinand saw that Aragon's destiny lay with its western neighbour, an appreciation that was doubly prescient in that at the moment when he joined its fortunes with those of Castile the latter was, if anything, rather the weaker partner.

Ferdinand's role in the most effective royal partnership known to history, supportive as it was, was appreciated by the later generations of Spaniards who looked back with awe and reverence to the reign of the Catholic Kings. Quevedo remarked that Ferdinand 'knew how to be a king himself and how to teach others to be kings', and Baltasar Gracián declared that 'a hundred kings could be forged from one Ferdinand the Catholic and there would be material left over to forge as many more'. They were paying these tributes nearly a century and a half after Ferdinand's death. Nevertheless it was the thought of Isabella rather than her husband that proved the more emotive in the minds of later Spaniards. There is something very stirring in the spectacle of a spirited young queen struggling against apparently insuperable odds. Isabella was an earlier Elizabeth of England, an earlier Maria Theresa or Catherine the Great. The courageous and matriarchal young woman personified emergent Spain as the Divine Gloriana was to personify emergent England. She gave form and focus to the chivalric impulses of a people long dedicated to the cult of chivalry. Her reign was the triumphant culmination of an epic. She and her husband bestowed on a country which has never ceased to be grateful for it not merely a political and religious unity: they gave it a national spirit, a national image; they gave it the identity for which it had been groping obscurely for eight hard centuries.

* * *

When Hernán Cortés was born, a Castilian in Queen Isabella's Castile, a mood of elation was in the air. Spain sensed that she was entering into the plenitude of her powers; she felt that a marvellous destiny was opening up before her. It was not for nothing that the memory of the Catholic Kings has always evoked such nostalgia. Américo Castro, in his monumental *Structure of Spanish History*, writes: 'In spite of the vastness of the Spanish Empire, still envied and feared in the eighteenth century, Spain has habitually longed for the moment of Ferdinand and Isabella, the moment she deemed unique. One thinks at once of the similar state of mind in Imperial Rome, which expressed with such frequency its nostalgia for the glorious centuries of the Republic.'

Cortés, his comrades in arms and his fellow *conquistadores*, were products of that 'unique moment'. They were the sons of a nation steeled in warfare, a nation in arms, at the summit of a towering triumph, poised and keyed up for a further flood of spectacular advances.

It must surely be an intoxicating sensation, to be part of a nation on the march, a nation which feels that its hour has struck.

2

Por lanças e por espadas avemos de guarir
si non en esta tierra angosta non podriemos bivir
e commo yo cuedo a ir nos avremos d'aquí

Since this harsh land will yield us no living, we must
rely on our swords and lances. For the same reason, we must move on.

IF THE moment of Cortés' birth is significant, so too is its place. He was an Extremeño: that is to say, in the words of Mario Sánchez-Barba, editor of the fullest and most recent edition of Cortés' letters and dispatches, he was *un hombre de frontera*, a man of the frontier—a frontiersman, with all that the word has always implied.

The term Extremadura—territory which is outlying, which is hard—was applied to different areas at different times. It was given traditionally to those lands which, during the centuries of the Reconquest, bordered on the Moorish domains. It was not until the late eleventh century that it was finally bestowed on the area which has born it ever since. But the name happens to be extremely apt when applied to the modern province in question. Extremadura is one of the most forbidding and inaccessible parts of Iberia, and except for the rich pastures and farmlands in the valley of the Guadiana it is indeed a *terra extrema et dura*, as the Romans termed it.

The Romans had reason to respect the ancestors of Cortés. His native town of Medellín was part of the homeland of the Lusitanians, a people who resisted the imperial legions with a singular ferocity. As William C. Atkinson writes in his *History of Spain and Portugal*: 'In 199 B.C. guerrilla warfare became more serious as renewed attempts at penetration brought the Romans into contact with the untamed and redoubtable Lusitanians and Celtiberians. By 179, when these tribes too had to all appearances been subjected, over 150,000 troops had been drafted to the conquest of this *horrida et bellicosa provincia*, whose fighting spirit had imposed on Rome the necessity for permanent military service. The peace was soon rudely shattered. In 154 a renewed confederation of Lusitanians launched a general rising which inflicted defeat after defeat on strong Roman armies. Twice the commanders of these had to sue for peace. Rome refusing to ratify such humiliating treaties, her generals were driven to humiliations greater still, resorting to perjury, treachery and massacre to bring low an enemy strong in his refusal to recognize when he was beaten.' A similar refusal to know when he was beaten was to be a cardinal quality of Cortés during the vicissitudes of his coming campaigns. Conditions had been hard and extreme for his forebears on the Roman frontier. To have crushed the Roman legions was a prouder boast, if anything, than to have crushed the Moors or the Aztecs. One Lusitanian leader, Viriatus, is called by Atkinson 'the first great figure in the peninsular scroll of fame'. A simple shepherd by origin, he became an outstanding exponent of guerrilla warfare (one should remember that the word *guerrilla*, with all the ferocity and cunning it implies, is Iberian in origin). For eight years he fought the Roman armies to a standstill in the mountains of Extremadura, and was finally killed only by the treachery of one of his own men in receipt of Roman gold.

Ultimately the Romans prevailed over the Lusitanians: but as if in appreciation of the stature of their late foe they founded at Mérida—which is only twenty miles from Medellín—one of the great cities of the civilized world. According to Ausonius, it ranked as the ninth city of the Empire, superior even to Athens. Today the visitor can still see the remains of the splendid Roman bridge, built in the first century B.C., over 850 yards long and with sixty arches; of the well-preserved Roman theatre, built at the time of the consulate of Agrippa, which held 6,000 people; and of the huge amphitheatre, dating from the reign of Augustus, which could accommodate no less than 16,000 spectators, almost half the present population of the city. Originally the resplendent city of Emerita Augusta also boasted a Temple of Diana, later to become the palace of the counts of Los Corbos, and a Temple of Mars, afterwards dismantled to provide material for the chapel of Saint Eulalia, built near the site of the oven in which she was martyred. It is worth mentioning that the walls of the Alcázar or Alcazaba, the fortress which stands beside the fine sweep of the Guadiana just south of the Plaza de España, are those of the oldest existing Moorish building in Spain. Thus Cortés grew up in close proximity to a famous and imposing city, a city that must have impressed upon his mind the grandeur of the classical epoch. This epoch, as we shall see, was in fact ever-present to him. The lofty walls of the Alcazaba were also a witness of the longer and no less stirring epoch which interposed between his own day and that of ancient Rome.

The taste for fortifications, bridges and military edifices persisted from Roman and Moorish times into the Middle Ages. The countryside around Medellín was distinguished for its castles. Concentrated into a relatively small area were the castles of Cáceres, Trujillo, Albuquerque, Elvas, Badajoz, Mérida and Zafra, some of them adapted from earlier Moorish strongholds. They were bastions of the military order of Alcántara, and were slighted when Queen Isabella made her attack on the military orders. Alcántara itself, the shrine of the order, was situated little more than sixty miles north-west of Medellín, on the banks of the Tagus. It was a renowned site, perched on a spur of rock high above the great river. Here stands the highest Roman bridge in Spain, built in the reign of Trajan, its arches constructed of blocks of granite without mortar or cement, the remains of a Roman temple still adorning its entrance, its centre crowned by a triumphal archway. The word for bridge in Arabic is *Al-kantara*, and the bridge dominated a strategic crossing of the Tagus. During the thirteenth century the crossing was wrested from the Moors by the knights of Calatrava and became the headquarters of a new military order of Alcántara. The knights of Alcántara held the bridge against the Moors, and the tombs of Masters of the order can be seen in the small church that stands in the ruins of the convent of San Benito.

Hernán Cortés grew up in a part of the world accustomed to military tradition and organization. It is not surprising that this particular nest of eagles should have produced other outstanding *conquistadores*. From beautiful Trujillo, fifty miles to the north-west, came ugly and rapacious Francisco Pizarro, bastard leader of a gang of bastard brothers, destined to be assassinated in far-off Peru by his own followers. From Badajoz, sixty miles to the west, came two of the most chivalrous and fearless of the Spanish adventurers: Vasco Núñez de Balboa, beheaded by the brutal Pedrarias Dávila at Panama, and Hernando de Soto, explorer of Florida, Georgia and Alabama, whose dead body was thrown into the Mississippi to prevent its capture by the Indians. The courtly and chivalrous Pedro de Valdivia, one of the most sympathetic of his kind, was also an Extremeño. Conqueror and governor of Chile, founder of the city of Santiago, it was his fate too to meet a violent end. It is a testimony to the cool character of Cortés, and to that streak of luck which Napoleon preferred to ability in his generals, that he was destined to die in Spain, rich, respected and elderly, in his own bed and in his own house. As La Rochefoucauld observed, 'However great may be the advantages she bestows, it is no nature alone, but nature helped by luck that makes heroes.'

When it was time for him to leave Medellín and go to the university, his parents sent him to an establishment within reach of his own province, albeit a fair distance to the north of it. Salamanca is almost two hundred miles due north of Medellín, but in its sense of gravity and reserve it is entirely Extremaduran in atmosphere. One recalls that Miguel de Unamuno, although a Basque, spent forty years of his life in Salamanca, was twice rector of its university, and survived demotion, exile and house-arrest to die there. The university of Salamanca has always been a famous foundation, but never more so than in the first three centuries of its existence and at the time when Cortés was a student. It was created in 1243 by Ferdinand III of Castile, in the same century as Alcalá de Henares and Valladolid in Spain, and Oxford, Bologna and Paris abroad. Its statutes were among the most enlightened in Europe. It quickly took a place among the most notable universities of the continent. It is interesting to note, in view of the difficulties encountered by university authorities in our own day, that by a decree of 1411 the rector and professors were elected by popular vote of the students. This did not prevent it from becoming a centre of advanced studies. Columbus and Copernicus both received a warm reception there.

Men matured earlier in those unprotected days. When Cortés took the highroad to Salamanca, by-passing his father's native village of Monroy by only a few miles, he was barely fourteen. His parents had set their hearts on his becoming a lawyer. He was a bright boy, and they wished him to make a positive career for himself. As the son of a country squire, the only other alternative would be for him to share the fate of the countless other young men in his position and idle his life away on his inadequate patrimony. The son of a petty squire or impecunious nobleman would inherit a horror of *el deshonor de trabajo*—the dishonour of work—without inheriting very much more. He could not sully his idea of himself or betray his caste by setting his hand to the plough or engaging in trade; in any case, a mercantile middle-class was almost non-existent in Spain at this date, and where it did exist was largely represented by Italians, Flemings and Frenchmen who, lacking the prejudice against earning a living of the Spanish gentry, flocked across the Pyrenees in thousands to make their fortune. Cortés' parents foresaw that the only alternative to allowing him to grow up as a scapegrace and petty Don Juan was to enter one of the three professions acceptable to a Spanish gentleman: the church, the law, or the army.

Supporting him at Salamanca would have entailed sacrifices; but the expense was lessened by the fact that his father had relatives in the city and that he could therefore lodge in the house of his aunt. Inés de Paz, wife of Francisco Núñez Valera. Nonetheless he spent only two years at the university before suddenly throwing up his studies and going home. Cervantes de Salazar indicates that his health had not been good at this time: but there must have been another and deeper reason for his leaving without graduating. Gómara, who was close to him, says that he returned home because he was 'either disgusted with school life, or having changed his mind or, perhaps, from lack of money. His return vexed his parents exceedingly, they being annoyed with him for having abandoned his studies. They had destined him for the law, the richest and most honourable career of all, because he was very intelligent and clever in everything he did'. Like so many parents, they were dismayed at the prospect of having a disgruntled teenager loafing around the house. It is surprising how many brilliant men have begun life by disappointing their parents, and by being restless and vacillating—perhaps it is one of the presages of their later brilliance; one recalls that Prince Eugène almost became a priest. However, as is the case with exceptional men, no experience is wasted. If Cortés realized early that he wanted to belong to the aristocracy of the sword and not to the aristocracy of the robe, his faculties were nonetheless sharpened by his sojourn at Salamanca. He pushed his studies to the point where Las Casas and Bernal Díaz were both convinced, after hearing him debate in fluent Latin, that he had actually acquired his degree at the university. This, as we have said, was the age of the *uomo universale*, when one man combined in himself the qualities of scholar, courtier, lover and man of action. Bernal Díaz claimed that Cortés wrote poetry. In any event, his curriculum at Salamanca included Greek, Latin and logic, and it is easy to appreciate from the study of his later life that these three grand and rigorous subjects made a permanent impression on his mind. As Madariaga observes, 'whether he was a bachelor of law or not, we can see him evince through his adventurous career an equal aptitude for letters and for arms; an astonishing capacity for being always *present*—presence of will in action, presence of mind in thought; a masterly hand with men; a masterly mind with things; a gift for expression, in action by doing the right thing, in thought by saying the right thing, always at the right time.'

There was a Spanish saying: 'Six Spanish adventurers, and one goes to the Indies, another goes to Italy, another goes to Flanders, another is in prison, another is engaged in lawsuits, and another is taking religious vows. And in Spain there are no other kinds of people except these six.' Cortés, as Gómara surmised, 'had changed his mind'. He wanted fame and he wanted money, but he would gain them by a livelier means than pleading dull cases in a dark and stuffy courtroom.

*   *   *

The father in Calderón's *El Alcalde de Zalamea* packs his son off to the army with the words: 'What can he do here with me but lounge his life away in dissipation? Let him go and serve the king.' The prospects of success in the army, where wealth and connections were of paramount importance, were slimmer than in the legal profession: but what active youngster would hesitate over such a choice? And it also happened that the opportunity to serve the king had not ceased with the conquest of Granada. The military impetus created by almost a millennium of warfare was not to be suddenly assuaged, and was soon spilling over into the world outside Spain. The Aragonese, who unlike the landlocked Castilians had early enjoyed access to the sea, had long shared with the Catalans a taste for intervening in the larger politics of the Mediterranean. As early as the later thirteenth century Tunis had been an Aragonese protectorate, a kind of back-door to the Reconquest; Sicily for a short period had passed by marriage to the Aragonese crown; and in 1420 Alfonso V of Aragon was declared titular ruler of Naples and took effective possession of the kingdom in 1443. He actually deserted Aragon for his new realm and never again returned to Spain, devoting the remaining fifteen years of his life to setting up a splendid court in his adopted country.

The ties between Naples and Aragon had weakened after the departure of Alfonso from Spanish shores, and after Alfonso had bequeathed Naples to an illegitimate son. The Spaniards became absorbed in their own dynastic tussles, and in the final phase of the struggle with the Moors. France, also beginning to coalesce into a nation at this time, with an attendant impulse to flex its muscles, was not slow to make trouble. The French stirred up strife in Catalonia and Navarre, seized the territories of Cerdagne and Roussillon, and in 1494 sent an army into Italy to claim Naples for the French crown. But in Ferdinand of Aragon they had picked a more implacable enemy than they knew. A year after the fall of Granada the troops of the newly merged kingdom of Aragon and Castile wrested back Cerdagne and Roussillon by force of arms. Nor were Ferdinand and his queen slow to counter-attack in Italy. They sent their best general, Gonsalvo de Córdoba, to settle matters with the French, and in a brilliant campaign that lasted less than a year he pitched them back across the Alps. In 1498 he returned home, to be received like a hero and showered with rewards, given the title of Duke of San Angelo, and granted large estates in the Abruzzi. This was the time when Cortés was about to set out for Salamanca. Must he not have found the news from across the sea unsettling? Must he not have found the prospect of buckling down to his text-books uninviting when compared with the opportunities for rewards and glory beckoning from foreign shores? Titles, lands and money were all there for a determined youngster to win by the exertion of his right arm and the cunning of his brain.

The Catholic Kings entered into an alliance with the Emperor Maximilian, with Milan and Venice, and with their old friend Pope Alexander VI. The participation of Spain in European affairs dates from this epoch. Nevertheless the French, as the French will, came again: the famous *furia francese* was not to be easily subdued. Gonsalvo de Córdoba was thereupon dispatched once more to Italy to give them a second taste of the *furia spagnola*. Europe had known that fury in the days of Imperial Rome when the Spanish legions alarmed their more realistic Roman comrades by their ferocity, their fanatical eagerness to fight to a finish, and their habit of advancing into battle shouting 'Long live death!' (The Navarrese troops during the Spanish Civil War used the same disconcerting war-cry.) Now Europe was to learn the lesson again. Led once more, as at the siege of Granada, by Gonsalvo de Córdoba, they first took Cephalonia and Zante from the Turks and handed them back to their allies, the Venetians. They then got to grips with the French. Gonsalvo won a remarkable victory at Cerignola, in Apulia, in 1503, and followed it up with an even more astonishing one on the River Garigliano, between Naples and Rome, the following year. Spain now took firm possession of half of Italy. As John Lynch notes in the first volume of his *Spain under the Habsburgs*: 'The victory was a sign of the times, for it gave further proof, if proof were needed, of the power inherent in the union of Castile and Aragon, and the success of their collaboration. The Castilian army was hitherto unknown outside the peninsula; now, after its apprenticeship in the war of Granada and its successful trial in the Italian campaign, it was the most powerful instrument of war in Europe.'

Gonsalvo de Córdoba had become a figure from legend, from romance. He belonged in one of those epics with which the heads of generations of Spanish boys before Cortés were stuffed, and the heads of generations after him. (What else but the recollection of those mighty men of former times drove Don Quixote to feutre his lance at windmills and flocks of sheep?) Gonsalvo entered into glory with Roland, with El Cid, with Palmerín and Amadis de Gaul. He has gone down to history under the resounding and immortal title of *El Gran Capitán*, the Great Captain. Was it any wonder that thousands of penurious young *hidalgos* flocked to his banner, and that, when his army was advancing through Italy to meet the regiments of the equally legendary Gaston de Foix, Cortés could bear his studies no longer and threw his school-books into a corner?

It is worth mentioning that after Isabella's death, in 1504, Ferdinand continued their policy of expansion with notable effect. In Africa, between 1504 and 1511, his armies took Mers-el-Kebir, Oran and Tripoli, and re-established the Spanish presence in Algiers. In 1512 his troops, under the command of the Duke of Alba, annexed Navarre, after the death of Gaston de Foix, and brought it back into the Iberian community after a lapse of almost three centuries.

Gómara tells us that, not surprisingly, Cortés' first thought on arriving home from Salamanca was to leave for Italy to join Gonsalvo de Córdoba. It is interesting to remark how many of the future *conquistadores* learned the trade of arms in the forcing-house of the Moorish or the foreign wars. To mention only a few, Alonso de Hojeda fought at Granada, Pedrarias Dávila at Oran, Pedro de Mendoza, Diego de Almagro and Pedro de Valdivia in Italy. In this, these provincial boys were only imitating the flower of Spanish knighthood and following the example of such men as Garcilaso de la Vega, the Sir Philip Sidney of Spain, killed fighting against the French at the age of thirty-three.

Cortés was about to profit from the same apprenticeship, when what appeared to be a more advantageous opportunity suddenly intervened. No doubt through family influence, because the person concerned was Master of the Order of Alcántara, he was offered a place in the suite of Nicolás de Ovando, a nobleman who was about to sail to take up the post of Governor of the Indies. Cortés was tempted by the offer not only because of the prospect of a connection with Ovando, but because, as Gómara adds in a very revealing detail, 'it struck him as the more promising on account of the quantity of gold that was being brought in from there.' In the upshot, he was prevented from leaving with Ovando because of a picturesque incident. The facts may have become somewhat embroidered in the form in which, as an old man, he related them to Gómara, but it would nonetheless throw light on the heightened way in which such men habitually regard themselves. 'While Ovando was arranging his departure and the fleet was being readied,' writes Gómara, 'Cortés went to a house one night to visit a woman and, as he was walking along the badly cemented wall of the garden, it gave way beneath him. At the noise made by the falling wall, and by the clatter of his armour and his shield, the jealous husband ran out and tried to kill him, but was prevented from doing so by his mother-in-law.' A somewhat *opéra bouffe* incident, but typical of the exuberant brand of knight-errantry in which Cortés indulged.

'He was injured by the fall,' Gómara continues, 'and was also stricken by a quartan fever which kept him in bed for a long time; so he was unable to sail with Governor Ovando.'

One way or another, fever or no fever, influence or no influence, he was determined to escape from Extremadura. Those readers who may have visited Extremadura will appreciate his feelings. Apart from the green and sheltered valleys and the plateaux where the flocks can feed in winter on the short, bitter grass, Extremadura is a harsh and uninviting land. On the other hand, anyone raised in Extremadura, anyone who can endure its winters, can survive the rigours of Central America. It was not for nothing that Cortés and Pizarro came from Extremadura. They were hard men from a hard province. And just as so much of the terrain of Mexico and Peru bore a conspicuous resemblance to Extremadura, so the regimes which they would establish there would be Extremaduran in character. However, it was Cortés and Pizarro who would then become the leaders and wealthy landowners. In Extremadura they were nothing; they would never own much more than their swords and their pride. The political powers of the aristocracy had been curtailed after the advent of the Catholic Kings, but its grip on its lands remained secure. It has been estimated that over half the land in Castile was owned at the close of the fifteenth century by the higher aristocracy, and almost all the remainder by the lower aristocracy and the church. Most of Castile was owned by three hundred noble families, who possessed their peasantry body and soul, lock, stock and barrel. Thus the Duke of Infantado, a Mendoza, was lord of 800 villages and 90,000 serfs. The noble estates were immune from alienation and tied in perpetuity to their owners by means of the sacred right of *mayorazgo*, or entail, a right which even the Catholic Kings were unable to shake. There was nowhere in such a tightly-knit system for even a young man of the mettle of Cortés to obtain a toehold. If he wanted to rise in the world he had to head for a frontier, where conditions were still fluid. He had to go to Italy or America. Once there, he could turn himself into a typical Spanish grandee, lord of serfs and villages. The Indians of the New World were to assume the role of the peasants of the Old. He would live the life of a Duke of Medinaceli, a Duke of Infantado, a Duke of Medina Sidonia. He would introduce and build up herds of cattle, and particularly flocks of sheep, in order to base his wealth on a typically Castilian foundation.

Cortés, like many of the other *conquistadores*, became a nobleman in the New World because there was no scope for him to become one in the Old. Other motives, of course, were at work: love of adventure; the typical curiosity of the age; the itch for fame; the desire to serve God, the King and the new Spain. But Cortés must also be regarded as a member of a precipitate band of needy young gentlemen on the make. Entire nations would be swept away in order to assuage that headlong drive towards wealth and success.

3

'*Ya cavelleros dezir nos he la verdad
qui en un logar mora siempre lo so puede menguar
cras a la mañana penssemos de cavalgar
dexat estas posadas e iremos adelant*'

Ah, knights, I want to tell you the truth: staying in one place can only make a man grow poor. Tomorrow morning let us move on. We will leave this camp and fare forward.

WITH the final conquest and consolidation of the kingdom of Naples and Sicily, emergent Spain had achieved an opening to the east. Only a few years later, in 1521, she was to tighten her grip on Italy by waging and winning a campaign to absorb the duchy of Milan into her possessions; and afterwards Sardinia and portions of the Tuscan coastline would be added to the inventory. Nevertheless, the way to further conquests in an easterly direction had already been barred by the incursions of the Ottoman Turks into eastern Europe and the Mediterranean during the fifteenth century. The infidel Muslims had carried all before them since Muhammed II had destroyed Constantinople in 1453. The siege of the great city, the second city of Christendom, had been going on for thirty years: but its eventual fall sent a fearful shock and shiver through Western Europe. More, the sack of Constantinople was only the beginning of a Turkish invasion that quickly submerged the ancient states of Transylvania and Hungary and brought the Turks to the gates of Vienna. And there they stayed for over a hundred years, an alien and sinister presence occupying fully a quarter of the continent.

Increasingly powerful on land, the Turks controlled Herzegovina, Albania and the Morea, which enabled them to dominate the Adriatic. They also controlled Greece and Rumelia, as well as Asia Minor and almost the entire coast of North Africa, which gave them mastery of the Mediterranean. We have seen how Gonsalvo de Córdoba had first to deal with the Turks before he could fight the French in Italy; and the countries of the Mediterranean, France and Spain included, were now scourged by Turkish fleets and landing-parties. The Turks were exceedingly proficient, both as soldiers and sailors. The most the Western powers could do was to form a somewhat ineffectual Holy League and indulge in a simple defensive action. There was no longer any talk of organizing a Crusade; the Crusades were tacitly acknowledged to be a disastrous if glorious failure of a bygone era. Spain, with her tradition of war with the Moors, would bear the main brunt of the struggle against the infidel. The price would be heavy, and her allies would leave her to shoulder the burden of preserving Christendom almost alone. The crowning victory of Lepanto in 1571 was to be a single-handed Spanish effort.

Blocked to the north by the Pyrenees, and to the east and south by the Turks, Spain had perforce to turn her gaze westward. Exciting events were taking place in the Atlantic. The Portuguese, with their privileged geographical location, had been quick to take advantage of the situation. Scarcely had Portugal achieved her definitive shape with the capture of the Algarve from the Moors in 1253, and established her independence from Castile at the battle of Aljubarrota in 1385, than she embarked on the building of her great maritime empire. The mariners of Henry the Navigator and his successors sallied forth into the unknown Atlantic even though they believed that in the tropics the sun poured down sheets of liquid flame, that the ocean boiled and the searing heat turned white men black; and Henry took their successes with the same 'virtuous obstinacy' that he took their failures. By the 1430s they had explored the coast of Africa as far south as modern Rio de Oro; by 1444 they had reached Senegal and Gambia; by 1455 they had visited the Cape Verde Islands; by 1460 they were at Sierra Leone. In the tremendous Portuguese ventures of the 1480s and 1490s, Diego Cão first reached the Congo, then Cape Cross, near Walvis Bay; then Bartholemew Diaz, leaving Lisbon in 1478, touched at Cape Cross, sailed on further south, doubled the Cape of Good Hope and named it, and touched the mouth of the Great Fish River before turning for home.

As a result of such initiatives, by 1500 Portugal was in control of valuable fishing grounds, important trading stations on the West African coast, and owned or leased such pieces of overseas property as Madeira and the Cape Verde Islands. The Spaniards were not slow to follow suit. After some preliminary skirmishing a regular war at sea broke out in 1475, when Isabella of Castile, who had been queen scarcely a year and was still fighting for her throne, ordered her subjects to wrest what they could of the spoils of Africa from their neighbours. The Portuguese emerged the winners in the murderous hostilities that ensued, and by the terms of the

Treaty of Alcaçovas, in 1479, the Spaniards had to be content with little more than the recognition of their occupation of the Canary Islands.

The Catholic Kings realized that in the lucrative area of the Atlantic they had a great deal of leeway to make up. Hence their decision to take a chance on Christopher Columbus when he presented himself at their court. It is one of history's little ironies that he had previously outlined his ideas without success to the Portuguese, who had given him a careful hearing but turned him down probably because he seemed more a theoretician and a geographer than a practical seaman. And this was the age of the practical seaman: the high seas, in those diminutive caravels, were no place for amateurs. The Portuguese were also concentrating at this time on finding both the eastward and overland routes to the Indies. The remarkable Pedro da Covilhã, posing as an Arab merchant, reached Cairo, Goa and Calicut, and in 1493 appears to have sent a letter back to Lisbon from no less a place than Abyssinia, where he spent the last thirteen years of his life in the service of that Emperor, whom all Europe took to be the fabulous lost Christian monarch, Prester John. In 1498 Vasco da Gama steered his way to Calicut by the sea route, following Diaz's route as far as the Great Fish River, then launching out with stupendous bravery across the Indian Ocean. The Portuguese error in judgment where Columbus was concerned was neither ill-considered nor dishonourable. For many decades it must have appeared that the Spanish Indies would have been a poor exchange for the rich factories at Ormuz, Socotra, Goa, Malacca, and later at Canton and Macao.

When Columbus sailed from Palos under the Castilian flag, four years after the Portuguese had rebuffed him, his intention was to anticipate the Portuguese landfall in Asia by discovering a shorter route to the East. When he sighted San Salvador (the modern Watling Island) he honestly believed he was off the Japanese archipelago. If the Portuguese and Spanish undertook their voyages primarily for reasons of commerce, they also had it in their minds that it might be possible to outflank the Turks in Europe and come at them from the rear. The desire to make contact with Prester John, to find a path round the Cape and tracks across the Atlantic and Indian Oceans, was bound up with the notion of stealing a march on the ancient Moorish enemy, recently expelled from Iberia but gathering strength for what threatened to be a second and more savage Conquest.

The Catholic Kings were characteristically businesslike in the accords they made with Columbus on the eve of his first voyage. They were equally businesslike in the speed with which they approached their great and good friend, Pope Alexander VI, in order to secure sanction for their putative gains. Columbus had scarcely dropped anchor in the Tagus before Spanish envoys were already on their way to Rome. Since the discovery of the New World was vitally related to the spreading of the Faith, it was felt that it should be for the Holy Father to make pronouncements regarding the apportionment of the territories in question. Nor was it a disadvantage, from the Spanish viewpoint, that the Holy Father happened to be a Spaniard, and that he was anxious to secure Spanish support for the cause of Papal expansion in Italy and for the ambitions of his son, Cesare Borgia. The four bulls which he lost no time in promulgating were therefore intended to favour Spain at the expense of Portugal. The first two secured to Spain the lands discovered or about to be discovered in the area just explored by Columbus. The third, known by the casual title of *Inter Caetera*—'Among Other Things', as if dividing up the globe was a casual matter—demarcated the Spanish and Portuguese spheres of influence. Alexander drew a horizontal line on the map a hundred leagues west of the Cape Verde Islands and the Azores, announcing that all land beyond it would henceforward belong to Spain. The fourth bull, in alarmingly vague terms, sought to extend the rights of Spain towards 'the west and south, in regions occidental or meridional and oriental, and of India'. At this, not unnaturally, the Portuguese balked. They were not particularly interested in the lands to the west; at that time those lands seemed likely to turn out to be nothing more than a string of islands on the fringes of Asia, and they were already in process of firmly establishing themselves there. The mention of the south, and of India, was a totally different matter. There the interest of Portugal might be radically affected. Unable to convince Alexander, they therefore entered into direct negotiations with Spain. After their recent clashes by sea and land, both sides were inclined to be reasonable, and by the terms of the Treaty of Tordesillas, ratified in 1494, the Spaniards agreed to move the Papal line of *Inter Caetera* two hundred and seventy leagues further out into the Atlantic. The Portuguese thus safeguarded their highway to India and China and took command of the south Atlantic: and if they had miscalculated with regard to the ultimate significance of the Spanish Indies, at least in the course of time, as a result of Tordesillas, the immensity of Brazil fell into their grasp.

The Spaniards were now legal masters of the Indies. Under the energetic direction of the Catholic Kings they set about the speedy exploitation of their new possessions. It is true that the course of history, like the course of our individual lives, is largely dictated by accident; as Pascal put it, the presence of a little bit of grit in Cromwell's bladder changed the course of English history. However, the realms and individuals who bear

2*

off the prizes are those who position themselves to take advantage of such accidents as they occur. We have said that the Aztecs would have been conquered, sooner or later, with or without the presence of Cortés; similarly the New World would have been discovered (or re-discovered) with or without Christopher Columbus. But Cortés and Columbus proved to be men who had the courage and determination to reach their goal ahead of their rivals. They had an unusually keen sense of what the Greeks would have called their *kairos*: 'that which one is ordained to do.' They were also willing, if need be, to surrender their lives in pursuit of their private vision. As Joseph Conrad, another seaman and venturer, points out in *Lord Jim*: 'A certain readiness to perish is not so very rare, but it is seldom that you meet men whose souls, steeled in the impentrable armour of resolution, are ready to fight a losing battle to the last.' Cortés and Columbus knew discouragement and despair, and the near presence of death. Neither of them were crude opportunists, but men of intellect and imagination. Their victories were hard-won. 'No victory without struggle', as Schopenhauer would put it. Their triumphs were neither perfect nor complete; such is not part of the universal compact. But though they emerged, at the end, sour and disillusioned, if also rich and honoured, each had achieved his individual and personal great deed. It is on the supply of such men as Cortés and Columbus, and of such statesmen as the Catholic Kings, all of them steeled in the impenetrable armour of resolution, that nations depend for their pre-eminence.

The Spaniards, through the instrumentality of a Genoese mariner, had stumbled on the Indies almost by chance. The fact that they were at their flood-tide of optimism and energy, coupled with the previous successes of their Portuguese neighbours in the field of overseas exploration, made them quick to follow up their advantage. Like the Portuguese, they too possessed a sea-faring tradition, dating back three thousand years to the time when Iberian sailors of the Neolithic and Bronze Ages ventured out into the cold grey Atlantic to make landfalls in England, Ireland, Scotland, and even further afield. Like the Portuguese, too, they possessed ports that gave them immediate access to the Atlantic.

On his first voyage, Columbus had touched on the Bahamas, San Salvador, Cuba, and the island that he called the Isla Española, or Hispaniola (the island now jointly occupied by the Haitian and Dominican Republics). On his second voyage, in 1493, with a fleet of seventeen vessels, he touched on the Virgin Islands, Puerto Rico and Jamaica, as well as re-visiting Cuba and Hispaniola. Materially, the second voyage was unsuccessful; but in 1496, when he himself had returned to Europe, his brother Bartholemew founded the future city of Santo Domingo, on Hispaniola, which was to be the metropolis of the Spanish Indies for more than half a century.

*   *   *

The Indies had been discovered, let alone settled, barely ten years before the nineteen-year-old Cortés travelled from Medellín to Seville to take ship for Santo Domingo. The pomp and glitter of Seville must have presented an extraordinary and exciting spectacle to the young man after the starkness and poverty of Extremadura. Seville in the year 1504 was the most important city in Spain and one of the leading cities in Europe. As I have written in *Diego Velázquez, Painter and Courtier*: 'For a century after its reconquest from the Moors by Ferdinand III in 1248 Seville had been the chosen capital of the rulers of Castile. Under Moorish rule the cities of Andalusia were the largest and wealthiest in Spain, and Seville was the first among them. Her position was consolidated in 1503, when she supplanted Cádiz as the official centre of trade with the New World. Here, in the ancient *alcázar*, was set up the Board of Trade or Casa de Contratación, which possessed its own separate judiciary and whose staff were all, indeed, called judges. The first Pilot-Major of the Casa de Contratación was Amerigo Vespucci, to be followed by Díaz de Solís and Cabot. During the sixteenth century almost the entire wealth of the Indies flowed over Seville's wharves and into its warehouses.'

Madariaga has a long and brilliantly evocative paragraph on Seville, as Cortés saw it, which should be quoted in full. 'Seville, Cádiz, Sanlúcar and Palos,' he writes, 'were teeming with the most glorious pageant that history had ever seen. The incoming caravels, radiant with the light of the New World: captains, pilots, adventurers, monks, soldiers of fortune, Indian caciques, now stark naked, now dressed in exotic attire with golden rings and headdresses of silver and plumes; slaves, men, women, children, shivering and hungry; gold, gold, gold, tales of monstrously big grains, as big as a pea, as a nut, as a good Castilian loaf, as a church bell, which had enriched So-and-so in one day; and So-and-so, himself, disembarking, his face gaping with a smile of success, his hat gorgeous, his gold necklace resplendent, and slaves galore; and now and then, the discoverer himself, passing through the streets of Seville at the head of one of his carefully organized processions, richly decorated with popinjays, glittering with golden chains and golden masks of strange design and profile; or perhaps by contrast, clad in the dark brown frock of a penitent monk or St. Francis, or even in iron chains, as a proud, shipwrecked, sullen prisoner; waves upon waves of excitement; new lands; banks of pearls; islands to be had for the asking. A crowd of discoverers-to-be, Vicente

Váñez, Hojeda, Bastidas, Guerra Alonso Miño, Nicuesa, Pedrarias Balboa, Ponce de León—keen, eager, anxious, watching one another—coming and going from the offices of the Royal Chancery to the office of Bishop Fonseca, the dignitary in charge of Indian affairs, to secure charter, a slice of the earth to be combed for gold or pearls, possibly subsidy for caravels, perhaps an appointment of Adelantado or Governo of the lands-to-be-discovered; thence to the quays of Seville and Cádiz t recruit sailors and youths eager to make a fortune or die, to find a pilot o shipmaster ready to risk his ship and his skin for so many shares in th gold and slaves to be had—everywhere the tension of that fantastic nev world pulling at the old Iberian oak and tearing from it roots, branche and foliage to feed the fire of discovery. . . .'

We can visualize with what high hopes Cortés left this bustling plac for the inviting continent that nursed and nourished it. He was quit alone, and the ship he sailed in was badly found and badly handled. O leaving the Canary Islands the vessel lost its mast and had to put bac into the Grand Canary. Then the pilot lost his bearings, and the shi drifted aimlessly about the empty ocean. 'They were in complete con fusion,' Gómara records. 'The sailors were filled with anxiety. The pilo was downcast, and the passengers wept. The captain blamed the pilot an the pilot blamed the captain. Provisions were scarce and water was givin out, and they only had rainwater to drink. All confessed; some curse their luck; others awaited the death that some had already suffered, o they expected to be cast away in the land of the Caribs, where men ar eaten. However, on Good Friday, about sunset, a dove alighted on th yard-arm. All considered this a miracle and wept with joy. They gav thanks to God and set course in the direction of the dove's flight, and o Easter Sunday they sighted the island of Hispaniola.' An eventful voyage and typical of the epoch.

What were the conditions which Cortés found in Hispaniola? Colum bus, during his remarkable third voyage of 1498, headed south, found th island of Trinidad, and became the first man to reach the American main land by landing at the mouth of the Orinoco. He then returned t Hispaniola in order to inspect his brother's handiwork. He found Sa Domingo in a lamentable condition, but although he was armed with th requisite authority he had neither the experience nor the skill to rectif matters. In 1499 the Catholic Kings sent out Francisco de Bobadilla t take the situation in hand. His first action, as is well known, was to sen Columbus home in chains. However, Bobadilla was only a stop-ga governor, and in 1502 he was superseded by Ovando. As befitted th Master of the Order of Alcántara, Ovando's *entrada* was exceptionall

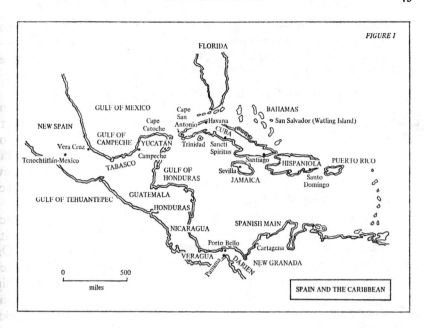

FIGURE 1

FLORIDA

GULF OF MEXICO

Cape San Antonio

Cape Catoche

NEW SPAIN

GULF OF CAMPECHE

Vera Cruz

Tenochtitlán-Mexico

YUCATAN

Campeche

TABASCO

GULF OF HONDURAS

GULF OF TEHUANTEPEC

GUATEMALA

HONDURAS

NICARAGUA

VERAGUA

Porto Bello

Panama

DARIEN

NEW GRANADA

Havana

CUBA

Trinidad

Sancti Spiritus

Santiago

Sevilla

JAMAICA

BAHAMAS

San Salvador (Watling Island)

HISPANIOLA

Santo Domingo

PUERTO RICO

SPANISH MAIN

Cartagena

0   500

miles

SPAIN AND THE CARIBBEAN

well organized. The handful of original settlers, numbering only 300, woke one fine morning to find thirty ships in the harbour, carrying no less than 2,500 new colonists. Ovando became the real *fundador* of Hispaniola. The Spaniards, as anyone who has travelled in Spain or the Americas can testify, possess a genius for building fine cities; and within a matter of months San Domingo was on the way to becoming, as Bernal Díaz described it a few years later, a city 'so well built there is no city in Spain better constructed, except the famous and very noble city of Barcelona'. Since Ovando was in holy as well as knightly orders, he lost no time in ornamenting the main square with a splendid cathedral.

While San Domingo made progress, the island at large was by no means so peaceful. A relentless war went on against the native population, who were called by the general name of 'Caribs', but were actually the Taino nation. Ovando led a number of expeditions himself, in one of which he captured and hanged the 'Queen' of the Tainos, together with her chiefs or *caciques*. The Tainos began rapidly to die out under the onslaught of European arms, supplemented by European diseases such as smallpox and consumption, to which they had no immunity. They also suffered as a result of the system of forced labour to which the Spaniards subjected them. Under the system of *encomiendu*, whole villages were assigned to Spanish overlords, like the feudal villages of Castile.

Cortés arrived in Hispaniola with little money but with lofty notions. Advised by Ovando's secretary to become a farmer, 'he scorned the advice, for it was his notion that he had only to land in order to be weighed down with gold. The secretary,' says Gómara, 'told him to think it over, for getting gold was a matter of luck and hard work.' However, according to Cervantes de Salazar, a period of poverty and hardship soon produced a more realistic attitude. He was glad to accept the gift of some Indians from the governor and the post of Public Notary in the town of Azúa. Professional men were scarce in the colonies, and his legal training at Salamanca was no doubt the decisive factor. In effect he was the most powerful man in his small community, and as part of the official apparatus he must have gained a useful insight into the workings of Government House and the colonial bureaucracy. It was not a lively existence for a young man of his energy and ambitions; he shared the life of those farmers whose way of life he had earlier disdained, raising exiguous crops of sugar-cane and cassava. The only interludes came from raids against the Tainos, from expeditions in search for gold, or from the hunting of wild animals or pigs and cattle that had escaped from domesticity and taken to the woods, where they were deemed common property. Nevertheless he was able by virtue of his office to cut a reasonably dignified figure, and Cervantes de Salazar records that he discharged his duties to the satisfaction of the whole town.

Las Casas has a nice anecdote that illustrates both the suavity of his manner and the ruthlessness of his will. 'He had a good way of keeping everyone in order. If he knew of anyone who was a disturbing factor, or who gave a bad example, and especially if he had been told that someone had set eyes on a married woman, even though his information went no further than that the man had only passed her in the street several times, he had the man summoned with much tact, received him with a pleasant countenance, and asked him to dine as if he intended to grant him a favour. Then Cortés would indicate the harbour and say: "Tell me, which of those ships down there will it be convenient for you to sail home in?" And the other man would turn white, then red, and ask: "But, sir—*why*?" And Cortés would reply: "Think now of nothing else." ' Thus would Cortés rid himself of any independent-minded young man who might threaten his own position. There might even have been another motive, for it seems likely that Cortés liked to reserve any personable young women in the neighbourhood for his own use, and would have little time for rivals. Bernal Díaz informs us that he heard it said that 'as a young man in Hispaniola, Cortés was rather sportive about women, and several times was at daggers drawn concerning them with brave and seasoned men, and always won. He had a knife scar close to his lower lip which could be seen by those who looked closely, though he covered it with his beard. It was from a wound he received in those quarrels'. Cervantes de Salazar also relates that when, at one time during these years, he wanted to join an overseas expedition, 'he was prevented from doing so because of a severe pain in the leg. His friends said it was the buboes, as he was always fond of women, and Indian women infect those who come to them more than Spanish women do.'

One of the men in whose company he made two major forays against the natives was the provincial governor, Diego Velázquez. The youthful Cortés attached himself to Velázquez and cultivated him assiduously. Las Casas has given us a characteristically shrewd portrait of this rich and important functionary, a former veteran of the Italian campaigns. 'He was much loved by all the Spaniards under his authority. He had a merry and attractive disposition, and talked continually about pleasures and festivities. He liked to speak in the style of one unruly young man confiding in another, but when necessary he knew well enough to make himself respected and obeyed. He had his lands in the province of Xaragua and in the area close to the harbour facing Cuba. He was very handsome in face and body, and was therefore the more imposing. He was growing fat, but had lost little of his good looks. He was actually very clever, though he liked to give the impression of being slow-witted' (see Plate 2a).

During his governorship, Ovando had sent a scouting expedition to Cuba, until then ignored by the Spaniards. Ovando's successor was Diego Colón, son of Christopher Columbus. Colón first moved east to conquer Puerto Rico, then annexed the comparatively small island of Jamaica. That done, he decided to launch an expedition against the much more important island of Cuba, which his father had insisted was not an island at all but a part of the mainland. For its leader Colón chose Diego Velázquez, and the latter in turn invited his sharp young friend Cortés to accompany him. Cortés had progressed as far as he could in Hispaniola; he had not made money, and his official position was a relatively humble one. The gold that he had come to seek had not materialized; in fact the overall supply of gold in Hispaniola had proved to be small, and even the little that existed was now in rapid process of running out. He had not crossed the Atlantic to finish his days as Public Notary of Azúa; his future lay elsewhere, and he had no hesitation in joining Velázquez. However, in his shrewd way he pretended to be reluctant, for an anonymous chronicler informs us that Velázquez 'begged him day after day to go with him, promising him oceans and mountains if Cortés would help him with the war'.

The expedition, which numbered three hundred men, sailed towards the end of 1511. It was the twenty-six-year-old Cortés' first experience of an armed *entrada*, his initiation into the obdurate brotherhood of the *conquistadores*. He went more in the capacity of quartermaster than as a fighting man, although all the members of an expedition were expected to lend a hand when the moment came for combat. The actual second-in-command was Pánfilo de Nárvaez, of whom we shall hear more later; but the same unknown chronicler tells us that, as Diego Velázquez was 'not very fitted for war, because of his obesity, he made Cortés his associate and adviser in all his decisions', and that Cortés 'behaved so bravely in the war that in a short time he became the most experienced man of all'.

We may suppose that Cortés made a large contribution to the speedy success of the expedition. The Spaniards quickly established themselves, and began the construction of the town of Baracoa, facing Hispaniola, which in 1514 became Santiago de Cuba (Havana, in the extreme west of the island, was not founded until 1515). Cortés, promoted to the positions of Secretary to the Governor and King's Treasurer, settled down to the next phase of his career as one of Baracoa's most prominent citizens. It was already a marked advance on the position of Notary Public.

He had spent seven years in Hispaniola, and was now to spend seven in Cuba. The ripening and tempering of his character continued, and by the end of his stay his material condition would so far have advanced that, when the time came for him to leave the island, he would do so as leader of his own expedition, a commander-in-chief in his own right. Nevertheless his progress was anything but smooth. He was developing the deft and sinuous side of his nature, but at the same time was still a young man, not yet fully in control of those volcanic impulses which had already ruffled the progress of his otherwise bland ascent. In fact it was a curious combination of his tastes for intrigue and women that almost caused his downfall and even his destruction.

He began well. Gómara writes that he 'raised cattle, sheep, and mares, and was the first to own a herd and a house. He extracted a great deal of gold with the help of his Indians'. Twenty-six, and sitting pretty. It was not to last. Among the first settlers in Baracoa was a man called Juan Juárez, originally from Granada, who had brought with him to the Indies his mother and several sisters. The sisters were poor, and looking for rich husbands. One of them, Catalina, had a high opinion of her charms, for Gómara says that she 'even said quite seriously that she was going to be a great lady, having dreamed it or heard it from an astrologer'. Gómara continues: 'The Juárez girls were pretty, for which reason and because there was a shortage of Spanish women they were much sought after.' Cortés courted Catalina. In doing so, he caught a shrew, for she proved a Beatrice to his Benedick. Their courting was lively. At first he refused to marry her. Her father and kinfolk went to the Governor to demand redress, and Diego Velázquez, who was himself having an affair with one of Catalina's sisters, threw Cortés in gaol for breach of promise. A nice instance of Satan reproving sin.

Velázquez had a more serious reason than an amatory one for putting his secretary in gaol. Juárez and the others, to bolster their case, had blackened Cortés' character by claiming that he was at the centre of a reasonable conspiracy. In later years Cortés—through Gómara—vigorously denied this charge, though the latter admits that it 'bore the colour of truth', as many men had been observed entering and leaving Cortés' house. It seems likely that the accusation against Cortés was well founded. He was not attempting to foment armed insurrection; reckless though he was at this period, his innate caution restrained him from such utter folly. Nevertheless he was almost certainly aiming to undermine his patron's position. Perhaps his idea was to unseat the Governor so that he himself, as King's Treasurer, could step into the vacant position. If so, he worked, as he would always do, strictly within the bounds of legality. Few men of action have had so marked a veneration for due form as Cortés; the man of action and the casuist were curiously intertwined. In the present instance, he appears to have been acting as the collector and transcriber into legal language of a number of serious complaints against Velázquez which were to be taken to Hispaniola for submission either to a visiting panel of justices that had arrived from Spain, or to a newly-established *audiencia*, a court of appeal independent of the Governor which had recently been established. Las Casas tells us that Cortés himself was planning to be the bearer of the petition, since the disaffected citizens could find nobody hardier or bolder in the face of danger, for he would have to make the crossing to Hispaniola amid high and stormy seas in a canoe or a native boat'.

His fat friend in Government House was certainly not slow-witted, and his spies had kept him informed of what was in the wind. He had Cortés seized and imprisoned, ostensibly for his refusal to marry Catalina, but actually to give himself time to formulate graver charges. The future conqueror of the Aztecs thereupon found himself sitting in a cell with his legs enclosed in the stocks. He had no illusions about what his fate would be after the trial that Velázquez was arranging for him, and Gómara tells us that, 'fearing a parade of false witnesses, as commonly happened in those parts, he broke the padlock, snatched the guard's sword and shield, opened a window, let himself down, and took sanctuary in a church'.

The escape seems to have been a put-up job, and the enraged Governor accused the head gaoler of accepting a bribe. 'Velázquez attempted,' says Gómara, 'to get Cortés out of the church by tricks and even by force, but the latter saw through the tricks and resisted the force.' What happened next is vividly conveyed by the same chronicler. 'One day, however, he grew careless and was picked up, while strolling outside the confines of the church, by the constable and a posse. They put him in a dungeon loaded with irons. Many people sympathized with him because they thought that the Governor's judgment was clouded by passion. But Cortés doubted that he would ever be set free, and was convinced he would either be sent to San Domingo or back to Spain. After many attempts, he finally managed to squeeze his feet out of the stocks, though it caused him a great deal of pain. That night he changed clothes with the boy who attended him and escaped from the gaol, slipping out of the side door into a skiff and cutting the painter of the boat moored next to it to prevent pursuit. As he was exhausted and alone, he was unable to make headway against the swift current, and was afraid that the skiff would capsize if he tried to land. So he took off his clothes and wrapped inside them some documents he had obtained that were unfavourable to the Governor. He placed the clothes in a bundle on top of his head, dived into the water and swam ashore.' There he promptly took sanctuary once more in a church.

Fortunately, at this juncture Velázquez found himself with a native rebellion on his hands. He had succeeded in preventing his fire-brand of a secretary from reaching Hispaniola, and judged it prudent to make friendly overtures to a young man whose courage and ability were otherwise useful to him. There was an armed peace-conference at a village outside Baracoa, where Velázquez was gathering his troops to march against the rebels. Cortés turned up without warning in the dead of night, armed with a crossbow, and strode into Velázquez's quarters without knocking. Velázquez was alarmed at Cortés' expression, as well as he might be, and hastened to placate him. The latter, for his part, realized that it was futile to continue the feud, for Velázquez held all the high cards. A reconciliation was effected between the two former friends. Next day he rode off with the Governor to help put down the insurrection.

'In this fashion,' Gómara observes, 'he regained the confidence of Diego Velázquez which he had formerly enjoyed.' We may take leave to doubt this. There had been too much anger and mistrust on both sides, and neither lived at an age or in a place where men habitually reposed confidence in one another. On the other hand, the relationship between the younger and older man was patched up. Cortés married Catalina, and the Governor was gracious enough to stand as godfather to a child born to Cortés by an Indian woman. We shall never know the rights and wrongs or the ramifications of these ancient quarrels. Nor at this distance do they greatly matter. What is significant is the light they shed on the tindery, explosive nature of the participants. It is not surprising that from such makeshift societies, led by such turbulent men, the breed of *conquistadores* should have sprung.

4

Andidieron los pregones sabet a todas partes
al sabor de la ganançia non lo quieren detardar
grandes yentes se le acojen de la buena cristiandad

The word went out, you know, in all directions.
At the lure of wealth nobody wished to delay.
From great Christendom large numbers flocked to him.

DIEGO VELÁZQUEZ, whatever his other shortcomings, was a first-rate officer and administrator. Under his guidance Cuba was subdued and settled more expeditiously than Hispaniola had been. Within five years he had established five townships, all well-sited and well-administered. Cuba was less mountainous than her sister-island, and better adapted for farming and planting sugar, and in a remarkably short time its first Governor made it productive and prosperous.

He was also an excellent businessman, and saw to it that he obtained his full share of the gold that was mined within his jurisdiction. Again, Cuba proved more prolific in this field than Hispaniola. As he waxed richer, he began to cast about for even more lucrative dominions to exploit. For the first six years the affairs of Cuba absorbed his energies; then, able, greedy and ambitious, he began to turn his eyes towards the more distant territories of the Caribbean and the Spanish Main, and more particularly the mainland. By 1517 he had entered fully into the potentially lucrative business of backing *conquistadores* by buying shares in their expeditions.

Christopher Columbus had reached the mainland in 1498. Within a year, two other captains had set foot there. Pinzón, one of Columbus' own captains on the great voyage of 1492, reached the coasts of Guyana and northern Brazil. Alonso de Hojeda, another of Columbus' former commanders, did not sail further than the coast of Venezuela, but his voyage is celebrated because his navigator was the Florentine geographer Amerigo Vespucci, whose contributions to the *Paesi novamente ritrovati*, published at Verona in 1507, led to the naming of the Americas. In 1500 Rodrigo de Bastidas entered the Gulf of Darien, on the north coast of modern Colombia; and in 1504 his companion on that voyage, Juan de la Cosa, yet another old comrade of Columbus, made the first of two more thorough investigations of the same area.

The Indies were beginning to open up. But to the dismay of the Spaniards, and the jubilation of the Portuguese, it was every year becoming clearer that the Indies were not the mainland of the rich continent of Asia, but a barrier cutting them off, seemingly forever, from those tantalizing riches. However, it was hoped that the barrier might prove to be merely a narrow strip of land. The crossing of the thirty-mile isthmus by Balboa, one of Bastidas' companions on the voyage of 1500, appeared to confirm this hope. Moreover, if the so-called mainland was so narrow at this and perhaps other points, then it might be possible to haul ships across and launch them into the vast new 'South Sea' towards elusive Asia. Surely the East could not now be too far off? Or might it not be possible to find a natural canal that would allow ingress into one ocean from the other? The *conquistadores* were to expend much energy and many lives seeking this much-desired waterway. 'The conquest of Central America,' writes J. H. Parry, in his *The Spanish Seaborne Empire*, 'was in a sense a race between Spaniards and Portuguese to reach the East. In the same year that Balboa crossed the isthmus, the first Portuguese ships reached the Moluccas. In the same year that Cortés landed in Mexico, Magellan sailed on the voyage which was to reveal both the western route to the East and the daunting size of the Pacific. Magellan's voyage also revealed that the Spaniards had lost the race; but in Central America they had a reward of a different kind: though they failed to find a strait, they founded a great empire.'

*　　　*　　　*

The first tentative settlements on the mainland gave no indication of the size which that great empire, of which Cortés was to carve out the first substantial portion, would assume in the matter of a few decades. In 1509 the Spanish crown authorized Alonso de Hojeda to establish a settlement on the Gulf of Darien, and Diego de Nicuesa to establish one at Veragua, in northern Panama. Veragua had been discovered and claimed as a personal possession by Christopher Columbus, on his fourth voyage; and in fact the permissions granted by the crown infringed the exclusive licences granted to the Columbus family. Diego Colón, the Governor of Hispaniola, not unnaturally put as many obstacles in the way of Hojeda and Nicuesa as he could. Nevertheless over a thousand men sailed with these pioneer *fundadores* on their joint expedition. It was a disaster. Hojeda had hardly landed before he was attacked by Indians with poisoned arrows and lost seventy men, including the great Juan de la Cosa himself. The body of the famous navigator, Las Casas tells us, was found 'tied to a tree, looking like a hedgehog bristling with arrows, swollen and misshapen, of frightful ugliness because of the poisonous herb'. Hojeda pressed on, saw the rest of his men drop like flies, was himself fearfully wounded, and led his last twenty men on a march through a four-hundred-mile swamp, chest deep in mud, that lasted thirty days. The survivors of the march were miraculously rescued and taken to Jamaica; and a little later Hojeda died in hospital in San Domingo, without even enough money in his purse to pay for his burial. As for his comrade in arms, Nicuesa, he founded a colony called Nombre de Dios and lost seven hundred of his eight hundred men there. Reinforcements arrived from Hispaniola. They were commanded by an inexperienced bureaucrat: but the contingent also contained Balboa, then thirty-five years old. The 'popular desperado' as Parry calls him, took over, shipped the bureaucrat home, and arranged for poor gallant Nicuesa to disappear at sea, ostensibly on his way back to San Domingo. First of the true line of *conquistadores*, he marched on to his great triumphs. He discovered the Pacific, founded the thriving colony of Castilla de Oro—Golden Castile—and prospered until 1517, when he ran foul of the sadistic Pedrarias Dávila, the new Governor of Castilla de Oro and *capo mafioso* of the *conquistadores*. The wreck of the Hojeda-Nicuesa enterprise, the first large-scale set-back in the colonization of the Indies, caused a sensation. We should bear in mind the fate of such men when we consider the similar undertaking shortly to be launched by Hernán Cortés. It was always odds-on, at that particular period, that a would-be *conquistador* would end up stuck with arrows, or cast adrift by a kind friend, or bankrupt, or sick, or loaded with chains, or with his head on the block.

* * *

The first attempts to settle the mainland from Hispaniola had gone south, deep into the Spanish Main. When explorers set out from Cuba, as they were soon to do, it made more sense for them to sail due west. In that way they kept out of the private back-yard of their rivals in Hispaniola. It had also been established that there were barely a hundred miles of open water between the westerly keys of Cuba and the eastern tip of Yucatán. By contrast, voyagers between San Domingo and the Gulf of Darien had to sail eight hundred miles.

The initial attempt to explore the coastline of Mexico and bring back a valuable cargo was made in 1517, by a wealthy Cuban landowner called Francisco de Córdoba. Velázquez had a finger in the pie, and hired out to Córdoba one of the three ships. To begin with the voyage went well. A landing was made somewhere in the vicinity of Cape Catoche, at the nearest point of the Yucatán peninsula, and the first contact took place between Europeans and Mexicans. Then trouble started. In an unexpected skirmish fifteen Spaniards were wounded, before the supernatural sound of firearms caused their assailants to flee. The Spaniards attacked the local village, got a first glimpse of the horrendous idols, temples and religious customs, and ransacked the place for gold. Short of water, they sailed on down the coast, looking for a site to land to replenish their supply. Ambushed at dawn by Indians as they were filling their barrels, a further fifty men were killed and many more wounded, including Córdoba himself, who sustained ten wounds. Thereupon the expedition turned towards home. Córdoba reached Cuba before he died; but the expedition could hardly be called successful. However, when the few scraps of gold and the Indian cult-objects that had been seized were circulated in Santiago de Cuba, they roused tremendous interest and served to whet the appetite of Diego Velázquez and his friends for more.

Soon after Córdoba's return, Velázquez fitted out a second expedition, this time providing two ships and some of the supplies and objects for barter. In charge he placed a relation of his, Juan de Grijalva. Grijalva's chief officer was Pedro de Alvarado, who was to become Cortés' second in command. The little fleet sailed on May 1, 1518, after being favoured with a florid address from the plump Governor. 'Gentlemen and friends, servants and connections,' he began, 'you will have gathered by now that my aim in spending money on such enterprises as this is the service of God and the King. Both will be well served if by our efforts new lands and peoples are discovered, and God will be sure to acknowledge your labour by giving you, at the very least, worldly wealth.'

Essentially the expedition covered the same ground as Córdoba's. After three days' sailing the Spaniards landed on the island of Cozumel, off the east coast of Yucatán, then proceeded across the narrow straits to the mainland. The Indians all took to the woods at their approach, and they entered a large village that was completely empty. Grijalva, who was a prudent and cautious commander (he had been strictly enjoined not to jeopardize the Governor of Cuba's investment), then decreed a return to Cozumel to refill the water-barrels; he was fearful of suffering the same misfortune as Francisco de Córdoba. Landing once more on the peninsula, the Indians emerged from their hiding-places and attacked him. He lost several men and was himself hit by an arrow in the mouth. Taking to the ships, the Spaniards sailed northwards around the coast of Yucatán, believing that, like Cozumel, it was an island. They rounded Cape Catoche and made an enterprising five-hundred-mile trip south-westwards as far as Tabasco, at the bottom of the Gulf of Campeche. Here they landed and managed to establish good relations with the local natives. Bartering took place. In exchange for some piffling objects—glass beads, scissors, mirrors, and a few bits of cheap or discarded clothing—the Spaniards obtained a respectable collection of gold vessels and ornaments, some of them sacred, and many of them set with turquoise and semi-precious stones. This was a minuscule return on the outlay of the complete expedition: but gold, that mysterious element, was after all the physical and psychological trigger of adventure and conquest. Grijalva turned for home. Apart from the fact that, unlike his predecessors, he brought most of his men back alive, and returned himself with a whole skin, his expedition could not be rated a success. But that little pile of gold, and the confirmation of the fact that the natives on the mainland appeared to be wealthy, that they lived in stone-built houses and erected substantial temples, produced lively excitement in Cuba. There were rumours of a fantastically rich civilization to be found further into the interior. The imagination of Diego Velázquez and his friends was inflamed so greatly, Gómara relates, that they were even inclined to believe tall stories brought back by Grijalva's men about 'the Amazons who inhabited certain islands', and other fabulous stories.

Slowly, as knowledge of the mainland grew, the enthusiasm of the young opportunists in Santiago de Cuba grew with it. But, unknown to the Spaniards, the accumulation of knowledge was a two-way process. Their haphazard comings and goings had been observed and studied by eyes much sharper than those of the humble villagers of Cozumel and Tabasco. It seems probable that observers and officials from the great hidden inland empire of the Emperor Moctezuma had witnessed the activities of the Spaniards. Reports were drawn up and swiftly carried by runners to Tenochtitlán, the beautiful white city built on a lake that was larger and more populous than San Domingo or Santiago de Cuba— larger, even, than Seville or Granada, Toledo or Valencia.

Before the ships of Córdoba or Grijalva had entered harbour, the Aztec leaders were taking counsel about them. When the next band of Spaniards waded ashore, they would receive a more organized welcome.

*   *   *

Diego Velázquez had begun to experience pangs of greed and anxiety almost before Grijalva's sails had dipped below the horizon. As the weeks passed, and Grijalva showed signs of becoming overdue, Velázquez was sure that his kinsman was engaged on some plan to cheat him, or would fail to plant the desired settlement, as instructed, 'in the name of Diego Velázquez and of the King'. Matters were becoming urgent. Diego Colón, the Governor of San Domingo, was now moving actively to spike Velázquez's guns as a freelance colonizer.

As a first move, Velázquez sent out a ship under Cristóbal de Olid to catch up with Grijalva, find out what he was up to, and if necessary stiffen his resolution. But Olid encountered a storm and was forced to return. However, in the meantime Pedro de Alvarado, Grijalva's chief lieutenant, arrived back in Cuba with the gold objects mentioned above: and the sight of them so stirred up Velázquez that, even before Grijalva's return, he began to make preparation for a third expedition.

Who was to command it? The first man he invited to share expenses with him turned him down. This was because, as Gómara says, Velázquez was 'stingy, and had little stomach for spending, and wanted to despatch a fleet at other people's expense, as he had done with Grijalva'. Thwarted, he turned elsewhere, and at length put the proposition to Cortés who, he knew, had been accumulating capital for just such a venture. Cortés accepted Velázquez's terms, close-fisted though he knew the latter to be. This was Cortés' chance, and he realized it. Diego Colón might put a stop to expeditions from Cuba, or a dozen other conclusive obstacles might arise. It was now or never. For several years he had watched other men set off on the hopeful voyage to the mainland. He had not been willing to serve in a subordinate capacity; he had waited until he was in a position to be the head of his own *entrada*. *Aut Caesar aut nihil*. He dared delay no longer. With each successive voyage the chances of a triumphant outcome appeared increasingly favourable. Grijalva's gold clinched it. On October 23, 1518, he signed an agreement with Velázquez in which the costs and objectives of the voyage were specified.

In fact, Cortés was now in a hurry. The speed at which he went to work on his own account, even before the agreement was drawn up, alarmed Velázquez, and would in any case have forced his hand. Furthermore, Cortés had two rich and powerful backers in Velázquez's entourage with whom he had already undertaken to divide any gold, silver and jewels that came his way. Once he had made up his mind, he threw himself into the venture with impressive energy. He spent all his own money and ran himself deeply into debt, so determined was he to ensure that his expedition would be the best-equipped of those that had sailed hitherto. Every biographer of Cortés emphasizes the fact that the hall-mark of his character was his carefulness and thoroughness. Never was this thoroughness so much in evidence as in the preparations he made for the coming voyage. When the future conqueror of the Aztecs landed on the coast of Mexico he would be bankrupt, but he would also be better provided with the necessities of war than any of his predecessors.

Cortés acquired his men and supplies piecemeal during the course of the next four weeks, which were weeks of furious activity. The bulk of them he assembled at Santiago de Cuba, others he picked up as he sailed around the south coast of the island on the way to Mexico; but it will be convenient to summarize here the totals of the troops and supplies he finally took with him. In Santiago de Cuba he enrolled upwards of 300 officers and men; later, when he wintered in the little port of Trinidad, staying in Juan de Grijalva's house and no doubt profiting from his host's advice, he enrolled 200 of Grijalva's men. In the end he found himself at the head of a fighting force of about 550 soldiers, and it was to his advantage that many of them were veterans not only of the two previous expeditions from Cuba, but that some of them had taken part in the conquest of Darien and served with Balboa and Pedrarias Dávila. They knew what to expect.

To transport them, he began by buying with his own money two caravels, one of which was the ship which Pedro de Alvarado had commanded during the Grijalva expedition. Velázquez, with what protestations of poverty we can imagine, provided another brigantine. These were the only four ships of any size in a fleet that eventually numbered eleven ships of all kinds. The caravel that was to serve as the flagship was 100 tons; the three others were between 80 and 100 tons. The eight remaining vessels were diminutive, and most of them had open decks. Conditions aboard during the voyage to Mexico must have been unbearably crowded, for in addition to his 550 troops Cortés had recruited 200 Cuban natives to act as servants and carriers. This swarm of people had to be packed aboard the vessels, together with their gear and a great mass of foodstuffs—live pigs, turkeys, salt pork, corn bread, cassava bread, wine, oil, chickpeas, maize, chili, sugar, yucca, and other commodities. The supplies of water alone must have occupied a great deal of space.

Then there were the soldiers' arms and armour. The principal weapon was the long, heavy ashwood lance, tipped with steel. This was the infantry weapon, and when a line of them were carried into battle they resembled an 'iron cornfield', as Calderón called them; they are the lances that can be seen rearing into the sky in *The Surrender of Breda*. It was this bristling thicket that the Spanish regiments had learned to wield with grim purpose during the Italian campaigns of Gonzalvo de Córdoba, and which had made the Spanish *tercios* supreme in Europe. Then there were the shorter, lighter javelins, also tipped with steel, which had been a standard item of military equipment since the days when Spaniards fought in the Roman legions; the name of javelin was derived from their usefulness in spearing the *jabalina*, the wild boar, in both Spain and the Indies. Next came the stout swords with solid hilts, the famous blades of Toledo, 'swords of Spain, the ice-brook's temper'. Also of steel were the characteristic Spanish helmets or morions, the breastplates, the shirts of mail, the arm-pieces and greaves. From their experiences on previous expeditions, however, many of the veterans would soon lay aside their metal armour in favour of body-protection made of a double thickness of leather, or of cloth stuffed with the cotton that was plentiful in Cuba. They had learned that such simple padding was cooler, less cumbersome, and equally efficient against the swords and darts of the Mexicans, who themselves wore such quilted armour. Finally, room had to be found for the specialist weapons which Cortés took with him. He had accumulated thirty-two crossbows and thirteen muskets, together with ten brass guns and four falconets. The firearms would require their full complement of powder and shot. One of these crude cannons can be seen in the museum of Chapultepec Castle in Mexico City; it resembles a primitive trench-mortar, a tube consisting of nine six-inch sections divided by fourteen separate iron rings. The weapon could therefore be easily dismantled for transportation: but it would have taken a brave man to fire the thing. Since Cortés, as Bernal Díaz says, 'was most careful about everything', he twice ordered his four gunners to parade the artillery for his inspection. He saw that the guns were clean, tested them, and provided wine and vinegar for their upkeep. So too with the crossbows. He made certain that all of them had 'two or three spare nuts and cords and forecords, that they were carefully stored, and that the planes and spokeshaves were in good order'. He ordered the crossbowmen to practise regularly at targets and acquaint themselves with the accurate ranges of their weapons.

He also paid special attention to the condition of the sixteen horses that he intended to take with him. Horses had been brought across to the Indies on Columbus' third voyage; but although they became common enough later on, they were still scarce and phenomenally expensive. One source tells us that Cortés' sixteen horses were valued at five hundred gold pesos each. Hardy as Spanish horses were, many of them died in their slings towards the end of the long voyage from Spain and had to be thrown overboard—hence, perhaps, the meaning of the Horse Latitudes. Cortés was therefore unable to buy or to persuade his officers to bring along more than sixteen of these precious animals. The fact that he took them on board at all is an indication of his determination to see the expedition through to the end. This was not to be a hit-and-run affair: this was to be a definite attempt at settlement. True, the horses would have been useful in any case as a small cavalry unit, but they would scarcely have been needed if Cortés had been contemplating merely the ship-based sorties employed by Córdoba and Grijalva. Clearly he meant this time to move inland, and the horses were to be the mode of penetration and reconnaissance. Of course, his decision to employ horses, which must have struck his contemporaries as bizarre and even astounding, was a stroke of genius. As Bernal Díaz wrote afterwards, those sixteen horses were to be 'their fortress', 'their one hope of survival'—in fact, 'they owed it all to the horses'. But the genius of great generals is based on their capacity for taking pains. Cortés must have had a clear idea from the outset of how decisive the presence of the horses was to be and of the exact manner in which he meant to employ them. No doubt, too, he had heard tales of the extraordinary effect that the first sight of a horse had produced on the natives of San Domingo and Cuba. As one of the first settlers of Cuba, one of the first importers of a horse into that island, he must have seen for himself the terrified reaction of the natives to this unfamiliar animal. It stayed in his mind, and he resolved to make use of that terror as a psychological weapon when he invaded Mexico.

What were those horses, the most celebrated horses in history, actually like? Bernal Díaz, with his marvellous powers of recall, describes them meticulously. Eight of them were bay or sorrel, three were grey, two were dappled or piebald, two were brown, and one was black. Not all were good for fighting, and some had more than one owner. In breeding they would have been a mixture of the Arab and the Barb, both of which had been brought to Spain by the Moors. The Barb was an offshoot of the Arabian steed that grew into virtually a separate type in the hands of the Arabs of North Africa: and the Barb-Arab horse, particularly as developed in Andalusia, was a magnificent creature. To the beauty and endurance of the Arabian, ancestor of the English Thoroughbred, the American Morgan, the Lippizaner, the Orloff, the Palomino, was added the additional staunchness of the Barb. The horses that the Spaniards took with them to the New World were fine specimens. J. Frank Dobie, in his classic study *The Mustang*, cites Sir Walter Raleigh as asserting that the horses in the West Indies were the best he ever saw in his life.

These were the horses with which the captains of Cortés and the other *conquistadores* subdued the New World, riding *a la gineta*, or Moorish fashion, as Garcilaso de la Vega said they did in Peru. Cortés himself appointed ten such captains, whose names are worth setting down not only because they will recur later in this narrative, but because they are the names of a group of fearless and singular men. They were Alonso de Ávila, one of Grijalva's companions, Francisco de Montejo—the future conqueror of Yucatán—Francisco de Saucedo, Juan de Escalante, Juan Velázquez de León, Cristóbal de Olid, and a man called Escobar. Most of these men, like their leader, were only in their early or mid-thirties. Ávila and Montejo were placed in charge of two of the ships, and Cortés divided his troops into eleven companies, giving one to each of these officers and retaining a headquarter's company for himself. Portocarrero was a cousin of the Conde de Medellín, and from Medellín itself came the man whom Cortés made his most trusted adviser and the second-in-command of the entire venture. This was a striking young man of twenty-four named Gonzalo de Sandoval. Bernal Díaz says of him: 'He was very brave. In his body and stature he was not very tall, but well-proportioned and sturdy. His chest was deep and his back was broad. He was rather bow-legged and an excellent horseman. His expression was vigorous, and his hair and beard, which were long, were chestnut-coloured and curling. His voice was not very distinct, and he lisped a little, but there was something impressive about the way he spoke. He was not scholarly or learned, but plain and simple, and he coveted nothing except fame and military honour. He appreciated a good soldier and did his best for him. He was the captain of whom our leader told the King that of all the brave men in our brave company, Gonzalo de Sandoval was head and shoulders above the rest.' Bernal Díaz also gives us one of his excellent thumb-nail sketches of the man who, without commanding a company, was captain of the fourth ship, and destined to become the most forceful single figure of the campaign after Cortés—disastrously so, for at a critical juncture he acted vigorously but injudiciously, with almost fatal consequences. This was Grijalva's lieutenant, Pedro de Alvarado, whom Bernal Díaz says 'was about thirty-four, well-built, with a very cheerful face and manner and an agreeable expression. He was so handsome the Indians nicknamed him *The Sun* (see Plate 2b). He was athletic and a good horseman, also generous and well-spoken. He was always punctiliously dressed and fond of rich and expensive clothes. Round his neck he wore a thin gold chain with a jewelled pendant, and on his finger was a good diamond'. After his exploits with

Cortés, Alvarado was to go on to take part in the conquests of Guatemala and Peru.

One more of Cortés' companions, not an officer but a remarkable man in his own right, ought to be signalized here. He is Bernal Díaz—Bernal Díaz del Castillo, to give him his full name—on whose *True History of the Conquest of New Spain* we have already drawn and will draw more extensively in the pages ahead. Bernal Díaz was born in 1492, the year in which Columbus discovered the Indies, at Medina del Campo, south of Valladolid, where his father had been the city governor. A young man of respectable lineage but no prospects, he joined the suite of a grandee going out as a governor to the New World, as the youthful Cortés had endeavoured to do. The governor in question was Pedrarias Dávila, and Bernal Díaz accompanied him to Darien in 1514 and was a witness of the events leading up to the execution of Balboa. A relative of Diego Velázquez, he crossed to Cuba with a hundred companions; but his kinsman disappointed him, and he received no grant of land or Indians. He and his friends thereupon 'decided to seek new lands in which to try our fortunes and find occupation', and joined forces with Francisco de Córdoba. Notwithstanding their arduous and disappointing experiences with Córdoba, most of the survivors, including Bernal Díaz, went out again the following year with Grijalva. By the time he sailed with Cortés, therefore, he was already, at the age of twenty-six, a seasoned veteran of the Caribbean—more seasoned, in fact, than his leader. He was a profound though not uncritical admirer of Cortés, and accompanied him not only throughout the campaigns in Mexico but also in the later and even more difficult campaign, if that were possible, in Honduras. He finished his days as governor of the town of Santiago de Guatemala, which was no great position for a man who had rendered Spain and her king such long and loyal service.

Though he never gained the fortune he sought, he had witnessed great events and known great glory, and as an old man (he died at eighty-nine) he lived increasingly in the golden days of the past. He began his *True History* when he was over seventy, to wile away the hours in Guatemala, but gave it up after a few chapters because, as he admitted, he was 'no scholar', and was ashamed of what he considered his poor style. Then, fortunately for posterity, a copy of Gómara's *History of the Mexican Conquest*, printed at Zaragoza in 1552, fell into his hands. Gómara, whom the old man regarded as an upstart young puppy, had not been present at the stirring scenes he described, and Bernal Díaz was filled with the desire of the old soldier to recount the battles from the point of view of a participant. He was also disgusted with what he regarded as the omissions and distortions of Gómara and other historians, so that notwithstanding his misgivings about his style he took up his pen and plunged once more, with a fine indignation, into his narrative.

Of course, his style is neither poor nor inadequate. On the contrary, as Prescott says of him, 'he is among chroniclers what Defoe is among novelists'. He is marvellously direct and down-to-earth, and his plainness gives an effect of complete accuracy and veracity. Although he claims to be unlettered, any poor Spanish gentleman of those days was a hundred times more literate than a college graduate in ours; and the hardness and sobriety of the Spanish mind, its lack of the cant and sentimentality which is the curse of many other nations and of modern times, gives his work a unique flavour. *The True History* is one of the world's classic books. Cortés, lucky in so many things, was doubly lucky in that his deeds were related by a man of such rare talents. Bernal Díaz not only possessed an astonishing memory, but was also a decent, intelligent and reasonable man. These qualities emerge on every page. His book is not a piece of propaganda, either for or against the Conquest, as so many of the later accounts were to be; he tried to tell his story honestly, nothing extenuating nor setting down ought in malice. The fascinating contradictions which are part of the warp and woof of historical events are all there. His was not the usual tidied-up history. Thus we see Cortés fighting against the Aztecs for gold *and* for the glory of God; we see him behaving altruistically *and* selfishly, generously *and* callously. Bernal Díaz grips our imagination and convinces us of the truth of what he is telling us because he is what he claims to be: 'an honest eyewitness, not twisting the facts in any way.' He states the truth about historical events: that they are compounded of both good and bad, and that the men enmeshed in them are themselves good and bad. He presents Cortés as he was: an extraordinary amalgam of seemingly contradictory qualities, not hag-ridden and rendered indecisive by such contradictions, but somehow rendered more energetic and effective by a very fusion of opposites. In fact, we will have to admit that it was largely what nowadays would be called his 'antisocial drives' that gave him his strength. We might perhaps do well to ponder Freud's contention, in his *Why War?* (1933), that far from being wicked or contemptible, the aggressive instinct, which Cortés possessed in such generous measure, is actually a vital and irreplaceable part of our nature. 'We must be chary of passing overhastily to the notions of good and evil,' says Freud. 'Each of these instincts is every whit as indispensable as its opposite, and all the phenomena of life derive from their activity, whether they work in concert or in opposition. It seems that an instinct of either category can operate but rarely in isolation; it is always blended ('alloyed', as we say) with a certain dosage of its opposite, which modifies its aim or even, in certain circumstances, is a prime condition of its attainment. Thus the instinct of self-preservation is certainly of an erotic nature, but to gain its ends this very instinct necessitates aggressive action. In the same way the love-instinct, when directed to a specific object, calls for an admixture of the acquisitive instinct if it is to enter into effective possession of that object.'

We are now on psychological and subjective ground, and are perhaps in danger of attempting to 'explain' Cortés in a way discountenanced earlier. However, a great part of the everlasting interest of Cortés—why one reads about him, and why one writes about him—lies precisely in the fact that he was, as Bernal Díaz painted him in his *Historia verdadera*, a creature of outstanding aggressiveness and outstanding contradictions—of outstanding virtues and outstanding vices, if one likes. Partly this can be explained in historical terms, for it was a legacy of the Middle Ages and almost an obligatory characteristic of the Renaissance that a man's virtues and vices, strengths and weaknesses, should be both exaggerated and unconcealed. But there is more than this. It would be evasive to write a biography of Cortés, of all people, without attempting to touch briefly on psychological matters. Hence, pursuing this direction a little, it is perhaps instructive to point out that Freud, in postulating his 'notions of good and evil', here approximates in an interesting manner to Nietzsche's ideas in *Beyond Good and Evil* (1886). The favourite pupil of the greatest of Renaissance scholars, Jacob Burckhardt, Nietzsche was in an exceptional situation to assess the personalities of that era. Cortés, more than Cesare Borgia, whom Nietzsche instances, surely qualifies as a type of the Super-man: 'He shall be the greatest who can be loneliest, the most concealed, the most deviant, the human being beyond good and evil, the master of his virtues, overrich in will. Precisely this shall be called *greatness*: being capable of being as manifold as whole, as ample as full.' Cortés to the life. Whether one believes with Maine de Biran that the will is good, with Schopenhauer that it is evil, or with Nietzsche that it is neither the one nor the other, there is no doubt that Cortés and the *conquistadores* are the classic embodiments of the Will to Power.

One would not wish to press this matter too far. After all, greatness and heroes are not much in demand these days. Perhaps Nietzsche is right when he asserts that: 'High and independent spirituality, the will to stand alone, even a powerful reason, are regarded as perilous; everything that elevates an individual above his fellows and frightens the neighbours is called evil, and only the modest, submissive, conforming, mediocre mentality is called good. Any high and hard nobility and self-reliance is almost felt to be an insult and arouses mistrust.'

Nietzsche must have approved of the *conquistadores*: and certainly to read or write about them demands a stomach stronger than the ordinary. And while the dangerous subject of the Conquest of Mexico and the dangerous philosopher Nietzsche are thus yoked together, may one not at least consider and speculate upon the point of view that Nietszche advances in Section 259 of the same book? 'Refraining mutually from injury, violence and exploitation,' he writes, 'and placing one's will on a par with that of someone else—this may become, in a certain rough sense, good manners among individuals: but as soon as this principle is extended and possibly accepted as the fundamental principle of society, it immediately proves to be what it really is—a will to the denial of life, a principle of disintegration and decay. Life itself is essentially appropriation, injury, overpowering of what is alien and weaker; suppression, hardness, imposition of one's own forms, incorporation and at least, at its mildest, exploitation. The incarnate will to power must strive to grow, spread, seize, become predominant—not from any morality or immorality, but because it is *living* and because life simply *is* will to power. However, there is no point on which the ordinary consciousness of the European resists enlightenment as on this: everywhere people are now rejoicing, even under scientific disguises, about coming conditions of society in which "the exploitive aspect" will be removed—which sounds to me as if they were promising to invent a way of life that would dispense with all organic functions. "Exploitation" does not belong to a corrupt or imperfect or primitive society: it belongs to the essence of what lives, as a basic organic function; it is a consequence of the will to power, which is after all the will to live. This is the primordial fact of all history: let us be honest with ourselves at least this far.'

This is a doctrine to which Cortés and his fellow *conquistadores* would have subscribed. So, to an even higher degree, would Moctezuma and the Aztecs, as we shall see. Of the two ruthless and self-assertive sets of people, the Aztecs were certainly the more brutal and belligerent. One might only suggest at this point that Nietzsche's remarks are worth consideration. It may be impossible to accept his view of human affairs in all its harsh finality—and we have had the experience in this century of watching a number of the more odious and self-styled Supermen in action: Stalin, with his Great Purge; Mussolini, giving his opponents the castor-oil and rubber-hose treatment; Hitler misinterpreting Nietzsche, whom he read at second hand in the fraudulent version of the philosopher's unscrupulous sister, to his own depraved ends. However, we might at least be inclined to follow Nietzsche's advice so far as to acknowledge the exploitative nature of our own century. The unconcealed exploitation by the Spaniards of the wealth of the Americas has been replaced, after all, only by their exploitation by another great power, nonetheless thorough for being more subtle and indirect. We might also acknowledge that our own century is not only militaristic and brutal; indeed, it is probable that we live in the most blood-sodden century known so far to history. This reflection should at least help us to study the actions and environment of the Spaniards and Aztecs with a minimum of the moral indignation and moral superiority which is an even more tiresome feature of our age than its mindless and hypocritical savagery. At least the Spaniards and Aztecs believed that they had solid reasons for what they did to one another. Marc Bloch, in his *Apologie pour l'Histoire*, abjures the craft of history 'to renounce its false angelic airs', and asks: 'Are we so sure of ourselves and of our age as to divide the company of our forefathers into the just and the damned?'

* * *

Alas, poor Superman. His path is by definition and of necessity beset with thorns. Governor Velázquez, as was his wont, began to regret his signature on the agreement before the ink was dry. He started to have second thoughts about allowing Cortés to assume command. In addition to his own chronic suspicions that his associates were always trying to cheat him, there were plenty of persons to pour poison in his ear concerning Cortés. The man who had previously refused the leadership was now regretting his decision, and seeking to oust Cortés; Velázquez's relatives were importuning the Governor on their own behalf; members of Velázquez's entourage were jealous at having been excluded and outmanœuvred. All these people conspired to bring Cortés down, even bribing the Governor's court jester and astrologer to keep up a whispering campaign. The astrologer reminded him that Cortés was proud and had a long memory, 'and would pay him out for putting him in prison'; while the court jester kept harping on the fact that Cortés was, after all, a crafty Extremeño—the equivalent of an Auvergnat in France, a Saxon in Germany, a Yorkshireman in England, a man from Cardiganshire in Wales, and an Aberdonian in Scotland. Gómara sums up the Governor's fears: 'He thought he could not trust Cortés, who was, after all, an Extremeño, cunning, haughty, touchy about his honour, and likely to seek vengeance for past wrongs.'

For Cortés, it was a serious matter to learn that Velázquez was huffing and puffing in this manner. The anonymous chronicler of the *Documentos ineditos* tells us that Cortés had spent more than 5,000 castellanos (a castellano was the equivalent of a peso) of his own in purchasing and equipping his fleet, had borrowed a further 1,800 castellanos from

3

Velázquez, and owed his two principal backers 4,000 gold pesos. No less than seven of the eleven ships he had bought outright. Velázquez had only put up one ship and the sum of 1,800 castellanos, and was not even a major shareholder: but as Governor he had absolute control over the activities of the residents of Cuba. He could place an official ban on every member of a projected expedition, not merely its leader. If Velázquez withdrew his sanction, Cortés would be ruined. It was a situation that called for the exercise of all his tact. Bernal Díaz tells us that he met the crisis by the clever expedient of 'never leaving the Governor's side, being most sedulously attentive to him, and telling him over and over again that, God willing, he would make him a very wealthy man in a very short time'.

Nevertheless, knowing how hesitant and slippery the Governor was, Cortés realized that the sooner his little fleet left Baracoa the better. The contract with Velázquez had been signed on October 23, and on November 18, less than four weeks later, the officers and men were given a sudden order to be aboard their ships by nightfall. Cortés spent as much of that evening as he could with the Governor, and brought him down to the port the following morning to give the men his blessing. In reality he wanted to slip away before the Governor had a chance to change his mind. He acted in the nick of time, for immediately he weighed anchor Velázquez, goaded by his hangers-on, promptly panicked. He was told that Cortés 'had been heard to say he meant to be captain in spite of the Governor and his relatives, and that he would have set sail immediately if any attempt had been made to detain him'. By the time Cortés reached Trinidad, two important personages had already arrived at Baracoa with orders to arrest Cortés as a rebel and to forbid the ships from sailing any further.

At Trinidad the expedition had passed well beyond the Governor's reach, and the orders were ignored. Cortés employed a characteristic mixture of threats and promises. The messengers were won over with promises of a share in the coming booty, and a threat was quietly conveyed to Velázquez that Cortés' men might possibly get out of hand, if their commander was arrested, and put Trinidad to the sword. The Council of the Indies did not look with favour on governors who allowed mutinies to break out in their territories. Velázquez was also reminded that Cortés did not lack for powerful friends in Baracoa. Overtly, Cortés wrote a honeyed letter to the Governor, 'expressing astonishment', as Bernal Díaz puts it, 'at His Honour's decision, and affirming that his only desire was to serve God and His Majesty, and to obey His Honour as the King's representative'.

All the same, Cortés judged it foolish to linger at Trinidad longer than he needed. After a brief stay of ten days, during which he garnered in as many men and supplies as that part of Cuba had to offer, the fleet set sail again. This time it sought shelter in the port of Havana, at the far end of the island, as far away from Baracoa and the writ of the Governor as it was possible to get. There was a moment of anxiety when the flagship, with Cortés aboard, failed to arrive with the other vessels; but the mishap was a minor indignity caused by the ship becoming stuck on a sandbank, and the commander put in a safe appearance two days later.

At Havana—which was not the modern Havana de Cuba, then known as Puerto de Carenas, but an earlier, smaller Havana—Cortés deemed it safe for the troops to go into winter quarters. There were final preparations to be made. As at Trinidad, he drew what reinforcements and supplies he could from the hinterland. There was also a repetition by Velázquez of his earlier pantomime. Furious at being outwitted in his previous attempt to bring Cortés to heel, he sent orders to his chief representative at Havana to arrest Cortés and conduct him under a strong guard to Baracoa. He instructed his relatives in the town to lend his representative every assistance. It took Cortés only a short time, by means of his customary mixture of flattery and promises, to bring the opposition over to his side. Obligingly, the chief representative wrote a letter to the Governor assuring the latter that Cortés was loyal and well-behaved, and that in any case he dare not molest him because his following was so strong and zealous that they might take it into their heads to burn down the town and carry all the settlers off to Mexico with them. This letter was accompanied by a politely insolent letter from Cortés himself, couched, as Bernal Díaz says, 'in those agreeable and complimentary terms that came so easily to him, saying that he was setting sail next day and would remain His Honour's most humble servant'. Cortés found it a simple matter to employ delaying tactics against his corpulent and wrathful partner during the three final months he needed to bring his company up to the standard of readiness he desired.

*   *   *

There are discrepancies in the historical accounts of the actual date on which the fleet eventually sailed; some say February 10, others February 18. It seems probable that the ships sailed for their rendezvous off Cape San Antonio on the 10th, and began the voyage proper on the 18th.

Five hundred men in eleven small ships, equipped with sixteen horses, a handful of muskets and crossbows, and a few rudimentary cannons. 'With such scant means,' says Gómara, 'did he win such a great kingdom.

And such, neither larger nor better, was the fleet that he led to strange and unknown lands; and with such a small company did he vanquish innumerable Indians. Never did a captain with such a small army do such deeds, gain so many victories, and win so vast an empire.' Or, as Prescott observed: 'With so paltry a force did Cortés enter on a Conquest which even his stout heart must have shrunk from attempting with such means, had he but foreseen half its real difficulties!'

Cortés himself, at this stage, was anything but discouraged. He was relieved to have eluded the Governors of Hispaniola and Cuba, to have brought his troops together, to have surmounted every obstacle, and to be on his way at last, commander-in-chief in his own flagship. He hoisted his banner: a cross surrounded by blue and white flames, with the motto: 'Friends, let us follow the Cross, and with faith in this symbol we shall conquer.'

Before he led his men aboard, he mustered them in their eleven companies on the beach, reviewed them, gathered them around him, and made them a short speech. It was a fine address, short and to the point, elevated and practical at the same time. It reflected the spirit of Cortés himself, and of the epoch in which he lived—the spirit of *quattrocento* man, skyrocket man, all-or-nothing man. It embodied the curiosity, the reverence for antiquity, and the desire for renown and immortality of a typical son of the Renaissance. It also reveals the attitude of a *conquistador* towards the enterprise which he had taken in hand. No doubt by the time that he was an old man, and was ready to dictate it to his secretary, the speech had become, over the years, touched up and generally improved, the carefully-edited peroration of an elder statesman. It is also just possible that the speech was never made at all: that Cortés merely felt that he ought to have made it, or wished that he had made it, or even dreamed that he had made it. That methodical chronicler Bernal Díaz makes no mention of such an address, and since he relates, at great length and word for word, many other speeches uttered by his leader on later occasions, he would surely have remembered this, the first and most important one of all. But whether it was actually delivered or not, it truly reflects the attitude and emotions of Cortés and his men as they marched aboard their vessels, saw the sunlight dancing on the open sea, and felt the strong salt offshore wind on their cheeks.

'Certain it is, my friends and companions,' Cortés begins, in the words of Gómara, 'that every good man of spirit desires and strives, by his own effort, to make himself the equal of the excellent men of his day and even those of the past. And so it is that I am embarking upon a great and beautiful enterprise, which will be famous in times to come, because I know in my heart that we shall take vast and wealthy lands, peoples such as have never before been seen, and kingdoms greater than those of our monarchs. Certain it is also that the lust for glory extends beyond this mortal life, and that taking a whole world will hardly satisfy it, much less one or two kingdoms.

'I have assembled ships, arms, horses, and the other materials of war, a great stock of provisions, and everything else commonly needed and profitable in conquests. I have spent large sums, for which I have put in pawn my own estate and those of my friends, for it seems to me that the less I retain of it the greater will be my honour. Small things must be given up when great things present themselves. As I hope in God, more profit will come to our King and nation from our expedition than from those of all the others. I hardly need mention how pleasing it will be to God Our Lord, for love of Whom I have willingly offered my toil and my estate; nor shall I speak of the danger to life and honour to which I have exposed myself getting this fleet together, because I would have you know that I do not seek gain from it so much as honour, for good men hold honour dearer than riches.

'We are engaging in a just and good war which will bring us fame. Almighty God, in whose name and faith it will be waged, will give us victory, and time will see the accomplishment that always follows upon whatever is done and guided by intelligence and good counsel. We must, therefore, employ a different way, a different reasoning, and a different skill from those of Córdoba and Grijalva. I shall not pursue the matter further because of the pressure of time, which urges us onward. There we shall do as we shall see fit, and here I offer you great rewards, although they will be wrapped about with great hardships. Valour loves not idleness, and so therefore, if you will take hope for valour, or valour for hope, and if you do not abandon me, as I shall not abandon you, I shall make you in a very short time the richest of all men who have crossed the seas, and of all the armies that have here made war. You are few, I see, but such is your spirit that no effort or force of Indians will prevail against you, for we have seen by experience how God has favoured the Spanish nation in these parts, and how we have never lacked courage or strength, and never shall. Go your way now content and happy, and make the outcome equal to the beginning.'

5

Passe la noche e venga la mañana
aparejados me seed a cavallos e armas
iremos veer aquella su almofalla
Como omnes exidos de tierra estraña
allí pareçra el que mereçe la soldada.

When night has passed and morning has come,
I would have the horses saddled and the
weapons made ready. We are exiles from a
distant land. Here we shall see who is
worth his pay.

WHILE he was making his initial preparations in Santiago de Cuba, Cortés had behaved in a manner that was unassuming, even self-effacing. It had been necessary to reassure the fretful Governor by a show of modesty.

When he reached Havana, he decided that it was time to throw off his constraint and act like a general confident of victory. No leader in history was ever more aware than Cortés of the importance of morale and the need to put on a brave show. What he could not supply by force of numbers, he would have to provide by means of bluff. 'It was here in Havana,' relates Bernal Díaz, 'that he began to form a personal entourage and assume a regal bearing.'

In his physical appearance he had always been something of a dandy—not flamboyant or outrageous, but the kind of dignified and methodical dandy that suited his character. Bernal Díaz first encountered him in Santiago de Cuba, when preparations for the expedition were in hand, and has left a vivid impression of him. 'He sported a plume of feathers, a velvet cloak trimmed with gold braid and a gold chain with a medallion. He was every inch the bold and gallant captain. On the other hand, he had no funds to meet the expenses of the undertaking. He was always in straitened circumstances and over his ears in debt, in spite of the fact that he owned a good *encomienda* of Indians and derived an income from the gold mines. This had never prevented him from spending his whole income on finery for himself and his wife, and on entertaining the guests who filled up his house, for he was extremely hospitable and fond of company. He had twice been chosen mayor of his town, which was considered a great honour.'

To Bernal Díaz, as to nine hundred and ninety-nine out of a thousand men of his age, Cortés was truly 'a bold and gallant commander', a man to be unconditionally admired and imitated. Yet even in his own time there was the thousandth man who was willing to question and denounce everything that Cortés, his fellow *conquistadores* and the Spanish colonists were undertaking in the Indies. That thousandth man was represented by Las Casas, the humble Dominican *clerigo* who was not afraid to plead the cause of the suffering of the natives to bishops, archbishops, even the King himself, and who in his *History of the Indies* has left us an incomparable if controversial work.

As noted earlier, it is the very ambivalence of what might be called 'the *conquistador* question' that makes it simultaneously fascinating and frustrating. It is always comforting to ask clear-cut questions and receive clear-cut answers. While the actions of Cortés and the others were, heaven knows, plain enough, the problem of how to interpret them is clouded. The word *conquistador* must be one of the most emotive words known to historiography; it provokes an immediate strong reaction, either for or against. Perhaps passions are dying down and prejudices, on either side, are not as violent as they once were. In an earlier generation, if an historian were anti-Spanish and anti-Catholic, Cortés could do no right; if he were a Spaniard and Catholic, he could do no wrong. If he were a nineteenth- or twentieth-century liberal, Cortés was to be condemned; if he were a Nietzschean or Bergsonian, he was to be praised. There are as many opinions about Cortés as there are historians.

Let us take a few examples. To Madariaga, a Spaniard, Cortés is one of 'the heroes of mankind'. To Obregón, a Mexican and partisan of the old *indigenista* school, Cortés was nothing but a robber baron, leading *compañeros codiciosos*, avaricious companions; while other Mexican writers refer to the *conquistadores* as *popalocas*, a popular word for barbarians. The English, having shed the anti-Papal and anti-Mediterranean prejudices which had roots in their own imperial rivalries, in Victorian snobbery, and in a natural resentment of the Spanish Armada, now tend to be favourable witnesses. Thus George Pendle, in his *History of Latin America*, calls Cortés 'a far-sighted, courageous, well-educated and charming Spanish gentleman', and V. S. Pritchett, in his *Spanish Temper*, declares that 'the conquistadors were governed by a great idea and represent Spanish character at its most splendid; they were not intriguers and tricksters without religion'. Prescott concurs. 'Cortés,' he writes, in the course of the best summary of the character of Cortés ever put on paper, 'was not a vulgar conqueror; he did not conquer from the mere ambition of conquest.' Neither, Prescott asserts, was he money-grubbing or cruel. But to the mass of Americans, with their eupeptic and utilitarian view of human affairs, one suspects that Cortés, apart from his undeniable spirit of get-up-and-go, is still a figure to be anathematized almost as severely as he would be by any Marxist. Here is Cortés as he is presented by one of America's best-selling writers, James A. Michener, in his *Iberia*. Mr. Michener's viewpoint is probably representative of that of the millions of people who buy his books. 'In the weed-grown plaza of Medellín,' he writes, 'stands one of Spain's uglier statues. Cortés in bronze looks over the land he deserted and he is brutal in his arrogance . . . In Medellín one looks in vain for the school established by the wealth he won, or the library, or the hospital, or the university, or even the factory set up for personal gain. The riches of Medellín, her men, was exported and nothing came back . . . When I see a defrauded village like Medellín, I am appalled at the bad deal Spain accepted in that crucial era.' Not for Michener the *conquistadores*' 'great idea'; to him, they were just indifferent businessmen, able to pile up a million dollars (the word *dolar* is actually Spanish) but woefully ignorant about how to invest it or about the operations of the market. In actual fact, the numbers involved in the emigration to the Americas in sixteenth-century Spain were not very large. It has been estimated that 69,000 went out to the Indies during that period: not a great number when one considers that between 1530 and 1540 the population of Castile alone increased by 65,000 a year, and between 1540 and 1590 by 40,000 a year. In 1590 the population of Seville was 90,000; so the total number of emigrants from Spain in an entire century totalled less than the population of that one town.

All manner of opinions of Cortés and the *conquistadores*, then, can be encountered, from the highest to the lowest. It is also possible, of course, to find an intermediate stance. Thus Jacques Soustelle acknowledges Cortés' courage and statesmanship, but alludes to him as 'cold and calculating' and speaks of his 'destructive will'. Soustelle is a profound admirer and advocate of the Aztecs, which makes it understandably difficulty for him to be an admirer of the Spaniards at the same time. This, of course, is precisely the nub of the matter: that for so many historians their instincts, background and training make it almost impossible for them to discuss the *conquistadores* and their opponents without adopting the cause of one side or the other.

We owe to a Spaniard, Ortega y Gasset, the classic exposition of the viewpoint that a man is born at a certain time, and formed by a definite tradition, and that his environment itself is also determined by historical circumstances. Thus, if one wishes to understand a man, one must throw overboard all rigid and immobile concepts and learn to think in ever-shifting terms. One should therefore try to be flexible in one's approach to Cortés—although, even if one seeks to be adaptable, one might perhaps be permitted to sum up, very briefly, the tangible and permanent elements in his individual situation and in the situation of the Spain of his time. To begin with, we know that he was a frontiersman and an Extremaduran, like Pizarro and other *conquistadores*. Unlike Pizarro, however, he was no unlettered ruffian, but a man who had read Greek, Latin and logic at Salamanca. The Roman era, moreover, was not something remote and theoretical, but something close and practical to him. All men of the *quattrocento* were steeped in classical culture, but Cortés was brought up only twenty miles from Emilia Augusta, one of the most imposing cities of the Roman Empire, and as a Spaniard he belonged to a race that had become central to the life of the Empire.

In addition, he was a child of the Reconquest. He inherited the ardour and fanaticism of a struggle that had lasted almost a thousand years. The Conquest of the Indies was a direct extension, without a temporal break, of the Conquest of Spain. With no more land to conquer, and their egress blocked to the east by a new upsurge of Mohammedan energies, they burst out to the west, with a vague notion of striking at the infidel from a new direction. The great legacy of the Reconquest, as it affected Spaniards, was a thirst for fame even more exaggerated than the thirst for it evinced by Renaissance man elsewhere. The *conquistadores* would have subscribed to the maxim of Vauvenargues that *Il n'y a pas de gloire achevée sans celle d'armes*, 'There is no glory except for that achieved in war.' To men of their generation, fighting the Aztecs or Incas was the next best thing to fighting the Moors.

It was a highly wrought-up generation. It was keyed to a pitch of fanaticism. Octavio Paz, most distinguished of modern Mexican writers, expresses this well in his essay on Rubén Darío, *The Seashell and the Siren*. 'The sixteenth and seventeenth centuries were the centuries of Spanish rage. During that period the Spaniards wrote, painted and dreamed in the same frenzy in which they destroyed and created nations. Everything was carried to extremes: they were the first to circumnavigate the earth, and at the same time they were the inventors of quietism. They raged with a thirst for space, a hunger for death. It was a delirium, whether boisterous or reserved, bloodthirsty or pious.' It is extraordinary to reflect that the lives of Cortés and Pizarro overlapped with those of Fray Luis de León and San Juan de la Cruz. Octavio Paz also pays tribute, in *The Labyrinth of Solitude*, his study of the Mexican personality, to 'Spanish vitality, which was affirmative and splendid in that epoch, expressing itself in a great *Yes!* to history and the passions'.

The vitality and affirmative nature of Cortés are not in question. He was a *conquistador*; his mind was bent on conquest; the word 'conquer' was emblazoned on his flag. Fate had appeared to cast a rather unlikely band of men in this glamorous role. Cortés overran a country larger than his native Spain, and broke up a powerful empire not in the guise of a great king at the head of a powerful army, but as a penniless adventurer, almost a man on the run. He knew perfectly well that if he returned in triumph, all would be forgiven; but if he was defeated, he would almost certainly suffer the fate of Balboa and of many more like him. His followers were no more romantic in appearance than he was, though men like Sandoval and Alvarado possessed an unmistakeable panache. In the main, his troops were not exuberant, colourful, swashbuckling figures, but sober and somewhat grim-visaged men in battered and rusty helmets, scuffed leather doublets and stained breastplates. However, what they lacked in appearance they made up for in spirit. Perhaps in their sense of being an élite and in their sense of mission they had something in common with the Puritan Ironsides, and Cortés could have said of his men as Cromwell said of his, when reproached with the appearance of his New Model army: 'I had rather have a plain russet-coated captain, that knows what he fights for and loves what he knows, than that which you call a gentleman and nothing else. I honour a gentleman that is so indeed.'

One point to note about Cortés and his relationship with his men is that it was curiously informal and egalitarian. Anyone who has visited Spain will know that Spaniards are incapable of servility; the idea that one man could be in any essential way inferior to another is foreign to them. The Spanish court was always a place where a beggar could look at a king. V. S. Pritchett, in *The Spanish Temper*, puts the matter in this way: 'The egalitarianism of the Spaniards is not like the citizenship of the French, nor the anonymity of the English or American democracy, where we seek the lowest common denominator and try to hide our distinctions. The Spanish live in castes, but not in classes, and their equality—the only real equality I have met anywhere in the world—is in their sense of nobility or, rather, in the sense of the absolute quality of the person. One will hear this sentence spoken of people living in the lowest wretchedness: "They are noble people." These words are not especially a compliment, nor do they convey resignation, pity, or regret; they are meant, almost conventionally, to describe the normal condition of man.' Gerald Brenan, in his *Literature of the Spanish People*, employs much the same terms: 'Where else but in Spain,' he asks, 'could the friendship that unites master and man be found? In England or France it would, then or otherwise, have been unthinkable. It says worlds for the temper of Spanish society that such mutual loyalty and affection should have been able to transcend the barriers of rank and fortune. This was possibly because the innate sense of dignity and self-esteem that is peculiar to Spaniards prevents them from thinking that any profession, however humble, can demean them. Even today, in out-of-the-way places, the servant who has eaten of his master's bread is a member of his family.'

Given this strong sense of equality, one can see that it was not possible for Cortés to dragoon his men in Prussian fashion. In any case, they were not regulars or pressed-men, but volunteers—gentlemen volunteers, many of them. What is more, they were not even in receipt of regular pay. It was therefore necessary to ride them with a light rein. Cortés needed all his arts of humour and persuasion. Discipline in Spanish armies has always been a tricky business; the ramrod and cat-o'-nine-tails never applied to the extent they did in other, class-orientated armies. Everyone who sailed with Cortés felt that he had a right to speak up and be consulted on important decisions. Bernal Díaz, then in his mid-twenties, and trailing a pike in the ranks, insists repeatedly that Cortés asked his advice on important matters, and took it. There is no reason to think he was boasting. Cortés appears at times to be acting more like a chairman of the board than a military commander: and indeed there is some reason to believe that during the course of the expedition he saw himself more in the role of director and diplomat than general, and that it was Sandoval and Alvarado, particularly the latter, who were the real military brains of the operation. Cortés, after all, was a novice in the military arts; there were many men in his company who were vastly more experienced in warfare than he was. There were also many men who were a great deal older, for he was only in his early thirties. On every count, and particularly at the beginning, he had to be tactful. All he could rely upon to impress his companions, in the early stages, was the fact that he was financing the venture, and that he had a certain flair and natural authority, an easy and rather insolent air of assurance. In the event, in the case of Cortés, the Spanish form of war-by-committee worked brilliantly. At other times in Spanish history its effect could be disastrous. We know what difficulties the triumvirate of Philip II, Medina Sidonia and Farnese had in working together at the time of the Spanish Armada, and what trouble Wellington had with his Spanish allies in his peninsular campaign; and in the Spanish Civil War the Government side was largely defeated because individual contingents, or even entire corps, felt free to pack up and go home if they disagreed with their leaders' conduct of the war. The Nationalists, in fact, owed their success largely to their superior and unquestioning discipline, deriving from the fact that they were mostly regulars or Guardia Civil, that they were closely associated with the German Condor Legion, and that they were led by Franco, the most professionally-minded soldier in the Spanish army of his day.

It was in this makeshift manner that Cortés marched to war for God, King and country. We have previously noted that the Spanish brand of Catholicism, which would have been pungent enough in any case, was rendered even more extreme by the long contest with the even more fanatical religion of Islam. It was the imperialism of Islam that lent a certain tone to the imperialism of Spain. Both creeds placed the utmost emphasis on the duty of their adherents to invade foreign lands in order to bring their inhabitants the one true faith. Las Casas himself, dissenter though he was, had no doubt at all that a Christian king was right to invade and annex the Indies in order to bring as many heathen souls as possible to God. His disagreement concerned the way it was done; he was protesting about means, not ends. We should also remember that in Cortés' band there were many soldiers, including Bernal Díaz, who had taken part in the Córdoba and Grijalva expeditions, and had already seen something of the grisly practices carried out in Mexican temples on the mainland (Cortés in his despatches significantly calls them 'mosques'). They were indignant, and they thought it right to put a stop to such appalling rites. Soon they were to come face to face with the full enormity of a state religion based on human sacrifice on a colossal scale, and their earlier determination was confirmed and strengthened.

As for the King, the second element in the litany of the *conquistadores*, it is worth noting that a very important development concerning the monarchy had occurred two years before Cortés set sail. In January 1516 Ferdinand of Aragon, who had reigned alone for twelve years since the death of Isabella of Castile, died. He was succeeded by a sixteen-year-old Habsburg prince, already the ruler of the Low Countries, claimant to the duchy of Burgundy, and heir presumptive to Austria, Tyrol and parts of Bavaria. From Ferdinand, who was his maternal grandfather, he inherited the throne of Aragon-Catalonia, with its dependencies of Sicily, Sardinia and Naples, and its entrepôts in North Africa; and simultaneously he came into possession of the throne of Castile because his mother, Joanna the Mad, had been declared unfit to rule and a successor was required. It will be remembered that it was against Joanna that Isabella had waged war in order to become ruler of Castile, although it seems very likely that Joanna had a more legitimate claim to the crown than she. By 1519, the young Archduke Charles had become acknowledged head of all these dominions. He was King of Aragon and Catalonia, regent of Castile, duke of Burgundy, ruler of Austria, the Tyrol, the Milanese, Naples, Sicily, Sardinia and the Low Countries, the latter including Holland, Flanders, Zeeland, Brabant, Hainault, Artois and the Franche-Comté. He also inherited the widening Castilian realm in the Americas. Before he was twenty, he was the most powerful ruler that the world has ever seen. It was logical that, on June 28, 1519, the seven Electors of the Holy Roman Empire should elect him Emperor. He was the secular head of Christendom. It seemed inevitable that his empire should grow even larger in the years ahead. His Grand Chancellor, Gattinara, told him: 'God has set you on the path to a world monarchy.'

For Spaniards like Cortés, the accession of Charles—who was Charles I of Spain and Charles V of the Holy Roman Empire—had an electrifying effect. For the first time the thrones of Aragon and Castile were united in a single person (though they were not to be joined formally for another two hundred years). Spain was no longer a country at the periphery of Europe: she was the prime mover and mainspring of a vast Empire. The sense of destiny induced by the Reconquest, and by the achievements of the Catholic Kings, was enhanced by the advent of Charles V. True, a faint cloud had been thrown over his first months in Spain by the fact that he was so obviously foreign—he spoke no Spanish—and by the unconcealed rapacity of his Flemish parasites and hangers-on. But from the young Emperor himself glorious deeds, deeds worthy of a King of Spain, were expected. Despite his somewhat unprepossessing appearance—he had the nutcracker profile of the Habsburgs, produced by a grotesquely under-slung lower jaw—he was a young man of spirit. Often called the first great modern monarch, he was also the last of the mediaeval monarchs (like Cortés, he was a man of both the old European order and the new), and dreamed of performing romantic deeds like a knight of the age of chivalry. In 1536 he astounded Europe by personally challenging Francis I of France to single combat. He was also a lover of hunting and tourna-ments. All this Burgundian swagger would endear his image to the *conquistadores* who were engaged on extending his empire overseas. As so many reigns do, Charles's reign began in a frenzy of expectation; and, as with so many reigns, it would end in disappointment and disillusion. But the enthusiasm of those early days must have contributed to the feel-ing of Cortés and his men that they could dare anything and do anything.

In his despatches, Cortés addresses Charles by his official title: 'Very High, Very Powerful, and Most Excellent Prince, Very Catholic and Invincible Emperor, King and Lord.' Also, after Charles had ascended to the dignity of Holy Roman Emperor, he addressed him as 'Caesar', or 'Your Caesarian Majesty'. This mode of address must have been very satisfying to Cortés, with his classical training and his upbringing in Roman Extremadura; it would have made him feel like a Roman general reporting to the Emperor and the Senate. We cannot truly understand Cortés and the men of his time unless we realize how strong was their longing to identify themselves with the heroes of antiquity. When Bernal Díaz first introduces Cortés to us, he does so in the following words: 'Although he was a valiant, bold and enterprising captain, I will henceforth give him none of these epithets, nor speak of him as Marqués del Valle, but simply as Hernán Cortés. For the plain name Cortés was as highly respected in Spain and throughout the Indies as the name of Alexander in Macedonia, or those of Julius Caesar, Pompey, and Scipio among the Romans, or Hannibal in Carthage, or Gonzalo Hernández, the Great Captain, in our own Castile.' Again, at the great scene of the burning of the boats at Vera Cruz, Bernal Díaz reports Cortés as making a 'honeyed and eloquent' speech, and 'developing to us comparisons with the heroic deeds of the Romans. And we all answered to a man that we would obey his orders and that the die would be cast for good fortune, as Caesar said at the Rubicon'. In another speech he told his captains that their observation that 'the most famous Roman captains had never performed deeds equal to theirs' was quite right, and added that: 'If God helps us, gentlemen, far more will be said in future history books about our exploits than has ever been said about those of the past.' Examples could be multiplied.

There is an extraordinary scene in the *Poema del Cid* where the Cid meets the King on the banks of the Tagus, and is so overcome at the sight of his monarch that he dismounts, gets down on his hands and knees, and literally chews the grass, weeping with joy. The relation of the Spaniards to their king was exceptionally personal and intense. It was this sense of identification with the ruler that often prompted them to fight the king's battles in spite of opposition from the king's ministers and representatives. Cortés and his men were serving 'their great Emperor Charles' in flat disobedience of the Governors of Cuba and Hispaniola. As Octavio Paz observes: 'Like the Reconquest of Spain, the Conquest of Mexico is equally complex from the point of view expressed in the various accounts by the Spaniards. Everything is contradictory. Like the Reconquest of Spain, it was both a private undertaking and a national accomplishment. Cortés and the Cid fought on their own responsibility and against the will of their superiors, but in the name of—on behalf of— the king. They were vassals, rebels and crusaders. Opposing concepts

fought within their own minds and those of their soldiers: the interests of
the Monarchy and of individuals, the interests of the Faith and of personal
greed for gold. Each conquistador and missionary and bureaucrat was a
field of battle. Considered separately, each one represented the great
powers that struggled for the control of society—feudalism, the church
and absolute Monarchy—but other tendencies struggled within them.
These were the same tendencies that distinguished Spain from the rest
of Europe and made her, in the literal sense of the word, an eccentric
nation.'

Finally, we must mention the love of the *conquistadores* for gold. It is
quite true that gold was their obsession. The words *gold gold gold gold*
ring out on every page of the chronicles. It was what drew them from
Seville, Cádiz, Málaga, Palos and La Coruña to the islands of the Indies,
and thence to the American mainland. There is no need to spell out the
mystique of gold. Although the open manner in which it was pursued by
the *conquistadores* is often condemned as odious, the economy of the
modern world, whether we like it or not, is still based on that same vulgar
metal. True, we do not have to soil our hands with it; in the tastefully
indirect way in which matters are conducted nowadays, the stuff is
extracted by Bantu labourers or Soviet convicts in forgotten parts of the
world. But it is hard to see why the frank appetite of the *conquistadores* is
somehow more reprehensible than buying mining shares, or why Cortés
should be considered less respectable than some modern, and far more
efficient, entrepreneur. If we choose to be censorious and delicate about
the *conquistadores*, we ought at least to face the fact that a dependence on
the gold-standard is even more widely marked in our world than it was
in his, even if our methods of grubbing it up and marketing it are somewhat more refined. At least they did their own dirty work.

Every war is fought for mixed motives. There is always the motive of
God and the motive of gold. Beneath the religious or ideological overlay,
quite genuinely believed in, is the solid substructure of economics and
self-interest. This was accepted as natural in the mediaeval world from
which the *conquistadores* sprang. A man was not expected to fight for his
king and country without receiving any reward. He would only go on
fighting if he felt he had a tangible economic incentive, and if he felt his
efforts were recognized. Gold and gifts were the accepted tokens of such
recognition, as were the bestowal of lands and titles. Nor was money or
loot a mere by-product of warfare: they were necessary for the actual
prosecution of the war, to enable the soldier to maintain the tools of his
trade and the king to replenish his treasury. It would be instructive to
compile a list of the presents exchanged in the *Poema del Cid* between the

king and his fighting-men. The poem is almost a continuous catalogue of such mutual exchanges: warhorses, draught-horses, palfreys, mules, saddles, furs, cloaks, garments of cloth and of cloth of gold, rings, jewels, swords, money. The note which is struck on every page is *siempre seremos ricos omnes*: 'We shall all of us be rich for ever!' 'We've got terrific and tremendous wealth!' they cry: 'We won't be able to spend it in a lifetime!'

The *conquistadores*, heirs of the Moorish wars, possessed the same philosophy. So, of course, as we shall shortly see, did the Aztecs, who deprived the peoples of their enormous empire of whatever they owned of any value. Again, one must remind oneself that the *conquistadores* enlisted without pay, and that what they could capture would be their wages. They were gamblers, and the stakes were high. If they won, they would hit the jackpot: but if they lost, they would not merely go broke but almost certainly lose their lives as well. This was the condition that lent such an edge to their pursuit of treasure. If they succeeded, they would become dukes and marquesses and landed gentry; they would satisfy the Spanish 'mania for aristocratic status', as Lynch calls it, a mania that an indigent Spaniard could not satisfy in any other way. Also, in helping themselves, they would be doing their duty to their king and country. No matter what they collected, of whatever nature, one fifth part of it, the King's Fifth, would be scrupulously set aside for transmission to Spain.

*   *   *

And if they failed? In that case they were confronted by a nameless grave in the jungle, five thousand miles from Castile. Or worse still, their skulls would adorn a skull-rack outside an Aztec temple, after their hearts had been cut dripping and palpitating from their living bodies.

*   *   *

PART TWO

MOCTEZUMA XOCOYOTZIN

Must I leave this place alone?
Must I perish like the flowers?
Will nothing remain of my fame?
Will nothing remain of my name?
                              Náhuatl Song

I

In the middle of the night
Before daylight and dawn
The gods assembled and took council together
Yonder in Teotihuacán

Codex Matritensis

THE contest between the Spaniards and the Aztecs was not to be an unequal struggle between an arrogant and aggressive culture on the one hand and a mild and pacific one on the other. It was to be a clash between two cultures that could both be described as advanced and self-assertive; both had reached a point in their development where they were accustomed to carrying all before them. Indeed, there is an irony in the fact that the Spain of Cortés and the Mexico of Moctezuma had both arrived, at much the same time, at a stage where, after many struggles, they had finally become unified and outward-looking. They were, to continue a metaphor used earlier, two sky-rocket cultures, shooting upwards and bursting into brilliant stars. The question was, which was destined to soar the higher, and to give out the denser heat?

There was to be no question here of an urban and sophisticated society attacking a society that was merely agricultural and primitive. Two splendid and virile peoples were about to pit their strength against one another. Perhaps the decisive factors, in the end, would prove to be three. First, there was the incontestable courage and superiority of Hernán Cortés. Second, there were certain political and psychological disadvantages suffered by his Mexican opponents. Finally, there was the fact that, despite all their manifest bravery, the Aztecs, to adopt an excellent distinction made by George Vaillant in his *Aztecs of Mexico*, were warriors, whereas the Spaniards were soldiers.

Although we have just spoken of the Aztecs as arriving at a point of unification and dominance, we must remember that conditions in pre-Conquest Mesoamerica were infinitely more complex than conditions in Iberia. Mexico, after all, is not a country of cities and civilizations, but a country of tiny villages: 65 per cent of the present population, Mexico City excepted, live in villages with less than a thousand inhabitants.

Iberia at its most diverse had never been divided into more than eleven or twelve distinctive kingdoms or counties; whereas the history of Mesoamerica is one of quite bewildering complexity. If we take the boundaries of Mesoamerica to be roughly contained between the Río Grande in the north, and Costa Rica in the south, then in the pre-Conquest era it would have been possible to distinguish no less than fifteen distinct language groups in that area, as well as several groups that still remain unidentified; and inside these language groups there were well over a thousand different dialects. Even today ninety separate languages are spoken in Mexico. Mexico, from prehistoric days onwards, was essentially composed of countless village communities, some of which can be linked together by modern scholars into roughly defined cultural groupings, and a very few of which can be dignified by the name of recognizable 'civilizations'. However, over this wide area a number of culture traits gradually evolved which can be characterized as typically Mesoamerican, though some could be found in some culture areas and were absent in others. Among the most important, as listed by Paul Kirchoff in the symposium *Heritage of Conquest*, are the following: A certain type of digging stick; the construction of gardens by reclaiming land from lakes; the cultivation of the *maguey* or century-plant for its fibres and for an intoxicating beverage called *pulque*; the cultivation of cacao; lip-plugs; polished obsidian; wooden swords edged with flakes of obsidian or flint; armour of padded cotton; sandals with heels; turbans; stepped pyramids; ball courts with rings; hieroglyphic writing; picture books folded like screens; certain forms of human sacrifice, such as burning children alive, dancing dressed in the flayed skin of the victim, tearing out the heart, and the tying of a victim to a gladiatorial stone; dances on top of a pole or flying game (*volador*); wars waged to secure sacrificial victims; cultivation of cotton, chili, pineapple, avocado, papaya and zapote; the eating of domestic turkeys and specially fattened dogs. Many of these traits continue into modern times; one can still eat the characteristic foods (though I have not tried edible dog) and drink the fiery and destructive *pulque*, or watch the brilliantly-clad *voladores* diving into the empty air at the end of ropes from a swaying platform eighty feet high. Náhuatl, the tongue of the Aztecs, and Mayan, the tongue of the Mayas, are still widely spoken. Nonetheless many of these traits were extinguished, of course, four and a half centuries ago, with the advent of the Spaniards.

In spite of the diversity of the village life of pre-Conquest Mexico, the heart-land of the country was the Valley of Mexico, the region round the modern metropolis of Mexico City. As it was the centre of the country's activity in ancient times, so it has remained in our own days; 25 per cent of the present population of Mexico is crowded into the Valley, which represents only 4 per cent of the total area of the country. According to Michael D. Coe, in his authoritative *Mexico*, there were only three forces that could have been called unifying in the entire history of pre-Conquest Mexico. These were the cultures of Teotihuacán, of the Toltecs and of the Aztecs. The first and third of these were situated in the Valley of Mexico itself, while the second was situated only sixty miles to the north-west of it. When the nomadic Aztecs fought their way into the Valley, and made their home there, they were therefore occupying the heart-land of Mesoamerica, and providing themselves with a powerful base for their imperialist ventures to come.

Of what might be termed the non-Valley civilizations, we might briefly mention the five most important. The first of these, by any standards, is the Mayan, one of the world's truly original and creative civilizations, greater by far than the later, upstart, parasitic civilization of the Aztecs. The Mayan country extended over modern Yucatán, Guatemala and Honduras. After two thousand years of humble farming, the Mayan peoples suddenly caught fire around the year A.D. 200 and established

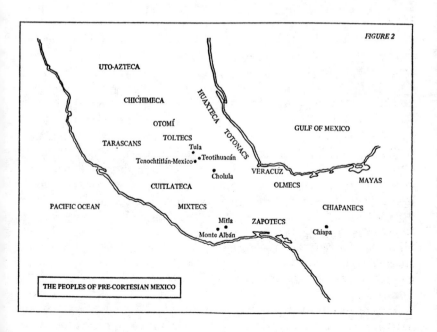

FIGURE 2

THE PEOPLES OF PRE-CORTESIAN MEXICO

literally hundreds of urban sites, which were centres of learning and religion rather than true cities. Many of them, like Chichén Itzá, Uxmal, Bonampak, Tikal, Palenque, Piedras Negras, Yaxchilan, Uaxactun, Copán, Kabah, Labná and Sayil, are truly extraordinary achievements, and many of them, only a few years ago concealed in the thick tropical jungle, can today be visited, particularly those clustered around the charming city of Mérida. The stately theocracy of the Mayas flourished for about seven centuries; it was by no means as static as was once supposed, and the Mayas also became outstanding voyagers and explorers. Then, after A.D. 900, the Classic Period ended; a decline set in. For some unknown reason the three million Mayas suddenly abandoned their magnificent urban centres. Finally, in 1527, when the Spaniards had firmly established themselves in Mesoamerica with the successive conquests of the Aztecs, the Guatamalans and the Hondurans, Cortés' former captain Francisco de Montejo invaded Yucatán with 380 men and 57 horses. After early setbacks, Mérida was founded in 1542, and by 1546 the Spanish conquest was complete.

The Mayans occupied the westernmost portion of pre-Conquest Mexico, and were very much a law unto themselves. Of the non-Valley civilizations in Mexico itself, the earliest was that of the so-called Olmecs. The Olmecs lived as forerunners of the Mayas on the Gulf Coast plain, around Veracruz and Tabasco. They were almost certainly the original seminal culture of all later developments in Mesoamerica, including the Maya, and appear to have flourished between 800 and 400 B.C. They were pyramid-builders and outstanding workers in stone, whether of small and delicate objects or of the massive 'baby-face' heads that tower nine feet tall, and which in later periods were buried, for some reason, deep beneath the ground. It may have been an Olmec offshoot that was responsible for the civilization of Monte Albán, at Oaxaca in southern Mexico, south-west of Mexico City. Marvellous jewellers and fresco-painters, creators of piquant and original sculpture, the Monte Albán civilization lasted for at least a thousand years, from 300 B.C. to A.D. 900. In turn, the Monte Albanians appear to have given rise to the Zapotec civilization, which after the fall of Monte Albán continued its traditions and built the beautiful city of Mitla. And finally, also in the Monte Albán-Zapotec area, we must mention the civilization of the Mixtecs. The Mixtecs, whose name means *People of the Clouds*, began late, in what is known as the Post-Classic Period, about A.D. 900. They were a clever, pushing people: and when Cortés landed in 1519 the Zapotecs and the Mixtecs, with the exception of the encircled Tlaxcalans to the north, were the only important peoples in central Mexico who had successfully defied the armies of the Aztecs, preventing the latter from completely dominating the region south of Mexico City.

* * *

In the Valley of Mexico, the earliest of the great civilizations was that of Teotihuacán, situated in the centre of the Valley, twenty-five miles north-east of modern Mexico City. Accessible to increasing numbers of visitors, a journey to Teotihuacán is an experience that rivals a journey to the Pyramids of Gizeh. Here, on the broad plain, within the great natural amphitheatre of the mountains, some time between 200 B.C. and A.D. 150 a priestly caste founded what was to be a carefully planned city—a true city, not a purely religious centre—around a great complex of temples and pyramids. The most important structures were the Pyramids of the Sun and Moon, joined by the majestic Avenue of the Dead, lined with minor pyramids. The Pyramid of the Sun—stepped, like all New World pyra-mids—is 215 feet high and 716 feet across the base, with a temple occupy-ing 130 square feet at its summit; it comprises a million cubic yards of material. Among the other wonders of this extraordinary city, which contained residential areas and special quarters for merchants and artisans, one might single out the miscalled *Ciudadela* or Citadel, a ceremonial plaza 400 yards long on each side, occupying 38 acres, and completely enclosed between high walls. There is also a magnificent Temple of Quetzalcóatl, now unfortunately rather weathered, but decorated with still-startling plumed serpents with fangs and ears, probably a fusion of serpent and jaguar, and rows of sea-shell motifs. The sea-shells might be a clue to the origin of the Teotihuacán people, as it is thought that they might have derived from the Classic Veracruz civilization, perhaps created by the Totonacs, an elegant and idiosyncratic culture that flourished on the Gulf Coast between A.D. 300 and A.D. 900.

The Feathered Serpent, Quetzalcóatl, and the Rain God, Tlaloc, were principal objects of worship at Teotihuacán, whose name means 'The Place of the Gods' in Náhuatl. So too were the Water Goddess, Chalchi-huítlicue, and the Old God or Flayed One, Xipe Totec. In fact the indi-vidual cults of most of the gods of Mexico, which had spread throughout the entire country and were universally worshipped, were elaborated and stabilized during the Classic Period, between A.D. 300 and A.D. 900, which saw the rise of Teotihuacán. The only major exceptions were the grim gods of the Post-Classic Period, Tezcatlipoca, the war-god of the Toltecs, and Huitzilopochtli, the war-god of the Aztecs. The gods of the Classic Period were not uniformly pacific, and human sacrifice was widespread; but ritual slaughter was not indulged in with the abandon of later centuries.

The Classic Period that preceded the Aztec empire was the most remarkable in the whole development of Mesoamerica, and constituted the true Golden Age of pre-Conquest Mexico.

Teotihuacán was not destined to survive to the end of the Golden Age. It began to disintegrate about 650 B.C., when barbarians and nomads found it easy prey, and spent the next three centuries slowly completing its ruin. However, it would appear that the forms of worship that had been developed at Teotihuacán were continued, after its collapse, at Cholula, fifty miles to the south-west, at modern Puebla. Here stands the largest ancient structure in the New World, the Great Pyramid of Cholula, sacred to Quetzalcóatl. It was built in the Classic Period, and possesses a greater volume than the Pyramid of Cheops at Gizeh. Its base extends for almost 500 yards, and it is now 210 feet high but was originally much taller. As with the Pyramid of Cheops, one can wander around the electrically-lit corridors of its interior. The *conquistadores* lost no time in constructing on top of it a Church of Los Remedios, which from the ground looks tiny but is actually quite large.

*   *   *

About the year A.D. 900 an awesome and mysterious convulsion engulfed all the leading states of Mexico, without exception. It ended the Classic Period, the Golden Age, and ushered in five hundred years of anxious and generally rootless existence. The two great civilizations which were to impose themselves on the others would be militaristic and tyrannical; and it was to be an overwhelming hatred of the second of these civilizations, the Aztec, that would constitute the Spaniards' chief advantage in the course of the Conquest.

Like so much else in the history of Mexico, it is impossible to account for the unprecedented cultural crash of A.D. 900. It was probably brought about by a combination of causes, chief among them an epidemic as severe as the Black Death in Europe. There also appears to have been a drought of unusual duration, which led in turn to a desiccation that drove whole communities into the wilds as hungry and savage marauders. We know that the great age of the pueblos of the south-western United States was brought to an end by a drought that lasted for twenty-three years, between A.D. 1276–99, causing tens of thousands of people to desert the areas in which they had lived for three hundred years, and where they had erected grandiose dwellings. Whatever the cause, the savage tribesmen who roamed the north of Mexico were as affected by it as the civilized city-dwellers of the centre and south. First they swirled around in a great

Völkerwanderung, then swooped down on the rich lands to the south and burst through their defences. In the manner of barbarians, they then settled among the unaccustomed glories of the cities they had ruined, embarking on the long process of teaching themselves the arts of civilization.

These wandering tribes had been given somewhat vague names by their more advanced contemporaries: 'Chichimeca', 'Teochichimeca', 'Otomí', 'Tamime'. One of the nomadic bands, however, comprising the Chichimeca with an admixture of the Otomí, were led by an extremely able ruler called Mixcóatl, or *Cloud Serpent*. He brought his people through the modern provinces of Jalisco and Zacatecas and about A.D. 980 established them at a place called Colhuacán, or *Crooked Hill*. This represented the birth of the Toltec nation, the forerunner of the Aztec empire, a nation whom the Aztecs revered and on whom they modelled themselves. Indeed, it seems likely that, at the apogee which it had reached a little more than a century later, the Toltec empire was larger in extent and as imposing in its trappings as the empire of the Aztecs.

It is not possible to understand the working of Moctezuma II's mind, with all that it entailed for the survival of his race, if we do not understand how much he admired his Toltec predecessors and how steeped he was in their philosophy. It was from Toltec lore that the Aztecs derived their knowledge of the legend of Quetzalcóatl, the Feathered Serpent, which was destined to be all-important during the critical early stages of the Conquest. The Quetzalcóatl whom the Aztecs worshipped was not altogether a mythical person, but partly an actual man. He was the son of Mixcóatl, *Cloud Serpent*, a boy who had received the name Topiltzín, *Our Prince*. The Aztecs were confusing myth with legend, compounding religious accounts of the Feathered Serpent with hazy recollections of an historical personage who had lived four hundred years before the dramatic rise of their own empire. The identification of Quetzalcóatl with Topiltzín was brought about by the disjointed nature of the whole era: the bloody and mysterious end of the Toltecs, reinforced by the desire of the Aztecs to identify themselves with the dimly-derived traditions of their illustrious predecessors.

Topiltzín was a remarkable figure in his own right. He was a culture-bringer and a man of outstanding individuality. He was born in the year A.D. 947, called in the Mexican calendar Ce Atl, *One Reed*. His birth occurred in circumstances typical of men destined to be of religious importance. His father was murdered by his brother, and his mother fled her native country to seek refuge elsewhere. She died in giving him birth, and he was brought up by his grandparents, who sent him to the school for priests at Xochicalco. The school was dedicated to the cult of Quetzalcóatl, whose splendid temple there can still be visited today. Topiltzín became a high priest of the deity, and since it was the practice of the high priests of Xochicalco to attach the god's name to their own, he became Ce Atl Topiltzín Quetzalcóatl. The grounds for the later fusion of prince and god were thereby laid.

Topiltzín sought out his father's murderer and killed him. To the pre-Conquest Mexicans, to avenge the death of one's father gave one a special reputation for sanctity. Then, becoming head of the Toltec nation, he moved its capital first to Tulancingo, then to Tula. The renown of the Toltecs, whose name means *The Artificers*, was so substantial that until only a quarter of a century ago it was believed that Tula must have been Teotihuacán, or at least Cholula. We now know that it was another site, almost as extensive as Teotihuacán but utterly smashed and comminuted, and therefore difficult to excavate and interpret. However, it was a very fine city, for the building of which Topiltzín called in a people known as the Nonoalca, the *Deaf and Dumb Ones*, or *Those Who Speak Incorrectly*. It may have been these people, perhaps of Mixtec-Puebla or even Gulf Coast origin, who brought to the Toltecs that accretion in the knowledge of the arts, crafts and agriculture which Topiltzín adopted and which gave him his reputation as a great culture-bringer.

Topiltzín himself, in spite of his act of vengeance on behalf of his father, was a man of peace. He wished to institute a mild and radiant worship of his patron Quetzalcóatl, devoid of any taint of human sacrifice. It so happened that the nation whom he ruled already possessed a cult of a warlike god called Tezcatlipoca, *Smoking Mirror*, divinity of the warrior caste. A contest between the devotees of the Feathered Serpent and of Smoking Mirror now ensued. The whole story is, in fact, extraordinarily reminiscent of the contest in the Eighteenth Dynasty of Ancient Egypt between the faction which worshipped the intellectual deity known as the Aton, a creation of the Pharaoh Akhenaton, and the faction which worshipped the traditional diety Amon-Ra, god of the established priestly hierarchy and the army. As in Egypt, in the end the forces of orthodoxy prevailed, and the reformer Topiltzín suffered the fate of the reformer Akhenaton. Topiltzín and his adherents, about the year A.D. 987, were driven out of Tula. There were various disgraceful versions, put about by the triumphant Tezcatlipocans, of the reasons for the holy heretic's departure; they included, as such attacks will, attacks on his undoubted virtue and rectitude, picturing him as a drunkard and the seducer of his own sister. There were also several versions of the actions of Topiltzín Quetzalcóatl after his departure from his native land. After burning or burying all his possessions, he left Tula, weeping as he looked back on the city he had founded. Preceded by gorgeously plumed Quetzal birds, he went first to Cholula, thence to the coast of Yucatán. The Mayan chronicles record that a foreign prince entered their land in A.D. 987 and conquered a portion of it. In the Mayan tongue he was called Kukulcán, *Feathered Serpent*. Archaeological evidence also lends solid support for a Toltec invasion by sea into Yucatán at this date, and there is a story that he settled at Chichén Itzá.

The accounts of his death are similarly conflicting, some incorporating myth, others legend. According to one, he built himself a funeral pyre on which he burned himself; the flames from the pyre turned themselves into Quetzal birds, and as he died a magnificent star arose from his ashes and soared into the sky. This was the planet Venus, appearing at dawn in the east and at evening in the west. According to another account, he set out across the Atlantic, 'the heavenly water', on a raft constructed of interwoven serpents. But before he departed, he sent four of his attendants back to Cholula with the promise that one day he would return, on his raft, from the direction of the rising sun, on his own name-day, Ce Atl.

We may judge the emotions of the Aztecs and their Emperor Moctezuma when news was brought to them that enormous ships with white sails, which they took for moving mountains, had been sighted approaching the shores of Mexico, on the eve of the date Ce Atl. The strange craft, which were of supernatural size and appearance, were crossing 'the heavenly water' from the east from the direction of the sun and the morning star. They carried men of a totally unknown breed, with novel dress and accoutrements, and accompanied by beasts of a quite extraordinary character.

*   *   *

Like so many Mexican empires before it, the Toltec empire was fated to collapse in blood and ruin. We may suspect that it was subject to the same maladies that had afflicted Mexico at the close of the Classical period—drought and desiccation, internal rivalries, a fresh onset of barbarian tribes from the north. It has been suggested that a civil war was sparked off by the disaffected Nonoalca, the foreign artisans, *Those Who Speak Incorrectly*. Whatever happened, the last king of the Toltecs, Huémac, moved the capital from Tula, perhaps after it had been sacked by the barbarians, and settled on the craggy hill of Chapultepec, which dominates modern Mexico City. There he killed himself, in 1156 or 1168. The remainder of the Toltecs infiltrated southwards through the Valley of

Mexico and on as far as Cholula, keeping some semblance of cultural coherence but with the glories of their great days irrevocably behind them.

Thus the region of Mexico City, where two hundred years later the Aztecs were to establish the famous city of Tenochtitlán, was already steeped in Toltec memories and traditions. As Jacques Soustelle states: 'The Aztecs and their neighbours knew that they were at the junction of two lines of descent, the one coming from the barbarians, who in no way shamed them and whose warlike virtues they cultivated, and the other from the Toltecs, the civilized people whose symbol was Quetzalcóatl, the inventors of the arts and of science, the protector of knowledge . . . We have in ancient Mexico a very clear case of cultural solidarity overlying political division, a markedly conscious unity, which took the traditional form of the Toltec myth—a myth which, it may be added, was rich in historical elements mixed with its symbolic figures.'

In the beginning, the omens for the future of the Aztecs were exceedingly unpropitious. As Michael D. Coe puts it: 'The beginnings of the Aztec nation were so humble and obscure that their rise to supremacy over most of Mexico in the space of a few hundred years seems almost miraculous. It is somehow inconceivable that the magnificent civilization witnessed and destroyed by the Spaniards could have been created by a people who were not many generations removed from the most abject barbarism, but such was the case.'

Abject they were. They were no resplendent, irresistible horde, but a small group of beggarly outcasts who crept and cringed their way into the Valley of Mexico in the footsteps of more impressive bands of barbarians. The people who were called by a variety of names—Tenochca, Mexica (the plural form of Mexícatl, a Mexican), Teochichimeca, Azteca—came from a homeland that has never been identified. They themselves asserted that they came from a place called Aztlán, the Place of the Herons, perhaps the Bajío of Guanajuato; but they themselves did not remember where it was. In later years they sent out an expedition to establish the place of their origin, but it got no further than Tula before giving up and turning back. All that is known of them is that they were one of a dozen humble tribes, all of them speaking the Náhuatl language—still spoken exclusively by a million Mexicans—who deserted their homelands in northern Mexico. The Aztecs started late, or were delayed along the way, and only arrived in the Valley of Mexico when the habitable land had already been pre-empted, either by peoples who were remnants of former civilizations, or by the destroyers of those civilizations who were now themselves progressing towards a more enlightened form of existence. The most important of the Náhuatl settlers, and also the earliest arrivals, were the

Tepanecs, who established themselves at Atzcapotzalco in 1230. A vigorous group of Chichimecs occupied Tenayuca in 1244; a group of Otomí occupied Xaltocán in 1250; and a group of Acolhuas occupied Coatlínchan in 1260 (see Figure 3). These were the pacemakers of the mettlesome newcomers, and into their orbit the Mexica insinuated themselves as the poorest of poor relations. Soustelle makes a neat summary of the situation when he writes: 'It was in this world, so reminiscent of Renaissance Italy, full of battles, plots, and astonishing reverses, that a poor, unwelcome, humiliated tribe managed to acquire a few little swampy islands in the lake from their powerful neighbours. The Mexica founded their capital, a wretched village of reed huts, around the temple of Uitzilopotchtli, the jealous and unyielding god who had guided them during a hundred and fifty years of migration. All about them stretched marshes, with no arable land, no timber or stone for building; the dry land was all owned by the established cities, and they rigidly held on to their fields, woods and quarries.'

It was in this way that, in 1325, the Aztecs took possession of the miserable bog where, within an incredibly short space of time, was to rise the capital of a potent empire. They were fortunate to receive even so little; their career in the Valley until then had been unenviable. As Michael D. Coe says, they were looked upon as little more than squatters, 'occupying territory that did not belong to them and being continually kicked out'. Nor was it simply the case that they were backward and brutish: they were downright squalid. Their little uncouth tribal war-god, Huitzilopochtli, was already notorious for the number of fresh, bleeding hearts he required, and his worshippers did not seem to be particular about where they got them. They gained a reputation for every kind of murder and brutality.

Why were these jackals and scavengers tolerated? Their neighbours put up with them because, though primitive, they were clever and fearless fighters. In that epoch of warring city-states, with petty 'empires' jostling each other around the great lake in the heart of the Valley—'empires' of forty or fifty square miles—the Aztecs were useful as mercenaries. Weightier states than those of Xaltocán, Coatlínchan, Tenayuca, Atzcapotzalco, Xico and Colhuacán have welcomed barbarians within their gates for that purpose, and lived to regret it. First the Aztecs stayed at Chapultepec, where the remnants of the Toltecs had found sanctuary. They were ousted because of their disgusting habits, and because they stole women from their neighbours. Thence they were driven to Colhuacán, where they worked as serfs for their masters in return for some land at Tizapán which no one else wanted. Frederick Peterson, in his

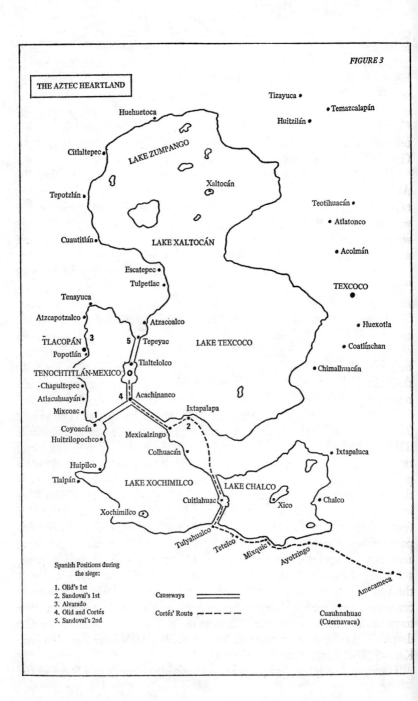

FIGURE 3

THE AZTEC HEARTLAND

Tizayuca •
• Temazcalapán
Huitzilán •

Huehuetoca •

LAKE ZUMPANGO

Citlaltepec •

Xaltocán

Tepotzlán •

Teotihuacán •
• Atlatonco

Cuautitlán •

LAKE XALTOCÁN

• Acolmán

Escatepec •
Tulpetlac •

TEXCOCO
•

Tenayuca •

Atzcapotzalco •

Atzacoalco •

• Huexotla

TLACOPÁN 3   5 Tepeyac

LAKE TEXCOCO

• Coatlínchan

Popotlán •

Tlaltelolco •

• Chimalhuacán

TENOCHTITLÁN-MEXICO O
• Chapultepec •

Atlacuhuayán •

4 Acachinanco

Mixcoac •

1

Ixtapalapa

Coyoacán •
Huitzilopochco •

Mexicalzingo •

2

• Ixtapaluca

Colhuacán •

Huipilco •

Tlalpán •

LAKE XOCHIMILCO

LAKE CHALCO

Cuitlahuac •

• Chalco
Xico

Xochimilco ⊙

Tulyahualco •
Tetelco
Mixquic
Ayotzingo

Amecameca

Spanish Positions during
the siege:

1. Olid's 1st
2. Sandoval's 1st
3. Alvarado
4. Olid and Cortés
5. Sandoval's 2nd

Causeways ═══

Cortés' Route ------

Cuauhnahuac
(Cuernavaca)

comprehensive *Ancient Mexico*, relates their fortunes at Colhuacán as follows:

'Coxcox (Pheasant), the ruler of Colhuacán, knowing that the land was barren and full of snakes; thought they would starve or be killed by the snakes; but the Aztecs liked rattlesnake meat, thrived on the snakes, and exterminated them all. When they built a temple to Huitzilopochtli, the Colhúa came and asked, "What are you going to put into such a big temple?" The Aztecs answered, "Fresh hearts and blood." In protest the Colhúa threw unmentionable rubbish into the Aztec temple.

'Colhuacán became engaged in a war with Xochimilco and asked the Aztecs for aid. Coxcox promised the Aztecs their freedom if they would take 8,000 Xochimilca prisoners. The Aztecs could not bother keeping score of the prisoners. They cut off the prisoners' ears and took these in several large bags to Coxcox, who, disgusted with their cruelty and savagery, gave them their freedom in order to get rid of them.

'The Aztecs then asked Coxcox for his attractive daughter in order to "pay a very special honour to her". They invited Coxcox to the ceremony, and took him into a dark temple where Coxcox made some offerings. When his eyes became accustomed to the darkness he saw a priest dancing around—dressed in his daughter's skin! Coxcox howled for his warriors to avenge the deadly insult. The bewildered Aztecs could not understand, because they had paid his daughter special homage in uniting her with their deity. They took refuge again in the reeds of Lake Texcoco and did not come out of hiding for several months; then they looked for a new home.'

They were to find that new home—and soon. In the year Ome-Acatl, *Two Reed*, an ancient prophecy attributed to Huitzilopotchtli was fulfilled. The god had promised that he would furnish them with a site to build their capital at a place where they would see an eagle standing on a prickly-pear cactus and devouring a snake. Moving among the reeds at the edge of the lake, one day they saw this longed-for sight. Filled with joy, they realized that their wanderings were at last an end. Thus was founded the city of Tenochtitlán, shortly to astound Cortés and his companions with its size and beauty. The etymology of the name is not clear; according to some, it means the place of the *tenochtli*, or prickly-pear; according to others, it signifies the place of Tenoch, the Aztec leader at the time of its foundation; yet a third explanation is that the name is connected with the words *metzli* (moon) and *xictli* (navel), and means 'the town in the middle of the lake of the moon'. Whatever its significance, the despised Aztecs, whose own name means 'the People Whose Face Nobody Knows', had found their Promised Land.

There was, in fact, a great deal of the ethos of the Chosen Race in the outlook of the Aztecs. In all their trials they had never lost their faith in themselves, which in turn derived from their faith in their tribal war-god. It was that faith which had brought them through, and which supplied the principal ingredient in the burst of psychic energy that was to take them so quickly to the heights. There are certain parallels here between the Aztecs and the Spaniards. The Spaniards too, at this time, had suddenly tapped a source of psychic energy, at the root of which was a burning religious faith. Both Aztecs and Spaniards, at the time of their confrontation, were military societies that had recently emerged in triumph from an epoch of trial and testing. They represented at that moment the most effervescent element in the life of the Old World and the New. If the men of the European Renaissance were ultimately to become the victors, they would not do so without a tremendous struggle.

The Aztecs proved no easy antagonists, as is sometimes supposed. What ultimately would undo them was that same aggressive spirit which now, at the moment when they founded Tenochtitlán, would be responsible for their brilliant imperial career. The bedrock of their success was the fact that every man's hand was against them, and that their hand was against everybody else. They were neither loved nor seeking to be loved. They were the Assyrians of the New World. It was their hatred of their neighbours that gave them their exceptional impetus. They never forgot the humiliations which their neighbours had inflicted on them; they never forgot that they had once born the festering brand of the slave.

For two hundred years, the power of that hatred would drive them onward and upward; but eventually it would pay diminishing returns. Bearing down too hard on their client states, they would drive them to a corresponding frenzy of hatred. Acting the role of a dominant military caste, they came to inspire in their vassals, who greatly outnumbered them, feelings of horror, terror and despair. These feelings reached a crescendo at the moment when the Spaniards landed. The Spaniards were therefore greeted not as enemies but as liberators, and the Aztecs would be unable to secure a single ally in their battle to expel the Europeans. The fate of the New World and the course of history would have been different if the principal champions of the indigenous way of life had been less unsympathetic and eccentric exponents of it.

*   *   *

The terrain where the Aztecs first settled was so infertile that in order to scrape a living they were compelled to construct artificial islands of soil on which to plant their crops. These *chinampas* or 'floating gardens'—

which did not actually float—were made by shovelling mud into a compact mass and bonding it firmly together by means of tree-trunks, canes or reed mats. Every year new mud was plastered on top of the old before the seeds were sown. The rafts of mud eventually put down roots and anchored themselves to the lake bottom, and were so fertile they produced two crops a year. This unusual and ingenious method of agriculture, which the Aztecs practised in common with other peoples around the lake, is still practised today at Xochimilco, now a distant suburb of Mexico City. There one can be poled Venetian-style in a gaily-bedecked *trajinera*, or flat-bottomed boat, through the canals between the fecund *chinampas* that still provide most of the vegetables and flowers for Mexico City. The early Aztecs also eked out their diet with a wide assortment of food from the lake—or, rather, from the four lakes linked together. Lake Texcoco, in the middle, was the largest, with Lakes Xochimilco and Chalco joined to it in the south and Lake Xaltocán in the north. The whole system was forty miles long and twenty miles wide. In addition to ducks, fish and shell-fish, the Aztecs ate frogs, newts, shrimps, and water-flies; they even made a kind of cheese from the scum that formed on the marshes. In addition, as we have seen, they had no aversion to snakes, which they supplemented with snails, ants, iguanas, and such vermin as rats and mice. From such lowly origins can great empires spring.

In 1367 the Aztecs were invited to ally themselves with the vastly more important Tepanecs of Atzcapotzalco. The gifted Tepanec leader Tezozómoc had embarked on a career of aggrandizement, and as a reward for their assistance in his successful campaigns he gave Tenochtitlán its first governor, Acamapichtli, *Handful of Reeds*. When the latter died, in 1396, his son had no hesitation in asking Tezozómoc for the hand of his daughter in marriage. This time they did not flay her and exhibit the skin to her father; they were learning manners now, although they did offer Tezozómoc what Peterson describes as 'an irresistible wedding gift of white edible fish, tiny minnows, frogs, and mosquito eggs'.

It was only a matter of time before the Tepanecs realized that they had been harbouring a cuckoo in their nest. The clash finally came in 1426 or 1427, when Tezozómoc's son Maxtlatzin, *Loincloth*, woke to the danger and sought to move against the increasingly arrogant Aztecs. The Aztec ruler, however, was the canny Itzcóatl, *Obsidian Serpent*, who contrived to bring the other peoples of the Valley into a common front against Maxtlatzin. Tenochtitlán headed a grand alliance of Texcoco, Tlacopán, Tlaltelolco and Xaltocán: and even two non-Valley peoples, those of Huejotzingo and Tlaxcala, joined in to help them. The territory of the Tepanecs was invaded, its capital Atzcapotzalco besieged and destroyed, and its ruler Maxtlatzin put to ignominious flight. It is interesting to note that at this stage, before it had grown too grand and ambitious, Tenochtitlán was merely *primus inter pares*. Other states did not hesitate to come to its aid. Ninety years later these states were only too ready to become allies of the Spaniards in order to destroy Tenochtitlán. In less than a century the Aztecs had contrived to turn their former comrades in arms into cowed and resentful helots, eager to seize any opportunity to strike at them. The alienation of the Tlaxcalans, who lived between Tenochtitlán and the Gulf Coast, and who managed to cling on to their independence only by the skin of their teeth, was to prove particularly calamitous.

Itzcóatl was the first of the Aztec empire-builders. He proposed to Tlacopán and Texcoco that they should divide between them the lands of the defeated Tepanecs, and himself took the lion's share. His successor Moctezuma Ilhuicamina (Moctezuma I) extended the boundaries of the budding empire even further. Between 1440 and 1469 this energetic monarch, the Tuthmosis III of the Aztecs, ranged southwards deep into Mixtec territory and northwards as far as Veracruz on the Gulf Coast. Unfortunately he also had a singular gift for antagonizing the former friends of the Aztecs, and it was from his reign that the deterioration of Aztec foreign relations began. The number of Aztec ill-wishers grew in inverse proportion to the number of people who had any close relations with them.

The expansion continued steadily under Axayácatl, *Water Face*, who reigned between 1469 and 1481; lagged a little during the five-year reign of the comparatively unwarlike Tizoc, *Bloodstained Leg*; then picked up again under the rule of the third son of Moctezuma I, Ahuítzotl, *Water Dog*. Ahuítzotl, who occupied the throne between 1486 and 1502, was the eighth king of the Aztecs, and brings the history of the Aztecs almost down to the time when Cortés set foot on Mexican soil. He was a truly manic conqueror, more avid and ruthless than any Spaniard. Peterson says of him: 'His well-deserved reputation for ferocity and vindictiveness exists to this day. Mexican people still say, "*Qué ahuitzote!*" "How fierce!" ' He brought fire and sword to territories as far afield as Guatemala, firmly established himself on the north and south coasts, and implanted Aztec rule throughout central Mexico. It was Ahuítzotl who dedicated the Great Temple of Tenochtitlán, begun by Tizoc, to Huitzilopochtli, the blood-soaked tribal totem who achieved his apotheosis at this time. At the ceremony of dedication, a conservative estimate of 20,000 prisoners had their chests opened and their hearts ripped out, waiting for their moment of immolation in four lines, each stretching for more than three miles.

It was this ferocious and awe-inspiring tyrant who was succeeded by Cortés' antagonist, Moctezuma Xocoyotzin, the *Young Angry Lord*, Moctezuma II. Ahuítzotl was not an easy man to succeed, but Moctezuma Xocoyotzin was by no means the weak-kneed and indecisive man that accounts so often picture him. Ascending the throne in 1502, he proved, in spite of a certain subtle and withdrawn habit of mind, to be as resolute and masterful as his people could have desired. True, he proved unable to deal with the Spaniards: but the causes of the downfall of the Aztec empire can be better attributed to the flaws in its own character than to the flaws in Moctezuma's.

Let us leave for a moment our examination of the career and personality of Moctezuma, in order to consider briefly the structure and appearance of mature Aztec society, as represented in the Tenochtitlán over which he ruled.

2

The city is spread out in circles of jade
Radiating flashes of light like quetzal plumes;
Beside it the lords are borne in boats:
Over them extends a flowery mist.

Náhuatl poem

IN A sense, the confrontation between the Aztecs and the Spaniards is the confrontation of the last of the great ancient civilizations with the first of the great modern civilizations. It has a bizarre and dreamlike quality which enhances its hold over the imagination. The encounter has an element of fantasy, as if there had been some slippage in time—as if the troops of Napoleon had found themselves fighting the ancient Babylonians. Encounters between opponents of a totally different character are not, of course, rare: one thinks of what Wellington must have felt at Assaye, Custer at Little Big Horn, or young Winston Churchill at Omdurman. But the struggle between the Spaniards and the Aztecs, like that between the Spaniards and the Incas, had a deeper and more tragic aspect. It was as if, with the disappearance of the Aztecs and Incas, mankind was saying farewell not only to a pair of marvellous regional cultures but to the whole a ncient world itself, to a portion of its own past and its own inheritance.

The Aztec empire had more in common with the Babylonian, Assyrian or Persian empires than with any of the European-based empires with which we are familiar. It is astonishing that such an empire should have been in full flower only four and a half centuries ago. When Cortés and his men stumbled on it they were overwhelmed. They had been prepared to encounter something very strange and unexpected, but they were completely unprepared for the extreme oddness of what they found. Instead of stepping on to the soil of Mexico, they might have arrived on another planet. Europe had already experienced culture-contact with Guinea, with Ethiopia, with Arabia, with the Moguls and Cathay, even with Tibet and Grand Tartary; they had witnessed the customs and manners of the Moors and the Turks. But the very existence of the high civilizations of the Americas, let alone their scope and character, was totally unsuspected. After the Lilliputian tribalism of the queen of the Tainos and her half-naked *caciques*, the Brobdingnagian ramifications of the Aztec empire were overpowering. The wonder is that Cortés and his men, when they saw what they were faced with, elected to press on with their expedition. They could scarcely have been blamed had they voted to turn round and straggle back to the sea-coast—except, as we shall see, that they had burned their boats . . .

*   *   *

First, there was the extraordinary spectacle of Tenochtitlán itself, a city unique in the annals of architecture (see Plate 3b). It is almost obligatory, in any account of it, to begin by quoting the celebrated passage in which Bernal Díaz describes the effect on the bone-weary Spaniards of their first glimpse of the Aztec capital: 'And when we saw all those cities and villages built in the water, and other great towns on dry land, and that straight and level causeway leading to the city of Mexico itself, we were astounded. These great towns and temples and buildings rising from the water, all made of stone, seemed like an enchanted vision from the tale of Amadis. Indeed, some of our soldiers asked whether it was not all a dream. It is not surprising therefore that I should write in this vein. It was all so wonderful that I do not know how to describe this first glimpse of things never heard of, seen or dreamed before. I stood looking at it and thought that no land like it would ever be discovered in the whole world.'

In fact, as we have seen, the Spaniards were viewing what was virtually a brand-new city; the temples that towered above its main square had been completed barely twenty years before. They were seeing it in its first mint-white splendour. Those Spaniards who had served in Italy compared it to Venice, to which indeed it bore an uncanny resemblance. Like Venice, built on its hundred islands, it was a city constructed on a lagoon, a city consisting of a series of swampy mud-flats and *chinampas* linked together by an intricate network of canals, over which wide beams had been laid to serve as bridges. The bigger buildings had been erected on the more dry and solid areas, but perpetual trouble occurred from subsidence even though these larger structures were specially built from a lightweight volcanic stone called *tezontle*. Subsidence has always been a major problem in Mexico City, where the subsoil is so spongy that when the subway was being constructed in the late 1960s it was possible to drive twelve kilometres of tunnel in ten months. The Mexicans, then as now, have always been ingenious engineers and architects; in our own time they have been pioneers of shell-roof construction, and the buildings of the University, the 1968 Olympics, and the forty-four-storey Latin American Building on its floating piers are greatly admired by specialists.

Surrounded by water, seamed and criss-crossed by Venetian waterways, Tenochtitlán could be approached from the lake-shore by three causeways. These could accommodate eight horsemen riding abreast, as Cortés noted, and were made of a bed of rocks, topped by tamped earth and held in place between revetments of wood. The northern causeway began at the satellite town of Tlaltelolco, two miles away, and ran for three miles to the mainland at the town of Tepeyac; the western causeway ran out two miles into the lake before dividing into two branches, one leading to Tlacopán and the other to Chapultepec, each another mile-and-a-half distant; and the third, which was the longest, extended no less than five miles over the water before dividing to reach the towns of Coyoacán and Mexicaltzingo. The causeways also served as dykes, and as the Spaniards observed there was nothing flimsy or jerry-built about them; like everything else at Tenochtitlán, they were beautifully fabricated. Parallel to the western causeway ran a gigantic aqueduct, built entirely of masonry, that carried the city's chief water-supply from a spring at Chapultepec. Built by Moctezuma I, it brought water right into the heart of Tenochtitlán. A subsidiary aqueduct, constructed by Ahuítzotl, ran parallel to the southern causeway, bringing water from Coyoacán. Water was always a problem at Tenochtitlán, even though its citizens were surrounded by it, and even though Mexico City, at least when the present writer has been there, appears to be almost the wettest and stormiest place in the world. The lake itself was either salt or brackish, and had a bad habit of rising unexpectedly or producing fierce waves and currents; there was either too much water at any given time, or too little. Nevertheless the Aztecs solved this problem, as they solved so many others, in a masterful way; much of their achievement, indeed, may be attributed to the theory of challenge and response. Fortunately there seem to have been small springs within the city itself which could always be relied on; but it is interesting to note that these early preoccupations with water have persisted through the centuries, and that today the inhabitants of the city refresh themselves with no less than 109 fountains—not far removed from Rome's champion tally of 150.

The rectilinear shape of the *chinampas*, divided by the straight lines of the canals—like miniature Dutch polders—made it easy to demarcate the various sections of the city where people were grouped according to class and occupation. In the lowlier quarters, on the fringes of the city, people lived in the simple reed huts that the Mexica had built for themselves in less exalted times. Then, moving towards the centre of the city, came quarters where the square, one-storeyed, mud-built, white-plastered houses were more prosperous, reminding the Spaniards, perhaps, of the houses in the Moorish villages of southern Spain. Next came the two-storey houses of the wealthier and more important citizens, standing on ground sufficiently solid to support them. And finally, on the solid core at the centre of the island were situated the palaces of the princes, of the rulers, and the temples of the gods. Every quarter possessed its handsome squares and market-places, where the commerce of the city was carried on. One of these markets, at Tlaltelolco, was a truly impressive place. Cortés said that it was 'twice the size of the town of Salamanca, completely surrounded by arcades, where every day there are all kinds of merchandise from all the provinces, whether it is provisions, victuals or jewels of gold or silver'. Bernal Díaz compared it to the fair in his native Medina del Campo, except that it was held every day. In the Museo Antropológico at Mexico City there is a model of the great market at Tlaltelolco, over which one can pore enthralled for hours; and Soustelle has a splendid description of the multiplicity of goods—human, animal, vegetable, mineral—which were on sale there, and the enumeration of which gives one an insight into the quality of everyday life in that bustling city. 'In one place,' he writes, 'there would be jewels of gold and silver for sale, and precious stones and the many-coloured feathers brought from the Hot Lands; in the next row there would be slaves, resigned and waiting for their purchasers, some untied, some wearing heavy wooden collars; farther on, men and women bargaining over cloaks, loincloths, and skirts, made of cotton or the cloth obtained from the fibre of aloes. Shoes, ropes, the skins of jaguars, pumas, foxes, and deer, raw or tanned, were piled up in the places kept for them: and there was a quarter reserved for the feathers of eagles, sparrow-hawks and falcons. Maize, beans, oil-bearing seeds, cocoa, peppers, onions, a thousand kinds of green stuff'—(the diet of the Aztecs had improved, now that they had come up in the world)—'turkeys, rabbits, hares, venison, ducks, and the little mute hairless dogs that the Aztecs so loved to eat; fruit, sweet potatoes, honey, syrup from the maize-stalks or the juice of the agave; salt; colours for dying and writing, cochineal, indigo; earthenware of every shape and size, calabashes, vases, and dishes of painted wood; flint and obsidian knives, copper axes; builder's wood, planks, beams, firewood, charcoal, resinous torches; paper made of bark and aloes; cylindrical bamboo pipes, charged and ready for smoking; matting, chairs, stoves . . . And up and down between the stalls the dense crowd, unhurrying, grave; not a noisy crowd, but one that hummed and murmured, as Indian crowds do to this day . . . And the impassive guardians of the market, pacing up and down the vast square, silently overseeing the crowd and the tradesmen. If any dispute arose, a buyer protesting that he was cheated, for example, or someone seeing his stolen goods exposed for sale, then instantly everybody concerned was taken off to the court that sat without interruption at one end of the market, where three judges continually took turns and gave their verdict on the spot.' The media of exchange for all these objects, apart from the immemorial method of barter, were cacao beans, often sewn up in bags in multiples of eight thousand; small copper axes; sea-shells; precious feathers; bolts of cloth, reckoned in multiples of twenty lengths; and the quills of turkeys or ducks carefully packed with gold dust.

Tenochtitlán was indeed a well-policed and well-run city. The Spaniards, used to the quarrelsome self-assertiveness of their own people, were impressed by the dignified deportment of its inhabitants, and by their sense of order and discipline. They were also impressed by Aztec cleanliness. Members of the poorer classes bathed once a day, and members of the upper classes twice. Every day an army of a thousand men descended on the streets and squares and washed and swept them until they were spotless.

This city, as Soustelle points out elsewhere, was a young city, a vital city, untouched by decline, neither primitive nor decadent, not 'one of those rich, sophisticated and ossified cities which are the elegant tombs in which their own civilization stiffens as it dies'. It was a capital city on the threshold of maturity: a maturity which it was destined never to attain.

*   *   *

The occupants of this spacious city had evolved in less than two centuries from a relatively undifferentiated tribal mass into a fully-developed society with distinct social classes. Its population has been variously estimated. Coe puts it at between 200,000 and 300,000 on the eve of Cortés' arrival—which, as he points out, is five times the size of Tudor London. Soustelle puts it at between 500,000 and 1,000,000, if one includes the outlying townships around the lake that formed part of the essential organism of Tenochtitlán, which functioned as the throbbing heart of an intricate nexus of communities. Soustelle holds that Tenochtitlán occupied the same land-area as that taken up by the present Federal District of the Republic of Mexico. If he is right, it was probably the largest city in the world at that time.

At the bottom of the social hierarchy were the *tlatlacotin*, the slaves. The institution of slavery had been widespread throughout Mexico before the time of the Aztecs, but the Aztecs, the most authoritarian of the ancient Mexican civilizations, extended and elaborated it in their usual thorough-going way. There was an enormous population of *tlatlacotin* in the Aztec state, divided into several categories. The foreign slaves were those who had been captured in battle, or sent to Tenochtitlán by vassal states as part of the prescribed tribute. They had not been designated for sacrifice, or, more likely, were awaiting their turn as victims; in the meantime they were put to work. Of the slaves of Aztec origin, the meanest were the criminals. Slavery, with its loss of civil rights, was the penalty for the more serious forms of theft, robbery or political offences against the state. A convicted thief or embezzler had to make full financial restitution for his crime or work off the amount as a *tlacotli* of the person or institution he had defrauded. Similarly, if a man borrowed money, or fell into debt, he could discharge his indebtedness by becoming a slave of his debtor, or by giving a child or member of his family to the debtor in his stead. This was an example of the voluntary slavery which was as common in the Aztec empire as compulsory slavery. If a man or woman came to the end of their resources, they could either sell themselves to the highest bidder or to a particular master; if to the latter, the purchaser paid over the price in advance, and the recipient remained free as long as the money lasted. This was a course often adopted by persons who were unable to cope with the business of everyday living. As *tlatlacotin*, they would be fed, clothed, housed, and relieved of the decisions and responsibilities they found irksome. They could depend on being as well-treated as members of their owner's own family, and had nothing whatever to fear unless they were idle or dishonest. In that case the master could give the *tlacotli* three solemn warnings, before witnesses, if his conduct was unsatisfactory. After three warnings, the *tlacotli* was put up for sale in the local market. And if he was considered unemployable by three successive masters, his fate was terrible indeed. He could be sold for sacrifice, and would be bought by some artisan or merchant guild which, precluded from capturing its own warrior for the purpose, was permitted to furnish a recalcitrant slave for its own honour and that of the gods.

Above the slaves were the common people, the *macehualli*, who constituted the greater part of the population. The humblest of these, the class known as *mayeques*, corresponded to the modern peons, people with little money and fewer rights, the immemorial poor peasants of the countryside. They were bound in service to a landowner and received little enough recompense for their labours. The *macehualli* of the capital and the towns were in a much more enviable situation. They were the equivalent of the modern proletariat. The lowest class, the *tamime*, worked as porters and carriers. Their more fortunate brethren cultivated a plot of soil on a *chinampa* near their modest dwelling, paying their tithes, fulfilling their military obligations, and performing their allotted share of the *corvée*, the duty to devote a number of days each month to road-building, bridge-building, or work on royal or religious enterprises. Nevertheless, as free men, they had the opportunity of rising in the social hierarchy, sometimes to the very top, and they had a voice in the election of the *calpullec*, the mayor or leader of the *calpulli* or district where they lived. Every town or city was divided into a number of *calpulli*, with its own council. They resembled the self-contained *barrios* of modern Mexico City. Tenochtitlán had about twenty of them, divided in turn into *tlaxicalli*, or streets.

Upon the mass of *tlatlacotin* and *macehualli* were superimposed the small and select groups of the craftsmen and merchants. These were professional men. Whereas the *macehualli* manufactured traditional handcrafts for general use, the craftsmen produced the luxury artifacts that ancient Mexico created in such marvellous abundance, or executed sculptures and murals for temples and palaces. Significantly, the craftsmen were called *tolteca*, or Toltecs. This was because the fine arts were inevitably associated with the Toltec culture which the Aztecs so much admired; but it might also have been because the artificers of Tenochtitlán were a separate caste, like the Nonoalca at Tula. It is possible that the artists of pre-Conquest Mexico were a peripatetic breed, moving from one centre of civilization to the next, according to which city happened to be in the ascendant. Artists, after all, have always been a race apart, contributing to a society more than they receive from it, owing their education, inspiration and loyalty more to their own kind than to the community

4*

around them. Granted the personal artistic preferences of different civilizations, to which they had to cater, there always appears to have been a great deal of cross-fertilization in Mexican art, much exchange and transmission of techniques and trade-secrets. Thus elements of the arts of the Gulf Coast cultures can be detected, as we have seen, at Teotihuacán; Teotihuacán elements appear later at Tula; and both, later still, at Tenochtitlán. The *tolteca* made the high-quality ceramics, clay figurines, portrait sculpture, and carved in such materials as obsidian, rock-crystal and Mexican alabaster, called *tecalli*. The wonderful Mexican pottery, be it noted, was not turned on the wheel, for the application of the wheel was unknown in the Americas, but was moulded from individual strips by sensitive fingers. The *tolteca* made fine jewellery from gold, silver and copper, by means of the *cire perdue* or lost-wax process, embellished with every description of precious and semi-precious stones. Von Humboldt called Mexico 'the treasure-house of the world', and although it provided the craftsman with no diamonds, rubies, emeralds or sapphires, it yielded them—and the *conquistadores* after them—magnificent turquoises, amethysts and opals, particularly the type of opal called by the Spaniards *arlequines*, *lechosos*, and *girasoles de fuego*. Of the precious stones which found their way to Tenochtitlán from the farthest corner of Mexico, by far the most valuable in Aztec eyes were turquoise and jade. Jade had a cult of its own, for it was a stone which, though commonly called *chalchihuitl*, also bore the name of *quetzalitzli*, or quetzal-stone, from its resemblance to the plumage of the quetzal-bird. It was thus sacred to Quetzalcóatl himself, and just as the emperor wore quetzal-feathers as his personal insignia, so he wore ornaments of jade. A piece of the stone was placed, according to the *Monarchia Indiana* of Juan de Torquemada, in the mouths of royal personages after their death. Jade had the first prerequisite of a precious material in that it was excessively scarce. The 'jade' palmed off on tourists in Mexico is actually nephrite, imported from the United States, for jade deposits are very seldom discovered in Mexico. To the Aztecs, jade was beyond price. When Moctezuma presented some jade ornaments to Cortés, as a gift for Charles V, he declared, according to Bernal Díaz: 'They are of such enormous value I would only give them to an emperor such as yours; each piece is worth two loads of gold.' The Aztec craftsmen were also adept at working in soft materials, and were responsible for weaving the exquisite cloth worn by the upper classes. A special kind of cloth had the feathers of quetzal-birds, parrots and other exotic birds woven into it, and the feather-workers or *amanteca* constituted a separate guild. In addition to brilliant feather cloaks and head ornaments, they incorporated feathers into flags, shields and body-armour. In a debased but still attractive form the art of the *amanteca* has lasted into modern times; the Tarascans in particular make pretty feather landscapes and altar-pieces. By a freak of fortune, a superb feather headdress that belonged to the Emperor Moctezuma himself was sent to Charles V by Cortés in 1519, and can be seen in the Natural History Museum in Vienna (and a magnificent modern copy of it in the Museo Antropológico in Mexico City). It was the sight of this and other objects from the Indies that prompted no less a judge than Albrecht Dürer to declare: 'These objects are so valuable that their price has been fixed at a hundred thousand florins. In all my life I have never seen anything that rejoiced my heart so much; I have found an admirable art in them, and have been astonished by the subtle spirit of the men of these strange countries.'

Associated closely with the craftsmen, though richer and more respected, were the merchants. Those who live upon the backs of artists —agents and entrepreneurs—are usually accorded a more prominent place in society than the originators of their wealth. The leading merchants formed a separate corporation, and were called *pochteca*. They were not to be confused with the petty tradesmen of the market place. The *pochteca* lived in the opulent two-storeyed houses near the centre of the city, as befitted men who organized caravans and armed expeditions to every corner of the empire and far beyond it. Sometimes they led the caravans themselves, literally fighting their way into distant territories to lay hands on the gold, silver, jewels, jade, pearls, obsidian, precious feathers, amber, cacao, and other commodities that were the source of their fortunes. It took courage to leave the safety of the Cold Lands, as the Valley of Mexico was aptly called, and fare forth into the uncivilized and tropical Hot Lands, where every sort of danger lay in wait. There was some excuse, therefore, for the *pochteca* to give themselves some of the airs of the military caste, the most sovereign caste of all. The latter much resented the pretensions of such mere tradesmen, and the *pochteca* had to act warily. They assumed a drab mode of dress and an obsequious and self-effacing manner. Nevertheless they had secured for themselves the privilege of being burned on a funeral pyre, like a warrior who perished on the battlefield, if they died while on an expedition; they could try cases in their own law-courts; they were permitted to make human sacrifice to the god Huitzilopochtli; their guild deity was installed in the pantheon with the more important gods; and they had their own private religious anthem. It was impossible for their detractors to deny the importance of their services to the state. They prospected the wealth of Mexico, brought it back and concentrated it in Tenochtitlán. They provided the *tolteca* with the raw materials they required to practise their crafts, and when the skill of the *tolteca* had enhanced their value they acted as salesmen for the finished article. More important still, when they ranged far afield with their expeditions, they scouted out likely territories for the emperor's armies to annexe. They were spies and secret-agents, submitting detailed reports on conditions throughout the whole of Mexico. They thus constituted a shrewd and efficient intelligence network. It was inevitable that in the course of time their influence should increase. In fact it seems likely that a struggle for power between merchants and military was well under way on the eve of the Spanish invasion. With the steady growth of empire, mercantile and civil considerations were bound to loom larger. The simple warlike virtues that had characterized the unsophisticated days of empire had to be supplemented by the skills of diplomacy and administration; and for these the merchants invariably possessed subtler qualifications than the soldiers. Tenochtitlán was already showing a tendency towards mushrooming into a bloated imperial condition when the Spaniards first entered it. Young and shining city though it was, one feels it might soon have been manifesting more than a hint of complacency and self-indulgence; and one wonders whether, had the Spaniards not appeared on the scene, the Aztec empire might not in any case have succumbed in the not-too-distant future to the mounting external pressure of hostile client states, coupled with internal pressures deriving from an increasingly hedonistic and extravagant mode of life.

*   *   *

The merchants could not yet aspire to membership of the higher echelons of society. The control of the state still lay wholly in the hands of the *tecuhtli*, a word which means 'lords'. The emperor himself was a *tecuhtli*, and the appointment of these eminent persons was a royal prerogative. The status of the *tecuhtli* was part civil and part military, and the chief priests were also *tecuilhuitl*, or noblemen. The only way to become a *tecuhtli*, which was open to every citizen, whatever his birth, was to distinguish oneself in the wars. Warfare, as we shall see, was a continuous condition; there were no intervals of peace; to the Aztecs, the concept of peace did not and could not exist. To preserve the framework of human society and to ensure the continuation of the universe it was necessary to wage uninterrupted warfare. Thus an ambitious young man had no need to wait long in order to test himself in battle. If he performed successfully, he was well on the path to becoming a *tecuhtli*; if he failed, he sank back into the mass of *macehualli*, or plebeians, never to emerge. During the reign of Moctezuma II, the aristocracy made an attempt to close ranks and establish the nobility on an hereditary basis, permanently excluding low-born persons; but the attempt had not succeeded, and on the eve of the Conquest the vigour of the Aztec state still derived from the fact that it was merit and achievement, not birth or influence, that supplied a man's credentials to a position of authority. A man might become rich and respected, but wealth and esteem were attached principally to the office and not the individual; and its present incumbent could not rely, in that intensely thrusting and competitive society, on holding any office permanently; disgrace and demotion were an ever-present possibility.

The son of a *tecuhtli* received the honorary title of *pilli*, 'child of a lord'. In the natural order of things, he possessed advantages that gave him a head-start in the race for promotion over his humbler rivals. He went to a special school attached to a temple, called the *calmecac*, to receive special training. However, if he proved mediocre, or a cowardly or inept warrior, his eventual lot in life would be a little better than that of any plebeian. The prize for which every Aztec strove was the esteem and high regard of his fellows; wealth and position were only the outward manifestations, the palpable rewards, of worthiness. A man's reputation was everything. The code of the *tecuhtli* was the code of the Samurai; and as in mediaeval Japan, the life of Tenochtitlán was a compound of a fierce and formal militarism allied to a sensitivity to whatever in life was delicate and beautiful: an appetite for the shedding of blood allied to an appreciation of music, poetry, dancing, drinking, making love. If he surmounted all the obstacles that bestrewed the path of the *tecuhtli*, the aspirant might eventually become one of the emperor's inner circle of advisers; or occupy a high position in the capital, such as becoming the *calpullec* of a fashionable *calpulli*; or proceed to one of the provinces as its *calpixqui* or governor. An Aztec *calpixqui* wielded more absolute power than any Spanish governor, and these 'major-domos', as the Spaniards called them, behaved with such lofty proconsular arrogance that their subjects heartily detested them. They were the inflexible representatives of a callous system.

The provincial governors and the bench of judges, who were also directly appointed by the emperor, were surrounded by a horde of minor officials, men occupying a kind of no-man's-land between the *tecuhtli* and the *macehualli*. The Aztecs were dedicated bureaucrats, and kept meticu-lous records. The local mayors or *capulli* compiled records of the families who inhabited their districts, together with details of agricultural holdings, all titles to which were officially registered. The officials filed all returns from the subject provinces. The priests supplemented the work of the bureaucrats with ambitious works of a literary nature. They composed detailed histories of the rise to eminence of the Aztec nation, and elaborate religious manuals.

The bulk of these texts, unfortunately, were destroyed before, during or immediately after the Conquest. The Aztecs themselves destroyed the records of the peoples whom they subjugated. The fame of Tenochtitlán alone was to descend to posterity. The Aztecs also destroyed, in the tenth century, their own early religious books, out of a sudden access of fear that the magic contained in them would lose its power if they fell into alien or unholy hands. A great many more codices were lost during the holocaust of the Conquest, when so many towns were put to the torch, particularly those that were stored in the library of the Great Temple in the main square of Tenochtitlán. The burning of the Great Temple was as grievous a loss to scholarship as the earlier burning of the library of Alexandria. In the aftermath of the Conquest, the Spaniards, with the best of intentions, made bonfires of every religious text that came their way. They had been appalled by what they had seen of Mexican religion, and regarded the religious books as filthy *grimoires*, the handiwork of Satan himself. Bishop Landa of Yucatán said: 'We found a large number of books of this character, and as they contained nothing but superstition and lies of the devil, we burned them all, which the Indians regretted to an amazing degree and which caused them great anguish.' Juan de Zumárraga, the first Archbishop of Mexico, also incinerated a mass of valuable books; however, he was a scholar and a man of the world, and sought to limit his anathema to religious works only, while sparing historical and legal ones. Nonetheless this nice distinction was not always observed, and the havoc was general. In addition the Aztecs and the other Mexicans added to the destruction by ridding themselves of books which, though precious to them, might have meant their death at the hands of the Inquisition if they had been found in their possession. Ironically, they had much less to fear at the hands of the Inquisition than they imagined, for during the three centuries that the Inquisition existed in Mexico only three Indians lost their lives in autos-da-fé. As some compensation, when the frenzy and demoralization of the actual Conquest had died down, the Spaniards began to develop a deep interest and respect for the pre-Conquest civilizations of Mexico; they commissioned new codices, many of them with texts in Spanish as well as in Náhuatl and Mayan, and carefully preserved those that by some accident had been saved from the wreck. The Spaniards also had a practical consideration in mind, in that they wished to confirm the ancient titles of the villagers and townsmen to their former property and agricultural holdings, and searched out the old records or had them rewritten in order to do so.

Among the books which the Spaniards caused to be written in the ancient Mexican manner, the most important is the Codex Mendoza, in the Bodleian Library. It was prepared for Antonio de Mendoza, first Viceroy of New Spain, and sent by him to Charles V to give the Emperor a notion, in native and picturesque terms, of the extent and character of his Mexican dominions. It portrays every aspect of Aztec activity, from birth to death, enumerates all the towns of the Aztec empire, listing the tribute they paid, and contains plans and genealogical tables. It is a marvellous and beautiful piece of work, all the more remarkable in that it was prepared in ten days on the eve of the departure of the treasure fleet for Spain. Three other books in this category are the charming Codex Maglia-becchiano, prepared in 1553 at the behest of Cervantes de Salazar, of which the larger and more comprehensive version is in Madrid; and the Codex Telleriano Remensis and the Codex Rios, both in the Vatican. Other important Mexican-Spanish manuscripts are the Codex Florentino in Madrid, prepared in 1558 to illustrate the great and exhaustive work entitled *A General History of the Things of New Spain*, written by Fray Bernardino de Sahagún, and the book commonly called the *Relaciones*. The latter was the result of a series of reports which Philip II, the supreme bureaucrat of all time, ordered from his overseas colonies. It provides us with a priceless statistical analysis of the state of Mexico a half-century after the Conquest.

These Mexican-Spanish books, with their parallel texts, were the Rosetta Stone by means of which the Mexican language could be deciphered. This was essential if the significance of Mexican painting, sculpture and architecture were to be appreciated, and also the meaning of the numerous pre-Conquest codices which by a fortunate accident were spared the general destruction. Of these purely native books, the out-standing example is the magnificent Codex Borgia, in the Vatican Library, rescued in Rome in the eighteenth century by a cleric who saw a child trying to burn it. The Codex Borgia is not an Aztec but a Mixtec compila-tion, ascribed by Alfonso Caso to the Puebla-Tlaxcala region, and with a definite affinity to Cholula. The Codex describes the birth and career of the gods, particularly Quetzalcóatl, whose personal links with Cholula have already been touched upon. A second Mixtec codex is the Codex Vindobonensis, or Vienna Codex. This too deals with the fortunes of Quet-zalcóatl, and is the longest and one of the finest of the codices. The Codex Borgia and the Vienna Codex enable us to catch a glimpse of the history of Mexico at least four centuries before the Aztecs came on the scene.

'Looked at in a purely detached way,' writes C. A. Burland in the introduction to his *Magic Books from Mexico*, 'ancient Mexican books strike one by the brilliance of their pattern and the excellent grouping and proportion of colour on the page. The designs themselves are strangely vivid and active. There is an insistent rhythm in the pattern that is almost like music—the music of drums and rattles, shell trumpets and pottery whistles which characterized ancient Mexico.' A Mexican manuscript was no mere succession of signs, but a vivid and dynamic presentation of life in its complexity and totality, part picture, part document. The Aztec mode of writing, developed from that of earlier cultures, resembled the writing of ancient Egypt. Egyptian writing, being that of an old and stable civilization, was the more firm and decisive, while Aztec writing was more spontaneous and exuberant; but in general lay-out and the technicalities of the written language the two systems had a good deal in common. Egyptian was more advanced, in that it made use of a regular alphabet in conjunction with purely pictorial signs, whereas Aztec had not yet begun to develop an alphabet. However, in addition to simple little pictures denoting obvious actions, Aztec like Egyptian had arrived at the phonetic principal, the principle of the rebus or pun which is at the root of so many early scripts, and which is now used in puzzlebooks for small children. Thus we could write the words 'You fly' by drawing a yew-tree followed by a house-fly; 'I flee' by drawing an eye followed by a flea; or 'I spy' by a cube of ice followed by a slice of pie. The system can be used in an ingenious and fairly extensive way, though its limitations are obvious; the expression of complex or abstract ideas is impossible. Until an accurate syllabary or a regular alphabet is perfected, no system of writing can be other than primitive.

The way in which the Aztecs wrote numbers was equally primitive, though perfectly adequate. Each unit up to twenty was represented by a little dot or finger, then each successive unit of twenty was represented by a little flag. For four hundred (20 × 20), and multiples thereof, a small sign like a fir-tree was employed, and for eight thousand (20 × 20 × 20) a bag of cacao beans was shown. Thus eight hundred and eighty-eight shields would be represented by a drawing of a shield surmounted by two fir-trees, four flags, and eight dots or fingers.

One individual and interesting feature of Aztec writing, not found in Egyptian writing, is the important place assigned to the use of colour. Spring crops are shown as green, summer crops as yellow; a bowl of water is blue, a bowl of blood is red. The Aztecs did resemble the Egyptians in that specific gods were usually painted in specific colours. Thus Tecatzlipoca, god of the night, is painted with a dark face; and Quetzalcóatl, god of the morning and the wind, is painted with a light one. This habit of representing Quetzalcóatl in their sacred writings was to have dire consequences for Moctezuma and his subjects. It so happened that not only did Cortés and his ships land on the appointed day, but Cortés was light-skinned in comparison to the Mexicans, had a black beard and long hair, and by a fantastic coincidence was wearing exactly the same kind of flat-brimmed, low-crowned hat which Quetzalcóatl could be seen wearing in many of the sacred books.

3

There is nothing like death in war:
Nothing like the flowery death
So precious to Him who gives life!
Far off I see it! My heart yearns for it!

Náhuatl Song

THE two supreme institutions in Aztec society were those of warfare and religion. The inner ordering of Aztec society is even more baffling and difficult for us to understand than it was for the *conquistadores*, who at least had the opportunity of observing it at first hand. Thus the Aztec concept of the goal and purpose of war, like their concept of religion, is wholly foreign to us.

There was, of course, the usual straightforward economic motive for waging war, common to all nations in all ages. The Aztec state was an exploitative and parasitic organism, entirely dependent on aggressive warfare for its existence. We have seen that, according to even the most conservative estimate, Tenochtitlán and its satellite towns were very densely populated. It is doubtful whether the lake and the *chinampas* alone, productive as they were, could have provided all the necessities of life for such a teeming conurbation. More important, the Aztec *tecuhtli* and *macehualli* had become accustomed, through a successful career of conquest, not merely to a comfortable but to a luxurious way of life. To have called a cessation to warfare would have entailed an immediate drop in living standards. The tribute from the conquered states was divided after every campaign among the citizens of Tenochtitlán and the other Aztec towns. It was what enabled the emperor to pay his household, his generals, his soldiers and civil servants. A good year for the army was a good year for the Aztecs. In any case, they had no alternative. Their naked cruelty and rapacity had made it a question of either getting on or of going under. Defeat had always been attended with unpleasant consequences in pre-Conquest Mexico: but for the Aztecs, as they knew too well, defeat meant annihilation. In the situation which they had created for themselves, their policy that the best defence was attack made good sense.

Fighting, as we have seen, was in their bones. Ever since they had left the Place of the Herons, in the shadowy north, it had been their avocation. To live was to fight. Indeed, they had early come to believe that heaven had appointed them its legionaries on earth, and that to them had been given the divine duty and privilege of fighting on behalf of the gods against the cosmic forces of destruction. It was only because the Aztecs were willing to shoulder the burden of battle that the cosmos remained intact. Until the advent of the Aztecs, the most warlike civilization which Mexico had known was that of the Toltecs. From the Toltecs the Aztecs took their principal example, not least their martial inspiration. But in this, as in every other respect, they went far beyond their exemplars. The most immoderate of Mexican civilizations, they pushed war to the point where it was not, in Clausewitz's well-worn phrase, the pursuit of diplomacy by other means, but a pursuit in itself, sanctioned by religion. Even more than nations in the modern world, which may sometimes feel a twinge of doubt about the rationalizations with which they mask their military undertakings, the Aztecs managed to combine profitability with unction. Even sixteenth-century Spain experienced doubt and dissent about the ethics of conquest. Not so the Aztecs.

It must be remembered how thoroughly saturated the Aztec state was with the ideal of militarism. It was not a question of a small devoted military caste overlying a largely passive proletariat; the proletariat too were warriors. The Aztec nation was permanently in arms, like Sparta, or the Germany of the Hohenzollerns or National Socialists. Moctezuma was not only head of state, but supreme war chief. We have seen that the only path to promotion lay through the battlefield. Success in war took a man upwards; failure took him down. Everyone in the Aztec state was a warrior, young and old, *tecuhtli* and *macehualli*. The priests themselves were combatants, forming a special corps with their own awards and decorations.

The martial spirit was inculcated in an Aztec boy from the instant he drew his first breath. The midwife who delivered him held him in her arms and addressed him in the following manner: 'My very loved and tender son, here is the doctrine that was given us by the gods. This place where you were born is not your true house, because you are a soldier and a servant of the gods. Your land is not here but in another place. You are promised to the field of battle, and your faculties are dedicated to war. Your duty is to give the sun the blood of your enemies to drink, and to feed the earth with the corpses of your opponents. Your land, inheritance and fortune is the house of the sun. There you will serve and rejoice in his service, and by some happy chance you may one day be worthy of dying the flowery death.' Into the baby's hands was put a tiny shield and a bow, and his umbilical cord was taken to be buried in foreign soil, so that when he grew up some mysterious force would draw him towards the lands of his country's enemies. When it was time for him to go to school, it made no difference if he went to the upper-class *calmecac*, attached to a temple, or to the ordinary *telpochcalli* or district-school; in either case military precepts and behaviour would be thoroughly implanted in him. Indeed, competition and outright hostility between the two types of establishment was encouraged officially in order to make the boys even more belligerent. Their rivalry was also sharpened by the fact that the students of the *calmecac* were considered to be the children of Quetzalcóatl, and those of the *telpochcalli* the children of Tezcatlipoca.

At school the boy was taught the necessary skills in handling weapons. These were the sling, the bow, the dart, the lance, the spear, the club, and the sword, called the *macquauitl*. The tip of the lance and the blade of the wooden sword were edged with razor-sharp slivers of obsidian, glued firmly into slots. They could inflict fearful wounds. The spear was shorter than the lance, and was hurled by means of a spear-thrower or *atlatl*, a short length of wood with a groove down the middle and a peg at the end on which rested the spear. A shield or *chimalli* completed the accoutrements. One of these shields is on view in the museum at Chapultepec Castle, in Mexico City. It is round, two feet in diameter, consisting of skin and woven material mounted on a light wooden frame, and bears a clan totem or regimental insignia executed in fur and feathers. For protection, there was the suit of padded cotton, stiffened in brine or vinegar, called the *ichcahuipilli*. We have seen that many of the Spaniards abandoned their leather corselets and chain-mail to adopt this lightweight gear. The Aztec warrior was no myrmidon clanking into battle, but prided himself on his swift reactions and fleetness of foot. Here the boys of the *calmacec* would have been helped by their addiction to *tlatchtli*, a ball-game not unlike American hand-ball, British Eton fives, or the marvellously fast game called variously *pelota* or *jai alai*, invented by the Basques but at which Mexicans and other Latin Americans are adept. The difference was that *tlachtli* was played with the thighs and knees instead of the hands. It was a gruelling game, requiring pieces of padding that covered almost the whole face and body. As the ball-courts were attached to temples, and the game had a sacred origin, it was allowed to be played only by the upper classes. We have noted that ball-courts are considered one of the characteristic cultural traits of Mesoamerica, and the Mexican ball-game goes back to the earliest antiquity in Mexico. The Mayans in particular built enormous and majestic ball-courts. It was left only for the Aztecs to turn it into a minor form of warfare. Wagering on it could be so intemperate that many Aztecs were ruined and were even reduced to selling themselves into slavery.

Almost as soon as he had finished school, the young man was off to the wars. In his early battles he was assigned to the care of a seasoned warrior. His principal object was not, as in any ordinary type of warfare, to share in the general victory and to kill the enemy, but to capture individual prisoners. To capture an enemy soldier was considered a thousand times more important than to kill him: in fact, to kill him outright was regarded as a stupid, clumsy and reprehensible act. The first step in rank occurred when a young man captured his first live prisoner, after which he was entitled to be called an *iyac*. When he had captured four, he became a *tequiua*, and had the right to sit on a special kind of stool. If he continued to mount the military ladder, he could become a *quauhchichimecatl* or Chichimec Eagle, or an *otomitl*, a grade named after the Otomí, both of them barbarian ancestors of the Aztecs. As a special distinction, he might be invited to enter one of the two élite orders, those of the Eagle Knights and the Jaguar Knights (Plate 4b). These provided the high officers of the army, and were devoted respectively to Huitzilopochtli and Tezcatlipoca. They were excessively austere and indulged in every form of abstinence and self-flagellation. Every step in rank meant an increment in wealth as well as in prestige for its recipient. He would receive a larger share of the booty allotted to his clan, or an additional grant of land, including the serfs who worked it, in the captured territories. He could also wear extra decorations on his breast or extra plumes on the elaborate wooden helm that possessed an ornamental rather than practical use. Eventually he might even aspire to be one of the 'four great ones', the four senior generals who commanded the army-corps drawn from the four principal divisions of Tenochtitlán.

The year's campaign took place during the summer. It was then, after the fields had been sown but before they were reaped, that the greatest number of men were available for warfare. The Spaniards, unfortunately for the Aztecs, contrived to land in the autumn, when the crops were being harvested, and also showed themselves superior in campaigning in bad weather; hitherto war had been a sport reserved for high summer in Mexico. The first move was to find an excuse for opening hostilities. The Aztecs were specialists at this, and rang the changes on several gambits. They could instruct the merchants, who had previously reconnoitred the land to be fought over, to act as *agents provocateurs*. The merchants would arrange to be insulted, and the insult would thereupon be interpreted as an insult to the emperor. Another method was to send a local ruler a statue of Huitzilopochtli, with a request to place it in his temple. If he refused, war followed. The tender susceptibilities of the Aztecs were well known throughout Mexico: but try as they might, states marked down for spoliation simply could not avoid wounding those sensitive feelings.

Once war was declared, mobilization was rapid. It was said that, within an hour of a *tecuhtli* reaching for his sword and shield, he was marching along the causeway leading out of Tenochtitlán at the head of his troops. The basic unit of the army was a platoon of twenty men; the platoon formed part of a battalion of a hundred to four hundred men; two or three battalions constituted a regiment; and the regiments in turn were grouped into divisions and corps. The warriors were summoned by the beating of the great war-drum, and assembled in the square outside their local temple. They then began the march to the seat of the war. The forced-marches of the Aztecs were celebrated. They went swiftly and in silence, with an impressive show of discipline.

Once on the ground selected for battle, the army deployed. Sometimes ambushes were staged, and occasionally fancy strategems were employed, like burying men in pits so that they could spring up in the rear of an army that had advanced over them. Normally, however, the Aztecs relied on the good old-fashioned frontal assault. It was a tactic that had usually proved effective. Indeed, the sight of the might of Tenochtitlán, drawn up in battle array and brilliantly bedizened, was in itself almost sufficient to bring victory. Their reputation for almost complete invincibility increased the enemy's apprehension. At a given signal, the Aztecs broke into howls and shouts, beat drums, blew conches and bone-whistles, performed threatening dances, and gradually worked themselves into the mood for attack. Another signal, and they moved forward, delivering a shower of stones from their slings. Closer, the bows and the *atlatls* were brought into play, and the sky which had been black with stones was now black with arrows and spears. Closer, and the lances were levelled in a bristling hedge. Closer still, and the bludgeons and the dreadful flint-edged *macquauitl* began to flail the air.

As the battle line advanced and rolled over the enemy, squads of specially trained men with ropes followed close behind to tie up the prisoners; and when the battle was over, the first thought of the Aztecs was to conduct the enemy wounded to the rear and bind up their wounds. There was no humanitarian motive involved; these captives were destined to provide the gods and the sun with the fresh blood which was their essential food—'precious water' or *chalchiuatl*—on the sacrificial altar. The gods had given their blood in making man, so it was right that man should give his blood in order to nourish the gods. And what blood could be more nourishing and sustaining than that of brave men who had acquitted themselves honourably in combat? Thus the dual purpose of the campaign had been achieved: the Aztecs had conquered a province ripe for present plunder and future tribute, and had also obtained a supply of victims to feed the sun and appease the gods. And next year the ceaseless cycle would bring the Aztec armies into the field all over again. The Aztecs were locked into an iron pattern, caught in a sinister and unbreakable rhythm. One wonders who, in the end, were the victims and the captives, the Aztecs or their wretched prisoners?

The Aztecs had always been warlike, and had always been partial to bloody sacrifices. We have seen how their grisly rites had resulted in their being expelled early on from Colhuacán. Quetzalcóatl-Topiltzín had failed to persuade the Toltecs to give up sacrificing human beings, and to sacrifice birds, butterflies and snakes instead. The Toltecs had rebuffed him and driven him out, but nonetheless they had kept the practice of human sacrifice within bounds. So had the Aztecs, in earlier times. In any case, they were a small, weak tribe, and their opportunity to secure victims was limited. But with the growth of their imperial mania and religious megalomania their appetites had grown. Like all primitive religions, the Aztec religion was convinced that there was a direct connection between the practice of a rite and the benefits it was intended to procure. If the rite was properly performed, the gods would be pleased; if not, they would be wrathful. It so happened that between the years 1451–6 there was a prolonged famine, due to crop failures produced by frost and heavy storms. The Aztec people were almost wiped out, and they ascribed this calamity to the anger of the gods at being offered insufficient food. Thereafter, for the remaining sixty years of their existence, they ensured that such a dangerous state of affairs should never occur again. In rites where two victims had been sacrificed, twenty were now offered up; where twenty, two hundred; where two hundred, two thousand; where two thousand, twenty thousand. What did the additional lives signify, where the well-being of Tenochtitlán—and indeed of the whole created world—was a question of placating the gods?

With these considerations in mind, they invented the *xochiyaoyotl*, the so-called *War of Flowers*, surely one of the wierdest institutions ever devised. Something like it appears to have existed in earlier centuries in the Valley of Mexico, but after the famine-years it was expanded and put on a regular basis. Briefly, the *xochiyaoyotl* was intended to ensure that, if no real war could be provoked or set in motion to procure the prisoners who were the gods' prime sustenance, then an artificial war would be launched for the same purpose. The War of Flowers was a tournament or gladiatorial combat where the contestants did not compete for a lady's favour but hazarded their actual lives. On one side were ranged the pick of the warriors of the three neighbouring Aztec cities of Tenochtitlán, Texcoco and Tlacopán; they constituted the home team, as it were. On the other side were the picked men of Tlaxcala, Huejotzingo and Cholula, the visiting team. We have seen how the last three cities had come to the help of the Aztecs when they were struggling against the Tepanecs in the 1420. Subsequently their enthusiasm for the Aztecs had waned, and it was only by means of bitter struggles that they had managed to cling to their independence in the face of Aztec expansion. They did not share the Aztec obsession for blood and sacrifice, and one suspects that they were not willing participants in the War of Flowers, but were afraid, lest worse befall, to refuse the Aztec invitation to join in this strange game. The two sides met at a chosen place and fought for a day or even longer. The prisoners were then taken home by their respective captors. The captors of the Aztec prisoners, one feels, would also not be slow to cut a few Aztec throats.

The most valiant of the captives taken in regular war or in the War of Flowers were accorded a special death. They were arrayed in a ceremonial uniform and a crown of soft white feathers was placed on their heads, emblematic of the dawn, the hour when the soul of a departed warrior winged its way towards the sun. They were then led to a special round stone, called the *temalacatl*, elaborately decorated and with a hole in the middle. To this stone they were tethered by a rope tied around the waist, leaving them ample room to move. They were then given wooden weapons with which to defend themselves against one or more Aztec warriors armed with the *macquauitl*. When the prisoner fell, mortally wounded, he was untied, carried to the altar, and his heart cut out in the usual manner.

It is almost impossible for us to comprehend the state of mind of the captor and the captive in these Aztec campaigns. The captive had a resigned and fatalistic attitude towards what awaited him that was even more marked, if that is conceivable, than the fatalism of the modern Mexican Indian when confronting the prospect of death. Sahagún records that: 'When a man took a prisoner, he said: "Here is my well-beloved son"; and the captive said: "Here is my revered father." ' It was all formal and predestined. Soustelle writes: 'The warrior who had made a prisoner and who watched him die before the altar knew that sooner or later he would follow him into the hereafter by the same kind of death. "You are welcome: you know what the fortune of war is—today for you, tomorrow for me," said the emperor to the captured chief.' Soustelle also observes, on military and other sacrifices: 'Blood was necessary to save this world and the men in it: the victim was no longer an enemy who was to be killed but a messenger, arrayed in a dignity that was almost divine, who was sent to the gods. All the relevant descriptions convey the impression not of a dislike between the sacrificer and the victim nor of anything resembling a lust for blood, but of a strange fellow-feeling or rather—and this is vouched for by the texts—of a kind of mystical kinship.' To an extent, this is rather like special pleading on the part of Soustelle, almost an argument for justification. Human nature being what it is, one suspects that many if not most of the captives were in the grip of terror and misery; it was the custom, indeed, to give drugs to sacrificial victims, which would not have been necessary if they had been in a tranquil frame of mind. But the actual moment of putting a man to death must always be awesome and mysterious, no matter how cruelly and unjustly he has been condemned; and the moment is rendered even more solemn by the victim who, all emotion and indignation drained away, strives to come to terms with his death and meet it like a man. One can sometimes see the special relationship between executioner and victim of which Soustelle speaks in the bull-ring, where a matador who possesses pride, nobility and imagination will accompany the bull to which he has just given the *estocada* across to the place beside the barrera, its *querencia*, where it has chosen to die. He will walk with his hand on the animal's neck—and sometimes, as it finally sinks to its knees, he will put his hand on its forehead in a kind of salute or benediction, a gesture of sorrow, regret and farewell. It is an intensely moving moment. One would hope that the sufferings of the prisoner of the Aztecs on the *temalacatl* and the sacrificial stone were softened, at the end, by some such compassionate expression in the eyes of the slayer.

At least, when the time of testing came for the Aztec nation, they were true to their salt, faithful to their dark creed. They neither complained nor asked for quarter. According to one account, after Cortés stormed Tenochtitlán only six hundred Aztec warriors were left alive; and although this is doubtless an exaggeration, it indicates the tenacity with which the Aztecs defended their city to the last.

The Samurai had a *tanka* or two-line poem that declared:

> '*Among flowers, the cherry:*
> *Among men, the warrior.*'

It was a sentiment that could also have been applied to the Eagle Knight or Jaguar Knight, with his own cult of flowers and blood.

* * *

There was a class, or rather caste, among the Aztecs even more rigorous and extreme than that of the warrior. This was the caste of the priest. If the warrior was the instrument who procured the wealth and external security of the empire, the priest was even more important, for he was the guardian of the spiritual security on which the success of the armies and the prosperity of the state depended. It is impossible to over-emphasize the intense religiosity of the Aztecs. Even in a land which since time immemorial had devoted a major part of its energy and imagination to religion, the Aztecs were a by-word for their piety. The Aztec year was divided into eighteen months, and every one of those months required its special observances from one or other sections of the population, and frequently all sections together. The observances went on for many days, and were of fantastic elaboration and complexity. It seems amazing that, bowed beneath this spiritual weight, the everyday life of the community could be pursued at all. Anyone who has witnessed, for example, the dances carried on day and night at certain times of the year in the pueblos of Arizona and New Mexico knows that there is nothing half-hearted about such rites: and the Aztecs were given up to these ceremonies to an altogether unheard-of degree. Every phase of national and individual life, every phase of the seasons and the agricultural year, every phase of the heavens above and the underworld beneath, were celebrated. In addition to the routine daily observances, there must have been no single day or hour when some special festivity, complete with processions, flowers and sacrifices, was not in progress in Tenochtitlán. In part this hectic religiosity can be attributed to youthfulness and aggressiveness, the phenomenal vitality and surging progress of the Aztec nation; but in part it can also be ascribed, no doubt, to an equally deep-seated sense of cultural anxiety and even neurosis which will be touched on a little later. It is possible that the frenzied character of so much of the life of the Aztecs was due to the restlessness occasioned by the fact that they were in the grip of a terrible psychic conflict or crisis. Their excesses were the galvanic twitchings of a deeply disturbed and tormented organism.

The Aztec priest was a man even more uncompromisingly set apart than the Catholic priest. He was the most ascetic product of the *calmecac*, in itself a very hard school. Run by priests, for the benefit of the *pilli* or sons of noblemen, the instructors of the *calmecac* were in a position to judge which of their pupils possessed the zeal and iron nerve necessary to serve the gods. The neophyte underwent the same military training as his comrades, but it would be noted that his enthusiasm was more unwavering than theirs, particularly when it came to the punishments which the boys were expected to inflict on themselves. Every day the aspiring warrior was expected to draw blood from himself with cactus thorns, usually by piercing the lobe of the ear; but the really fervid did more than this: they scarified their flesh, drove sharp sticks through their tongues, or stuck needles through their penises in order to smear the sacred images with their blood. They painted their bodies black, undertook fasts and vigils until they became emaciated, and took massive doses of violent and unpredictable narcotics. These drugs were derived from such sources as tobacco, Jimson weed, certain species of mushroom and fungus, and the *peyotl* of the Chihuahuan desert. *Peyotl* or *peyote* is the Náhuatl word for the button of some of the larger agaves, from which mescaline is derived, and which when chewed produces hallucinations. From various species of the agave or century-plant—which actually lives ten or twelve years—the ancient Mexicans also extracted the liquors that produced the divine drunkenness of feast-days. Tequila, pulque, and mezcal were distilled from the roasted hearts of the agave, and sotol from the roasted heart of the sotol. These unforgiving liquors are still standard beverages in Mexico today. The agave, the sotol and the yucca, be it noted, were truly remarkable growths, in that they provided the ancient Mexican not only with drink, but with fertilizer, soap, medicaments, needles, thread, and fibres for making paper, cloth, rope, sandals, baskets and mats.

The aspirant priest entered his profession when he was twenty-two or twenty-three, presumably after intensive instruction and when he had undergone considerable military experience. Now he was entitled to wear the black robe, embroidered with skulls and bones. The Spaniards found the Aztec priest a fearsome sight: sombre, skinny, eyes glittering from a mass of unkempt hair matted with blood. The young priest was henceforth sworn to an existence apart, and to celibacy. It may have been the priests who, forbidden women, practised the sodomy which was widespread in Aztec domains, and which shocked the Spaniards; but sodomy is so common a feature of militaristic cultures that it is probable that the young men were introduced to it in their *calmecac* and *telpochcalli* and continued it thereafter. Once he was ordained, the young priest was called *tlamacazqui*, a holy title which he shared with Quetzalcóatl, Tlaloc and other principal gods. He might proceed no further than the rank of parish priest or *quacuilli*, serving out his time in an obscure local temple; but if he rose in the priestly hierarchy, which was as precisely demarcated as the military, he could become a *tlenamacac*, a priest of superior grade. Finally he might rise to one of the leading administrative positions in the Aztec church, an organization of immense extent and complexity controlled by two supreme pontiffs, the *quetzalcóatl totec tlamacazqui*, Plumed Serpent, Priest of Our Lord, presiding over the cult of Huitzilopochtli, and the *quetzalcóatl Tlaloc tlamacazqui*, directing the cult of Tlaloc.

While the individual priest was dedicated to complete poverty, abstinence and celibacy, the church itself was the richest single entity in the Aztec state. Each temple received official revenues and was endowed with estates and the serfs and slaves to work them. The larger temples possessed whole tracts of conquered territories, and every temple shared in the gains from the year's campaigns. In addition the emperor was lavish with gifts from his own purse. The predominance of the priesthood was symbolized by the fact that the temple was always the tallest and most imposing building in any city. When the *conquistadores* first set eyes on Tenochtitlán they thought that the two great temples rearing up out of the main square must be the palaces of the ruler. In warfare, the recognized culminating act of hostilities was for one side or the other to burn the temples of its rivals. This betokened the destruction of their very soul. The temple of a captured city was always put to the torch. When Tenochtitlán itself fell, the Great Temple was set afire, and with its disappearance the Aztec empire was annihilated—not temporarily, but for all time. The Aztec religion, like the religions of all primitive or semi-primitive peoples, was the framework on which the whole fabric of the life of the Aztec people was woven, the thread on which the beads were strung. When the frame was broken, the thread cut, there was no longer any basis on which that life could be reconstituted.

The Great Temple of Tenochtitlán, dedicated jointly to Huitzilopochtli and Tlaloc, stood in the centre of the city, where the three causeways intersected. The main square, a sacred area that was delimited by its own Serpent Wall, a crenellated wall with three entrances, was almost exactly 430 yards square (Plate 3a and Fig. 7). When the Spaniards began to construct modern Mexico City, they built their Plaza Mayor or Zócalo on the rubble of the old main square; thus, although a precious sense of historical continuity was maintained, the remains of the old buildings were buried beneath the structures of the new. Without dismantling the entire north-west corner of magnificent Zócalo, one of the most majestic squares in the world, it is impossible to excavate and examine in any detail the old sacred precinct of the Aztecs. Thus far, the most intensive excavations have been those of Gamio in 1916 and Cuevas in 1933.

The Great Temple, the largest structure in the precinct, was a gigantic stepped pyramid, built during four reigns between 1450 and 1494. There were four steps or layers, and the two temples that rested on the upper platform were approached by two parallel staircases. Cortés put the number of stairs at about 100, Díaz says precisely that there were 114, and Durán, writing later, states that there were 120. We shall probably not be far wrong if we accept Ignacio Marquina's figure, in his *Templo Mayor de Mexico*, of a height of about 33 yards from the ground to the top of the pyramid, with an extension of perhaps 15 yards for the temples on top. Marquina puts the base at about 110 yards square. While it is of modest dimensions by Egyptian standards (the Great Pyramid at Gizeh is over 130 yards high and covers thirty-one acres), the Great Temple of Tenochtitlán was imposing, and was only one among an elegant and harmonious group of buildings placed within the enceinte. It has to be remembered that the Aztec temples could be neither too heavy, because of the spongy nature of the city's foundations, nor too high, because constant access was required to the temples with which they were crowned. Almost as massive as the Great Pyramid was the adjacent Pyramid of Tezcatlipoca, and in the vicinity were four smaller temples, also pyramidal and surmounted with temples approached by staircases; these were the Sun Temple, the Snake Temple, the Temple of Xipe Totec, and the Temple of Colhuacán. There was also space for a ball-court, two calendar stones, a platform on which was mounted the round stone for the *temalacatl* or gladiatorial combat between captive and captor, and a gigantic *tzompantli* or skull rack, on which were strung the grinning fleshless crania of sacrificed victims. Sahagún, best informed of the post-Conquest chroniclers, lists seven large *tzompantlis* in the proximity of the Great Pyramid, which would represent a number of skulls running into many hundreds.

What gods were worshipped in these temples? The gods of the Aztecs were legion. Vaillant lists sixty-five principal members of the Aztec pantheon, dividing them into ten main categories: Great Gods, Creative Deities, Fertility Gods, Gods of Rain and Moisture, Fire Gods, Pulque Gods, Planetary and Stellar Gods, Gods of Death and the Earth, Variants of Great Gods, and 'other gods'. With sixty-five major gods alone, not bothering about minor ones, one can appreciate why the Aztec worshippers were kept continually busy. Like so many other traits of their culture, the religion of the Aztecs was a mushroom growth. They were a *parvenu* people, and in the space of only two centuries they had cobbled together a state religion which they considered appropriate for their elevated situation. This religion was meant to impress: it was an instrument of terror, of propaganda, part of the system of coercion that constituted the Aztec empire. That is not to say that the Aztecs did not believe in it and give themselves to it: it means only that their religion was a reflection of their own restless, uneasy, questioning nature. There was nothing detached or intellectual about it; nothing lofty or olympian. It was sorcery on a grand scale. The Aztecs bore much the same kind of relation to their fellow-Mexicans as the Apaches or Comanches bore to their fellow Indians, and one would expect them to worship more savage and relentless gods.

Having been hurriedly assembled, the Aztec pantheon was a rag-bag of deities of all types and ages. The oldest were the deities of the northern barbarians, those tribal deities—almost fetishes or ju-jus—which the Aztecs had brought into the Valley when they arrived with the Chichimecs, Otomí and Tamime. Then there were the more sophisticated deities whom they had inherited from earlier dwellers in the Valley. And finally there were the older, grander deities, the immemorial gods of Mexico, whose name and fame had outlasted the fall of a thousand cities and temples. In particular, the Aztecs had taken over the gods of the Toltecs, prominent among them Quetzalcóatl, in his guise of Tlahuizcalpantecuhtli or *Lord of the Dawn*, Tezcatlipoca, and Tlaloc, the rain god, *He Who Makes Things Sprout*, whose cult had been prominent many generations before at nearby Teotihuacán.

It is interesting, however, that although the Aztecs venerated Quetzalcóatl, according him his feast-days and giving his name as an honorific to their priests, he was not a principal object of worship. They revered him as a creative presence: but he was, after all, an intellectual and philosophical deity, not really in tune with their extroverted ethos; furthermore he was pacific, and had set his face against human sacrifice. The Aztecs were not pacifists, and human sacrifice was the cornerstone of their religious practice. The gods they preferred were gods susceptible of more downright and earthy adoration. These included the gods whose temples stood in the centre of Tenochtitlán, Tlaloc and Tezcatlipoca, and the important and characteristic god Xipe Totec, the *Flayed One*, god of seedtime and planting, sometimes called the Red Tezcatlipoca. Several of these gods had numerous avatars; Tezcatlipoca was especially protean, being worshipped at various times under the guise of Metztli, the moon god, Itzli, the *Stone Knife*, Itzlacoliuhqui, the *Obsidian Knife*, Chalchiuhtotoliu, the *Jewelled Bird*; he also had a close connection with

Tonatiuh, the sun god. Among the many other divinities, one might perhaps single out a few of the more important. These included the agricultural deities: the several earth goddesses, Ilamatecuhtli, Coatlícue, Chicomecóatl, and Teteoinan or Tlazoltéotl; the god and goddess of the maize, Centéotl and Xilonen; the fire god, Xiuhtecuhtli; the deities of death and the land of the dead, Mictlantecuhtli and his wife Mictecacíhuatl; and the goddesses Chalchiutlícue, *She of the Jade Skirt*, goddess of water, and Huixtocíhuatl, *Salt Woman*, goddess of salt. The one truly unique Aztec god in the Aztec assemblage was Huitzilopochtli, *Left-handed Humming-bird*, the ubiquitous war-god, recipient of the most frequent and substantial honours of all. He was the tribal totem who had guided his people on the weary journey from far-off Aztlán to the Valley of Mexico; he had shown them the place on the lake-shore where they were to build their city; he was the touchstone of their success. He had developed close links with other leading Aztec gods, for example with Tonatiuh, the sun god. On occasion he was called the Blue Tezcatlipoca, bringing him into contact with the great cult of Tezcatlipoca which the Aztecs had received as a legacy from the Toltecs and Mixtecs. Quetzalcóatl himself, as well as appearing in the form of Ehécatl, the god of the wind, was sometimes called the White Tezcatlipoca. Thus he was confused with the aggressive figure who, at Tula, had been regarded as his deadly enemy. Perhaps, for the Aztec, his image had actually been swallowed up by that of his rival. But in effect Huitzilopochtli reigned alone and supreme, and was perhaps the most sanguinary deity known to history.

The Aztec gods, despite their pretty-sounding names and attributes, were exceedingly menacing of aspect. This can be verified by a visit to the Aztec section of the Museo Antropológico in Mexico City. One is struck by the contrast between the objects that represent the cheerful, colourful existence of the humble people and the mournful statuary that represents the priestly and military castes who governed them. When they were not shouldering their spears and marching off to the seat of war, the *macehualli* could be merry and relaxed enough. Not so their rulers and their gods. Fortunately for mankind, sooner or later the principalities and powers pass away, no matter how pompous and callous they might be, but the careless and amiable *hoi-polloi* go on for ever. The art of the Aztecs, in its official aspect, is always sinister, although the jewellery and mobiliary art can be light-hearted and even gay, particularly when it reflects that love of nature in all its aspects which was part of the Mexican soul, and which even the Aztecs shared. The statues of the gods, however, are frightening. They have none of the benevolence and humanity, for example, of their counterparts in the Cairo Museum (though in speaking

of ancient Egypt one is referring, of course, to the most radiant and
tolerant civilization which the world has possibly ever seen). The Aztec
sculptures remind one of the despotic gods pictured on the walls of the
palaces of Assyria. The gods of the Aztecs, as one views them in the
museum, are four-square and ponderous. They are always carved to be
looked at directly from the front—blocks of dull blackish volcanic stone,
squatting massively on their pedestals, glowering down as if they meant
to topple over and crush the spectator. One searches in vain for any
relieving touch of elegance or simplicity, unfailing ingredients in the art
of other Mexican peoples and cultures. The Mayas and other tribes of
Yucatán and the Gulf Coast evince everywhere in their art an outstanding
sense of colour and refinement; even the prehistoric Olmecs were capable
of a certain wit and pathos. The Zapotecs and Mixtecs, and the warlike
Toltecs who followed them, had been capable of introducing a strain of
playfulness and fantasy into their art and artifacts; while at Teotihuacán,
although some of the heavier aspects of the statuary were later adopted by
the Aztecs, the pottery in particular demonstrated a rare charm and grace.
The enormous unfinished statue from Teotihuacán of Chalchiuhtlícue,
She of the Jade Skirt, which stands outside the Museo Antropológico and
is 23 feet high, 17 feet wide, and weighs 168 tons, is as square and
uncouth as any of the similar earth goddesses later made by the Aztecs;
but the Aztec statues are a hundred times more gruesome. The statue of
her sister-goddess Coatlícue in the Museo Antropológico, though only
half as high, is an altogether nightmarish figure (Plate 4a). It could have
been conceived only by a morbid imagination, seeking to express an
ultimate vision of monstrosity. She was found in the eighteenth century,
buried beneath what is now the Zócalo. That she was not a negligible
deity, an occasional or accidental demon, is shown by the other representa-
tions of her to be found in the Museo. As described by Ignacio Bernal, in
3,000 years of Art and Life in Mexico, she is here portrayed as 'a beheaded woman from whose neck two large serpent-heads emerge. She
wears a necklace made of human hearts, two hands with palms turned
outwards, and a skull containing lifelike eyes. Her petticoat or skirt is a
mass of serpents whose bodies are interlaced like a rhomboidal keyboard.
She wears a sash made of two serpents knotted in front; serpents that
resemble enormous claws take the place of hands. Her feet are like eagle's
talons with the nails grasping the earth'. (She is represented as beheaded,
by the way, because, after she had given birth to the Four Hundred Gods,
they showed their affection by decapitating their mother.) To other
cultures, the goddess of the earth is a tender, benign, all-welcoming, all-
embracing personage; to the Aztecs, she is an effigy from Lucas Cranach,

Hieronymus Bosch or Matthias Grünewald. Another and equally intimidating statue of Coatlícue was unearthed in 1969; and in the Museo Antropólogico can be seen other ill-favoured relatives of this disagreeable lady: Mictecacíhuatl, the goddess of death; Itzpapálotl, the *Obsidian Knife Butterfly*, a Chichimec goddess of death and battle; and the four goddesses or witches called the Cihuateteo, the spirits of women dead in childbirth, who had the unpleasant habit of shouting and screaming in the middle of the night, or wandered abroad at twilight and struck anyone who met them with paralysis.

It was not to be expected that the worship of gods and goddesses of this character would be a predominantly joyous affair. In fact it was associated with execution, torture and the infliction of ingenious modes of suffering on an altogether unprecedented scale. It is interesting and rather amusing to remark, as one inspects the great Aztec hall of the Museo Antropológico, that this feature of Aztec civilization, which was perhaps its single most distinctive component, is deliberately glossed over. It is ignored almost as thoroughly as the three centuries of Spanish rule are ignored in the historical museum at Chapultepec Castle. There is one small display, illustrating some of the details of a sacrifice in a somewhat sketchy fashion; it consists of a reproduction of a sixteenth-century Spanish woodcut, together with an obsidian knife. The blade of the knife is an excellent specimen of the flint-knapper's craft, and the handle, fashioned in mosaic in the shape of a crouching man, is a most original conception. The deadly instrument is so attractive that it is easy to overlook the purpose for which it was used.

There is no point, at this late date, in waxing indignant or censorious about this aspect of Aztec civilization. We must remember Marc Bloc's advice to historians to renounce their false angelic airs. We must also remember, when we discuss the hundreds of thousands of victims put to death by the Aztecs, that in our own time tens of millions of human beings have been exterminated in Europe, Asia and Africa. As for the Americas, the massacres committed by the Aztecs can be parallelled on almost as large a scale and practically within living memory by the systematic extirpation of the American Indian. Nevertheless, in dealing with the question of the Aztec sacrifices, we are confronted inescapably with a moral problem of an even larger magnitude than that presented by the actions of the *conquistadores*. We cannot evade it, if only for the reason that it made such a deep and painful impression on the minds of Cortés and his men. They regarded it as an abomination, and considered themselves justified in all their undertakings by the fact that, if nothing else, they were putting an end to this one custom. More, they regarded it as not merely abominable but blasphemous, in that the rites of sacrifice seemed to be an obscene parody of their own Christian rituals. The sacrifice of the pagan victim bore a certain resemblance to the crucifixion of Christ, while the offering of blood and the eating of the dead man's flesh bore a kind of correspondence to Christian communion. The similarities were more definitely remarked at a later date, after the Conquest, by the Mexicans themselves. Used to equating blood and suffering with religion, they found it correspondingly easy to accept as their own the bleeding, suffering and essentially sacrificial figure of Christ on the cross.

The salient feature of Aztec sacrifice was the scale on which it was practised. One post-Conquest chronicler suggested in all seriousness that there may have been more people in fifteenth-century Mexico who died on the sacrificial stone than who died natural deaths. It was noted earlier that at the dedication of the Great Temple of Tenochtitlán 20,000 victims were sacrificed in four days. Peterson says: 'We know that at the dedication of the main temple of Huitzilopochtli the ruler Ahuítzotl began the sacrifices, and the rulers and priests of the neighbouring provinces also took turns opening chests and plucking out hearts until their arms were exhausted. The slaughter continued four days, from sun-up until sunset, until the city was permeated with the smell of blood. Some historians say 20,000 were sacrificed on that occasion, and Torquemada gives 80,000. After the sacrifices the city stank horribly, and several epidemics took many Aztec lives in ironic retribution.' When we visit or study photographs of Aztec temples, we should picture to ourselves those tall staircases as they frequently appeared: covered from top to bottom with a tacky, crimson sheath of blood (see Plate 8).

Zumárraga stated that the number of people sacrificed annually at Tenochtitlán was 20,000; Gómara gives the figure as 50,000. Obviously it is impossible to make an accurate estimate. We do know, however, that each of the eighteen months of the Aztec year, each month divided into twenty days, was accorded its individual tally of victims, male or female, adult or infant. Thus in the months when rain was sought, a band of children were drowned, or walled up in a cave, or exposed on a mountain-top; and the more they wept, the better the augury for rain. At harvest-time, victims were thrown into a fire or furnace, and their bodies pulled out with hooks before they were totally consumed so that the precious hearts could be extracted in the usual way. At the periods when growth and fertility were required, the commonest practice was to behead a priestess and flay her, and for a priest to insert himself into the skin and lead a ritual dance. Flaying was the type of sacrifice particularly associated with the powerful god Xipe Totec, the *Flayed One*.

5

Sir James Frazer, in *The Scapegoat*, has assembled from the works of the Spanish chroniclers an account of the rite of Xipe Totec, filled with his characteristic dry humour, that deserves to be quoted at length. 'On the day of Xipe's festival,' he writes, 'all the prisoners, with the exception of a few who were reserved for a different death, were killed in the usual way. The scene of the slaughter was the platform on the summit of Huitzilo-pochtli's temple. Some of the poor wretches fainted when they came to the foot of the steps and had to be dragged up the long staircase by the hair of their heads. Arrived at the summit they were slaughtered one by one on the sacrificial stone by the high priest, who cut open their breasts, tore out their hearts, and held them up to the sun, in order to feed the great luminary with these bleeding relics. Then the bodies were sent rolling down the staircase, clattering and turning over and over like gourds as they bumped from step to step till they reached the bottom. There they were received by other priests, or rather human butchers, who with a dexterity acquired by practise slit the back of each body from the nape of the neck to the heels and peeled off the whole skin in a single piece as neatly as if it had been a sheepskin. The skinless body was then fetched away by its owner, that is, by the man who had captured the prisoner in war. He took it home with him, carved it, sent one of the thighs to the king, and other joints to friends, or invited them to come and feast on the carcase in his house. The skins of the human victims were also a perquisite of their captors, and were lent or hired out by them to men who had made a vow of going about clad in the hides for twenty days. Such men clothed in the reeking skins of the butchered prisoners were called Xixipeme or Tototectin after the god Xipe or Totec, whose living image they esteemed and whose costume they wore. Among the devotees who bound themselves to this pious exercise were persons who suffered from loathsome skin diseases, such as smallpox, abscesses, and the itch; and among them there was a fair sprinkling of debauchees, who had drunk themselves nearly blind and hoped to recover the use of their precious eyes by parading for a month in this curious mantle. Thus arrayed, they went from house to house throughout the city, entering everywhere and asking alms for the love of God. On entering a house each of these reverend palmers was made to sit on a heap of leaves; festoons of maize and wreaths of flowers were placed round his body; and he was given wine to drink and cakes to eat. And when a mother saw one of these filthy but sanctified ruffians passing along the street, she would run to him with her infant and put it in his arms that he might bless it, which he did with unction, receiving an alms from the happy mother in return. The earnings of these begging-friars on their rounds were sometimes considerable, for the rich people rewarded them handsomely. Whatever they were, the collectors paid them in to the owners of the skins, who thus made a profit by hiring out these valuable articles of property. Every night the wearers of the skins deposited them in the temple and fetched them again next morning when they set out on their rounds. At the end of the twenty days the skins were dry, hard, shrivelled and shrunken, and they smelt so villainously that people held their noses when they met the holy beggars arrayed in their fetid mantles. The time being come to rid themselves of these encumbrances, the devotees walked in solemn procession, wearing the rotten skins and stinking like dead dogs, to the temple called Yopico, where they stripped themselves of the hides and plunged them into a tub or vat, after which they washed and scrubbed themselves thoroughly, while their friends smacked their bare bodies loudly with wet hands in order to squeeze out the human grease with which they were saturated.'

*　　　*　　　*

What are we to make of these manifestations, which were not only extraordinary but carried out, as we have said, on an unprecedented scale? It always goes against the grain to make value-judgments, to evaluate one human culture in terms of another. It is a commonplace that the various facets of a culture, good or bad, pleasant or unpleasant, harmonious or discordant, straightforward or obscure, are bound up into a unique totality, a living whole. It is dangerous and frequently useless to isolate individual traits and analyze them separately. Moctezuma made a shrewd observation when Cortés lectured him on the shortcomings of his religion. 'Throughout all time we have worshipped our own gods,' said Moctezuma, 'and thought that they were good. I do not doubt the goodness of the god whom you worship, but if he is good for Spain, our gods are equally good for Mexico, so do not trouble to speak to us any more about them at present.' However, where such a startling institution as human sacrifice is concerned, particularly when it results in the killing of 20,000 captives in the space of four days (which works out at about one victim every twenty seconds) one cannot help asking whether, in fact, it is 'good'. We are bound to find ourselves reflecting to some degree on the moral considerations involved. As Arnold Toynbee, speaking of Cortés in the supplementary volume to his *Study of History* puts it: 'It is not only conquerors and rulers who have found themselves forced to pass summary judgements on the respective merits of their own standards and those of alien peoples. Anthropologists and historians are in the same plight. Their hands too are forced by the relation into which they have entered with the human objects of their study. They cannot study without finding themselves also compelled to judge.' Entering more fully, in another book, into what he calls the problem of 'relativity in studying human affairs', Toynbee observes: 'In what cases ought we to pass judgement on the strength of our belief in the existence of such common human standards, and in what cases ought we to suspend judgement in deference to our recognition that some human standards, including some of our own, have only a relative validity? Here there is no *a priori* rule to guide us; we can only feel our way; and, all the time, we are perpetually being forced into taking a line by the pressure of events. Were the Roman authorities justified in forcibly suppressing the practice of human sacrifice in North-West Africa, or the Spanish authorities in forcibly suppressing it in Middle America? Were the British authorities in India justified in suppressing infanticide, suttee, and the self-immolation of the devotees who used to throw themselves under the wheels of Juggernaut's car? From the point of view of the Punic, Aztec, and Hindu addicts to these rites, their alien conquerors were misusing their military power to suppress religious practices whose significance and value these aliens did not understand. Ignorant prejudice militant is certainly an ugly thing, and the Aztec citizens of Tenochtitlán can have seen nothing but an outrageous act of sacrilege in the overthrow of their gods' images and altars and the slaughter of their priests by Cortés' indignant soldiers. On the other hand, Cortés and his companions saw nothing but an atrocious barbarity in the tearing of human hearts out of living human bodies by priests whose locks were matted with their victims' blood. And the Spanish intruders had to take a line. Now that they were in Mexico and in power there, they must either suppress the local practice of human sacrifice or else condone it. How is the voice of humanity to decide between Spaniards and Aztecs in this case? Perhaps it has delivered its verdict already. If not, it will surely deliver it in time.'

*　　*　　*

Moctezuma asserted that the practice of human sacrifice was 'good'. Viewed in its most favourable light, the Aztecs regarded death on the sacrificial stone as an honourable end. The slave or criminal gave up his life to feed the sun and to ensure the continuation of the world; this ennobled and redeemed him. As for the captured soldier, death on the altar-block was a substitute for death on the battlefield. There was nothing shameful in it. 'Your turn today, my turn tomorrow.' Was it not preferable that the fatal wound that terminated a soldier's life should be struck by a man of god rather than a simple soldier, on sacred rather than on unhallowed ground? As for the young girls, or the mothers who yielded up their children, they too were suffering in the same supreme cause. And although the final act was ugly—four priests seizing the limbs of the victim, spreadeagling him back over the saddle-shaped stone, the executioner stabbing the knife below the left nipple, wrenching it down the rib cage, rummaging with his free hand through the welling blood to tug at the pumping heart—the rituals that preceded it were not devoid of beauty and dignity. The elaborate costumes, the deference shown to victims, the preliminary ceremonies and processions, the feathers, the flowers, the high colours in the sunlight—these were lovely. The preliminaries were not coarse or casual.

It would not be necessary to dwell on the custom if it had not assumed such importance at the moment of the Conquest. More than any other factor, it induced the subject peoples to side with a foreign invader instead of with men of their own blood. Cortés was Theseus, come to rid them of the obligation of despatching their choicest young men and maidens to King Minos. Their masters had involved them in their own demented system; they were caught up in a state of perpetual war, losing their able-bodied men, on whom their economy depended, in Wars of Flowers and on the Aztec altars. When the opportunity for uprising came, it was all the keener for being imbued with such desperation and hatred. Cortés and his men felt the same sensation. Sacrifice not only struck them as impious and inhuman, but on occasion they were forced to listen to the yells of their own comrades as, a few moments after falling into the hands of the Aztecs, they perished under the knife. This was a powerful incentive to fight to the end and, when victorious, to give no quarter.

To some extent, the Aztecs were not to blame. After all, they had inherited the practice; it had been wished on them by the civilizations which had preceded them. Human sacrifice had been practised in Mexico from prehistoric times. The Mayas had thrown men, women and children into their *cenotes* or sacred wells. The Toltecs had made human offerings to their stately *atlantes* or towering statues of warriors. From Teotihuacán had come the powerful and impressive notion that the sun was a sick, pustular, dying god who could only be renewed in his youthful strength at the end of every universal cycle by kindling a flame on the shattered breast of a sacrificial victim. These ancient and sensational concepts were bound to take deep hold on the mind of the Aztecs. Lacking roots of their own, they had come to the Valley as nomads and barbarians, seeking cultural forms and a cultural identity. As such people do when they begin to settle down, they are forced to borrow their cultural forms and notions of civilized behaviour from their neighbours. Among the norms which they borrowed was that of human sacrifice. If, then, their cultural career seems to demonstrate what Aldous Huxley, writing of them in *Ends and Means*, calls 'the disastrous practical effects of wrong metaphysical beliefs', we should remember that those metaphysical beliefs were implanted in them by others. The curse of the Aztecs, their doom, was that, being a people of exceptional vitality, they could inherit nothing without exaggerating it. Men who live with sword and shield always to hand, who every day stick needles through their ears, tongues or penises, cannot be expected to indulge in a significant amount of calm and ratiocinative thought.

It would be possible, I think, to argue that the Aztec empire was not the flower and culmination of the centuries of civilization in Mexico. Instead, it constituted a tumour on the Mexican body, a hot and feverish growth that drained Mexico of its strength and reduced its capacity to resist. The Aztecs weakened Mexico. If the Spaniards had made their *entrada* at a more settled and stable epoch, at a time, say, resembling the great Classical Period, then it is not impossible that the Mexicans, the populous inhabitants of a vast country, might have repulsed them. Of course, the Mexicans were divided into village-cultures which did not make for political unity, and to that extent were vulnerable; but the expeditions of sixteenth-century Spain, cannons and horses notwithstanding, were puny and hazardous. It was the universal loathing of the Aztecs that gave the Spaniards their chance. Had the Mexicans been able to combine against Cortés, they might have achieved both a sense of unity and a breathing-space to build up a resistance against future onslaughts. In that case the history of the New World—and of Spain and the Old World—would have been different, and the invasion of Cortés would not have been a turning-point.

There seems to be no reason why a nation cannot take a wrong turning in life, cannot go down a cul-de-sac, in the way that an individual can; nations, after all, are only collections of individuals. The Aztecs had chosen to follow the road of Tezcatlipoca rather than the road of Quetzalcóatl. It is permissible to ask whether that road had not led them into an impasse. Freud once suggested that whole nations might, under certain pressures, become neurotic; and whether or not one would accept that conditions had rendered the Aztec nation neurotic, it seems reasonable to postulate that something had gone very seriously amiss. A. L. Kroeber, in his *Anthropology*, writes: 'Almost any trend or inclination familiar from individual psychology might be recognized in culture. For instance, for cruelty, or sadism, peoples like the Aztecs and the Assyrians immediately come to mind. The Aztecs are notorious for the bloodiness of their religion. Their art portrays scenes of cruelty over and over again with the utmost unconcern, or rather, with pleased predilection. Death, skulls, flayed skins, rattlesnakes, and jaguars are among its favourite symbols. We think of Roman gladiatorial exhibitions as an example of cruelty; but the Romans, except for some degenerate emperors, were limited in their sadism as compared with Aztecs and Assyrians; they were only callous and brutal. It is also clear that such extreme cases represent local and temporary exaggerations. Human sacrifice with flaying and tearing out the heart was a practice common to all southern-Mexican peoples; but it was reserved for the Aztecs to riot in the practice. The Maya followed the custom, but much less frequently; and it was only occasionally that they expressed it in their art. The difference accordingly was one of weighting; it was a relative or quantitative one.' Sadism, particularly when employed by a notable anthropologist, is a strong word. It signifies the impulse to derive satisfaction by inflicting pain, which suggests an impulse of murkier character than that of a purely religious or philosophical one. Brussel and Cantzlaar define it in their *Dictionary of Psychiatry* as 'the psychic force behind any act or pattern of behaviour by which the individual derives pleasure from the psychic pain (fear, sense of indignity, embarrassment) which he causes in another'. They add that it may or may not be pathologic. This casts a different altogether less sympathetic light on the religious practices of the Aztecs.

A severe view of Aztec religion is put forward by Mlle Laurette Séjourné in her authoritative *Burning Water*, a study of thought and religion in ancient Mexico. Her thesis is that the only form of religion the Aztecs brought with them into the Valley of Mexico was a 'low witchcraft'. She asserts that they seized and perverted the noble religion of the Toltecs, in the forefront of which stood the majestic figure of Quetzalcóatl, in order 'to prop up their bloody State'. 'Late arrivals in the Valley,' she writes, 'they at once set to fighting cruelly for the land and for political dominance over the tribes which, having adopted more civilized customs, let themselves be caught unaware by the newcomers' brutality. Piling one atrocity upon another, the Aztecs imposed themselves first upon the communities of the plateau, then upon the whole country, including Central America; till the kingdom of the chosen people, the dream of a few fanatics, became a reality.'

Mlle Séjourné dismisses the pretence of the Aztecs to genuine spirituality as essentially a sham. 'It seems evident,' she says, 'that the Aztecs acted simply from political motives. To take their religious explanations of war seriously is to fall into a trap of State propaganda. Their lying formulae are shown up by one fact. The Aztec nobles were never themselves impatient to achieve the Solar glory in whose name they were slaughtering humanity. Their lust for life equalled their desire for power. If they had really believed that the one aim of existence was to give up their lives, sacrifice would not have been limited to supposedly inferior beings—slaves and prisoners—but would have been a privilege of the "élite". In fact everything points to the conclusion that the Aztec lords, although brought up in the doctrine of Quetzalcóatl, which taught men that inner perfection and spiritual sacrifice were supreme goals, had come to think of ritual slaughter only as a political necessity. Thus two strong and opposed currents of thought existed in this society: on the one hand degenerate mysticism supporting an ambitious plan of conquest; on the other, Quetzalcóatl's doctrine as the one moral basis. So deep a contradiction must necessarily produce serious conflict.'

In the light of these observations, Mlle Séjourné proceeds to an interesting analysis of the fundamental character of the Aztec State. 'How are we to account,' she asks, 'for the degree of authority and implacable discipline that ruled in Tenochtitlán? According to the testimony of all the chroniclers, Spanish and native alike, it appears on the surface that any freedom of thought or action was inconceivable in the Aztec world. Laws, penalties, and innumerable prohibitions, indicated to each person in detail the behaviour he must follow in all circumstances of his life; in such a system personal decision did not exist, dependence and instability were absolute, fear reigned. Death lurked ceaselessly everywhere, and constituted the cement of the building in which the individual Aztec was prisoner.

'There were those who, by their social status, were by law destined to extermination: the slaves—and anyone might become one through losing his fortune or civic rights; captive warriors; children born beneath a sign favourable for sacrifice and offered to the gods. Capital punishment was another constant threat: to anyone who dared without authority to wear a garment that reached below the knee; to the official who ventured into a forbidden room of the palace; the merchant whose riches had made him too proud; the dancer taking a false step . . .

'Judging by the laws the rulers were apparently obliged to pass, this mechanism for breaking men down was not established as easily as might be supposed. We know, for example, that every person—priest or spectator—who retired from the ceremony before the child-sacrifices to Tlaloc had been consummated was held to be despicable, declared unworthy of all public office, and converted into a wretch without the law. We cannot just be satisfied by explanations which talk of "mysterious magic rituals". Sahagún throws an interesting light on the picture when he tells us that: "the parents of the victims submitted to these practices, shedding many tears and with great sorrow in their hearts." The chronicler Tezozómoc describes how the chiefs and lords were invited to witness the human sacrifices on pain of being sacrificed themselves if they did not attend. There were, beside, precautionary measures in case those who went to the sacrifice, instead of climbing the temple steps happily as the moral directive prescribed, had the bad taste to be seized with panic, to faint or weep.

'These texts represent authentic human cries and show clearly what struggles and resistance undoubtedly resulted from such a system of terror, the perfection of which causes us all too easily to forget the individual. They show that so-called Aztec religious concepts were little more than a political weapon in the hands of the despots who promulgated them.

'How could it be otherwise? Can we seriously believe that any religion —that is, a revelation to free man from the anguish of his destiny—can be built upon laws of human destruction? If it is admitted that a religious doctrine could arise out of a concept so lacking in love—and this not only in the acts of the administrators, which would not surprise us, but in its very origin—then all possibility of understanding has been removed.

'How can we suppose that belief in the Sun's tyranny over physical life could have taken such root in human hearts? It is more likely that it could only have been planted there by force. Clearly, the spirituality of some aspects of Aztec life must have sprung from an old pre-Aztec tradition, later betrayed in its most sacred essence so that the interests of a temporal structure ruled by an implacable will to power might be upheld. A careful reading of the historic texts confirms this view.'

*   *   *

We have spoken, in connection with Cortés and his fellow *conquistadores*, of the aggressive tendencies of mankind, and quoted Freud to the effect that such tendencies may not be wholly reprehensible. It is the nature and the lot of man to fight, to struggle, to venture forth; without these activities, life would have no salt, no savour, little meaning. Perhaps Nietzsche was right, in the wider view, when he described all human existence and all human relations as essentially and ineradicably exploitative. But there must be some acceptable boundary to the extent of the exploitation involved. The difference between Cortés and Moctezuma is that the former, though an exploiter and an adventurer, strove as a reasonable and sensible man to limit the damage, whereas Moctezuma was the representative of a society which had long since passed the point

5*

of what might be termed tolerable or permissible exploitation. When that point has been exceeded, a natural and human law appears to come into operation whereby the oppressed arise and rid themselves of the exploiters. Perhaps this is what we call the imperative of human freedom.

The Aztecs were a highly intelligent people. Although they were not unduly given to contemplation, there must have been men among them, as Mlle Séjourné indicates, who questioned the wisdom of the path on which they were set. Except in the very lowest types of social organization, important institutions are never accepted unquestioningly. Even in Aztec society there must have been controversy and debate: not as vigorous and vocal, of course, as the dissent of Las Casas in Spanish society, but sufficient to give rise to uneasiness. Perhaps Moctezuma himself, with his somewhat veiled and withdrawn character, was one such person. In the tragedy that lay ahead, he acted as one whose actions were inhibited because he was afflicted with a crippling psychological burden. Perhaps it was some subconscious sense of guilt, some dim feeling that for the Aztec nation retribution was inevitable, and just. Perhaps it was an unconscious longing for the return of Quetzalcóatl, the gentle and humane god who alone could cast out Tezcatlipoca and set the Aztec nation on a path to psychological recovery. Any thoughtful Aztec, regarding the condition of his country, must have recognized, in his heart of hearts, that to continue on the same course could only result in disaster. The economic situation of Tenochtitlán, though apparently prosperous, was based on the rickety premise of uninterrupted conquest; and the religious situation increasingly maddened the subjugated peoples and—who knows?—may have alienated increasing numbers of Aztecs themselves.

Would the situation have ameliorated, given time? Would the Aztecs have matured and, while preserving their independence, have continued to soften the edges of their fanatical institutions? Could they have grown humane, without growing weak? There is no means of telling. My own theory, for what it is worth, is that when a nation is confronted with a dilemma of the first magnitude, that dilemma is never directly resolved; if it is resolved at all, it is resolved only because society is confronted by another and graver dilemma. The second dilemma dwarfs the first one, diminishes it, and often causes it to be forgotten or to disappear. This is what might be termed the crisis view of history: one crisis dissolves in the crisis that succeeds it. The view is, admittedly, somewhat pessimistic; however, there is no need to suppose that humanity is likely to run out of crises, and at least it means that, if one is patient, the danger or tedium of the present crisis is bound to yield to another and perhaps more interesting one in the not-too-distant future.

History, or destiny, or whatever we wish to call it, decreed that the world of the Aztecs was to yield to the world of the Spaniards. Slowly the two continents, separate since the beginning of the world, were coming together. As Thomas Hardy, an authority on destiny, wrote in *The Convergence of the Twain*:

> *Alien they seemed to be:*
> *No mortal eye could see*
> *The intimate welding of their later history.*

> *Or sign that they were bent*
> *By paths coincident*
> *On being anon twin halves of one august event.*

> *Till the Spinner of the Years*
> *Said 'Now!' And each one hears,*
> *And consummation comes, and jars two hemispheres.*

4

> *Oh, if only one lived for ever.*
> *Oh, if only one never died.*
> *We live with our soul torn apart,*
> *Lightning flashes upon us,*
> *We are spied upon and attacked.*
> *We live with our soul torn apart. We*
> *   have to suffer.*
> *Oh, if only one lived for ever.*
> *Oh, if only one never died.*

> *Náhuatl Poem*

MOCTEZUMA XOCOYOTZIN, the two words of whose name mean respectively *Angry Lord* and *Younger*, was, as we have seen, the second emperor of that name to rule the Aztecs. The correct rendering of his name is *Moctecuhzoma*, but in modern works the simpler form of *Moctezuma* is often employed. Prescott's familiar *Montezuma* is completely wide of the mark as a transliteration from Náhuatl, and should be allowed to lapse into oblivion.

Seventh and last emperor of the Aztecs, he ascended the throne in 1502, on the death of the much-feared Ahuítzotl, who had died of a strange and horrible wasting disease. He was the younger son of the emperor Axayácatl, who reigned between 1469 and 1481, and he would not have become ruler if his elder brother had not been killed fighting in a War of Flowers against Huejotzingo. Moctezuma, who had already created a reputation as a soldier, was elected emperor in his brother's stead on the death of Ahuítzotl.

His mother was a Toltec, from the Toltec capital of Tula, which had remained a sizeable urban centre even after its imperial monuments had been razed to the ground two centuries earlier. He was thus imbued from birth with Toltec traditions and philosophy. He would be particularly familiar with the legend of the departure of Quetzalcóatl-Topiltzín from Tula with his Toltec companions, promising that one day he would return. When the Spaniards reached Mexico, for Moctezuma they were not only supernatural beings but Toltecs, his own kindred, his own ancestors. In later years he showed himself to be a man who was profoundly interested in and influenced by the past, and of a deeply religious caste of mind. Often when he was emperor he would make a pilgrimage on foot to Teotihuacán, twenty-five miles away, to meditate among the ruins.

Though given to these inward-looking preoccupations, he did not neglect his duties as war-chief. In the manner of the Aztec emperors, he led his armies personally into the field and fought a series of highly successful campaigns. The Aztec empire was not marking time during the reign of Moctezuma: its boundaries were being vigorously extended. He understood as clearly as his predecessors that the rule of life for such a nation was either to grow or to perish; there could be no standing still. He struck due south, extending the conquests of Ahuítzotl in the modern state of Guerrero, and consolidating his grip on the coastline from modern Acapulco to modern Playa Azul, 150 miles east. The warlike Yope people called the Yopotzingo held him at bay, but he thrust southwest of them into the modern state of Oaxaca. Here he took twelve thousand prisoners, whom he sacrificed to Huitzilopotchtli. This was the Zapotec-Mixtec country, and the Mixtecs fought fiercely but without success to preserve their ancient capital of Mitla. The Aztecs were exerting unrelenting pressure on them, and would have harried them further in later campaigns if Moctezuma had lived to continue his drive along the southern coast towards modern Guatemala. Already Ahuítzotl had reached the Gulf of Tehuantepec by taking the towns of Tehuantepec and Xochictlán (modern Juchitán). The Aztecs had earlier established a distant outlying province of some size far down the coast on the modern Mexican-Guatemalan border, and Moctezuma appears to have set himself the task of enlarging the empire in this direction. He took no less than forty-three towns during the course of his activities, many of them in such inaccessible situations that their walls could only be reached by means of scaling ladders.

What was the extent of the Aztec dominions on the eve of the Spanish invasion? It occupied an area of 100,000 square miles, and comprised a population of between ten and twelve millions (see Figure 4). It comprised practically the whole of the thickly-populated central zone of Mexico, the wealthiest and most civilized area of Mesoamerica. Its northern border ran roughly from the River Pánuco on the Gulf of Mexico, at the point where Tampico now stands, to the River Balsas on the Pacific Ocean. There were considerable indentations in this northern border, occasioned by the resistance of the barbarian tribes. These were the Huaxteca, the Chichimecs, the small state of Metztitlán which held out stubbornly in modern Hidalgo province, and the Tarascans in the south. The Tarascans were not barbarians, but a superior people who knew the arts of metallurgy, and who with their copper weapons had twice, on one occasion in the reign of Moctezuma II, given the Aztecs a bloody nose. They were first-cousins of the Aztecs, having reputedly come out of the north with them in the years of wandering. Their war-god was a relative of Huitzilopotchtli, and their capital bore the beautiful name of Tzintzuntzan, *Green Hummingbird Town*. They had established the kingdom of Michoacán, which had never looked in serious danger of being overrun by the Aztecs.

The north of Mexico, of course, was largely barren, and the Aztecs had no powerful incentive to conquer it. They contented themselves with their occupation of the lusher portion of the coast of the Gulf of Mexico, from Tampico 300 miles to the south-west, almost 100 miles below modern Veracruz. There they were blocked by the Totonacs, a once-powerful people who may perhaps have been the founders of Teotihuacán, and who were still energetic enough to withstand the Aztecs. To the east of the Totonac country lay Yucatán and the Mayas. The Aztecs had never indulged in much contact with the Mayas because of the enormous distances involved and the daunting nature of the jungles of Yucatán. From the western shore of the Bay of Campeche, their boundary turned and ran south-west through Oaxaca to the Pacific at the River Ometepec. The resistance that defined the border in this region was provided by the Coatlimacacs, backed by the Chiapanecs, who gave their name to the modern state of Chiapas, and, as we have seen, by the

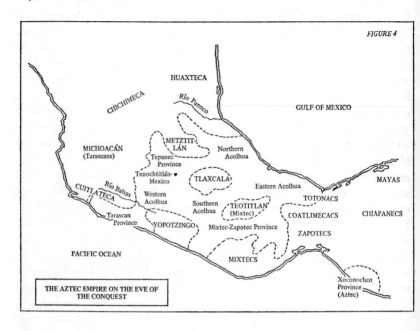

FIGURE 4

THE AZTEC EMPIRE ON THE EVE OF THE CONQUEST

Mixtecs and their older Zapotec substratum. The Mixtecs had refused to yield the southern coast, where their lands were almost contiguous with those of the Yopotzingo. In time the Aztecs would no doubt have pinched out the southern Mixtecs and Yopotzingo, as well as Metztitlán in the north-west. In addition, there were two large enclaves buried deep inside the Aztec empire which, although they were required to pay danegeld to the Aztecs, had preserved their independence. The larger of these enclaves was that of the Tlaxcalans, maintaining a sizeable realm in the mountains only seventy-five miles north of Tenochtitlán. Tlaxcala had beaten off an attack by Moctezuma, but existed more or less on Aztec sufferance because the continuous state of hostilities provided prisoners for sacrifice. Understandably, shortly after the most recent Aztec assault on them, the Tlaxcalans were delighted to become the principal allies of the Spaniards. The other enclave was the little state of Teotitlán, 150 miles south-west of the Aztec capital and fifty miles north of modern Oaxaca. All these four boundaries, of course, were fluid, and the armed columns of the Aztec traders constantly probed into hostile territory to bring back slaves and precious commodities.

From the thirty-eight provinces of the empire the Aztecs, concentrated in Tenochtitlán and its sister-towns around the central lakes, extracted heavy tribute. From the Codex Mendocino and the Codex Matrícula de Tributos, which itemize the goods which were sent annually to Tenochtitlán, we learn that Moctezuma received 7,000 tons of maize, 4,000 tons each of beans and grain amaranth and sage seed, 200,000 pounds of cotton, and other primary products such as salt, pepper, cacao, tobacco and honey. Then there were manufactured products, or items suitable for manufacture, which included 100,000 loads of cloth, 150,000 loincloths, 30,000 bundles of precious feathers, 250,000 cotton mantles, together with amber, gold, turquoise, jade, incense, rubber, shells and birds. There was also the human tribute in slaves and victims for sacrifice. When one reflects that these articles were not paid for, and were additional to those secured by the Aztec traders for what were probably nominal sums, one can appreciate the weight of the yoke which the subject peoples bore. Each province rendered to Moctezuma the pick of its particular crops and manufactures, and whatever luxury articles were to be found in the area. The Aztecs were an efficient people, and their efficiency is nowhere shown to greater effect than in the practical manner in which they assessed the tribute to be levied from individual provinces and the promptitude with which it was collected. The Inland Revenue department of our modern bureaucracies could regard their Aztec counterparts with envy and admiration. There was nothing primitive about Aztec mathematics when it came to counting bags of maize and bolts of cloth. Native-born Aztecs themselves paid taxes: but usually this consisted of making a certain village responsible for the upkeep of the palace of a prince or a great *tecuhtli*, who thus lived like feudal barons on the labour of their tenantry.

At his palace in Tenochtitlán, Moctezuma kept a household of three thousand servants. In his own way, he lived with greater state than his counterpart, the Emperor Charles V, who shared his taste for jewels, for fine art, and for rare and curious objects of all kinds. His palace was situated, like those of the other notables, in the heart of Tenochtitlán, adjoining the sacred precinct. It stood on the south side of the square, immediately behind the temple of Tezcatlipoca, divided from it only by the Serpent Wall. It was called the 'New Houses' of Moctezuma, to distinguish it from the old imperial palace, that of his father Axayácatl, which stood on the east side of the square. The palace of the President of the Mexican Republic is built directly above the site where the palace of Moctezuma once stood.

Cortés, when at length he met Moctezuma, with whom he developed a close and curious relationship, and for whose death he would be directly or indirectly responsible, was at a loss to describe the pomp by which Moctezuma was surrounded. In his Second Despatch, he told the Emperor Charles V that 'the ceremonies which this sovereign used in his services were so many that I believe none of the Sultans, nor any infidel sovereign of whom we have ever heard, has had such a ceremonial at his court'. He insisted on the 'greatness of the state' which Moctezuma kept, and noted that 'no prince in the whole world was ever so greatly feared'. He related that when the Aztec nobles spoke to Moctezuma, 'they did not look him in the face, out of respect and reverence. I know this was a matter of respect, because some of the lords reproached the Spaniards that when they spoke to me, they would behave with a lofty demeanour and look me in the face, which seemed to them disrespectful and shameless. When Moctezuma went out, which happened rarely, all those who accompanied him and those whom he met in the street, turned their faces aside, and did not look at him, and they prostrated themselves until he had passed. One of the lords, who carried three long thin rods, always went before him, and I believe this was done to give notice of his approach. When he descended from his litter, he took one of the rods in his hand and carried it as far as he went'. Clearly, where 'the divinity that doth hedge a king' was concerned, Moctezuma was the equal of the pharaoh of Egypt, whose person or even whose shadow it was death to touch, even accidentally.

Bernal Díaz, throughout his *True History*, almost consistently prefixes the name of the emperor with the word *great*. When he first saw Moctezuma, he was struck, like his chief, by the extreme deference that was paid to him: 'There were four other great *caciques* who carried the canopy above his head, and many more lords who walked before the great Moctezuma, sweeping the ground on which he was to tread, and laying down cloaks so that his feet should not touch the earth. Not one of these chieftains dared to look him in the face. All kept their eyes lowered most reverently except those four lords, his nephews, who were supporting him.' The ruler of Tenochtitlán was not actually worshipped as a god, like the ruler of ancient Egypt, but he was paid a god-like deference.

With all his state, Moctezuma was affable. Bernal Díaz records that he was capable of laughter, and that despite his princely manner 'he spoke very gaily'. The emperor was open-hearted and hospitable, and freely gave the Spaniards the run of his palace. This establishment was duly described by Cortés for the delectation of Charles V; but the best and most extended description was penned by Bernal Díaz. It may be quoted at length, although a substantial portion of it is here omitted, because quite simply it could not be bettered. The marvels of the place made such an impression on the writer that, nearly fifty years after their tragic destrucion, which he deplored as bitterly as any, he was able to recall them in their entirety.

He opens with one of the shrewd and succinct character sketches with which he brings history to life for us, and for which we are forever in his debt. 'The great Moctezuma,' he begins, 'was about forty years old, of good height, well proportioned, spare and slight, and not very dark, though of the usual Indian complexion. He did not wear his hair long but just over his ears, and he had a short black beard, well-shaped and thin. His face was rather long and cheerful, he had fine eyes, and in his appearance and manner could express geniality or, when necessary, a serious composure. He was very neat and clean, and took a bath every afternoon. He had many women as his mistresses, the daughters of chieftains, but two legitimate wives who were *caciques* in their own right, and when he had intercourse with any of them it was so secret that only some of his servants knew of it. He was quite free from sodomy. The clothes he wore one day he did not wear again till three or four days later. He had a guard of two hundred chieftains lodged in rooms beside his own, only some of whom were permitted to speak to him. When they entered his presence they were compelled to take off their rich cloaks and put on others of little value. They had to be clean and walk barefoot, with their eyes downcast, for they were not allowed to look him in the face, and as they approached they had to make three obeisances, saying as they did so, Lord, my lord, my great lord!" Then, when they had said what they had come to say, he would dismiss them with a few words. They did not turn their backs on him as they went out, but kept their faces towards him and their eyes downcast, only turning round when they had left the room. Another thing I noticed was that when other great chiefs came from distant lands about disputes or on business, they too had to take off their shoes and put on poor cloaks before entering Moctezuma's apartments; and they were not allowed to enter the palace immediately but had to linger for a while near the door, since to enter hurriedly was considered disrespectful.

'For each meal his servants prepared him more than thirty dishes cooked in their native style, which they put over small earthenware braziers to prevent them from getting cold. They cooked more than three hundred plates of the food the great Moctezuma was going to eat, and more than a thousand more for the guard. I have heard that they used to cook him the flesh of young boys. But as he had such a variety of dishes, made of so many different ingredients, we could not tell whether a dish was of human flesh or anything else, since every day they cooked fowls, turkeys, pheasants, local partridges, quail, tame and wild duck, venison, wild boar, marsh birds, pigeons, hares and rabbits, also many other kinds of birds and beasts native to their country, so numerous that I cannot quickly name them all.

'Let us now turn to the way his meals were served, which was like this. If it was cold, they built a large fire of live coals made by burning the bark of a tree which gave off no smoke. The smell of the bark from which they made these coals was very sweet. In order that he should get no more heat than he wanted, they placed a sort of screen in front of it adorned with the figures of idols worked in gold. He would sit on a soft low stool, which was richly worked. His table, which was also low and decorated in the same way, was covered with white tablecloths and rather long napkins of the same material. Then four very clean and beautiful girls brought water for his hands in one of those deep basins that they call *xicales*. They held others like plates beneath it to catch the water, and brought him towels. Two other women brought him maize-cakes.

'When he began his meal they placed in front of him a sort of wooden screen, richly decorated with gold, so that no one should see him eat. Then the four women retired, and four great chieftains, all old men, stood beside him. He talked with them every now and then and asked them questions, and as a great favour he would sometimes offer one of them a dish of whatever tasted best. They say that these were his closest relations and advisers and judges of lawsuits, and if he gave them anything to eat they ate it standing, with deep reverence and without looking in his face.

'Moctezuma's food was served on Cholula ware, some red and some black. While he was dining, the guards in the adjoining rooms did not dare to speak or make a noise above a whisper. His servants brought him some of every kind of fruit that grew in the country, but he ate very little of it. Sometimes they brought him in cups of pure gold a drink made from the cocoa-plant, which they said he took before visiting his wives. We did not take much notice of this at the time, though I saw them bring in a good fifty large jugs of this chocolate, all frothed up, of which he would drink a little. They always served it with great reverence. Sometimes some little humpbacked dwarfs would be present at his meals, whose bodies seemed almost to be broken in the middle. These were his jesters. There were other Indians who told him jokes and must have been his clowns, and others who sang and danced, for Moctezuma was very fond of music and entertainment and would reward his entertainers with the leavings of the food and chocolate.' (Cortés records that 'there was an apartment in which there were men, women and children, white of face, body, hair, and eyelashes from the day of their birth'; so Moctezuma also kept albinos for his entertainment.) 'The same four women removed the tablecloths and again most reverently brought him water for his hands. Then Moctezuma would talk to these four old chieftains about matters that interested him, and they would take their leave with great ceremony. He stayed behind to rest.

'As soon as the great Moctezuma had dined, all the guards and many more of his household servants ate in their turn. I think more than a thousand plates of food must have been brought in for them, and more than two thousand jugs of chocolate frothed up in the Mexican style, and infinite quantities of fruit, so that with his women and serving-maids and breadmakers and chocolate-makers his expenses must have been considerable.

'One thing I had forgotten to say is that two more very handsome women served Moctezuma when he was at table with maize-cakes kneaded with eggs and other nourishing ingredients. These maize-cakes were very white, and were brought in on plates covered with clean napkins. They brought him a different kind of bread also, in a long ball kneaded with other kinds of nourishing food, and *pachol* cake, as they call it in that country, which is a kind of wafer. They also placed on the table three tubes, much painted and gilded, in which they put liquidamber mixed with some herbs which are called tobacco. When Moctezuma had finished his dinner, and the singing and dancing were over and the cloths had been removed, he would inhale the smoke from one of these tubes. He took very little of it, and then fell asleep.

'I remember that at that time his steward was a great *cacique* whom we nicknamed Tapia, and he kept an account of all the revenue that was brought to Moctezuma in his books, which were made of paper—their name for which is *amal*—and he had a great house full of these books.

'Let us pass on to the aviary. I cannot possibly enumerate every kind of bird that was in it or describe its characteristics. There was everything from the royal eagle, smaller kinds of eagles, and other large birds, down to multi-coloured little birds, and those from which they take the fine green feathers they use in their feather-work. These last birds are about the size of our magpies, and here they are called *quetzals*. There were other birds too which have feathers of five colours: green, red, white, yellow, and blue, but I do not know what they are called. Then there were parrots with different coloured plumage, so many of them that I have forgotten their names. There were also beautifully marked ducks, and bigger ones like them. At the proper season they plucked the feathers of all these birds, which then grew again. All of them were bred in this aviary, and at hatching time the men and women who looked after them would place them on their eggs and clean their nests and feed them, giving each breed of birds its proper food.

'In the aviary there was a large tank of fresh water, and in it was another type of bird on long stilt-like legs with a red body, wings, and tail. I do not know its name, but in Cuba birds rather like them are called *ypiris*. Also in this tank there were many other kinds of water birds.

'Let us go on to another large house where they kept many idols whom they called their fierce gods, and with them all kinds of beasts of prey, tigers and two sorts of lion, and beasts rather like wolves, and foxes and other small animals, all of them carnivores, and most of them bred there. They were fed on deer, fowls, little dogs, and other creatures which they hunt and also on the bodies of the Indians they sacrificed, as I was told.

'I have already described the manner of their sacrifices. They strike open the wretched Indian's chest with flint knives and hastily tear out the palpitating heart which, with the blood, they present to the idols in whose name they have performed the sacrifice. Then they cut off the arms, thighs, and head, eating the arms and thighs at their ceremonial banquets. The head, they hang up on a beam, and the body of the sacrificed man is not eaten but given to the beasts of prey. They also had many vipers in this accursed house, and poisonous snakes which have something that sounds like a bell in their tails. These, which are the deadliest snakes of all, they kept in jars and great pottery vessels full of feathers, in which they laid their eggs and reared their young. They were fed on the bodies of sacrificed Indians and the flesh of the dogs that they bred. These snakes and wild beasts were dedicated to their fierce idols, and kept them company. As for the horrible noise when the lions and tigers roared, and the jackals and foxes howled, and the serpents hissed, it was so appalling that one seemed to be in hell.

'Now to speak of the great number of performers whom Moctezuma kept to entertain him. There were dancers and stilt-walkers, and some who seemed to fly as they leapt through the air, and men rather like clowns to make him laugh. There was a whole quarter full of these people who had no other occupation. He had as many workmen as he needed, too, stone-cutters, masons and carpenters, to keep his houses in repair.

'We must not forget the gardens with their many varieties of flowers and sweet-scented trees planted in order, and their ponds and tanks of fresh water into which a stream flowed at one end and out of which it flowed at the other, and the baths he had there, and the variety of small birds that nested in the branches, and the medicinal and useful herbs that grew there. His gardens were a wonderful sight, and required many gardeners to take care of them. Everything was built of stone and plastered; baths and walks and closets and rooms like summerhouses where they danced and sang. There was so much to see in these gardens, as everywhere else, that we could not tire of contemplating his great riches and the large number of skilled Indians employed in the many crafts they practised.'

*   *   *

The gardens were of particular importance, for flowers were an obsession of the Aztecs, and particularly of Moctezuma II. Brutality and sentimentality often go together (one recalls the flower-gardens of Dachau and Sachsenhausen), and are united in the phrase *War of Flowers*. In his *Guide to Mexican Flora*, P. Clark points out that: 'The cultivation of ornamental plants was a major industry in the Mexico of that early day. At the time of the Conquest, the Aztecs were cultivating double-flowered marigolds and dahlias, indicating that, through scientific selection and hybridization, these varieties had been developed by a horticulturally sophisticated people.' No doubt because Mexico possesses such an outstanding diversity of flowers, shrubs and trees, for which the wide variation in climate is responsible, the ancient Mexicans became devoted botanists. Their system of plant nomenclature was far in advance of anything known in the Old World at that date. They had given names and recorded exact descriptions of three thousand medicinal herbs alone, many of them depicted and labelled in the Codex Badianus, which was translated into Latin in 1552. Xochipilli, the *Flower Prince*, the god of pleasure, feasting and frivolity, was an important deity, and in the Codex Magliabecchiano there is a charming vignette of him being carried in a flowery litter by his devotees.

Then as now, Xochimilco, 'the Place of the Fields of Flowers', was the leading horticultural centre in the country. The flower gardens there have been in continuous cultivation since they were established in 1265 by the city's first ruler. Another famous garden was that established by the great poet and philosopher Nezaualcóyotl, the ruler of Texcoco, at Tezcatzingo, on the western shore of the lake. This garden, beautifully described by the Hispanicized Mexican Ixtlilxóchitl in his *Historia Chichimeca*, was superior, if anything, to the gardens of Moctezuma. The latter, beside the garden of his royal palace, of which a pathetic relic survives in a small garden of the Presidential Palace, possessed other gardens too. According to Cervantes de Salazar, writing in 1554, he laid out groves and hanging gardens at Chapultepec, on the heights above his summer palace. Some of the *ahuehuete* cypresses, Mexico's national trees, which he planted there can still be seen, with the broken relics of a few of the royal walks. He also revived the garden at Oaxtepec (modern Yuatepec), between Cuernavaca and Cuautla, forty miles south-east of Mexico City. The garden had been laid out by Moctezuma I and allowed to run to seed. Cortés visited it after the Conquest and wrote in glowing terms to Charles V of its 'grandeur and exquisite beauty'. Moctezuma settled forty Indian families there as gardeners, and as in his palace garden, says Cervantes de Salazar, 'did not permit any fruit or vegetable to be grown, saying that it was not kingly to cultivate plants for utility or profit. He said that vegetable gardens and orchards were for slaves and merchants'. He ordered every type of plant and tree to be brought to Oaxtepec from the farthest reaches of the empire, and orchids, vanilla trees, cocoa trees and other exotic species were to be found there. He nurtured a similar exotic garden at the town of Cuitláhuac, which stood on an island at the confluence of Lakes Chalco and Xochimilco. Cortés and his troops stayed there on the march to Mexico, and were amazed at the beauty of the town, its royal residence of Iztapalapa, and its sumptuous gardens. Moctezuma was so enamoured of rare plants that, when he heard that the ruler of a town in Oaxaca had a tree which bore remarkable blossoms, he demanded that it be sent to him. The ruler refused. The Aztec army was sent to raze the town, kill the ruler, and seize the tree. When it was transplanted to Tenochtitlán, it died.

*　　*　　*

Moctezuma was the master of a country the size of the Iberian peninsula. His rule was undisputed. The Aztec empire was at the peak of its power. Its vigour and stamina were undiminished.

Why, then, should the Aztecs have been uneasy, as they undoubtedly were, about the future? Many scholars have pointed out the deep strain of pessimism in the Aztec soul. To anyone who has travelled in Mexico, the sense of insecurity and hopelessness which one encounters in that harsh and impoverished land offers a retrospective insight into the state of mind of the pre-Conquest civilizations. It seems safe to assert that the pessimism of the Mexicans, though reinforced by the experience of the Conquest, was not implanted by that experience but was a product of the centuries that preceded it. The experience of the post-Classic period in particular, the period of the warring states, was incomparably darker than the so-called Dark Ages of Europe.

The Aztec view of the world was akin to the pagan view of the world which had been in retreat in Europe since the era of Greece and Rome.

The Christian religion, dominant even during the Dark Ages, was a religion of hope and consolation. The religion of post-Classic Mexico, on the other hand, was shot through with witchcraft, sorcery and the baser manifestations of superstition; it was a religion in which fear and cruelty were primary ingredients. It knew nothing of the humane spirit of Christianity which, though often violated and betrayed, was humane nonetheless. The Aztec did not look forward in a mood of serenity and expectation; he inhabited a world which threatened constantly to run down or fly to pieces; his gods were not mild and forgiving but malevolent and ailing. The gods of Mexico fought among themselves with the never-ending hostility with which the Mexicans, emulating them, fought each other. The universe was an anxious place.

The Aztecs suffered from a fundamental sense of disequilibrium. Their civilization had two distinct faces which it was impossible to reconcile: a Janus civilization. They oscillated between moods of extreme exhilaration and extreme despair. On the one hand, Moctezuma was Bernal Díaz's 'great prince', cultured, intelligent, enlightened, sagacious, graceful, a man of exquisite manners and deportment; on the other, he was a capricious tyrant like Shaka Zulu, obsessed with irrational fears, capable of irrational cruelties, the author of such actions as the sacrifice of twelve thousand Mixtec prisoners. It was hard for the Spaniards, as it is hard for us, to associate this smiling, gracious prince with the holocaust carried out when he celebrated what was to be the last of the New Fire rituals in 1502. This ritual was enacted every fifty-two years, when the sun had fallen into a semi-moribund condition and needed to be revived by cataracts of blood. Up to that time, no battle or series of battles ever fought in the Old World had remotely approached such hecatombs. The reaction of the Spaniards was understandable. It was perhaps to be expected that sooner or later this civilization, so violent, so schizoid, so infected with the dread of demons, would shake itself to bits. There was no core of sanity to ensure its continuity and survival.

Moctezuma was as superstitious as the least of his subjects. He was a student of witchcraft, and a recent succession of evil omens had profoundly agitated him. His misgivings began in 1509, when the wise men of Nezahualpilli, the ruler of the neighbouring Aztec town of Texcoco, predicted the imminent fall of the empire. Moctezuma scoffed at them, and his own wise men produced counter-predictions. When Nezahualpilli would not retract, Moctezuma decided to ridicule him by challenging him to a game of *tlachtli*, the ball-game already described, to decide whose view would prevail. Moctezuma was so confident that he wagered his kingdom against three turkey-cocks, the winner to take three out of five games. Moctezuma won the first two games: but his opponent won the last three games running. Thus Moctezuma had not only lost face, with the loss of his ridiculous bet and the implied rebuff to his wise men, but there was an even more disturbing implication. Ball-courts were attached to temples and, like everything in Aztec life, *tlachtli* had religious over-tones. It was as if the gods themselves had spoken out against Moctezuma.

The omens continued and grew more ominous. They were afterwards collected and recorded in Náhuatl, at the behest of Fray Bernadino de Sahagún, in the Florentine Codex, accompanied by graphic little illus-trations. Sahagún's informants were eye-witnesses of the events they describe, and they list eight 'dismal presages'. The first were tongues of flame that began to appear in the heavens ten Aztec years before the coming of the men from Castile, continuing until the year of the invasion and prompting general fear and speculation. The second was a sudden fire that broke out in a temple of Huitzilopochtli, and the more water that was poured on the blaze the worse it grew. The third was the spon-taneous combustion, in a particularly dry season, of part of the Great Temple. The fourth was a comet-like emanation with three tails. The fifth was a storm on the lake of Mexico so furious that the water appeared to be boiling. The sixth was the crying of many voices, including that of a woman who wailed at night and cried out: 'My children, let us flee! My children, where can we hide ourselves?' The seventh was the presentation to Moctezuma of a strange ashen-coloured, heron-like bird that had been caught by fishermen on the lake. It had a kind of mirror set into the top of its head, and when Moctezuma looked into the mirror he was dismayed to see a vision of the stars, followed by a vision of a number of warriors, striking about them, moving rapidly, and some of them mounted on what looked like a species of deer. The eighth was the appearance of monstrous and deformed beings with two heads, who showed themselves to the emperor in the palace and then vanished.

It has been worth dwelling at some length on these omens because they afford us some insight into the Aztec mind, and show us how it differed from that of the Spaniards. The omens are exactly the kind of *espantos*, or 'frights', which are commonly believed in all over Mexico today, and are thought to be one of the principal causes of ill health. The wailing woman, similarly, is the *Llorona* of modern Mexico, often heard in Mexican villages at night and descended from the old Aztec Cihuateteo. The preoccupation of a people so advanced in many ways as the Aztecs, in some respects superior to their European counterparts, indicates the tribal leaven in the Aztec soul which placed them at a disadvantage when dealing with Cortés. Moctezuma shared this mode of primitive thought and perception with the rest of his subjects. Sahagún's informants record that the last two omens were brought to him in 'the Black House', a part of the palace where he dabbled in witchcraft.

The primitive soul is filled with fear, with a nameless dread. To the primitive, the universe is inexplicable, the behaviour of the gods—and the gods are everywhere and in everything—is unpredictable. This explains much of that anxiety and pessimism which was present in the Aztec as in every primitive psyche. The primitive cannot, except in the simplest everyday activities, understand the principle of cause and effect; he cannot see that some links in a chain of events are more important than others. To him, every occurrence, however trivial—even a game of *tlatchtli*— reveals the mysterious will of heaven, if only he could interpret it. Indeed, the more seemingly trivial the occurrence, the more subtle and important the supernatural message might be, and the easier to overlook. The primitive seeks every moment of the day to put himself into a proper relationship with a universe that he feels no real hope of understanding. He has, moreover, no tools or aids for understanding it; the Aztecs could not have perceived and taken comfort from the fact that the fountains of fire in the sky might have been simply an unusual appearance of the zodiacal light, or that the flame with three tails was probably nothing more than a comet. Lévy-Bruhl, in his *Primitives and the Supernatural*, has a passage that sheds light on what the omens must have meant to Moctezuma and the Aztecs, and explains much of their singular, to our eyes, behaviour thereafter. 'The primitive,' he says, 'is not entirely una- ware of the actual connections between phenomena; on the contrary, he has noted some of them very carefully, and also successfully. He knows very well how to turn them to account in his "technique" of hunting, fishing, agriculture, manufactures, arts, etc. But such knowledge as this maintains its exclusively practical character. Although he profits by it, he never seems to reflect upon it. He does not realize that if he were to pursue such knowledge further it would contribute to an understanding of things and events, and would give him more control over them. His mind is oriented in another direction. It is immediately carried beyond the confines of what we call nature. In any occurrence that makes an impression on him he immediately recognizes that an intervention of supernatural forces has brought it about. When, therefore, he experiences failure or misfortune, even if, like ourselves, he perceives its cause (as we understand the term), he does not stop short there. He asks himself what evil influence is being exerted upon him, and why this should be. The cause that is of supreme interest to him lies outside the shackles of circumstance.

'Herein precisely lies our difficulty in comprehending the workings of primitives' minds. Given the way in which they picture to themselves the relations of unseen forces with the ordinary course of nature, they regard the supernatural cause as intervening in this course, but not as integrated with it. It dominates and modifies it, but it does not take any definite place in it, and accordingly they do not know when its action has begun, nor when its operations are completed. Since it is "supernatural", it is, in a certain sense, outside time and space. To our minds, from the very fact that phenomena necessarily react upon each other, they have a definite existence in themselves and in their results. All that happens seems to be capable of explanation merely through the consideration of what has previously occurred. In every way an event is surrounded by a network of phenomena and, if it has any result, that will take its place there also.

'To the primitive mind, on the contrary, the most serious part of a misfortune is not the misfortune itself, however disastrous it may be. It is what the misfortune reveals—that is, the evil influence which has just been exerted on the victim, which will no doubt be exercised again, and which makes fresh disasters imminent—who knows what may yet await the victim? Here the affective category of the supernatural is brought into play in a direct and almost reflexive fashion. Thus every accident, misfortune, check, loss, failure, and the like, is regarded and interpreted as a harbinger of other accidents and misfortunes that will not fail to occur, as long as the evil influence that causes them has not been neutralized, paralyzed, or induced to adopt a more favourable mood. Immediately the blow has fallen, the primitive's mind is directed towards the world of supernatural influences, and he inquires of it so that he may know whether fresh blows await him. This unvarying attitude of his largely accounts for some of his proceedings which seem strange to us, and in particular it throws a little light on the tremendous importance so often assigned to witchcraft in the primitive's mental preoccupations.'

*   *   *

Moctezuma and the Aztecs, then, were at a disadvantage even before the Spaniards arrived. They were already overwrought and half-demoralized before the ships of Cortés were sighted. Their demoralization was complete when the person of Cortés seemed to fulfil all the prophecies concerning the physical appearance of the man destined to overthrow the Aztec empire. To receive messages from the gods is unnerving in itself; but when the messages appear to be accurate and explicit, it must be more unnerving still. We have to admire the courage of the Aztecs in pulling themselves together, after such a series of *espantos*, and fighting against the Spaniards with determination and tenacity even when the gods had already spoken out against them, and when they felt no real hope of winning.

In the coming contest, the Aztecs were hampered by the fact that, owing to the way in which their minds worked, they were not free agents. They were weighed down with superstitious baggage, and were as much occupied with trying to divine how the gods wished them to fight as with conducting the actual fighting. This is a poor basis for an effective strategy. The Spaniards had no such mental encumbrances. They did not have to wrestle with the cloudy will of the gods: for them there was only the clear and simple Will of God. They could concentrate entirely on the task in hand. Moctezuma was less capable than Cortés of forming independent judgments, in any case. Like all primitives, he was not an individual: he could only think, feel and function in and through the tribe; he was embedded in the tribal body, incapable of thinking or acting outside its frame of reference. Cortés, on the other hand, was very much an individual; he was more than capable of distinguishing between cause and effect, and of appreciating the relative importance of each event in a series. He was, as it were, a triple individual: individual as the product of fifteen centuries of Christianity, which is based on the concept of the unique being, the unique soul; individual as a Spaniard, most independent of nationalities; and individual as a man of the Renaissance, born at the supreme moment of the European cult of individuality. Thus he possessed a liberty and a determination to think and act which was denied Moctezuma. So it was with Cortés' companions. Though a mere six hundred strong, and though no one would claim that most of them exactly represented the fine flower of Christian chivalry, it could not be denied that at least they were outrageous and uninhibited individuals, to a man. Otherwise they would not have been sailing, in an improvised flotilla, towards the shore of a vast, unexplored and admittedly hostile continent.

In the last analysis the Spaniards believed, through their cultural inheritance, in what V. S. Pritchett called, in a phrase quoted earlier, *the absolute quality of the individual*. The Aztecs, through their own inheritance, did not. It was to prove, perhaps, the decisive consideration.

PART THREE

CONQUEST

I am looking for two things most men
would try to avoid—namely, to bring
trouble to myself, and trouble to
other people.

Machiavelli: Mandragola

I

> *I beg you, follow your star, and don't budge an iota for anything in the world. I believe, used to believe, and always will believe that what Boccaccio says is true: It is better to act and repent, than do nothing and repent.*
>
> *Machiavelli: Letter to Francesco Vettori*

THE expedition did not enjoy a smooth voyage to the mainland. The small vessels were cruelly tossed about by a Caribbean storm and scattered over the sea. One was lost for several weeks. The bulk of the little fleet required four days to cover the two hundred miles between Havana and Yucatán. The vessels found shelter first among the five islands called the Islas Mujeres, then sailed on to the more substantial island of Cozumel, seventy miles to the south. The general landing took place on Good Friday, April 21, 1519.

The flagship had been blown off course. It only managed to catch up with the other ships some days later. This was the second time since he had formed his expedition that Cortés had sailed bravely off in the lead only to find himself bringing up the rear. He was angry, and when he landed he ordered the pilot of the flagship to be put in irons. In San Domingo and Cuba he had been content to play what he termed 'the gentle pirate': but the necessity for that kind of ultra-tactful behaviour had passed. He now needed to exercise the rigour and authority he knew would be required if the enterprise was to be pushed to a successful conclusion. To remind him of what happened to leaders of expeditions who were insufficiently decisive, he had the examples of Alonso de Hojeda, Diego de Nicuesa and Juan de la Cosa; and within the previous two years had occurred the disastrous failure of Francisco de Córdoba and the unimpressive sortie of Juan de Grijalva. The latter had taken place as recently as the preceding summer.

When he rejoined the main body at Cozumel, he discovered that in his brief absence Pedro de Alvarado had taken command and given rein to his impulsive appetite for action. Alvarado had been Grijalva's chief lieutenant, and was therefore familiar with the terrain; it held no terrors for him. When he found that the local Indians had taken to the woods on the approach of the Spaniards, he at once allowed the men of the expedition to forage among their empty villages and carry off what booty they could. This was not at all to Cortés' liking. His first action was to coax one of the native *caciques* out of the woods, treat him civilly, load him with presents, and persuade him to bring his people back to their dwellings. The incident is revealing. First, it shows that Cortés was determined to show his men who was the commander and who was the subordinate; he set the flamboyant Alvarado firmly in his place. Alvarado's willingness to take the initiative could be an advantage or it could be a danger. Many expeditions to the mainland had already been ruined by colourful underlings trying to wrest control from their superiors. Nor would Alvarado have been without allies: in addition to the comrades with whom he had served under Grijalva, he had brought along with him on the present expedition no less than four of his equally volatile brothers. More important, however, the incident showed that, right from the outset, Cortés possessed a well-defined grand strategy. This was not to be a smash-and-grab raid: it was to be a calm and well-conducted operation of which the successive stages would be carried out in an orderly manner. The natives were not to be treated as a pack of irredeemable savages: they were to be studied, their point of view was to be considered, and wherever possible their aid was to be enlisted. Admittedly, Cortés embarked on this policy largely out of self-interest. He was not so simple as to believe he could conquer what promised to be an enormous and populous land by methods that were entirely conciliatory and pacific. He knew that hard fighting lay ahead, and wanted to seize any opportunity to husband the strength of his limited forces. He also knew that in addition to hard fighting there would be hard marching. During those marches his men would have to live off the land, and it made more sense to march through friendly country and obtain supplies from friendly natives than to fight every step of the way and battle for every mouthful of food. Most of his men were looking forward to a brief, bitter but lucrative campaign; they were professional soldiers and adventurers, temperamentally attuned to the notion of a short life and a merry one. Cortés was not. From the beginning he demonstrated his methodical turn of mind and showed that the taste for negotiation was as strong in him as the desire for action. He would never fight for the sake of fighting; first he would patiently exhaust every possibility of compromise and accommodation. He was as much a politician as a general. He had grasped the fact that, if he was eventually to settle down in this great new land, as he fully intended to do, he would be wise to begin as he meant to go on. Why antagonize the Indians at the outset? Why alienate them by means of a brutal and bloody conquest that would forever symbolize repression and terror? If there was an element of cunning in this policy, if we can detect the cold logic of the lawyer of Salamanca, I think we must also credit the brain that framed it with a sense of moderation and responsibility. If, as was suggested earlier, it is characteristic of an ambitious and vigorous man to delight in strife and contest, it is also a mark of a civilized one to appreciate the damage that might result and seek to limit it. According to this definition, Cortés, much more than other *conquistadores*, was an eminently civilized man. It was his fixed principle to attempt persuasion instead of combat. He would not reach Tenochtitlán without being compelled to fight a series of stubborn engagements; but on each occasion he fought only when his peaceful overtures had been rejected. When finally he entered Tenochtitlán, he would do so as a guest rather than as a conqueror. His relationship with Moctezuma was, at first, to be one of mutual esteem—forbearing, deferential, curiously tender. Up to the last it appeared possible that he might achieve a relatively bloodless take-over. Sooner or later, of course, the Spaniards would have encountered spirited resistance: the Aztecs of all people would not have permitted themselves to be mesmerized into parting with their freedom. But there was a honeymoon period even in the relations between Spaniards and Aztecs, most aggressive of the Mexican peoples. It is fascinating to reflect on the course that history might have taken if, as Cortés wished, the Aztec empire had been dismantled in a benign manner instead of by violence. After all, large portions of the British and other European empires were originally acquired without undue bloodshed, and when the time for disengagement came the break between the imperial power and its colonies was effected, in those cases at least, without acrimony and ill-feeling. The 'black legend' or *leyenda negra* concerning the Spaniards in Mexico was born primarily as the result of such incidents as the coming massacre within the city of Tenochtitlán. This Cortés would have striven hard to prevent, and his grip on his troops was strong enough for him to have stood an excellent chance of doing so had outside factors not intervened. Unfortunately, he was to be called away from the city at a crucial moment. In his absence an irresponsible attack was to be launched on the populace by the officer whom Cortés had left in charge. The officer was Pedro de Alvarado.

*　　*　　*

Having restored peace on the island of Cozumel, Cortés now performed another characteristic act. Three days after landing he held a review of his troops. They were drawn up in regular order and properly inspected. Their leader was again impressing on them that they were not a free-wheeling gang of opportunists but an army: a tiny army, yet an army nonetheless, and an army that was subject to a strict code of discipline. Bernal Díaz, on parade that day, gives precise numbers of the men present at that important muster: five hundred and eight soldiers, thirty-two crossbowmen, and about a hundred sailors. There were ten brass guns and four falconets. Cortés went to great pains to ensure that each man's arms and equipment were in first-class condition.

He also enjoyed a small and unexpected piece of luck. He had heard through his interpreter, an Indian dubbed with the name of Melchior, who had somehow acquired a few words of Spanish, that some Spaniards who had been shipwrecked on a previous expedition were living as slaves somewhere in the hinterland. He sent out a message by Indian traders, and a few days later an extraordinary apparition walked up to him, dropped to its knees, and saluted him Indian-fashion. The man was indistinguishable from a native, and as Díaz describes him 'he carried a paddle over his shoulder, had an old sandal on one foot, wore a very ragged old cloak and a tattered loincloth to cover his private parts, and in his cloak was tied an object which proved to be an ancient prayer-book'. He was Jerónimo de Aguilar, a Spaniard in holy orders who had been cast ashore eight years before while carrying official documents and the King's Fifth from Darien to Santo Domingo. The documents related to the quarrel between Balboa and Nicuesa. He had been one of seventeen survivors, including two women, but all were now dead except him and a certain Gonzalo Guerrero. He and Guerrero, with some of the others, had been put in cages to be fattened up for sacrifice, but had managed to escape and find their way to the territory of a friendly *cacique*. There they worked as common slaves, but on receipt of Cortés' message the *cacique* had consented to release them. Guerrero, however, refused to obey the summons, for he was happily settled in his present situation with a wife and three pretty children. He was also ashamed of the fact that he was tattooed like an Indian, wore heavy earrings, and had a stone plug through his lower lip. Gómara adds the picturesque detail that when Aguilar's mother, in Spain, was told that her son had been shipwrecked on a coast whose inhabitants were cannibals, she went mad. 'From that time on, whenever she saw meat being roasted or broiled, she would scream: "Ah! that's my son! that's my son!"' Aguilar had indeed had a miraculous escape from that gruesome fate: and it may be worth mentioning in passing that, in his *Short History of Mexico*, J. Patrick McHenry offers an interesting sidelight on the subject of cannibalism. He suggests that the practice might have had a dietetic as well as a religious significance. 'The Indian's diet,' he points out, 'was perniciously low in proteins. His meals consisted almost entirely of corn and beans. Perhaps it was his craving for proteins that drove him to cannibalism, and to the practice of fattening up his hairless, elephant-hided dogs for eating at special repasts.'

Aguilar was fluent in several of the local Mayan dialects. He was therefore to be invaluable to Cortés in the weeks ahead, when the latter was waiting for his lost vessel to arrive and making his final preparations. Aguilar had heard rumours of populous towns further to the west; but whether these were actual Mayan communities in the heart of Yucatán, or folk-memories of the once-great cities of the Mayas, or genuine intimations of the mighty Aztec empire, it is impossible to say. The Spaniards were still five hundred miles away from anyone who could have given them definite information about the Aztecs: although, as was noted earlier, Toltec and Aztec influence had filtered into Mayan territory along the coastal routes, and Quetzalcóatl himself had come to reside at the temple of Chichén Itzá, only a hundred miles due west of Cozumel. The practice of cannibalism itself may have reached Yucatán from the direction of the Valley of Mexico. Nevertheless, the bare mention of lusher pastures elsewhere would have whetted the eagerness of Cortés and his men to move on. There was little to keep them in a remote island which boasted nothing more than three poor little towns.

*   *   *

Before leaving Cozumel, however, Cortés had one more act to perform. It was a solemn act that he would carry out in every town through which he passed. It consisted of the ceremonial casting-down of the local religious images, or 'idols' as the Spaniards called them. The procedure was always the same, although sometimes, as at Cozumel, the natives would eagerly co-operate in the work of rolling the idols down the steps of the temple and breaking them up, whereas at other places there would be anger and resistance. The events at Cozumel may stand for most of the remainder. Cortés called the priests and *caciques* together and, after Jerónimo de Aguilar had preached them a sermon in their own tongue, he delivered a no-nonsense, proconsular type of speech. In the words of Díaz: 'He told them as best he could, through our interpreter, that if they wished to be our brothers they must throw their idols out of this temple, for they were very evil and led them astray. He said they were not gods, but abominations which would bring their souls to hell. Then he spoke to them about good and holy matters, telling them to set up an image of Our Lady, which he gave them, and a cross, which would always aid them, bring them good harvests, and save their souls. He told them other things too about our holy faith and in well-chosen words. Next he sent for some lime and for some Indian masons, and set up a very fair altar, on which we placed the image of Our Lady. He also ordered two of our carpenters to make a cross of rough timber. This was placed in a sort of shrine beside the altar, and one of our priests said mass. Meanwhile the *caciques* and the priests and all the Indians stood watching us intently. Cortés consigned the image of Our Lady to their care and told them to worship the cross, which they must keep clean and decorate with flowers. He said they would then see what benefits they gained, and the Indians promised to obey him. Then he embraced them.'

Maurice Collis, in his excellent short account of the Conquest, makes a characteristically shrewd observation, as befits a writer who is also an art historian, concerning the effect which the native 'idols' produced on the Spaniards. The latter would have been nauseated by the blood-smeared appearance of the images, the blood-soaked walls of the shrines in which they stood, and the blood-stained garments and bodies of the priests who served them. They would have been revolted by the nature of the rites carried out in honour of the images. But, suggests Collis, their fear and loathing would also have been enhanced by the unfamiliar artistic idiom in which the images were carved. Often Aztec religious sculpture is sufficiently sinister and frightening in itself—'devilish', to use the word the Spaniards so frequently employed. But Aztec art was also aesthetically strange: and aesthetic strangeness often provokes an exaggerated reaction. One thinks of the manner in which educated and civilized Westerners greeted the canvases of the Impressionists, the Cubists, the Fauves, the Expressionists, the Futurists, the Surrealists, the Tachistes, right up to the time of the hard-edge painters; the very names of the movements were often terms of contempt and disapprobation. Anything unfamiliar produces uneasiness. How much more uneasy, then, must the Spaniards have felt, confronted in a remote and hostile country by these fearsome and to them excessively wierd-looking objects. If anything existed in their own experience to which they could compare them, it was to the demons represented in their own religious art. To eyes attuned to the Romanesque style as represented at Compostella, or to the Gothic style of the cathedrals of Burgos, León, Toledo or Seville, the temples of Mexico would naturally appear barbaric and shocking. The Arabic, Mozarabique and Mudéjar styles of the Moors would have seemed miracles of grace and refinement in comparison with the gloomy sanctuaries of the Aztecs. Once again the sharp clash of two opposed worlds, two fundamentally different cultures, can be discerned.

In the speech which Cortés delivered to the village elders we can detect the same tone of conciliation mentioned earlier. The tone is purposeful, but more paternal than autocratic or tyrannical. Had he been a cynic or an outright opportunist, he would have left the Indian cults untouched, however depraved he considered them; but in his own way and in his own generation he was a man of principle. He tried to be fair-minded; he was not wantonly and capriciously destroying the native idols, he was attempting to set up in their place something which he sincerely felt to be superior and more humane. In substituting the image of the Virgin for the Indian images, he was also executing a move that was psychologically shrewd. When he spoke of the Virgin bringing them good harvests and other benefits, he showed insight into the pragmatic relationship which natives enjoy with their gods. The Virgin, the Christian counterpart of the earth-goddesses and mother-goddesses so prominent in pre-Columbian religion, sprang into immediate popularity. It was a mere twelve years after the Conquest that the Virgin appeared to the poor and elderly Indian Quahtlatohua, called Juan Diego, and with a beautiful gesture filled his robe with roses. The place near Mexico City where the miracle of Guadalupe occurred in 1531 was the hill which had previously been the shrine of Tonantzín, the 'Mother of the God'. Ironically, the Virgin of Guadalupe, whose cult was established by the Spaniard Juan de Zumár-raga, first Archbishop of Mexico, later became the patroness of the Mexican troops during the War of Independence. The Spanish royalists adopted a rival Virgin, the Virgin of Los Remedios, whose shrine tops the Pyramid of Cholula (see p. 88), and whose image was said to have been carried by a soldier of Cortés. In spite of the fact that the Spaniards made the Virgin of Los Remedios a full General of the Army, she was defeated by her blessed opponent and captured in battle. Then, as James Norman puts it in the latest edition of Terry's monumental *Guide to Mexico*, 'she was stripped of her uniform by a Mexican general, and ordered to be deported from Mexico. She was allowed to remain on, only when it was promised that she would stay out of politics'.

It is a touching scene: the *caciques* and village notables wrapped in the habitual dark Indian silence while they watch the Spanish carpenters erecting the makeshift cross in its homely shrine. The shrine of Cozumel was the forerunner of scores of thousands of such shrines in the New World. It is always a moving experience, even for a non-Catholic like the present writer, to visit these humble dwelling-places of God, whether in South or Central America or in the pueblos of the south-western United

States. In Arizona or New Mexico these little chapels of whitewashed adobe, with their floors of beaten earth and their primitive *retablos*, are tiny specks of sanity and simplicity in an ocean of materialism. One feels the same at Santa Fé, two thousand miles from Cozumel and nearly the northernmost point which the *conquistadores* reached, when one stands in a little shrine in Bishop Lamy's cathedral in front of a diminutive doll-like virgin dressed in the robes of a Spanish queen. She is called La Conquistadora, and was brought to Santa Fé by Frey Alfonso de Benavides in 1625. The holy images which the Spaniards set up in place of those they tumbled down the stone staircases were certainly much milder than those they had superseded.

Prescott offers us a fair summary of this aspect of the Conquest at the point in his majestic narrative where he describes Cortés' sojourn on Cozumel. 'The Spanish cavalier,' he writes, 'felt he had a high mission to accomplish as a soldier of the Cross. However unauthorized or un-righteous the war into which he had entered may seem to us, to him it was a holy war. He was in arms against the infidel. Not to care for the soul of his benighted enemy was to put his own in jeopardy. The conversion of a single soul might cover a multitude of sins. It was not for morals that he was concerned, but for *the faith*. This, though understood in its most literal and limited sense, comprehended the whole scheme of Christian morality. Whoever died in the faith, however immoral had been his life, might be said to die in the Lord. Such was the creed of the Castilian knight of that day . . . and no one partook more fully of these feelings than Hernán Cortés. He was, in truth, the very mirror of the times in which he lived, reflecting its motley characteristics, its speculative devotion and practical licence—but with an intensity all his own.'

*　　　*　　　*

There are discrepancies in the two principal accounts, those of Gómara and Díaz, concerning the length of time which the miniature armada spent at Cozumel; nor do they agree on the date on which it weighed anchor, doubled the north-eastern cape of Yucatán, and set sail towards the west. Both accounts agree, however, that after a few days, as on the former voyage, the fine weather changed and a tempest sprang up, again causing the ships to be scattered. The opening of Cortés' campaign was not encouraging, and some of his soldiers were already beginning to grow dispirited as a result of seasickness and of an intestinal affliction called *el vómito*, which sometimes vanished rapidly but on other occasions could have fatal results.

The ships crawled down the long coastline, hugging the land as closely as they dared, striving to keep together as they sought anchorages. They made a brief rendezvous off Campeche, now a large modern township of the same name, then ran south-westwards again, considering but not effecting another pause at Champotón (see Fig. 5 for the course of their voyage). They were following the track which Córdoba and Grijalva had taken shortly before them, and which had at least yielded a little of that gold which they had failed to find in Cozumel.

They were afforded a welcome breathing-space when they reached the huge lagoon called the Puerto Escondido, or Hidden Port (now the Laguna de Términos). There they were overjoyed to find awaiting them the brigantine which they had presumed lost. They were also intrigued when they were greeted by a handsome greyhound bitch that had been left there by Córdoba or Grijalva, and which had not only managed to survive but grown sleek and fat. She had become a cunning hunter, and was invaluable in helping her rescuers to run down the deer, rabbits and hares they needed to replenish their stocks of fresh meat.

At length, after an anxious eight- or ten-day journey, they dropped anchor at their destination. This was the mouth of the Río Grijalva. This river, still called by that name, flows through the important city of Villahermosa, capital of the province of Tabasco, but is now a tributary of the larger Río Usamacinta. It was either off the delta of the Usamacinta or more probably off the Laguna Mecoscán, thirty miles to the west, that the fleet anchored. The whole of that part of the coast is marshy and uninviting, and the Spaniards were unwilling to commit their vessels to the evil-smelling mangrove-swamps. Instead, they rowed ashore in small boats: and were dismayed to find that the people whom Grijalva had named Tabascans, and whom they had expected to be friendly, were in fact hostile. The Tabascans, who took their name from a chief called Tabasco, had been cordial enough to Córdoba and Grijalva; but their neighbours had called them cowards, and they were now anxious to show their mettle. They were to provide Cortés' troops with a first sharp taste of action.

When Cortés' men landed, Díaz says that 'the whole bank was thick with Indian warriors, carrying their native arms, blowing trumpets and conches, and beating drums'. Cortés ordered restraint ('for he wished to be justified in all that he did') and spoke to them through Aguilar in the presence of Diego de Godoy, the Royal Notary (the official recorder of the expedition, and the accredited collector of the King's Fifth). 'He asked them to let us land, take water, and speak to them about God and His Majesty. He added that if they attacked, and if in self-defence we were to kill or hurt any of them, it would be their fault and not ours.' As Gómara put it, 'Cortés endeavoured to treat these barbarians with every civility, as is right, and as is laid down in the instructions issued by the monarchs of Castile: that is, to offer them peace one, two and many times before making war on them or invading their lands and taking their towns.'

It was to no avail. The Indians discharged their arrows and a free-for-all took place. Cortés and his immediate entourage were surrounded, and only rescued by the tardy arrival of a force led by Alonso de Ávila. Cortés himself lost a shoe in the mud during the fighting. It was fortunate that the Spaniards, caught in such an exposed position, had not had to reckon with the main force of the Indians, which was still gathering a few miles inland. Shouting their war-cry, 'Santiago, Santiago!', the combined forces of Cortés and Ávila carried all before them, and by nightfall were in occupation of the small town of Potonchán, or 'stinking water', the first town captured by the Spaniards in Mexico. They counted eighteen Indian bodies. It is significant that at this stage in the *entrada* it was the gruff, bad-tempered Ávila who had been named second-in-command, not the brilliant but impetuous younger man, Pedro de Alvarado.

The skirmishing continued the next day, after Cortés and the local *caciques* had indulged in some ineffectual negotiations. Another small inland village was taken, and the Indians lost a further fifteen men and the Spaniards two. All this was merely a prelude to the main battle that took place on the third day, March 25, a battle that has been dignified with the name of the Battle of Cintla. Cintla was the principal town of the area, and it was there that the Tabascan mobilization had taken place. It may be the modern town of Comalcalco, twelve miles inland, which possesses the remains of a large stone temple.

Cortés realized that a set-piece engagement was now inevitable, and the two armies met next day on a level plain between the town and the sea. Cortés picked his position carefully, and sent back to the ships for six of his cannon and thirteen of the horses to be brought ashore. There was some anxiety lest the horses should be stiff after the sea-voyage, but they soon limbered up, and their harness was hung with little brass bells to make their onward rush more awe-inspiring.

The Spaniards marched on to the field in a disciplined manner, with banners flying. Cortés was not disposed to carry out impromptu little forays from shipboard in the manner of Córdoba and Grijalva. The force of five to six hundred men gathered around Fray Bartolomé de Olmedo, one of the two priests who accompanied the expedition, in order to hear Mass. They then prepared to receive the onslaught of the Indians, which was not slow in coming. 'Their squadrons, as they approached us, were so numerous that they covered the whole savannah,' said Díaz. 'All the men wore great feather crests, they carried drums and trumpets, their faces were painted black and white, they were armed with large bows and arrows, spears and shields, swords like our two-handed swords, and slings and stones and fire-toughened darts, and all wore quilted cotton armour. They rushed on us like mad dogs and completely surrounded us, discharging such a rain of arrows, darts and stones upon us that more than seventy of our men were wounded at the first attack.'

The brunt of the battle was born by the infantrymen, commanded by Ávila, Alvarado and Sandoval. Cortés had placed himself in command of the cavalry unit, and had removed it before the conflict had started to ground on the left of the infantrymen. At first he had difficulty in picking his way through marshy terrain to the rear of the enemy; but his charge, when it finally took place, was all the more effective for being delayed. It is extraordinary what havoc a baker's dozen of horsemen could inflict on a vast horde of Indians: and indeed it seems as if the horsemen did not do the damage directly, but that the sudden appearance of these 'centaurs' (to use Díaz's word) caused so much demoralization that the Indians faltered and enabled the Spanish infantrymen to dash at them with renewed force. The horsemen, that is, were essentially a diversion at this stage of the campaign, though they inflicted much mischief in their own right. The Indians had no idea how to deal with this supernatural beast, half animal and half man, and simply stood paralysed while the pounding hoofs and flashing swords cut them down.

*   *   *

All Spanish writers on the Conquest are agreed that the Indians, at Cintla and at all the battles thereafter, were exceptionally brave opponents. They always mastered the initial panic which the novel weapons of the Spaniards aroused in them, and pressed home their attacks again and again. The pitched battles were not hit-and-run affairs but long-drawn-out contests lasting several hours and usually ending, from the Spanish viewpoint, none too soon. The Indians not only showed courage when confronted by cavalry, which must have seemed as terrifying to them in terms of the warfare of the time as the spectacle of the first line of British tanks looming out of the mist at the Battle of Cambrai; they also showed courage when confronted with the flash-and-bang of the muskets, the whirr of the bolts from the crossbows, and the flame-and-crash of the cannon. It is indeed a proof of their exceptional valour that in such circumstances they were always willing to turn about and come back for more.

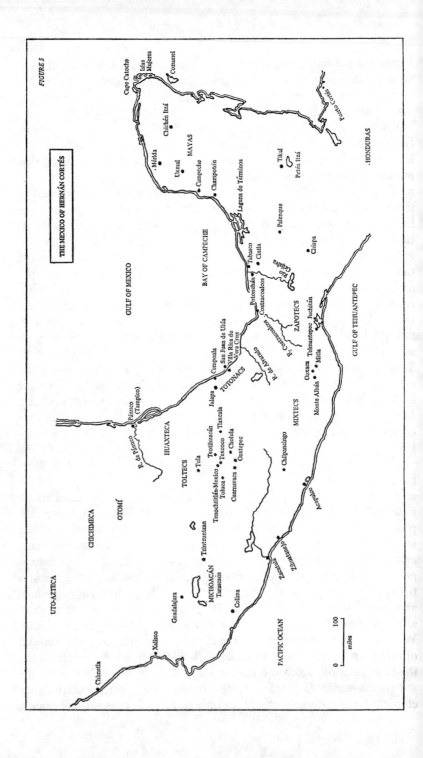

FIGURE 5

THE MEXICO OF HERNÁN CORTÉS

The superiority of weapons is the perennial explanation of the ability of a handful of Europeans to defeat a host of natives:

> *Praise the Lord that we have got*
> *The Gatling gun, and they have not.*

On the other hand, it should be appreciated that the sixteenth-century brass gun or falconet was vastly less reliable than the Gatling, and that muskets and crossbows were prone to develop all sorts of unexpected maladies at the moment when they were most needed. In their final phase, therefore, most of Cortés' tussles with the Indians culminated in hand-to-hand fighting. The Indian masses pressed on, trampling over the fallen bodies of their comrades, enduring the cavalry, shrugging off the arrows, ignoring the musket-balls, brushing past the wicked tips of the long pikes that, on Cortés' orders, jabbed directly at their faces. At the climax of the action the Spaniards stood toe-to-toe with their bedizened adversaries, exchanging a deadly cut-and-thrust, the swords of Spain against the swords of Mexico. Of course, the steel sword was technically superior to the wooden *macquauitl*, or *montante* as the Spaniards called it: but even a steel sword was of little use if its owner lacked the will and skill to use it. The Spaniards lacked neither. Like the Aztecs, they were trained from childhood in the use of arms. The Mexicans were hardly likely to prevail in hand-to-hand combat against men who had traded blows with the Moors at Granada or the French at Cerignola. Of the eight hundred enemy dead counted by the Spaniards after Cintla, the majority had been killed by sword-thrusts.

The Spaniards not only knew how to use their weapons: they knew how to keep their ranks. When surrounded, they fought back-to-back in an unbreakable square. In contrast, the Indians sallied forward in an undisciplined mass, and in that way squandered much of their energy and potential effectiveness. Also, since they tended to think and react in tribal rather than individual terms, they were prone to impulsive errors and *espantos*. Individual groups would give up and retire from the field if their personal chieftain was killed—if the head, as it were, had been stricken from the body. They lacked the cohesion, the professional phlegm and ability to improvise which characterized the European soldier. They were also confused by the conventions of previous wars, and particularly of the War of Flowers, as to whether they ought to kill their opponents outright or capture them alive for sacrifice. The Spaniards felt no such confusion: they went straight for the jugular vein.

In the fields of strategy and tactics the Mexicans were hopelessly outclassed. They possessed no grand strategy and their day-to-day tactics were rudimentary. Although they were observant, and picked up many tricks, they were like the bull in the bull-ring: it learns, but it can never learn fast enough, for the matador will not give it time, and the end comes too soon. At the beginning the Mexicans had no tactic more subtle than the simple ambush. They had no conception of how to divide or how to concentrate their forces; of how to attack a weak flank and roll up the enemy line; of how to choose an advantageous position; or any of the hundred other stratagems familiar to any soldier brought up in the European military tradition.

*   *   *

The next day, when a deputation of forty Indian notables came to talk peace, this time with a serious intention, Cortés arranged a special demonstration of his two principal weapons. Before the Indians arrived, he ordered his biggest cannon to be loaded with a large ball and plenty of powder; and he instructed two of the horses, a mare and a stallion, to be brought out. The mare was in season, and she was led off to a place where the stallion would not get wind of her. When the notables were assembled, Cortés gravely explained that some of his *tepuzques*, or 'irons', as the interpreter called the cannons, were still angry at having been attacked the previous day. As he spoke he signalled for the big cannon to be fired, and the ball whistled through the air with a roar and a bang that thoroughly terrified the Indians. Then he signed for the mare to be brought closer—still in concealment—to the stallion. The stallion began to whinny and clatter fiercely with its hoofs, again terrifying the Indians, who thought the animal was about to charge and eat them. Cortés declared that the horses too were angry, but that he had told them that the Indians were now friendly and wished to talk peace.

Cortés already considered that he had taken *de facto* possession of this new land in the name of the King. He had done this on the first night of his arrival, after the capture of the village of Champotón. In the main square stood a large *álamo* or cottonwood tree, and Cortés, in the presence of his troops and the Royal Notary, solemnly struck its trunk three times with his sword and declared that he and his men would defend the King's right with their lives. It was therefore somewhat academic when he now invited the Indians to enter the royal service as the King's vassals; but his manner throughout the negotiations was mild and gracious, and a 'treaty' between Spain and Tabasco was formally entered into. As an earnest of good faith, the *caciques* presented Cortés with some objects made of gold, about a score in number; but it was apparent that here, no less than at

Cozumel, supplies of this coveted metal were in short supply. However, the *caciques* indicated that more of it was to be found to the west, in the direction of the setting sun, in the great kingdom that they called *Colhúa* or *Mexico*. *Colhúa*, Culhua or Acolhua was a generic name for the eleven tribes who were the last to arrive in the Valley of Mexico, including the Tepanecs, Colhuans and Aztecs. They took their name from Colhuacán, a town seven miles south of Tenochtitlán (now Coyoacán, a suburb of Mexico City), which was the first important centre of Colhuan activity in the Valley. It was the men of Colhuacán who conquered the Toltecs and overran Tula; but later, when the Mexica-Aztecs became the dominant power and built their great city, Colhuacán, together with the other cities round the lake, became first the ally and then the vassal-state of a people whom it had once despised.

This was the first time the Spaniards had heard the tantalizing word 'Mexico', signifying the land of the Mexica. When they saw the fingers of the *caciques* pointing towards the sunset, they felt contradictory emotions of elation and gloom. They had already travelled a long way and had fought hard: now they must travel farther and fight harder. Their goal continually eluded them, and the country seemed increasingly more vast and intimidating. On the other hand, they had at last received a definite intimation that a rich kingdom in fact existed, and that they had only to press on to secure the gold they sought.

A few fortunate ones, friends of their commander, received a small immediate bonus. As if to atone for the poverty of their presents, the Tabascans gave Cortés twenty beautiful girls. These he distributed among his captains. One of the girls, who in the words of Díaz was 'good-looking, intelligent and self-assured', was bestowed on Alonso Porto-carrero, the native of Medellín, kinsman of the Conde de Medellín, and particular favourite of Cortés. In Cuba, Cortés had even snipped the gold buttons from his own cloak in order to buy Portocarrero a horse for the expedition. It was natural, therefore, that he should give Portocarrero the pick of the girls. La Malinche, for that was her name, probably in deriva-tion from the Náhuatl name Malinulli, was indeed exceptional. She rapidly established herself as a person of importance in the Spanish camp and soon became indispensable to Cortés. Her early life was singular and melancholy. Her parents were aristocrats, her father being *cacique* of a town in the region of Coatzacoalcos, which is also the name of an im-portant modern town (see Fig. 5). Her father died when she was young, and her mother, on re-marrying, gave her daughter away to slave-traders in order that her son by the second marriage should enjoy the undisputed status of heir to the family fortune. The slave-traders sold her to the Tabascans, who lived a hundred miles to the west of the Coatzacoalcans. And now the Tabascans, in their turn, consigned her to the Spaniards.

La Malinche was a quick-minded young woman, and she was familiar not only with the languages of the Tabascans and Coatzacoalcans, but with the languages of the Mayas to the east and the Aztecs to the west. She at once assumed a key role as the expedition's main interpreter. Melchior, the original interpreter, had never been much use, and after the battle of Cintla he had defected and run away to his own people. Jerónimo de Aguilar spoke Mayan, but the Mayan country was now behind them and the country of the Aztecs was looming ahead. His usefulness as a linguist was almost over. Now Cortés could speak Spanish to Aguilar, Aguilar could speak in Mayan to La Malinche, and La Malinche could speak in Tabascan to the Tabascans. Later she would speak in Náhuatl to the Aztecs. In a matter of weeks she acquired fluent Spanish, and throughout the Conquest was continuously at Cortés' elbow. In the eyes of the Indians they formed an inseparable pair, so much so that Cortes was also called Malinche, or *Malintzin*, which means 'Malinche's Captain'. It is clear that she was much more than a simple interpreter. Cortés consulted her on matters of general policy and on all matters relating to Indian psychology, and both Díaz and Gómara accord her a whole section to herself in their respective accounts. Her contribution to the Conquest was acknowledged by the Mexicans of her own time and by later generations. Typically, the Mexican attitude to her, as to so much besides, was ambivalent. On the one hand, she was accorded quasi-divine honours as a goddess, as the grieving deity *La Llorona*, almost as another Mexican Blessed Virgin, interceding with the Spaniards on behalf of her own people and softening the rigours of defeat. On the other hand, she was reviled as a female Quisling, a collaborator who sold both her soul and her body to the invader and exposed the sacred soil of her country to corrupt foreign influences. The Mexicans have always tended to be xenophobic (with sufficient reason) and have coined the word *malinchista* to describe any person who is guilty of the crime of *malinchismo*—that is, who wishes to open Mexico to the outside world, thus betraying its supposed aboriginal purity. Moctezuma and La Malinche have been elected respectively the male and female devils in the history of Mexico, though it seems a trifle hard to stigmatize her as a traitress in this way. We are advised that we should not ask what our country can do for us—but what, exactly, did Mexico do for La Malinche? Her mother sold her to slavers; slavers sold her to strangers; and strangers gave her to the men who had conquered them and stolen their land. It would be surprising if, after her earlier trials, she did not welcome becoming the chattel of Portocarrero, who at least was a Spanish hidalgo.

Soon after her transfer to the Spanish camp, she was the first Mexican to become a Christian. She then took the baptismal name of Marina, a name which is never written in the records without the respectful suffix *Doña*. This alone indicates that the Indian woman was regarded as a person of consequence. She is depicted in the Codex Florentino, the Lienzo de Tlaxcala and other codices as standing beside Cortés and translating his words or issuing her own instructions (Plate 5). It was understandable that such a close relationship should move from the political plane to the physical. In his despatches to the Emperor, Cortés refers to her twice, and the references are fleeting. She is merely 'the female interpreter', 'an Indian woman of this country whom I obtained in Potonchán'. Cortés was always careful, in his correspondence with the Emperor, to reserve all possible credit to himself and apportion very little to anyone else. Besides, it would never have done to let the Emperor know that his captain, who yearned for a Spanish patent of nobility, and who was married to a Spanish woman, was cohabiting with an Indian. For this is what happened only four months after she became the mistress of Portocarrero, when Cortés had written the first of his despatches to the Emperor Charles. Whom did he select to carry the despatch to Spain? No less a person than Portocarrero. True, he sent Portocarrero because, as a close friend and Extremeño, he could trust him utterly, in an epoch and in circumstances when few men were to be trusted. But it also seems reasonable to suspect that Cortés might already have been attracted to La Malinche, and wished to remove her first protector from the scene as tactfully as possible. He took Marina to himself, and had a son by her. This was Don Martín Cortés, the first of his two sons of that name, older by ten years than the legitimate brother who succeeded to his father's title and estates. Then, probably because by that time Cortés regarded the liaison as socially disadvantageous, or was genuinely concerned to end the anomaly of her position, he married her off years later to one of his soldiers called Juan Jaramillo, described by Díaz as 'a gentleman'. She had a daughter by Jaramillo, and received from Cortés on her marriage a handsome estate at Jilotepec, a village fifty miles north of Mexico City. That she continued in his thoughts, and that his sense of gratitude and obligation had not lessened, is shown by the fact that in 1528 he gave her a plot of land attached to her house at Chapultepec, and another plot in the vicinity that had once belonged to Moctezuma.

Díaz was present when Cortés travelled through Coatzacoalcos in 1523 on his expedition to Honduras. Doña Marina accompanied Cortés, although it was on this journey that she married Jaramillo. She was now a very great lady, and she ordered her mother and the stepbrother who had been the cause of her childhood rejection to be brought before her. Not surprisingly, as Díaz puts it, 'they were very much afraid of Doña Marina; they feared that she had sent for them to put them to death, and they wept'. Instead, she comforted them, 'pardoned the old woman, and gave them many golden jewels and some clothes. Then she sent them back to their town, saying that God had been very gracious to her in freeing her from the worship of idols and making her a Christian, and giving her a son by her lord and master Cortés, also in marrying her to such a gentleman as her husband. Even if they were to make her mistress of all the provinces of New Spain, she said, she would refuse the honour, for she would rather serve her husband and Cortés than anything else in the world'.

It would appear that Doña Marina was not only beautiful and clever but, which is rarer, steadfast, generous and magnanimous. She deserved a better fate than to have her name degraded into a cheap epithet.

* * *

It was time to leave Tabasco. After the ritual of casting-down the local idols and substituting a Christian altar had been performed, and Palm Sunday had been solemnly celebrated, the Spaniards embarked once more and set sail westwards towards the land of Colhúa, still following the track of Grijalva.

In some ways it was unfortunate that they had landed at Tabasco and been compelled to fight a major battle there. Tabasco, though they could not have known it, was far removed from their ultimate destination; pacifying it served no purpose; and the affair at Cintla had only strained their resources and caused the faint-hearts to start grumbling. However, it may have been useful as an introduction to Indian modes of warfare and Indian modes of thought. It had served as practice for the sterner battles that awaited them.

They sailed past the town of Coatzacoalcos, past the landmarks of Grijalva's voyage, in particular the Río Alvarado where Pedro de Alvarado had landed the previous year (modern Laguna de Alvarado), and finally cast anchor at a place which was called San Juan de Ulúa. They had covered a distance of 250 miles, and put ashore on Holy Thursday.

Certain of the members of the expedition were now showing overt signs of disaffection. The *vómito* and the violence of the battle of Cintla had affected the nerve of some, while others thought that the expedition

was in a fair way to suffer the same inconclusive fate as those of its predecessors. In particular, the numerous spies and adherents of Velázquez
who had tacked themselves on to the expedition grew increasingly alarmed
the further they went. The cavalier way in which Cortés had ignored the
orders of the Governor made them uneasy. They reflected on the wrath
that might descend on them when they returned to Cuba, and wished they
had been less carried away by Cortés' blandishments and had dropped out
of the business while there was still time. It was also becoming clear to
every member of the expedition that, in the person of Hernán Cortés, they
had caught a tiger by the tail. They were going to be involved in this thing
right to the end: they might as well make up their minds to it. The calm,
quiet, self-possessed young man of thirty-four who led them had no
intention, in any time or in any circumstances, of cutting his losses like a
sensible man, or like one of the opportunist leaders they had been used to.
They had underrated that unemphatic and composed manner: it concealed a power of the will and a determination to push things through to
a final conclusion that were unshakeable. Some of them began to regret
that they had flocked so gaily to the banner with the blue-and-white
flames and the injunction '*Conquer!*'.

These were only the waverers. The confidence of the majority was
expressed by young Portocarrero who, immediately after landing, strode
up to Cortés and, pleased with his commander, pleased with himself, and
pleased with the mistress he had just acquired, addressed him in the
words of one of the old metrical romances of the Reconquest in which the
men of that era were steeped. He recited from the ballad of Count
Montesinos the triumphant lines: '*Now look on France, Montesinos! Look
on Paris! Look on the waters of the Seine as they flow to the sea!*' He added:
'You too are looking on rich lands! May you know how to govern them
well!' Cortes replied in his collected manner, also alluding to one of those
heroes who were never far from the thoughts of himself and his companions: 'With you, sir, and with these other gentlemen for my captains,
I shall know how to acquit myself. God give us the same good fortune
as he gave to the Paladin Roland.'

*   *   *

'Cortés,' says Díaz, 'understood the reason why Portocarrero had spoken
in the way he had.' Indeed he did. Since leaving Cuba, Cortés and his
intimates had been hatching a plot among themselves, and now was the
moment to put it into operation. Portocarrero, perhaps indiscreetly, was
letting the cat out of the bag. It was that word '*govern*' which gave the

clue to what was afoot: 'May you *govern* these lands well.' Officially, Cortés was only the instrument of the Governor of Cuba, who would automatically become Governor of any territory which Cortés was able to seize. Cortés, as Portocarrero indicated, intended at the outset to be governor of these great new lands himself, and he and his friends had already concocted a legalistic device to shuffle off the thrall of Diego Velázquez and make themselves the legitimate rulers of the country.

The way to do this was to transfer their allegiance from Velázquez to the Emperor Charles, thus becoming direct liegemen of the crown, answerable to Spain and not to Cuba. Spain was far away; the Emperor had no first-hand information about what was happening in Mexico, except what Cortés chose to tell him. If Cortés could represent the expedition as a success-story, and play on the Emperor's cupidity and chronic need for cash by sending respectable amounts of treasure and promising more, then it was unlikely that Charles would interrupt the progress of a prosperous enterprise or interfere with its personnel. What did Charles care who governed Mexico, as long as the Royal Fifth was ample and arrived punctually?

To whet the imperial appetite, Cortés informed the Emperor in the despatch which he was shortly to send that: 'In our judgment, it is entirely possible that this country has everything which existed in that land from which Solomon is said to have brought gold for the Temple.' What money-hungry monarch could resist such a promise? The despatch went on to blackguard the Governor of Cuba in astonishingly frank terms. They reveal the all-or-nothing nature of Cortés' mood: after the transmission of this despatch, there could never again be any hope of accord between Cortés and Velázquez. The despatch stated that Velázquez had given assent for the expedition 'more out of greed than anything else', and went on to say that: 'We have good cause to fear him, for we have seen what he has done in Cuba. He renders justice as he pleases, punishing those whom he chooses from anger or passion and not from reason or justice. He is involved with dishonest men, seeking always his own advantage, and nobody dares oppose him because they know he can ruin them. Your Majesty has not been told of this because those who should have done so are his lackeys, whom he bribes with grants of Indians.' (We may see a reflection, in this last sentence, of Cortés' adventure after his escape from prison, when he tried to sail to Hispaniola carrying documents concerning the Governor which he wished to lay before the *audiencia*.) 'We pray you,' added the despatch, 'not to grant him the *adelantamiento*, nor the perpetual governorship of this land, nor the charge of justice; and if any of these has already been granted, to revoke it.' The despatch concluded with the damaging accusation that Velázquez coveted the Royal Fifth himself, explaining that this was why Cortés had sent the gold and jewels which accompanied the despatch to Spain and not to Cuba.

Cortés regarded himself as justified in addressing the Emperor directly in this manner because he had already, by means of an ingenious dodge, severed his responsibilities to Velázquez. His legal training and casuistic mind were of great assistance to him here. In clandestine discussions with his closest friends, he had hit upon the contrivance of founding a new city and having himself elected its mayor. He could then assume his duties by means of an oath which would be administered to him in the name of the Emperor, not in the name of the Governor of Cuba, and his instructions from the latter could thereupon be pronounced legally void.

It was an elaborate pantomime. A deputation led by Alvarado, Sandoval, Portocarrero, Escalante, Ávila and Olid waited formally on him. They told him that they had concluded that, in the words of the First Despatch, 'it seemed to them that it was not in His Majesty's interests to do as Diego Velázquez had ordered Cortés, but seemed better that a town should be founded and peopled there in the name of His Majesty. In this town there would be a court of justice, so that the King would have his jurisdiction in this country just as in his other realms and dominions. And once this country was peopled by Spaniards, thereby adding to His Majesty's kingdoms and dependencies, and also to his incomes, he might see fit to bestow his favours upon us, and upon the future colonists who would come here'. They then looked around for the best man to become Governor, Captain-General and Chief Justice, and were delighted to find that, by a happy chance, such a man happened to be at hand. Cortés, having ceremoniously handed in his resignation as leader of the expedition, was now invited to assume an even more exalted position. He put up a great show of modesty and reluctance, but was at length persuaded to accept. Of course, he did so 'not because of the profit he might gain', but because he was 'exclusively devoted to the royal service'.

Alvarado and the others were appointed to the principal offices of the new town. The central plaza was laid out, and two of the appurtenances indispensable to civilized living—a pillory and a gallows—were installed therein. The town, of which Cortés laid the first stones with his own hands, was hopefully and artfully named Villa Rica de Vera Cruz. It is now the town of Old Veracruz, twenty miles north of modern Veracruz, the handsome capital of the province of that name, a city with a population of 150,000. The modern town was shifted southwards in later years to take advantage of a better harbour. The castle of San Juan de Ulúa, marking the spot where the *conquistadores* landed, stands on the reef of La Gallega. A short distance to the south are the sizeable towns of Medellín and Alvarado, founded only two years later, comprising respectively 15,000 and 12,000 people, and with names equally redolent of those vivid events which took place four and a half centuries ago.

Cortés not only achieved independent status, but by employing his phenomenal talent for persuasion, he also induced his colleagues to vote him one fifth of whatever treasure might accrue to the expedition. The entire episode was an exercise in impudence. He and his friends were nothing more than rebels, and although they made a great parade of legality their actions were at bottom transparently extrajudicial. They were gambling that the Emperor would decide that Cortés was likely to make a weightier contribution to the royal coffers than Diego Velázquez. Cortés had no illusions that Velázquez would hit back at him with all his strength. The Governor of Cuba not only had the letter of the law on his side, he was actually related by marriage to Juan Rodríguez de Fonseca, Bishop of Burgos and Archbishop of Rosano, who had controlled the direction of Spain's colonial empire since its inception. He was one of the most powerful men in Spain, virtual dictator in his own sphere, a dry, hard, spare, active man, more suited by all accounts to practical than ecclesiastical affairs. He had set up the Casa de Contratación in Seville in 1503, and in 1524 would become the first President of the newly-constituted Council of the Indies. He was a dangerous man to defy and a difficult man to circumvent. Cortés knew the risk he was running. As soon as he was installed in his pseudo-position as Governor, he sent off two of his senior officers to Spain with his first despatch, which purported to be written by the administrative body of Villa Rica and not by himself. He also took care to send with them the most substantial amount of gold and treasure he could scrape together; cash on the barrel can speak louder than words. He gave his followers a few marks to enable them to pay their more pressing debts, but kept none of the gold or silver for himself to defray his own crushing expenses. He wanted this first royal instalment to be as impressive as he could make it. The officers to whom he entrusted it were the ardent young Portocarrero, as before mentioned, and Francisco de Montejo. They were both *alcaldes* or justices of Villa Rica. Portocarrero was a loyal friend, but Montejo had been Velázquez's man until Cortés had presented him with a thousand pesos. From that time onwards he served Cortés faithfully. He and Portocarrero reached Spain in October to discover that Velázquez and Fonseca had already laid charges of treason against Cortés and petitioned the Emperor to arrest his envoys and confiscate their treasure. They managed to elude Fonseca's henchmen for five months, and finally obtained an audience with the Emperor at Tordesillas in which they and Cortés' father, Don Martín Cortés, successfully pleaded the cause of their self-styled Captain-General. Montejo returned to the New World to find fame as the conqueror of Yucatán, a task in which he was assisted by Alonso de Ávila, whom we have already encountered.

It was fortunate that these weeks on the coast, when Cortés was caught up in diplomatic preoccupations, were otherwise peaceful. The people whom they called the Cempoalans received them amiably and proved tractable. Today there is a Punta Zempoala on the coast above Veracruz, and thirty miles north of Villa Rica is the village of Zempoala where squatters live among the impressive and extensive ruins of what was once the Cempoalan capital. The Cempoalans were Totonacs, a people whose origins rested on an ancient Olmec base, and who at that period were spread over an area that stretched from the coast a hundred miles inland almost as far as modern Puebla. Today there are still 60,000 people who speak the Totonac language. Cortés and his captains made a number of route-marches around the Totonac country, overthrowing idols, erecting altars, and generally suppressing those 'cruelties and obscenities', as Díaz put it, which seemed to become increasingly gruesome the closer they came to the territory of the Aztecs. Hearts were ripped, Aztec-style, from the breasts of five or six victims a day; cannibalism was widespread; and sodomy was commonplace and featured young male prostitutes dressed up in women's clothes. Cortés' harangues grew increasingly sharp and imperative. On the other hand, he was elated when the Totonacs brought him lavish offerings of gold and silver. After the meagre showing of Yucatán the golden sun-discs, silver moon-discs, golden bracelets, diadems, cartwheels and rough nuggets of the Cempoalans were welcome. The Cempoalans were so generous because they were convinced that their visitors were in fact *teules* or gods; the Spaniards had made their first contact with the Quetzalcóatl legend. One of the Cempoalan chiefs was much struck with an old rusty helmet worn by one of the Spaniards. It was exactly the same shape as the helmet worn traditionally by the war-god Huitzilopochtli, and the chief supposed that it had been brought back to Mexico by supernatural comrades of that god. He wished to fill the battered helmet with grains of gold as a gift for the Emperor Charles. Cortés did not dissuade him.

It was at Cempoala that the Spaniards also first heard the name of Moctezuma. The Totonacs were vassals of the Aztecs, and the Spaniards learned later that the Totonac leaders had ordered painters to make portraits of Cortés, his ships, his officers and captains, his horses, even his greyhounds, and sent them off to Tenochtitlán (Plate 5). But Cortés was also gratified to learn that the Totonacs hated their overlords. In Diaz's words, 'they told us that every year many of their sons and daughters were demanded of them for sacrifice, or for service in the houses and plantations of their conquerors. They added that, if their wives and daughters were handsome, Moctezuma's tax-gatherers took them away and raped them, and that they did this in all the thirty villages in which the Totonac language was spoken.'

Cortés was always a quick man to spot an advantage, and he realized immediately the implications of the Cempoalan grievances. 'When he learned that Moctezuma had enemies,' writes Díaz, 'he was greatly delighted.' Gómara uses almost the same words: 'Cortés was well pleased to find the lords of that country at odds with each other, which would allow him the better to carry out his plans and intentions.' This was the inception of the policy of *divide et impera*, the Roman strategem re-stated by Machiavelli, which Cortés was to practise so expertly and which was to pay such dividends. Indeed, it would have been utterly impossible for Cortés and his diminutive band to have encompassed the fall of the Aztec Empire if such internal dissensions had not existed. Had the tribes of Mexico lived together in unity and amity, six hundred Spaniards could have made little impression on that dense mass. Cortés' ability to turn a simple *entrada* into a full-scale civil war is the key to the Conquest. The moment when he suddenly saw that the Mexicans were at odds among themselves might be represented as one of the psychological turning-points of the campaign. As he wrote fifteen months later in his Second Despatch, when the campaign was mounting towards its climax: 'I was very pleased to see discord between the various parties. It strengthened my design, and later I would find means of overcoming them. I was reminded of a quotation from scripture which ran: *Omne regnum in seipsum divisum desolabitur*. I treated with one faction, then the other, privately thanking each side for the advice it had given me, professing to be friends of all equally.'

He was given an immediate opportunity to put his new policy into execution. While he was in conversation with the *cacique* of a village near Cempoala, he saw coming towards them across the square, as Gómara puts it, 'twenty men looking like constables, each carrying a short, thick wand and a feather fly-flap. The *cacique* and his friends started to tremble at the sight of them. Cortés asked the reason, and they told him they were Moctezuma's tribute collectors, whom they feared would report the presence of the Spaniards to Moctezuma and bring down on them his wrath and punishment'. Cortés not only reassured them: he performed an action that astonished them—and, as he intended, astonished the whole country round. He motioned to his guards and ordered them to seize Moctezuma's henchmen, beat them, truss them like chickens to poles, their feet lashed to one end and their hands to the other, and cart them off to a nearby house under a heavy guard. The sensation which this high-handed procedure caused can be imagined.

Cortés' fertile mind had already discerned how the business could be put to double advantage. In the middle of the night, when the Cempoalans were asleep, he instructed his men to untie two of the prisoners and bring them to him secretly. He explained to the two bewildered Aztecs that what had occurred was all the result of a misunderstanding, that he himself had been unaware of exactly what was afoot, but that he had pretended to arrest them in order to save them from the murderous designs of the Cempoalans. He told them to make their way to Moctezuma and give him a message. They were to say, in Gómara's words, that Cortés 'would not fail in his service to Moctezuma whenever the occasion required it, nor fail to seek his grace, favour and friendship by all possible means. He was convinced that nothing but love and goodwill need exist between them, and that Moctezuma would not deny his friendship. God was coming to Moctezuma and his subjects in the persons of the servants of the Christian Emperor, who brought with them great benefits and the knowledge of mysterious and holy things'. The messengers were also to assure Moctezuma that the tribute collectors who remained prisoners would not be harmed. He then gave them a meal and had them rowed up the coast and landed at a safe and suitable spot from which they could begin their long journey to Tenochtitlán.

The Cempoalans were terrified at what they took to be the accidental escape of two of the Aztecs. An urgent and hectic conference took place at which Cortés was a calm and indulgent spectator. As Gómara relates: 'Some were certain the runaways would report to Moctezuma the insult and abuse they had suffered. Tribute should be sent immediately to appease his wrath, and he should be informed that it was the fault of the Spaniards that they had behaved in such a mad and impudent way. Others declared that it was better to shake off the yoke of the cruel and arrogant Aztecs and seek the help of the invincible Spanish demigods. In the end a decision was taken to rise up and rebel, and they begged Cortés to act as their leader.' Cortés gravely assented to their request. 'He told them that he would command and defend them because he valued their friendship more than that of Moctezuma.' He asked them how many men they could muster, and was delighted to be given a figure of a hundred thousand.

At his suggestion 'they despatched messengers at once to all the towns round, praising the Spaniards to the skies. Open war was declared against Moctezuma. Cortés meant to rally the whole countryside to his support, since without their assistance he could accomplish little'.

* * *

Cortés and his companions, after a busy three months among the Totonacs, were now in the mood, in the phrase of Díaz, 'to go and take a look at Moctezuma'. Cortés had a few remaining pieces of business to attend to. In a sharp and vigorous action he successfully reduced the principal Aztec garrison in the region, a small victory that maintained the enthusiasm and morale of his new allies. He also found it necessary to stamp out a conspiracy within his own ranks, fomented by the partisans of Velázquez. Here he decided to use a heavy hand. When the ringleaders were brought before him they admitted that they had planned to steal a ship, sail to Cuba, and inform the Governor of what was happening. In his capacity of Chief Justice, Cortés sentenced two of them to be hanged, two to be flogged, and one to have his feet cut off. As he signed the sentence, Díaz says, 'he gave a deep and sorrowful sigh' and uttered a classical tag attributed to Nero, in one of that Emperor's few mellower moments: 'It would be better not to know how to write, for one would then be unable to confirm death sentences.' As J. M. Cohen indicates, in his translation of the *Historia verdadera*, it is possible that Cortés' sentences were not carried out, as one of the men sentenced to be hanged survived to put his name to a letter the following year; and in the Second Despatch the matter is dismissed somewhat evasively: 'I punished them according to the dictates of justice and the best interests of Your Majesty.' Nonetheless 'with this action', Gómara writes, 'Cortés made himself more feared and respected than before. It would have been fatal to have been soft, or even negligent, since if Diego Velázquez had been warned he could have seized the vessel in which Portocarrero and Montejo were taking their despatch and the treasure destined for the Emperor Charles to Spain.'

To offset the effect of the conspiracy, the Spaniards received a small fillip in the shape of a caravel that arrived at Villa Rica under the command of Francisco de Saucedo. Saucedo had managed to sneak away from Santiago de Cuba under the nose of Velázquez, and brought a reinforcement of sixty Spaniards and nine horses. Any addition to the cavalry was welcome; Cortés own mount had recently died of sickness. The extra troops meant that, after detaching a hundred and fifty men to police the Totonac area and man the base at Villa Rica, putting his close friend

Juan de Escalante in charge of them, he was still able to take fully four hundred troops with him on the advance to Tenochtitlán.

He had been putting his finishing touches to his preparations for that great event, and now bowed to the inevitable and named Alvarado as his second in command. Alvarado had shown himself in every way superior in personality and ability to Ávila; it would have been wrong to resist his claims. Nevertheless Cortés appointed his closest friend Sandoval as Alvarado's watchdog and coadjutant.

He was planning a final dramatic touch before turning his back on the coast. Like most of his strokes, it combined low cunning with a high Renaissance flourish in the direction of posterity. It was actually such a gamble, such a melodramatic gesture, that he did not even dare to mention it in his Second Despatch. There, as always in his reports to his royal master, he strove to put his conduct in a thoroughly sober and responsible light.

When all was ready, he destroyed his fleet. He ordered his shipmasters to strip the ships of their guns, provisions, anchors, cables, sails and other useful articles; and then he told them to scuttle some vessels and bore holes in the others. This drastic action was performed secretly. When the troops got wind of it there was a howl of rage and dismay. Many of the men complained that he wanted 'to send them to the slaughterhouse', as Gómara puts it: to which he answered, in Díaz's account, that they could 'now look for help from no one except from God, and would have to rely on their own good swords and stout hearts'. By this bold proceeding he was securing a number of different ends. First, he was imbuing his troops with his own all-or-nothing attitude to the enterprise. Next, he was destroying the possibility of a group of men thinking, at some time in the future, that they could desert, return to the coast, and find a ship to carry them to safety. Third, he was preventing any of Velázquez's sympathisers from sailing to Cuba as soon as he had marched inland, perhaps taking the entire fleet back with them to be used to ferry over Velázquez's own troops to Villa Rica. Lastly, he was freeing a sizeable body of sailors to take part in the march to Tenochtitlán, though many of them balked at being pressed into land service.

Cortés gathered the entire company of Spaniards around him and treated them, after a solemn mass had been celebrated, to one of his most forceful and brilliant discourses. He developed classical parallels. He spoke of Caesar crossing the Rubicon, and quoted the Roman Emperor's *alea jacta est*, 'the die is cast', the pronouncement attributed to him by Suetonius. Cortés also had in mind a more recent performance of the same type, when one of the famous Barbarossa brothers, the Moorish admirals, had, in Gómara's words, 'sunk seven galliots and foists in preparation for the taking of Bujía'. What a Moorish captain could do, a Spanish captain could do better. It might almost be said that it was the moment when Cortés sank his boats that constituted the physical turning-point in the Conquest and, by extension, the historical moment at which the Hispanization of a large part of the globe was decreed.

Gómara states that Cortés left the coast for the interior on August 16, 1519 (see Plate 6), with a force of between four and six hundred Spaniards, fifteen horses, three hundred Indians, and most of his guns. The latter were carried by native porters, the *tamemes* referred to earlier, professional carriers who were skilled in transporting heavy loads for exceptional distances. Some guns and a few horses he left with Escalante to guard the rear, to drive away any expeditionary force that might be sent by Velázquez, and to create a relatively secure sanctuary to which he could retire in case of extreme emergency.

The preliminaries were over. The tempo was quickening. Cortés was getting down to business.

2

A man must not only know how to ride: he must know how to fall.

Mexican proverb

THE route which Cortés took from Villa Rica to Tenochtitlán was circuitous (see Fig. 6). Had he elected to march along the southern route through modern Orizaba, instead of the northern route through Jalapa, he would have travelled through easier terrain. There was not a great amount of difference in point of distance, which in each case was about 250 miles; but he would have saved his little force a good deal of hard climbing in a land remarkable for its rugged mountains. He chose a roundabout method of approach because he was informed by the Totonacs that the Tlaxcalans, whose lands adjoined theirs on the west and north-west, would welcome the Spaniards even more warmly than they had themselves. In this the Totonacs, though they gave their opinion in good faith, were grossly mistaken.

We have already met the Tlaxcalans. Although their principal city of

Tlaxcala lay a bare sixty miles due east of Tenochtitlán, this ancient and vigorous people, whose culture like that of the Totonacs had Olmec antecedents, had managed to keep their independence. In part this was due to their own warlike exertions, in part to the fact that the Aztecs found it convenient to tolerate them as an alien enclave. The Tlaxcalans on their own constituted no great threat to the powerful Aztec league in the Valley of Mexico, and were permitted to survive on sufferance as long as they consented to take part in the deadly mock-battles of the War of Flowers. This, in turn, was to prove a serious mistake on the part of the Aztecs; they would have done better to have extirpated the Tlaxcalans, as they had extirpated other dangerous rivals, before the arrival of Cortés. The Tlaxcalans comprised five large tribes, and were proud, warlike, well-armed and prosperous; the word *Tlaxcalli* was the same as *tortilla*, and meant 'The Land of Bread'. They had much to fight for, and were consumed by a passionate hatred of their Aztec neighbours.

Hardly had the Spaniards passed through the village of Jalapa, now a large city with more than 100,000 people, than they were given an indication of the character of the Tlaxcalans and the conditions under which they lived. They came upon a gigantic wall of uncemented stone that had

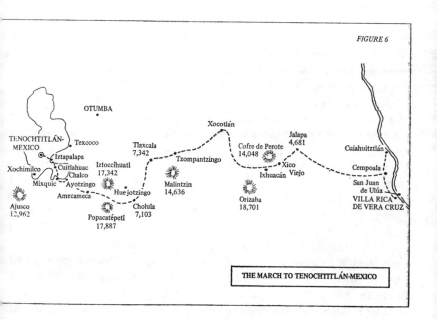

FIGURE 6

THE MARCH TO TENOCHTITLÁN-MEXICO

been built as a defence between Tlaxcala and the outside world. Both Gómara and Díaz describe this fortification, although the former comments that it was easily outflanked and was therefore as useless, presumably, as the Great Wall of China. It appears to have stood somewhere between Jalapa, which was still in Totonac territory, and the village of Xico, ten miles south of it, an outpost of Tlaxcala. Nothing remains of it today, for the stones were no doubt carted off in later centuries to make the walls of haciendas.

The line of the Spanish march is not known with exactitude. The Mexican historian Carlos Pereyra takes the Spaniards from Xico to Ixhuacán, at which point what is now only a secondary Mexican road becomes a cart-track and then peters out into wild hunting-country. The expedition would then pass south of the Cofre de Perote and cross a wilderness to join up with the road between Jalapa and Tlaxcala in the neighbourhood of Oriental and El Carmen. Whatever the route, it was an adventurous journey, marked by those harsh extremes that are the particular attribute of Mexico. Pereyra describes it well when he speaks of the Spaniards leaving a coastal landscape whose appearance was familiar to them from other parts of the New World, and passing into 'a region entirely new to them. The calendria, the sapodilla, the red cedar, the mahogany, the palm and other species began to give way to grand and mountainous country whose rises and falls were a challenge to Castilian intrepidity. Here the oaks grew in tangled thickets that wrapped the invaders in a balmy atmosphere. One tree, the *Xochiocotzoquáhuitl*, produced an aromatic turpentine or liquidambar that was so powerful that the perfume could be smelled long before the tree came into sight. The army crossed a zone in which the vapours of the Gulf condensed into curtains of pearly mist that wreathed the stands of conifers, their crests looming through the glistening rain as they guarded the rims of plunging chasms in whose depths rustled a sinister tropical life. Then came the cold country. They marched across a vast plain covered with salt pans and lakes of stagnant water whose presence added to the cause of desolation. For three days they were short of food and water. The winds off the fourteen thousand-foot peak of the Cofre de Perote punished them and killed the naked Indians brought from Cuba. A hailstorm added to their miseries'.

It was indeed a hard march, from the Hot Country of the coastal region into the Cold Country of the interior, a contrast in flora and climate that was dreaded even by those hardy Aztec traders mentioned earlier. The march would have been an arduous undertaking under any circumstances: but what made it almost intolerable for the Spaniards was the fact that the

Tlaxcalans compelled them to fight every step of the way. Situated as they were, the Tlaxcalans were not likely to assume that an armed force that had entered their territory had done so with a friendly intent. Cortés sent repeated messages to assure them that he came in peace, and that he wished merely to pass through their country on his way to Tenochtitlán. But they had too much reason to fear the Aztecs. Guile and deception had always been a feature of life in Mexico, and the Aztecs had lifted the arts of treachery to new heights. The Cempoalans and the coast peoples were vassals of the Aztecs: what if Moctezuma had ordered them, in concert with this curious regiment of foreigners, to launch an attack from the east, while the Aztecs themselves prepared to attack from the west? What if the Actecs had tired of tolerating a hostile enclave and were ready to eliminate it?

Fatigued, footsore, unable to sleep because of the freezing winds cutting through the high passes, the Spaniards were further worn down by the continuous combat. They were also at an altitude of between six and seven thousand feet, and were affected by the rarefied atmosphere. The Tlaxcalans ambushed them in the defiles, hurling down rocks, spears and slingshots. Tormented, they stumbled on. On the more open ground the Tlaxcalans harassed them with groups of skirmishers, and the Spaniards were unable to deploy their horses because of the broken and boulder-strewn nature of the terrain. When finally, on September 2, the Spaniards were able to offer something like regular battle, the horsemen were still hampered. As a result, one of them was fatally wounded and his mount captured. The horse was cut in pieces and the pieces were circulated in Tlaxcalan towns before being offered up in religious rites. Already the shock-value of the horse was beginning to fade.

There was a second major encounter three days later. The situation was so grim that even the sick and wounded were pressed into the ranks. The enemy general, an old blind chieftain called Xicotenga, came on at the Spanish phalanx with five separate columns, each of which contained, at a conservative estimate, at least two thousand men. Once more the dour discipline of the Spanish soldier prevailed over the pell-mell attacks of the enemy; but the price was heavy. Not more than a handful were actually killed (it was difficult to kill a Spaniard of that era) but one man in six had been wounded—and a man had to be wounded very seriously for the chroniclers to mention it at all. 'I too was hit twice,' remarks Díaz, 'once on the head with a stone, once in the thigh by an arrow; but this did not prevent me from fighting and later performing my watch.'

They were nearing the end of their tether. They buried their dead comrades as secretly and as deeply as possible, so that the enemy would not find the bodies and discover that they were not gods but humans. They had no oil and salt to dress their wounds, and had to pour into them the rendered-down fat of Indian corpses. They had no protective clothing to shield them from the icy winds eddying around the crown of the Volcán de Malintzin, as it came to be called, a volcano even higher than the Cofre de Perote. They prayed for Xicotenga, the enemy chief, to free them from some at least of their misery by making peace: but no encouraging word came from the Tlaxcalan camp. On the contrary, they were badly shaken by a fierce night assault, and if they had not as usual been sleeping in their armour, with weapons to hand and horses saddled, they would have been lost.

Some of the Spaniards were becoming disheartened. A deputation waited on Cortés. They told him in plain terms that his obduracy would kill them all. They compared him with the legendary Pedro Carbonero, who during the Reconquest had led his company into the land of the Moors, where they had all disappeared without trace. They reminded him that neither Caesar nor Alexander had been reckless enough to wage war against such odds. They asked him to turn around and take them back to Villa Rica, where they could build a ship to summon assistance from Cuba. They added nastily that the ships which had been scuttled would have proved very useful at the present juncture. In short, they made it clear that they and the men they represented thought the expedition was a failure, and wanted him to retire while he could still do so.

It is impossible not to admire the firmness of Cortés' reply. Had we ourselves been stranded in those cheerless cordilleras, at that bleak moment, the feelings of the deputation would no doubt have been our own. Furthermore Cortés was suffering from fever, and from an intestinal upset he was treating with thrice-daily doses of castor-oil. Appropriately, he was one of the first victims of the undignified complaint that modern tourists call *Montezuma's Revenge*. It is not easy to sit a horse, swing a sword, conduct a campaign and cope with a mutiny under such circumstances. It was fortunate that none of his principal lieutenants was the kind of man to abandon his general in a crisis; and one wonders whether it may not have been during this trying period that he began to be attracted by and seek comfort from La Malinche. 'Let me say,' reports Díaz, 'that Doña Marina, although a native woman, possessed such manly valour that, though she heard every day that the Tlaxcalans were going to kill us and eat our flesh with *chiles*, and though she had seen us surrounded in recent battles and knew we were all sick and wounded, yet she betrayed no weakness but a courage greater than a woman's.'

Cortés began his reply to the deputation with a mild reproof, observing that they spoke rather haughtily for men who were proffering unasked-for advice. Then he launched out into an eulogy of the general courage and conduct of his army, concluding the first part of a speech which would have done credit to any professional advocate with the words: 'As for your observation, gentlemen, that the most famous Roman captains never performed deeds equal to ours, you are quite right. If God helps us, far more will be said in future history books about our exploits than has ever been said about those of the past. For, I repeat, all our labours are devoted to the service of God and our great Emperor Charles. Under his true justice and the Christian law, God in His mercy is aiding us and will turn our good fortune to better.' Warming to his theme, he enlarged on the impracticality of retiring and its shamefulness. 'What would the great Moctezuma say on hearing that we had retreated? He would say that our whole expedition was a childish joke.' And he finished with a magnificent peroration: 'As for your statement, gentlemen, that we have lost fifty-five soldiers since leaving Cuba from wounds, starvation, cold, sickness and hardship, and that we are now few in number and all wounded and sick, God gives us the strength of many. It is clearly true that wars destroy men and horses and that we only occasionally eat well. But we did not come to this country to take our ease, but to fight. Therefore I pray you, gentlemen, kindly to behave like gentlemen. The duty of a gentleman is to encourage those whom they see displaying weakness. From now on, keep Cuba and your families and possessions there out of your thoughts. Try to act, as you have done until now, like brave soldiers. For after God, who is our aid and support, we can rely only on ourselves.'

In fact, relief was closer at hand than his listeners suspected. No doubt, being a bold and clever commander, he had it in mind that, although one may be in a bad condition oneself, it is quite possible that one's enemy may be in a worse. This was the case. On their side the Tlaxcalans had grown despondent at their failure to halt the onward progress of these fair-skinned strangers, and the majority of their chiefs were ready to make peace. Xicotenga alone, backed by his son Xicotenga the Younger and his chief captain Chichimecatecle, held out for continuing the war. He was overruled, and under the guise of seeking a truce he sent forty envoys to Cortés with gifts of parrot feathers and of the aromatic incense called copal (Náhuatl *copalli*), the fossil resin from various tropical trees that was universally used in Mexico. Cortés soon saw that these envoys were spies, sent to learn the disposition of his camp in preparation for one final onslaught; and after extracting a confession from one of their number he cut off the thumbs or hands of seventeen of them and sent the severed members to Xicotenga. The latter took the point, and soon made serious overtures for peace, much to the relief of the Spaniards. 'We gave thanks to God,' says Díaz, 'for at that moment we were lean, weary, and unhappy about this war, of which we could neither see nor forecast the end.'

*   *   *

'The city of Tlaxcala is so large and admirable,' wrote Cortés in his Second Despatch, 'that the little which I shall say is almost incredible. It is more extensive than Granada, and better fortified. Everywhere good order and good manners prevail. The people are full of intelligence and understanding. Their way of life is superior to anything to be found among the Moors. Their kingdom is ninety miles in circumference and contains many wide and beautiful valleys. These valleys are all well cultivated. The form of government seems to resemble that of Venice, Genoa or Pisa, as there is no supreme ruler.'

He and his men were very glad to linger in this agreeable town for three weeks, reorganizing and recouping their strength. The attitude of the Tlaxcalans towards them became extremely cordial, and when Xicotenga and his fellow *caciques* discovered that Cortés, in spite of his amiable manner, was keeping up his guard and maintaining piquets each night, they were deeply offended. As a proof of his good faith, Xicotenga bestowed his own daughter upon Cortés. The latter, after making a graceful and tactful speech of thanks, gave the girl to Pedro de Alvarado, telling Xicotenga to rejoice because she would be honourably treated. Four other principal chiefs offered a daughter in their turn, and these Cortés bestowed on Sandoval, Olid, Ávila and Juan Velázquez de León. The girls were then baptized, and after the Conquest became, like La Malinche, great ladies in their own land. One must remember that, in this and similar transactions, Cortés would have given serious offence had he refused so personal a gift; and although the young women were undoubtedly welcome perquisites to his war-weary captains, their acceptance by the Spaniards was also in the nature of ratifying a solemn treaty between the representatives of the King of Spain and the leaders of the Indian peoples. It would have been undiplomatic as well as churlish of Cortés to refuse.

He put his time at Tlaxcala to good use, holding a series of earnest conferences with Xicotenga and the other war-chiefs. He ascertained as accurately as possible the strength of the Aztec army and its probable tactics; discussed the most promising line of march on Tenochtitlán; and worked out a joint plan of battle. Xicotenga pleased and startled him by declaring that the Tlaxcalans would be able, at a pinch, to put no less than 150,000 warriors in the field, and he realized that henceforth the Tlaxcalans would be his main and indispensable allies.

The Tlaxcalans too had come to appreciate that they had at last found a staunch ally against the dreaded Aztecs. They had suddenly been given an unlooked-for chance to crush Moctezuma and ensure their own survival. The Spaniards had proved that they were invincible, and that they were truly gods: they would lead Tlaxcala to victory, after which they would show their Indian friends their gratitude. After the Conquest, the Tlaxcalans did in fact receive preferential treatment. They were totally exempted by the Spanish crown from taxation, and their leaders were allowed to use the prefix *Don* and to ride horses; and it must be said of them that, once they had thrown in their lot with the Spaniards, they supported them to the end, through fair times and foul. As in so many other things, Cortés was fortunate in his confederates.

He knew how to utilize their fanatical hatred for the Aztecs. In order to avoid antagonizing them, he even went as far as to modify his strictures on their religion. When they showed anger at his attempt to destroy their idols he contented himself with building a single small Christian altar and leaving their shrines intact. He told himself that there would be plenty of time, when the hurly-burly was done, to attend to the matter later. Today, in the small provincial capital of Tlaxcala, a city with not more than ten thousand inhabitants, the towers of the great cathedral church of San Francisco soar to the sky. In its Capilla del Tercer Orden can be seen the first pulpit from which Christianity was preached in Mexico.

Cortés quickly shed his own early suspicions concerning the Tlaxcalans. These suspicions had been nourished by no less a person than Moctezuma, who had now interrogated the two tax-collectors whom Cortés had first seized and then released at Cempoala. Moctezuma immediately sent off six high officers of state, who reached the Spanish camp soon after Xicotenga had started to sue for peace. The Aztec envoys presented some fine gold jewellery and featherwork to Cortés, warmly urging him not to trust the Tlaxcalans, who meant to lure the Spaniards to Tlaxcala in order to kill them. Cortés had grasped firmly by this time the fact that the teeming peoples of Mexico lived in an atmosphere of mutual fear and perfidy, and though he placed a qualified trust in the Tlaxcalans, he placed none at all in the Aztecs. In a land where treachery was endemic, the Aztecs had acquired a well-merited reputation as masters in that art.

Events soon verified his judgment. Against the advice of his Indian allies, he decided to direct the next stage of his march through the celebrated city of Cholula (see pp. 88, 165), twenty miles to the south. The

Tlaxcalans despised the Cholulans, whom they considered abject lick-spittles of the Aztecs. Cortés took note of their objections, but appears to have felt that, even with the support of a large Tlaxcalan army, it would be foolish to leave a hostile population in his rear. He must go to Cholula, where he would either secure the neutrality of the *caciques* by negotiation, or, failing that, disable them by means of rougher measures. Even before he left camp, he received a second embassy from Moctezuma, now growing increasingly uneasy. The embassy included a number of the leading Aztec noblemen. The Aztecs, alarmed by the unmistakable friendship between the Spaniards and Tlaxcalans, disbursed further quantities of gold, and conveyed their master's astonishment that Cortés should linger so long among a backward and poverty-stricken people. They extended to him an invitation to visit Tenochtitlán, where they assured him that a suitable reception was being prepared for him. Cortés had a private idea of what that reception might be: but he contented himself with thanking the envoys in his usual bland and amiable manner. He would be delighted to accept the great Moctezuma's kind invitation. It was not for nothing that the name *cortés* in Spanish means courteous or polite.

Probably he had already worked out a method of neutralizing the Cholulans, if that proved necessary. The peoples of Mexico did not retain sole title to the precept of *per fas et nefas*. When the *caciques* of Cholula refused his invitation to come to Tlaxcala and confer with him, one bright morning he took the road to their city notwithstanding. When he reached his destination, all seemed to be well. The Cholulans accorded him a lavish reception. In reality, Moctezuma had sent twenty thousand picked troops to reinforce the warriors of Cholula; they were hiding in the houses and in nearby ravines, and pits lined with sharpened stakes and covered with reed mats had already been dug in the streets to trap the Spaniards and their horses. Next day, at a given signal, the Spaniards were to be massacred, except for twenty who were to be captured alive and sent to Tenochtitlán to be offered up to Huitzilopochtli.

Cortés must have guessed what was in the wind. He entered Cholula with his Spaniards and left the Tlaxcalans outside the city walls, though warning Xicotenga to keep them standing to arms and on the alert. His surmise was proved correct when an old Indian woman, the wife of a *cacique*, apprised La Malinche of the plot, wanting to save one of her own countrymen from the slaughter. In consequence it was Cortés who delivered the first blow. He had the Cholulan chiefs dragged before him, upbraided them, and ordered a musket to be fired. At the sound of the shot the Tlaxcalans burst into the town, the Spaniards joined them, and the town quickly became a shambles. The Tlaxcalans went about their

Diego Velázquez

Photo: Mas, Barcelona

Pedro de Alvarado

Photo: Mas, Barcelona

Reconstruction of the Central Square of Tenochtitlan

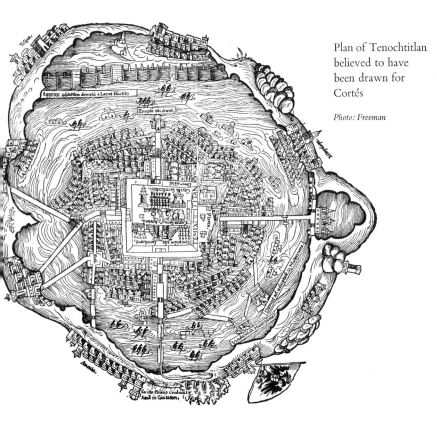

Plan of Tenochtitlan believed to have been drawn for Cortés

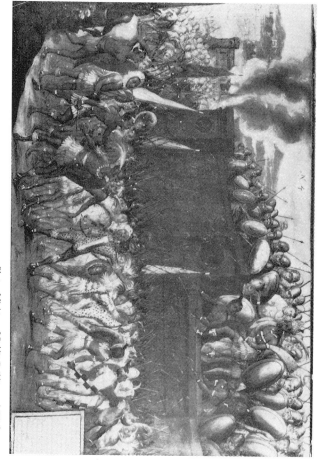

Photo: *Ministry of Public Building and Works*

Moctezuma addresses his countrymen

teçiquauhtitlā

The Spaniards and Tlaxcalans fight their way down the causeway

yeqnnnualtocaquecaltzatan:

The Spaniards break into the city

Cortés is nearly captured during the siege of Tenochtitlan

Coatlicue: 'The Lady of the Serpent Skirt'. Goddess of the earth and of spring, and mother of the great war-god Huitzilopochtli

Photos: Museo de Antropologia Cultura Mexica

Eagle Knight: A member of one the three great military orders the Aztecs (the others being t Arrow and Jaguar Knights)

Photo: *Freeman*

Cortés, by Diego Rivera

The statue of Cortés in Medellín

work so enthusiastically that Cortés had trouble in calling them off.

Needless to say, Moctezuma purported to be horrified. His ambassadors, who had actually accompanied Cortés from Tlaxcala to Cholula, disclaimed all responsibility and blamed everything on the Cholulans. A further deputation arrived post haste from Tenochtitlán bearing a third offering of gold and jewels from the Aztec Emperor. Moctezuma disparaged the Cholulans as earlier he had disparaged the Tlaxcalans, again assuring the Spaniards of his friendship and pressing them to visit his capital.

There was no need to offer Cortés such bogus encouragement. He was on his way, invited or not.

*   *   *

Moctezuma's behaviour had been marked by terror and indecision ever since he had first learned of the advent of the foreigners. It is not at all easy to account for the appalling dread which had laid hold of him and which incapacitated him during the months that lay ahead. The *caciques* of Cozumel, Campeche, Cempoala and Tlaxcala had all been dismayed and fearful when they first came face to face with the interlopers, but they quickly regained control of themselves and began to react to the newcomers in a normal fashion. Why was Moctezuma so timid and apathetic when a lesser chieftain like Xicotenga had already made the Spaniards struggle for their very lives?

To some extent, of course, Moctezuma's inactivity was deliberate. He was playing a waiting-game. The invaders had shown themselves in several pitched battles to be unstoppable and unkillable; and at Cholula the Aztecs had already lost one encounter, largely because they had made the error of underrating their opponents. For the moment it would be wise to try a completely different policy, a policy of guile. It was desirable to observe the enemy in order to find his weak points. In a contest of wits an Aztec ruler had no reason to suppose he would prove inferior to any newcomer. And the further he lured the Spaniards into his empire, the more vulnerable they were. They were advancing towards the centre of the web. There was also the possibility that the strangers had not come to conquer the country, but only to obtain a haul of gold, silver and precious stones; if these were given them, they might be satisfied and withdraw. Or they might be intending nothing more than a reconnaissance, in which case it was surely wise to treat them kindly and allow them to depart in peace.

These practical explanations have not satisfied later generations of his countrymen. To them, Moctezuma was a coward, a man suffering from a straightforward loss of nerve. Cortés himself and his fellow Spaniards considered that the Emperor, despite his kingly and agreeable presence, was weak and lacking in courage; but those whelps of the Renaissance were not burdened with the same supernatural baggage or sense of guilt as their opponent. Until recent years, when a more tolerant and objective attitude has prevailed, Mexican historians have tended to represent Moctezuma as a sybarite who was never a genuine warrior-king, but a ruler whose will to resist had been sapped by the life he led in his luxurious palace. His early reactions to the arrival of the Spaniards had certainly been immoderate to the point of panic. After the fiasco at Cholula he is said to have shut himself up for two days in his private apartments, surrounded by his priests. As the Spaniards drew closer, he was seized with an altogether extraordinary anguish. Sahagún records that his Indian informants told him that when the Emperor heard that the 'gods' were asking questions about him, and were eager to meet him face to face, 'his heart was heavy and he was filled with dread. He thought of flight; he wished to flee; he longed to take to his heels. He wanted to slip away and hide himself from the "gods". But he was unable to flee and unable to hide himself. He had no will or desire; he was powerless. The words of the magicians with whom he had drawn apart weighed upon his spirit. He wavered; he was languid and apathetic; he was completely irresolute and unable to make up his mind whether to stay or run away. In the end he decided that his only course was to await the arrival of the "gods". He felt he had to resign himself to simply submitting to whatever was going to happen'.

We might be more disposed to blame Moctezuma if his behaviour had been exceptional. In fact it was shared in the same degree by his subjects. Just as they had been reduced to a state of terror by the eight omens that had preceded the coming of the Spaniards, so now they were overcome by a universal *espanto*. According to Sahagún, 'everyone was in the grip of fear. There was general consternation and dismay. Everyone talked about what had happened and what would happen. There were meetings, conferences, discussion groups, and widespread weeping and wailing. People went about with their heads bowed. They greeted each other with tears. They tried to hearten and encourage one another. They embraced each other and hugged their children tightly. Fathers cried, "Oh, my little ones, what will become of you?" Mothers cried, "Little ones, how can you bear the horror that is coming to you?" '

Hardly a cheerful picture. It seems, then, that Moctezuma has become a scapegoat for what was a general condition, although as the leader of the nation he was scarcely setting a spirited example to his people. Everyone in the Valley of Mexico, the sophisticated courtier no less than the humblest peasant, was touched by a contagion of fear. How is one to account for this reaction, or rather over-reaction, on the part of the Aztecs? It would seem to be one more indication that they were an unusual and abnormal people. To some extent they were manifesting the familiar inability of a race of relatively primitive character to cope with the unexpected: but there was also a curious undertone of hysteria. It was as if, in their collective soul, they bore an intolerable burden of guilt. They acted as if they expected a divine punishment to fall on them, as if they were aware that their Empire was overripe and that its fall was finally at hand.

*   *   *

It was in this mood of fatalism that Moctezuma went out to meet Cortés. The Spaniards had had a cold and miserable journey, but otherwise the last seventy miles had been untroubled. After two weeks at Cholula, they set out with a force of four thousand Indians, drawn from the territories through which they had passed. Along the way they assured the people who flocked to meet them that their purpose was to rid the country of the tyranny of the Aztecs; they were therefore greeted as conquering heroes. Cortés was careful, nonetheless, to remain vigilant, and his little army marched in regular order, with scouts, flankers, advance guard and rear guard.

A piquant little episode took place twenty miles from Cholula, as they proceeded from Huejotzingo towards Amecameca, with the volcanoes of Ixtaccíhuatl on their right hand and Popocatépetl on their left. Cortés gave one of his more madcap young officers, Diego de Ordaz, permission to scale the latter, which was the higher peak, with two companions. Ordaz managed to reach the summit, and thereby became the first Spaniard to set eyes upon the marvels of Tenochtitlán, forty miles to the west. After peering into the crater, which reminded them of a glass oven boiling at its hardest, the three men were making their descent when an eruption started. 'It began to rain ashes and flames,' recounts Gómara, 'then hot cinders, and finally very large pieces of burning stone. If they had not found shelter under a rock they would have been burned to death. When they finally returned alive and well, the Indians crowded round and stared at them, kissing their garments as if they were miraculous beings, or gods. The Indians gave them little presents, such was their amazement at the feat, for these simple people believe the volcano is the mouth of hell, where bad rulers and tyrants are sent when they die to purge their sins.'

From Amecameca they began the last stage of their epic journey, climbing up through the high pass, labouring in the thin air and enduring a snow storm. It was a gruelling ten miles. Then finally it was downhill once more, to the village of Mixquic and the edge of the vast lake. At last they had reached the kernel of the Empire. At intervals messages and petitions arrived from Moctezuma. Four Aztec chiefs, one of them a brother of Moctezuma, brought a rich offering of gold and precious stones, and begged Cortés to turn back. 'They brought me about three thousand dollars in gold,' wrote Cortés in the Second Despatch, 'and told me it was from Moctezuma. He urged me not to insist on coming to his city. His country had little food, the roads were bad, the city was on the water and could only be entered by means of canoes. I had only to say what I wanted and it would be given to me. He would pay me an annual tribute which would be taken to the coast or to any place I named.' We can detect the plaintive and demoralized note that had characterized Moctezuma's utterances from the outset.

The plea served no purpose. Cortés had not crossed the Atlantic, the Caribbean and the freezing cordilleras to be fobbed off with lesser promises now the larger prize was at hand. He brushed aside a similar petition presented to him by Cacama, the young lord of Texcoco, a nephew of Moctezuma, who came down twenty miles from the north to throw himself across the Spanish path. The same treatment was accorded the lord of Ixtapalapa, the beautiful city which could be reckoned an actual suburb of Tenochtitlán. On reaching Ixtapalapa, Cortés had now set his foot on the southern causeway that would bring him to the centre of the great city which his men had glimpsed when they were among the mountains, and whose extent and loveliness had so much excited them. They traversed the causeway, as they had traversed the ultimate miles, in a mood that combined awe, elation and self-congratulation with unrelieved watchfulness, for they knew Moctezuma would destroy them if he could summon up the nerve to do it. They pushed ahead surrounded by the swirling throngs of Indians who had streamed out of their towns to see the 'gods'—Tlamanalco, Chalco, Coatepec, Coatlínchan, Xochimilco, and as far afield as Chapūltepec, Tlacopán and Atzcapotzalco. Mexicans love a show. There was also the horde of their own Indian supporters whom they had pressed into service along the way, and of whose loyalties they could never be completely sure. 'With such wonderful sights to gaze on,' relates Díaz. 'we did not know what to say, or if this was real that we saw before our eyes. On the land there were great cities, and on the lake many more. The lake was crowded with canoes. At intervals along the causeway were many bridges, and before us was the great city of Tenochtitlán. As for us, we were scarcely four hundred strong, and we well remembered the many warnings we had received to beware of entering the city, since they would kill us as soon as they had us inside. Let the reader consider whether there is not much to ponder in this narrative of mine. What men in all the world have shown such daring?'

The most arresting account of the historic meeting which took place on November 8, 1519, when a great man of Europe first encountered a great man of the Americas, was that later given by Indian eye-witnesses to Sahagún. The sharp ears of the Indians even captured the very words in which their Emperor expressed himself. There is no doubt from the tenor of his speech that Moctezuma considered the Spaniards to be gods; and if he did not take Cortés to be Quetzalcóatl himself, then he took him to be at least the surrogate of that god, whom the forerunners of the Aztecs had injured and driven out. We must remember, as we note the fear and despair in Moctezuma's voice, that the Spaniards not only appeared as eerie in Aztec eyes as if they were visitors from another planet, but that they also came as deities, as overlords, as avengers, in accordance with ancient prophecy. Their advent had been accompanied by signs from heaven. Their godhead had been demonstrated by the supernatural weapons they brought with them, their invulnerability by their ability to defeat armies fifty times larger than their own. What use was it to struggle against the gods? One can only admire the dignity and fortitude with which Moctezuma, like a hero in a tragic drama, went forth to meet what he took to be his doom (see Plate 7).

But first, as so frequently, let us allow honest old Bernal Díaz to set the scene, in his own incomparable fashion:

'Who could now count,' he asks, 'the multitude of men, women and boys in the streets, on the roof-tops and in canoes on the waterways, who had come out to see us? It was a wonderful sight. As I write, it all comes before my eyes as if it had happened only yesterday.

'We marched along the causeway to a point where another small causeway branches off to another city called Coyoacán, and there, beside some towerlike buildings, which were their shrines, we were met by many more *caciques* and dignities in very rich cloaks. The different chieftains wore different brilliant liveries, and the causeways were full of them. Moctezuma had sent these great *caciques* in advance to receive us, and as soon as they came before Cortés they told him in their language that we were welcome, and as a sign of peace they touched the ground with their hands and kissed it.

'There we halted for some time while Cacama, the lord of Texcoco, and the lords of Ixtapalapa, Tlacopán, and Coyoacán went ahead to meet the great Moctezuma, who approached in a rich litter, accompanied by other great lords and feudal *caciques* who owned vassals. When we came near to Mexico, at a place where there were some other small towers, the great Moctezuma descended from his litter, and these other great *caciques* supported him beneath a marvellously rich canopy of green feathers, decorated with gold work, silver, pearls, and turquoises, which hung from a sort of border. It was a marvellous sight. The great Moctezuma was magnificently clad, in their fashion, and wore sandals, the soles of which were of gold and the upper parts ornamented with precious stones. And the four lords who supported him were richly clad also in garments that seem to have been kept ready for them on the road so that they could accompany their master. For they had not worn clothes like this when they came out to receive us. There were four other great *caciques* who carried the canopy above their heads, and many more lords who walked before the great Moctezuma, sweeping the ground on which he was to tread, and laying down cloaks so that his feet should not touch the earth. Not one of these chieftains dared to look him in the face. All kept their eyes lowered most reverently except those four lords, his nephews, who were supporting him.

'When Cortés saw, heard, and was told that the great Moctezuma was approaching, he dismounted from his horse, and when he came near to Moctezuma each bowed deeply to the other. Moctezuma welcomed our Captain, and Cortés, speaking through Doña Marina, answered by wishing him very good health. Cortés, I think, offered Moctezuma his right hand, but Moctezuma refused it and extended his own. Then Cortés brought out a necklace which he had been holding. It was made of elaborately worked and coloured glass beads called *margaritas*, and was strung on a gold cord and dipped in musk to give it a good odour. This he hung round the great Moctezuma's neck, and as he did so attempted to embrace him. But the great princes who stood round Moctezuma grasped Cortés' arm to prevent him for they considered this an indignity.'

Now Sahagún:

'And so the Spaniards reached the fork in the causeway. They had reached their goal. And there Moctezuma had been making ready to meet them, with his noblemen, grandees and magnates. They had all come out to greet the newcomers. Magnificent flowers had been arranged in huge floats: the heart-flower, the shield-flower, and in the centre the rare yellow-flowers of heavenly perfume. There were wreaths and garlands of flowers, also collars of gold, collars of massive hanging beads, and collars of finely-woven material.

'Then came the strangers to the place where Moctezuma waited. Then the captain and his soldiers were given gifts, garlands, wreaths, strings of flowers to circle their breasts, chaplets for their heads. They were given gold collars and all manner of gifts and tokens of welcome. And after an exchange of collars, Cortés said to Moctezuma:

' "Is it you? Is it really you? Are you truly Moctezuma?"

'And Moctezuma answered:

' "I am he."

'At that he put his foot to the ground. He approached Cortés and bowed to him, bending his head. He addressed him as follows:

' "Lord, you have reached your destination. You are tired and weary. You have arrived in your city of Tenochtitlán. You have arrived to take possession of your throne. For what a short time have we, your substitutes, guarded and preserved it for you. For what a short time have our kings Itzcóatl, the elder Moctezuma, Axayácatl, Tizoc, Ahuítzotl, governed the land and held sway on your behalf. Its people lie beneath your hand and under your protection. What would those rulers think if they could see what has happened to their descendants, if they could return and witness what has come upon me—me, the last remaining survivor of my line? No, I am not dreaming. I am not waking from a dream. I am not asleep. Now I have seen you. Now my eyes have rested on your face. For five to ten days I have been troubled; the features that regarded me from the Region of Mystery were stony. But now you have come through clouds and snow. This is what our kings and those who ruled this your city told us: that you would come to assume your rightful place. And it has come to pass. You have come, eager but fatigued. Weary, you have come to earth to occupy your palaces. Rest now. Welcome to your kingdom, lords!"

'When Moctezuma had finished speaking, La Malinche gave Cortés a translation of his words. Then Cortés, through the mouth of La Malinche, replied in his strange and foreign tongue:

' "Be glad, Moctezuma. Fear nothing. We love you greatly. Our heart rejoices. We have seen and spoken with you. We have wished for many months to set eyes on you. We have reached your house in Tenochtitlán. Hear what we say with an easy mind."

'Then they took one another by the hand, and their followers did likewise. They embraced each other to show their affection for one another.'

* * *

The mutual respect was not destined to last, although the first six days were uneventful. The newcomers were escorted to the centre of the city, and Cortés and his officers, as befitted gods, were lodged in one of the palaces of the Aztec emperors. They occupied the palace of Axayácatl, adjoining the Serpent Wall on the east side of the sacred precinct. It is now buried deep below the foundations of the Zócalo. Facing it, on the opposite side of the square, was the palace of the earlier Moctezuma, in which his later namesake was living at that time; and on the south side was Moctezuma II's larger, personal establishment (see Fig. 7). Cortés and his captains were therefore almost within touching distance of the Great Temple jointly dedicated to Tlaloc and Huitzilopochtli and the adjacent Temple of Tezcatlipoca. They were thus able to watch the gory rites of Aztec religion at the closest possible range.

The following morning they crossed the square to pay Moctezuma a ceremonial visit. The 'old palace' of Moctezuma, like the palace of Axayácatl, has long since disappeared; in its place stands a handsome baroque edifice, built on the site of a viceregal palace later constructed by Cortés himself, and which since 1775 has been used as the Monte de Piedad or national pawnshop. If one cannot view the actual palace in which the two men conferred with each other, it is nevertheless still possible to tread the place where they walked and stand beneath the same sky.

Their meeting was agreeable. Afterwards the Spanish captains left on a guided tour of the city that occupied them fully for several days. There is no space here to describe the marvels of Tenochtitlán as seen by Cortés and his friends. Cortés himself devoted to them a large section of his Second Despatch, written in October of the following year for the instruction and edification of the Emperor Charles; and both Gómara and Bernal Díaz gave extended lyrical accounts of them in their narratives. One can imagine the sense of wonder on the faces of the Spanish soldiers as they wandered around the royal palaces, the royal zoos, aviaries and gardens, the teeming markets and the squares with their lofty temples, or were rowed like tourists in Venice around the sparkling spiderweb of the canals. Most of them had never seen a real city in their lives, except perhaps for a few days in Seville on their way to the Indies. Santo Domingo and Santiago de Cuba were shanty-towns compared to Tenochtitlán. Those of Cortés' officers who had fought in Italy had seen Naples and Rome; but Cortés himself, to our knowledge, had never visited a city larger than Salamanca, Córdoba or Seville. And now he and his captains were confronted by the dreamlike vistas and airy whiteness of the most original capital city that ever existed.

While they were strolling or sailing about with their Aztec guides, many of the Spaniards were conscious of a chill in the air that could not be ascribed to the advent of winter. They were treated like kings; their

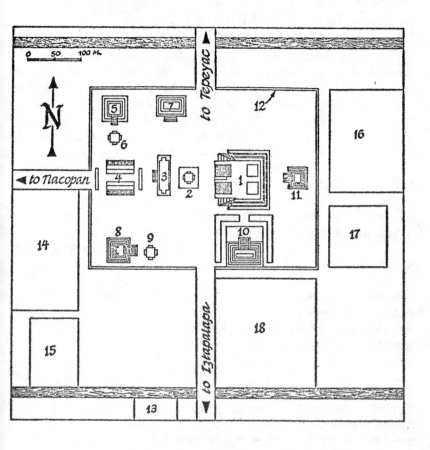

THE CENTRE OF TENOCHTITLÁN-MEXICO IN 1519
(After Michael D. Coe)

1. Great Temple of Tlaloc and Huitzilopochtli. 2. Platform for stone of Tizoc. 3. Tzompantli (skull rack). 4. Ball court. 5. 'Eagle House' of the Sun Temple. 6. Platform of the 'Eagle House', base for Calendar Stone. 7. Snake Temple. 8. Temple of Xipe Totec, God of Spring. 9. Platform for gladiatorial stone. 10. Temple of Tezcatlipoca. 11. Temple of Colhuacán, the former temple of Huitzilopochtli. 12. Snake Wall, enclosing the sacred precinct. 13. 'Black House' of the Temple of Coatlicue. 14. Palace of Moctezuma I (1440–69). 15. 'House of the Songs'. 16. Palace of Axayácatl (1469–81). 17. Royal Aviary. 18. Palace of Moctezuma II (1502–20) horses were fed on corn and bedded down each night in flowers; but beneath the smiling surface they detected hostility and treachery. It needed very little reflection to appreciate that they were in a truly frightening situation. One small accident or incident, one signal from Moctezuma, could mean their annihilation. As Cortés observed to the Emperor Charles: 'We Spaniards are somewhat touchy and importunate, and if by some chance we should provoke him and make him angry he could do us such injury with his enormous power that no memory would remain of us.' True, they had managed to repulse the Tlaxcalans by forming squares on an open plain, where there was room to manœuvre: but how could they hope to repulse the Aztecs, caught as they were at the heart of a crowded city? Would they barricade themselves in one or other of the palaces? There could only be one end to such a course. Before many days had passed they would be starved out or burned out, and those who survived would be dragged to the summit of the Great Temple where black-clad priests awaited them, glistening stone knives in their hands.

It was foolish to remain passive and await the inevitable. They must seize the initiative: that was the Spanish way. They had observed how unquestioningly Moctezuma was obeyed by his subjects, how precious his person was to them. They had grasped that in this community which was still in many respects barbaric the king was the lynch-pin of order and authority. They should kidnap him and hold him as a hostage. A number of them went to Cortés and urged that this course should be taken. Even Sandoval, Cortés' closest associate, was among the group headed by Alvarado, Ordaz and Velázquez de León who waited on him.

Cortés hesitated. In later years he admitted to Gómara that during those critical days 'he paced back and forth for a very long while, alone and very apprehensive about the great enterprise of arresting Moctezuma'. He temporized, unwilling to take so drastic a step. His instinct was always to attempt mildness and cajolery before using naked force. Like the true diplomat he was, he knew the danger and inadvisability of driving an opponent to extremes. He therefore returned a refusal to his captains' proposal—but overnight an event occurred that made him change his mind. Two Tlaxcalan messengers arrived with the news that there had been a rising at Villa Rica. Some of the Totonacs, at the instigation of agents of Moctezuma, had ambushed and killed Cortés' representative, Escalante. They had also killed Escalante's horse and six Spanish soldiers. Cortés' situation had suddenly become more precarious than ever. It now appeared highly likely that he and his men would probably have nowhere to go even if they managed to fight their way clear of Tenochtitlán.

He assembled an armed squad of thirty men and marched across the square to Moctezuma's palace. In words that were courteous but firm he informed the Emperor that he was under arrest, and that he should make ready to return with the Spaniards to the palace of Axayácatl. Moctezuma was dumbfounded. Immediately he gave orders for the arrest of the Aztec *provocateurs* who were alleged to have been guilty of Escalante's murder: but he refused to leave the palace. Cortés argued with him. The Spanish captains grew impatient. 'What's the use of talking?' broke in Velázquez de León. 'Either take him or knife him. If we don't, we're dead men.'

For Cortés, the matter was not quite so simple. He was a man of foresight; he could project himself beyond the immediate problem. He foresaw that his behaviour with regard to Moctezuma would affect the fortunes of Mexico and of himself in the days to come. He would be accountable to the Emperor in Valladolid for his conduct towards the Emperor in Tenochtitlán. Moctezuma, after all, was a monarch, and this was the age of Divine Right. Men who laid violent hands on barbaric emperors in the New World might be the sort of men who might be tempted to lay hands on civilized emperors in the Old World. The surest way for Cortés to acquire a reputation as an unprincipled adventurer was to deal harshly with Moctezuma. It was not a reputation he wanted, either in the eyes of his king, his fellow-countrymen, or of posterity—the latter an ever-present preoccupation to a man of the Renaissance.

His instinct was sound: many of his frustrations and disappointments in the years ahead were to stem from the allegedly brutal way in which he treated Moctezuma. But at the present moment he had no choice. He continued to try and soften the blow—'but Juan Velázquez de Léon burst out in his high and terrifying voice, and when Moctezuma asked La Malinche what they were saying so loudly she, in her quick-witted way, replied: "Lord Moctezuma, please accompany them immediately to their quarters and make no protest. I know they will treat you very honourably as befits your station. But if you stay here, you will die." '

So Moctezuma bowed to the inevitable, and was hurried across the sacred precinct to the Spanish stronghold in the palace of Axayácatl. There he was placed under constant guard, in secure and inaccessible quarters. And with his arrest and incarceration, the tempo of the tragedy quickened, its note grew darker.

*   *   *

Cortés sought to make Moctezuma's imprisonment as tolerable as possible.

With his ingrained habit of playing off one side against the other, he made it privately clear to Moctezuma that he, Cortés, was also a virtual prisoner of his own lieutenants. He had already done his best to show Moctezuma, at the moment of arrest, that he had only adopted his present course with reluctance. He now saw an opportunity to impose his will on the Aztec Empire, and through the Aztecs on the rest of the country, by standing behind Moctezuma and using the Emperor as his mouthpiece. Therefore it was to his advantage to keep Moctezuma in his present passive and compliant mood.

On the other hand, he could not ignore the recent events at Villa Rica, nor Moctezuma's part in them. When two to three weeks later, the Aztecs whom Moctezuma had ordered to return from the coast reached Tenochtitlán, they freely admitted that they had instigated the attack on Escalante at Moctezuma's behest. It was necessary to take action to show that the Spaniards would not vacillate and could not be intimidated. Cortés arrested all fifteen of the Aztec *provocateurs*, tried them for murder and rebellion, convicted them, and sentenced them to death. To heighten the effect, on the day of the execution he had Moctezuma put in chains. Then the fifteen offenders were solemnly burned in the sacred precinct. Both actions were probably a mistake, though it is difficult to see what else Cortés could have done under the circumstances. Chaining Moctezuma, though it served to frighten the Emperor himself, was an unforgivable affront to the pride of his subjects. As for the so-called criminals, Cortés wished to make their execution an example of Spanish justice: but it would hardly have been understood in that way by the Aztecs. First, in the eyes of their countrymen the victims were patriots and heroes; secondly, the violent and unfamiliar manner of their death would suggest that the Spaniards themselves, for all their protestations of humanity, were no more averse than the Aztecs to shedding blood. In fact, they had methods of killing people every bit as gruesome as a ritual death beneath the priest's knife.

Cortés, as if acknowledging that he had made a tactical error, released Moctezuma the same day, removing the fetters with his own hands, speaking as soothingly to him as if he were gentling a scared horse. From then onwards Moctezuma was accorded every consideration and mark of respect. He was attended by his own people, and apart from a restriction on his movements he led his normal life in every particular. Cortés had demonstrated who was master; he now sought to reduce the sense of crisis and excitement and bring about, if he could, an atmosphere of normality and stability.

He took, of course, an early opportunity to give his deeds the gloss of legality. He required Moctezuma to make a formal act of submission to the Emperor Charles. It was not a matter that could be hurried, as Moctezuma had been instructed to summon his chiefs and administrators from the furthest corner of his dominions and hold conferences with them. Moctezuma was allowed to consult the chiefs at leisure and in private. Several of them refused to come to the capital, declaring their implacable hostility to the Spaniards; and even among the chiefs who obeyed the call there was not complete unanimity. But eventually Moctezuma persuaded the majority to swear fealty to the White Emperor whom none of them had ever seen and could scarcely visualize. In December, 1519, in the great hall of the palace of Axayácatl, the Aztec noblemen and Spanish captains, dressed in all their finery, met to ratify a solemn act binding the Empire of the Aztecs to the Empire of the Habsburgs. Cortés, who was later careful to assure the Emperor Charles that he had treated Moctezuma with all due deference, set forth Moctezuma's speech in his Second Despatch as follows:

' "My brothers and friends, you know that for a long time you and your fathers and grandfathers have been and are subjects and vassals of my forefathers and myself, and that you have always been well treated by them and by me, and that you have likewise done what good subjects are obliged to do towards their rightful sovereign. I also believe that you have kept in mind, from your forefathers, that we are natives of this country, and that they came to it from another, very far off; that they were brought here by a sovereign whose vassals they all were, who left them in it, but who returned after a long time; that he found our forefathers already settled and established in this country, and married to the women, and having a great increase of sons, so that they did not choose to return with him, nor much less to receive him as their sovereign; and that he departed, saying that he would return, or send such a force that they would be compelled to submit. You also know that we have always expected him, and according to what the Captain has told us of that King and Lord who has sent him here, and according to the direction whence he says he comes, I hold it to be certain, and you must also hold it thus, that his sovereign is the one we have been expecting, especially as the Captain says that they have had information there respecting us.

' "Since our predecessors did not act justly towards their sovereign lord, let us do so, and let us give thanks to our gods, because that which they looked for has come to pass in our times. I heartily pray you, inasmuch as all this is well known to you that, as you have obeyed me as your sovereign, henceforward you will regard and obey this great king, because he is your rightful sovereign, and, in his place, you must hold this, his Captain; also, that all the tributes and services, which until now you have paid to me, you do give to him, because I also shall pay tribute, and serve in all that he may command me. In so doing, you will do your duty as you are obliged to do, and you will, moreover, in doing this, give me much pleasure."

'As he told them all this, he wept the greatest tears, and heaved the greatest sighs a man can give vent to. And all those lords who heard him wept so much that they were unable to answer for a long time. And I assure Your Sacred Majesty that there was not one among the Spaniards who did not feel great compassion.

'After they had restrained their tears, the assembled lords answered that they regarded Moctezuma as their sovereign, and they promised to comply with all that should be commanded them in the royal name of Your Majesty, and that they would give to Your Highness the tributes and services which heretofore they had given to Moctezuma. All this passed before a notary public, who at my request recorded it in due form, in the presence of many Spanish witnesses.'

Salvador de Madariaga has a significant comment on that day's ceremony. He calls it 'a strange ceremony which bears all the stamp of Cortés. His Salamanca days, his "letters" side, his legalistic turn of mind, his implicit belief in a universal commonwealth of men of reason, within which things must happen according to recognized rules, are all alive in it. Just as he would not take any native girl to his private rooms before she had been christened, so he would not "accept" the wealth and power of the Empire he had conquered until the visible head of that Empire had signed away his own independence before the royal notary of the Christian Emperor whose crown symbolized the unity of all mankind. Such is the psychological background on which we must imagine that historic day, in order to form an adequate estimate of its meaning. On that day, the Christian world acquires a new dominion; the Middle Ages, or in other words, the Roman Empire baptized in the Jordan, opens a window on to a different sector of mankind, and, historically, the Renaissance begins: the Christian widens into man. The experience was, as usual, saddened by grief, for man cannot rise one step up the steep *teocalli* of history without covering with blood and tears the step he has just left behind'.

*   *   *

Both in the personalities of the men involved, and the manœuvring in which they were now engaged, one might draw some interesting parallels between King Charles I and Oliver Cromwell. Their association is reminiscent of the period after the Great Civil War when King Charles was confined to Carisbrook Castle in the Isle of Wight. Cromwell had won the war, but was finding it difficult to rule the conquered kingdom; and the deposed monarch, in comfortable captivity, was plotting secretly with the victor's enemies. Cortés had a Cromwellian resoluteness and a Cromwellian rigour, though it was overlaid with an urbanity and smoothness of manner that had no part in the make-up of the Great Protector; while Moctezuma had the mildness, guile and cultured air of the Stuart king, together with the pathos engendered by the spectacle of a great man brought low.

Cortés took pains to allow the royal captive every latitude. He cast himself in the role of Moctezuma's prime minister or chief courtier, sedulously meeting the Emperor's wishes and tending to his well-being. No opportunity was lost to make the imperial figurehead happy or to cater to his amusement. Cortés was delighted when Moctezuma became very attached to the young Spanish page who was assigned to wait on him, and Moctezuma and the Spanish captains were on the friendliest terms possible under the strained circumstances. There is no doubt that the Spaniards genuinely liked and admired Moctezuma. They played games of chance with him, they took him on hunting trips, and they sailed with him up and down the lake in one of the four sloops which Cortés had ordered to be constructed. The Emperor loved to sit under a painted awning as the Spanish mariners tacked from one shore to the other, laughing with pleasure when the gunners were ordered to fire a *feu de joie* in his honour. There were one or two disagreeable incidents. Several of the officers or guards were coarse and tactless. One night a sentry made water in the corridor outside the Emperor's room. Moctezuma was shocked by this crude behaviour, and reported the man to the captain of the guard; but when the sentry received a tongue-lashing, the kind-hearted Emperor gave him a present. Thereupon the man relieved himself again, in the logical but simple-minded expectation of getting another present. He was then permanently removed to less congenial duties at the other end of the palace. In general, however, relations between the captive and his foreign masters were cordial, so that it was scarcely noticed when Cortés also quietly incarcerated three other leading men of the kingdom, including Cacama, lord of Texcoco, who might otherwise have caused trouble. The Spanish commander was making his usual play with the velvet glove.

The building of the sloops was only one indication that, as usual, he was looking ahead. Sailing-ships would constitute a powerful weapon in any future warfare, for they could attack any of the lakeside cities or be employed as troop-carriers; they might also prove useful to effect an escape from the wharves of Tenochtitlán in the case of a sudden emergency. Cortés was not a man to allow time to slip by without utilizing it to the utmost. During these months of uneasy truce he sent out, under safe-conduct from Moctezuma, small parties of intelligent and experienced Spaniards with Aztec guides. They ranged far and wide, prospecting for gold and precious metals. He also sent an expedition to the coast of the Caribbean to make a more thorough search than had been possible hitherto for a good deep-water port. Already he was looking forward to the time when his treasure-fleets would set their course for Spain.

Gold was the first cause and justification of all his exertions. He never relaxed his search for it. However, his feelings, now that it was at last beginning to flow in so abundantly, were probably not unmixed. It was not difficult to foresee that in the present delicate situation a sudden shower of gold could prove a distracting and even demoralizing influence. Soon after their arrival in Tenochtitlán the Spaniards had made an electrifying discovery. In sounding the wall of a room in the palace of Axayácatl, looking for a place to erect an altar, a Spanish carpenter stumbled on a hidden cache of treasure. An incredible wealth of gold, silver and precious stones was revealed to the astonished eyes of the Spaniards. Its value was so enormous that Cortés, at a loss what to do, immediately ordered it to be sealed up again. This inevitably caused suspicion and discontent among his more importunate followers. Moreover, in addition to this Aladdin's Cave, more treasure kept accumulating in the palace of Axayácatl during the weeks ahead. Cortés had instructed Moctezuma to secure tribute from the Aztec cities and from his client states for transmission to the Emperor Charles. No doubt the elaborate ceremony by which Moctezuma swore allegiance to the White Emperor had been partially designed to enable Cortés to take possession by comparatively legal means of this mountain of wealth.

It was splendid to hit upon treasure in such awesome quantities, but embarrassing to have done so at such a ticklish time. The day came when the counting and distribution of the treasure could be put off no longer. Curiously, the ceremony was precipitated by Moctezuma himself, who summoned Cortés and his men and told them: 'I wish you to know, my lord, and my lords, captains and soldiers, that I am indebted to your great king and bear him good will, both for being such a great king and for having sent from distant lands to make enquiries about me. Take this tribute which I have collected: only haste prevents there being more. What I have got ready for the Emperor is the whole of the treasure I received from my father, which is under your hand in your own apartments. I know very well that as soon as you came here you opened the door and inspected it all, then shut it up again as it was before. When you send it to him, tell him in your letter: "This is sent to you by your loyal vassal Moctezuma." '

It took three days to remove the gold objects from the sealed room, list them, and sort them into three heaps whose combined value was estimated at six hundred thousand pesos. The more beautiful pieces of jewellery were spared, but the rest were broken up, melted down into gold bars, and officially stamped with an iron die. Then the royal notary and the men designated as the Emperor Charles' representatives removed and took charge of the Royal Fifth. It was at this stage that trouble started. It began when Cortés, the poor boy from Medellín, who was no more immune to gold-fever than any other normal human being, demanded and took a second full fifth of the treasure for himself. We must remember, in fairness, that his men had promised this to him after the landing at Villa Rica, and that he was naturally interested in recovering the money—his entire capital—which he had originally sunk in the expedition. He was not being greedy or unreasonable. However, there followed a long series of other deductions. These included compensation set aside for Diego Velázquez for his ships which were destroyed at Villa Rica—a nice example of Cortés' lawyer's sense of property, and also of his ever-functioning impulse towards conciliation. Double shares were next drawn by the captains, by the horsemen, by the musketeers, by the crossbowmen, and even by the two priests. As usual, there was little left over for the infantrymen. The footsoldiers were therefore disgusted, as they had every right to be, by the mean treatment accorded them. They were so angry they refused even the paltry amount offered them, telling Cortés that since he had stolen everything else he might as well take that too. Cortés attempted to soothe their feelings by slipping a few pieces of gold to one man or another; but this satisfied no one. All manner of quarrels and squabbles arose. Fights over cards and dice broke out. The royal notary and Juan Velázquez de León drew their swords and dealt each other two wounds apiece. Predictably, the presence of such a treasure-trove resulted in a general moral degeneration, accompanied by a serious weakening of soldierly standards.

If part of the coming *débâcle* could be blamed on ordinary venality, it might be argued that Cortés was also betrayed by his idealism and piety. From the beginning of his sojourn in Tenochtitlán he had indulged in religious debates with Moctezuma. The conversations continued almost daily, and since both men were endowed with outstanding intelligence their discourse was conducted on a high level. Cortés, having induced Moctezuma to accept a Christian king, now wished him to accept the

Christian god. He also wished to persuade Moctezuma to give up the practice of human sacrifice. During the whole of the Spanish visit to Tenochtitlán the daily quota of victims was offered up. As at Tlaxcala, Cortés was simply not in a sufficiently dominant position to ban outright the particular aspects of Indian religion that revolted him. The surest way to bring a nest of hornets around his ears was to interfere with the Aztec religion. Moctezuma, notwithstanding his conviction that his gods had deserted him, still continued to pay them a pathetic respect.

Nevertheless Cortés chafed. Although he was a dedicated practitioner of diplomatic double-dealing, this kind of spiritual hypocrisy did not sit well with him. As Madariaga says of him, 'under his clear mind, there was a hot, religious heart'. The intensity of his religious belief was that of any Spaniard of his age; the flame of faith burned high in the men of the Siglo de Oro. As Octavio Paz pointed out, in a passage already quoted, this was the epoch of Spanish fanaticism, of Spanish extremism. It is often assumed that Cortés was a religious cynic—but in fact he depended on his religion even more firmly, if that were possible, than Moctezuma. He had, as his words show, a mature and philosophic grasp of the fundamentals of his creed; but his faith was not merely abstract, it was practical. It was that faith that had brought victory to Spanish arms in the long centuries of the Reconquest; it was that faith that had brought Cortés and his little legion from Villa Rica to Tenochtitlán. When the Spanish troops shouted the names of Saint James or Saint Peter it was not a simple war-cry, it was a sacred talisman. Cortés was a vigorous young man of thirty-four, and he believed in the martial efficacy of his spiritual patrons as fervently as his opponents believed in Huitzilopochtli and Tezcatlipoca. Andrés de Tapia, in his *Relación sobre la Conquista de Mexico*, relates the remarkable scene that took place when Cortés finally and unexpectedly lost patience, during a visit to the shrine in the Great Temple: 'Cortés went up, just to pass the time with eight or ten Spaniards. All the inside walls were composed of stone images of idols, and in their mouths and bodies they had much blood, as thick as two or three fingers. He inspected the idols, sighed sadly, saying, for we all heard it: "O God, why dost Thou allow the Devil to be so much honoured in this land?" By this time many priests and others had come upon the scene, warned by the noise of the bells, and Cortés said to them: "God, who made heaven and earth, made you and us and all, and created that whereby we live. If we are good He will take us to Heaven, and if not, we shall go to Hell, as I shall explain at more length when we can understand each other better. I desire that, here where you have these idols, there shall be the image of God and of his blessed Mother. Bring water to wash these walls, and we shall remove all this stuff from here.'

They laughed, as if it were an impossible thing, and said: "Not only this city, but the whole land, as one, hold these as their gods, and all this is here by the power of Huitzilopochtli, whose creatures we are. Everyone holds his parents and children as nothing compared to this god, and would rather die, and on seeing you come up here, they have all run to arms and wish to die for their gods." Cortés told a Spaniard to go and see that Moctezuma's person was well secured, and that thirty or forty men should come to support him. Then he told the priests: "I shall be happy to fight for my God against your gods, who are nothing." Then, before the Spaniards he had sent for had arrived, he was angered by some words he heard. Taking hold of an iron bar, which happened to be there, he began to smash the idols: and I pledge my faith as a gentleman, and swear to God that it is true, that I can see now how he leapt up in a supernatural way, and swung forward holding the bar midway, striking the idol high up on its eyes, and smashing its gold mask, saying: "We must risk something for God". '

Madariaga, commenting on this passage in a chapter to which he gives the revealing title *Cortés Throws Away His Conquest*, writes: 'This remarkable narrative confirms in every way our reading of Cortés' character. He was at the time the virtual, undisputed owner of an Empire which he had conquered by a masterpiece of foresight, caution, shrewdness, patience and astuteness. And one morning, as a pastime, he went to see the Great Teocalli. He sees the idols, and the gruesome traces of their inhuman worship, and he grows sad, wonders, questions God, offers to serve Him by freeing the land from that abomination; then, he argues about it with the priests; hears their resolution to die for their gods, and the cautious captain in him rapidly takes a few tactical precautions. But, does he change his strategy? Does he for one second reflect that in one minute he may destroy the magnificent success of a whole winter of hardship, courage and intelligent perseverance? Does he think of his gold now safely stowed, of his power now safely established? Not for a second. He seizes an iron bar, even before the Spaniards he has sent for have arrived, and leaps on the idols to smash them to pieces before the dumbfounded priests. Tapia, and no doubt also his companions, saw him at this moment as greater than himself, rising in space as high as the gigantic idols he was challenging and destroying. He *was* greater than himself. "I consider that God is above nature," Cortés had written once to the Emperor. So, now, drawn always upwards by God, Cortés rose "supernaturally". The march begun on the swamps of Veracruz, higher and higher and ever higher up the slopes of the mountains to the very heart of lofty Mexico, had to end in this highest of all ascents—on top of that tower of the Chief Teocalli, where Cortés hit Huitzilopochtli between the eyes. That morning was the culminating moment of the conquest. It was the triumph of man's yearning for ever higher things over his contented enjoyment of the ordinary; of ambition and endeavour over success, of faith over reason. Had he been a less reasonable man, his action might have to be discounted as that of a hothead, below the standard which man must reach to be fully grown to manhood; but no. Cortés was caution and reason incarnate. His action was not below reason, but above reason. And that is why it is legendary, as are all those acts whereby man rises above men.'

Cortés' own account of these religious proceedings agrees with that of Andrés de Tapia. He told the Emperor Charles in his Second Despatch: 'The figures of the idols exceed in size the body of a large man. They are made of all the seeds and vegetables which they eat, ground up and mixed with one another, and kneaded with the hearts' blood of human beings. The breasts are opened while these unhappy creatures are still alive; the hearts are removed, and the blood which comes out is kneaded with the flour to make the quantity necessary for a large statue. When the statues are finished the priests offer them more hearts, which have also been sacrificed, and smear the faces with the blood. The idols are dedicated to different things. To obtain favours in war these people have one idol, for harvests another, and for everything they desire they have special idols whom they honour and serve. I overturned the idols in which these people believe the most and rolled them down the stairs. Then I had those chapels cleansed, for they were full of blood from the sacrifices; and I set up images of Our Lady and other Saints in them. This disturbed Moctezuma and the natives a good deal, and they told me not to do it. They said that if it became known, the people would rise against me, as they believed that these idols gave them all their temporal goods. If the people allowed them to be ill-treated, they would be angered and give nothing, and would take away the fruits of the soil and cause the people to die of want. I made them understand by the interpreters how deceived they were in putting their hope in idols made of unclean things by their own hands. I told them that they should know there was but one God, the Universal Lord of all, Who had created the heavens and earth and all things, and them, and us, Who was without beginning and immortal; that they should adore Him and believe in Him and not in any creature or thing. All of them, especially Moctezuma, answered that they had already told me they were not natives of this country and that it was a long time since their forefathers had come to it. Therefore, they might err in some points of their belief since it was so long since they had left their native land, while I, who had arrived only recently, should know better than they what they should believe, and if I would explain to them, they would accept what I told them as being for the best. Moctezuma and many chiefs of the city remained with me until the idols were taken away, the chapels cleansed, and the images put up, and they all wore happy faces. I forbade them to sacrifice human beings to the idols, as they were accustomed, for besides its being very hateful to God, Your Majesty had also prohibited it by your laws and commanded that those who killed should be put to death. They abolished it, and in all the time I remained in the city I never again saw them sacrifice any human creature.'

We may take the assertion that the bystanders 'all wore happy faces' with a pinch of salt. Such spirited tampering with their religion, the central core of their existence, only added to the deepening atmosphere of resentment and menace.

If this were not serious enough, a storm that had long been brewing in Spain and Santo Domingo suddenly burst upon him from the direction of Villa Rica.

* * *

The two envoys who had brought the First Despatch and the King's Fifth to Spain, Portocarrero and Montejo, had scored a signal success in obtaining personal access to the Emperor in spite of the opposition of Bishop Fonseca. Their despatch had reached the Emperor at Barcelona; their meeting with him had taken place at Tordesillas, while he was visiting his mother and technical co-ruler of Spain, Joanna the Mad; and the Royal Fifth had eventually been delivered to him, after many delays, at La Coruña, on the eve of his departure for the Low Countries. The young monarch was already distracted by the Cyclopean problems of European polity for which he was to strive all his life to find solutions—and for which no solutions existed. He was delighted with the promising tidings from the New World, pleased by the token instalment of gold, and diverted by the two Indian men and two Indian women whom Cortés' deputies presented to him. He showed a close personal interest in the progress of the expedition that served to give notice to Fonseca that in seeking to crush Cortés he would have to tread carefully.

But Fonseca was not a timid man, and the Emperor's half-endorsement of Cortés did not deter him. When the Emperor sailed from La Coruña, the Bishop had a clear field. He thought it wiser not to arrest Portocarrero and Montejo, as he had originally planned. He did not need to, for he had already given orders for the impounding at Seville of the money they had brought for their own expenses. His agents there even stripped them of the sum which they were carrying as a gift from Cortés to his father, for whom, as we have seen, Cortés had a close and filial regard. When the two men rode to Medellín to pay their respects to Martín Cortés, who thereupon decided to travel with them to see the Emperor, they scarcely possessed a peso between them. A pair of penniless adventurers constituted no obstacle to Fonseca. He had already been gathering soldiers, ships and supplies and sending them to Velázquez in Cuba. Now he instructed the Governor to act speedily, with the injunction that the rebel Cortés was to be captured and put to death with the full approval of the Council of the Indies. Like Cortés, the Bishop was a proponent of the *fait accompli*. The Emperor was not yet so attached to the cause of an obscure mercenary that the man's death could not be smoothed over and explained away.

Diego de Velázquez assembled a fleet of no less than nineteen ships. Aboard them he put fourteen hundred men, including nine hundred Spaniards, eighty horses and twenty-three cannon. At their head he placed a man who, like him, had a personal score to settle with Cortés, a man from his own Spanish province of Cuellar. This was an experienced and hard-bitten professional called Pánfilo de Narváez. Narváez sailed from Cuba early in March, made a quick crossing, and anchored close to Villa Rica at San Juan de Ulúa, where Cortés had made his own landfall twelve months before. His force was in every respect superior to that of Cortés, and he looked forward to the latter's quick and easy extinction.

However, if Cortés could reach Tenochtitlán by the exercise of his wits and with a handful of men, there was no reason to suppose that he would be unable to deal with Narváez. And he had an important advantage in his favour: the men who had fought their way to Tenochtitlán with him were veterans. They had long ago learned to master the lesser kinds of fear; they were hardened by battle and inured to the country and its climate. They were the people in possession, with a large slice of the country's wealth in their hands, and with the prospect of acquiring more. Nonetheless, the threat posed by the arrival of Narváez' armada was a formidable one. In dealing with it, Cortés was to display, yet again, the astounding range of his abilities and the adamantine nature of his will.

After the death of Juan de Escalante, he had sent his energetic and trustworthy friend Gonzalo de Sandoval to the coast to take charge and re-establish order at Villa Rica. It was Sandoval who now received Narváez' three envoys and, notwithstanding the fact that he commanded only a pitiful handful of troops, most of them the old and sick members of the original garrison, he seized the emissaries, tied them up in hammocks, and had them carted off to Cortés in Tenochtitlán. From Cortés' point of view Narváez could not have appeared at a more unfavourable moment. His men were widely dispersed, as a result of that series of exploratory undertakings described earlier. Not only was Sandoval detached at Villa Rica with seventy men, but Velázquez de León with a hundred more was a hundred and fifty miles further down the coast in the region of Coatzacoalcos, making an intensive search for the deep-water port which Cortés was so anxious to find. It must always have been clear to Cortés that Diego Velázquez would sooner or later send an avenging army against him, and he was guilty of carelessness in dividing up his forces and being caught unprepared.

Cortés paraded the three hundred Spaniards at Tenochtitlán and made one of his speeches. It was larded with his customary classical allusions—to Caesar and Pompey, Marius and Sulla. He professed to be deeply shocked that the Governor of Cuba had set one Spaniard against another, and had shamefully incited the Indians to attack his own fellow-countrymen. At the end of the speech he received an ovation, which considerably raised his own spirits and that of his troops. He then divided the company into two parts. The larger part, about two hundred strong, he entrusted to Pedro de Alvarado. They were to remain in Tenochtitlán while he took the other hundred men and marched for Villa Rica. After making sure that the palace of Axayácatl had been turned into a fortress, that it was well provisioned, and that Moctezuma was secure there, he took the road for the coast on May 4, 1520.

He marched by way of Cholula and the southern villages of Tlaxcala, hoping to pick up Indian support on the way. The *caciques* proved to be long on promises and short on performance. They sent polite assurances but furnished no troops. No doubt, like Moctezuma, whose agents were soon in contact with Narváez, they believed that Cortés' luck was running out and that they would have to look around for other ways of defending themselves. Undismayed, and keeping excellent discipline, the little band of Spaniards pressed on. As they went, their leader kept up a constant exchange of letters with Narváez. His aim, as ever, was to try to prevail by means of bribery and blandishment before putting the matter to a wasteful trial of arms. He was unsuccessful with Narváez himself, but by employing one of his priests ostensibly as a peacemaker, but actually as a secret agent, he was able to suborn a number of Narváez' more important followers. He treated Narváez' own emissaries with elaborate courtesy, buying them over to his side by means of substantial gifts of gold. Narváez also sought to employ bribery, but without effect: for on this occasion Cortés' men had complete faith in their leader's star. The chief object of

Narváez' attention in this respect was Velázquez de León, who was a kinsman of Diego Velázquez, and whom the latter was confident could be induced to desert Cortés. In an interview with Narváez, the stalwart Velázquez de León, who at that moment could be said to have held Cortés' fate in his hands, contemptuously refused to change sides. Instead, he contrived to escape from Narváez' camp and join his forces with those of the advancing Cortés.

While Cortés was working out and adhering to a businesslike plan, Narváez was wasting time. He was careless and over-confident, devoting his energies to plundering the villages of the Totonacs instead of girding himself for the coming battle. While he was making leisurely preparations to barricade himself in the town of Cempoala, in order to repel Cortés, who was rumoured to be somewhere in the neighbourhood, the latter was actually a mere four miles away, drilling his men in the details of a night attack. The fact that the rain was pouring down and that it was pitch dark did not discourage him. Placing Sandoval in the vanguard with seventy to eighty men (Bernal Díaz among them), and instructing them to attack Narváez' twenty guns, he put himself at the head of the main body. Another bout of oratory—and in the dead of the night he launched his men at Cempoala. Sandoval overran the guns in a single charge, with a loss of three men, driving the bulk of Narváez' sleepy troops right back to the central plaza, where many of them tried to take refuge at the top of the temple. The eighty enemy horsemen galloped away into the deluge. Cortés and his troops arrived in time for their leader to accept the capitulation of Narváez himself, who had lost an eye in the brief but brutal encounter.

*   *   *

Cortés, Velázquez de León and Sandoval anticipated a period of rest and consolidation before returning to Tenochtitlán. Velázquez de León went back down the coast with the bulk of the men to resume his search for a port at Coatzacoalcos, and to secure fresh supplies, which were running low. Cortés and Sandoval remained at Villa Rica, where they were soon called upon to cope as best they could with an outbreak of smallpox. The disease had been brought over by a negro in Narváez' fleet, and it ravaged the Indian population of Cempoala who, of course, had no natural immunity to European viruses. It was the first of a succession of such visitations that within the course of the next two centuries would reduce the population of Mexico to as little as a twentieth or even a thirtieth of what it had been in pre-Cortesian times.

Cortés had written a cheerful letter to his men in Tenochtitlán to give them good tidings from the coast. From Tenochtitlán, however, came other news, brought by Tlaxcalan messengers. It was grave. It caused him to recall Velázquez de León and start inland immediately. There had been an Aztec rising in the capital. Spanish soldiers had been killed. Pedro de Alvarado and his men were penned in their palace, their food and ammunition running low. Hard on the heels of the Tlaxcalan messengers came four Aztec *caciques* to complain, with bitter invective, that Alvarado's troops had set upon the citizens of Tenochtitlán and murdered scores of them while they were innocently celebrating the feast-day of Huitzilo-pochtli and Tezcatlipoca. The *caciques* were relating the facts of what was to become known as the massacre of the Great Temple, to employ the the term later used by the informants of Bernardino de Sahagún. It seems that Aztec representatives had approached Alvarado with a request to be allowed to observe the feast-day with full ceremonial. They were eager to assure him that the gathering would be devoted to purely religious pur-poses. Alvarado gave them the formal permission they wanted, and the festivities began. Then, as the dense crowd in the main square was swaying and dancing and singing, groups of Spaniards secretly shut the three gateways leading into the main precinct, the Gate of the Eagle, the Gate of Reeds, and the Gate of the Mirrored Serpent. A stream of Spaniards then issued through the one remaining gate, outside the palace of Axayácatl, and laid about them with cold fury. They spared no one, slaughtering indiscriminately, killing men, women and children, even chopping down the flute-players and drummers. The square was covered with blood and littered with lopped-off heads, arms and legs. Alvarado was not the sort of man to do anything by halves. Some of the Aztecs tried to escape by scaling the Serpent Wall or feigning dead, but most were put to the sword.

Alvarado's true motive for acting as he did was never revealed. It is possible that, on the day of the feast, he grew uneasy as the hours went by and the dancing and singing became increasingly frantic. We must imagine the square crammed with humanity, everybody in gorgeous gala costume adorned with plumes and feathers dyed all the colours of the rainbow, yelling, clapping, the dust rising beneath their thudding feet as they circled to the throbbing of the drums. As the celebration rose towards its wild climax the Spaniards could be forgiven for wondering, amid all the din and excitement, whether the Aztecs were not working themselves up to an insensate and irresistible attack. That was the reason that Alvarado himself gave. The real explanation was probably less creditable. Alvarado was the last man to lose his nerve and order the slaying in a moment of near-panic. Cortés himself was careful in his Second Despatch to leave the question in abeyance and not to impugn the honour of a Spanish officer; but he later told Gómara, or Gómara had gathered from another leading source, that the actual cause was Alvarado's well-known greed. 'The Spaniards,' says Gómara, 'went to see them perform this much-praised and famous dance, and, seeing them so rich, they coveted the gold the Indians were wearing, so that Alvarado blocked the entrances with ten or twelve Spaniards at each one, and himself entered with more than fifty, and cruelly and pitifully stabbed and killed the Indians and took what they were wearing.' These are strong and indignant words, and not the kind of angry accusation that one Spaniard would ordinarily level against another. Cortés must have had serious reservations about leaving Alvarado in charge in the first place. We have seen how badly Alvarado had behaved at the outset, in Cozumel; and within recent months Cortés had been forced to pull him up short for a second time when Alvarado had tortured the *cacique* of one of the towns in the Valley in order to extract gold from him. It was not feasible to pass over so forceful and influential a man in favour of someone lower in the chain of command, such as Sandoval; and Alvarado was in any case a good man to rely on in a fighting situation. Cortés could only pray that the volatile Alvarado would manage to keep his more wayward instincts under restraint. It had been Cortés' hope that, after disposing of Narváez, he might be able to reduce the tension at the heart of the Empire and so re-establish a general atmosphere of tranquillity in which his diplomatic gifts would have a chance to operate. Alvarado had destroyed that hope, and had stirred up such irreversible feelings of hatred against the Spaniards that henceforth it could only be war to the death—the kind of extreme situation that Cortés had always struggled to avoid. We are not surprised to learn that Cortés was furious at what Alvarado had done, and brooded about it all the way back to Tenochtitlán. As Díaz puts it, he was disgusted, and when the confrontation between the two men eventually took place it was pungent. 'When Alvarado told his story,' relates Díaz, 'Cortés exclaimed very angrily that it was a bad thing and a great mistake, and that he wished to God he had never heard of this business. Then he turned away and said no more on the subject.' Notwithstanding his statesmanlike determination to put the past behind him, the incident rankled with Cortés. This is the first occasion on which we find him losing not his courage nor his faith in himself, but what was almost equally important, his equanimity. For the first time he was ruffled, disconcerted. From this point on he was not the man he had been during the earlier phase of the Conquest. He became given to outbursts of spleen. Evidently the strain of those extraordinary months was beginning to tell even on that iron temperament. Alvarado had inflicted a serious blow on his leader. *Vivit sub pectore vulnus.* He felt betrayed; he felt alone; it seemed that he had to do everything for himself —be everywhere, supervise everything, make all the decisions. The load seemed unbearable. He was further weakened by the colic that had plagued him since the time of his entry into the country. And he was bone-tired; he had just completed one more exhausting march over some of the harshest country in the world, with the prospect of all-out conflict at the end of it.

The welcome which the Spaniards received at the city of Tlaxcala was reassuring. When Cortés reviewed his army there it comprised thirteen hundred Spanish infantry, ninety-six horsemen, eighty musketeers, eighty crossbowmen, and two thousand picked Tlaxcalan warriors. By adding Narváez' levies to his own veterans, Cortés had more than doubled his forces. On paper it looked impressive: but Narváez' men were raw, they were afraid of the country and its inhabitants, and they had only been induced to throw in their lot with Cortés by heavy bribery that caused dissatisfaction among his own troops.

Neither newcomers nor veterans were reassured by the increasingly deserted aspect of the towns through which they made their way as soon as they reached the Valley. Texcoco was empty. Its people had left it on the approach of the Spaniards. The silence was unnerving. Across its empty streets and squares wandered a few turkeys and chickens. Cortés had promised his new recruits a triumphal progress, but this was a funeral procession. Their eventual entry into Tenochtitlán was even more unnerving. When they halted outside the palace of Axayácatl they might have been at the centre of a dead and abandoned city. Even the circumstances of their admission to the palace were peculiar. For some minutes Alvarado postponed opening the doors, either because he wished to delay the coming interview with Cortés or because he feared that Cortés may have done a secret deal with Narváez that might entail arresting his own lieutenants. Everyone was in a sad state of jitters. When Moctezuma, aware that Cortés knew of his collaboration with Narváez, sent him a timorous message of welcome, Cortés boiled over, repeatedly shouted that the Emperor was 'a dog', and refused to visit him.

Cortés returned to Tenochtitlán on June 24. The next day the Aztecs launched their attack, as if they had only been waiting for the Spaniards to come back and run their heads into the noose. They began their onslaught without bothering to offer a pretext. Early that morning Cortés had sent out Diego de Ordaz with four hundred men to reconnoitre the hushed streets: and almost immediately there was a sudden explosive roaring noise and they came running back in disorder, with Ordaz bleeding in three places. The sky above the palace was darkened by a rain of arrows and slingstones, and as the Spaniards rushed to man the walls and windows the first wave of Aztecs were already setting fire to the building. They were only driven back when Cortés opened up on them with his muskets and cannons.

The *élan* of the Aztec rising was not attributable to simple hatred alone; they had acquired a new leader, a new war-chief, a new Emperor. Moctezuma had been deposed at a meeting of the royal council, and his brother Cuitláhuac had been appointed to rule in his place. In all probability Moctezuma had been dismissed because his noblemen were tired of his pacific policy; but it was also possible that it was a device, to which Moctezuma himself had acceded, whereby his people could acquire a general and chief-priest free to act independently and rally the nation. To judge by the will and energy with which Cuitláhuac infused his followers, the former was the case. The Aztecs behaved like men who until that day had been sleepwalkers, or men under a spell. They now came on with such spirit that they were repulsed with difficulty, at a loss of ten Spaniards dead and eighty wounded. Cortés' left hand was so badly injured by a sling-shot that he permanently lost the use of two fingers.

The next day's fighting was equally severe. Another ten dead and eighty wounded were added to the tally. It quickly became obvious that the Spaniards could not long continue in this way. Soon they would all be incapacitated. The Aztecs had declared that they would wipe out every single Spaniard if it meant losing twenty thousand Aztecs for every enemy they killed. There was no alternative: Cortés would have to retreat; he would have to leave the city—if he could. We can imagine with what bitterness, after all his hopes and exertions, he took the decision.

On the night of June 26, and during the day of the 27th, he ordered three mobile wooden towers to be built. They were large enough to give protection to twenty crossbowmen and musketeers, who would shoot from slits in the sides over the heads of the infantry, horsemen and artillery marching on either side. The plan was for a general organized break-out along one of the main causeways. While the carpenters were building the towers, the Aztecs assailed the palace from all points, and the muskets and cannon thundered back at them without cessation. Between attacks the Aztecs treated the defenders to vivid descriptions of what awaited them. Their hearts would be ripped out, their heads struck off and put in the skull-racks, their arms and legs cooked and eaten, their limbless trunks thrown to the wild animals in the royal gardens.

The next day the Spaniards and their Tlaxcalan allies made their sortie.

It was beaten back. The bridges had been destroyed and the drawbridges on the causeways demolished. The infantry were showered with missiles and rocks from the rooftops. The horsemen could not deploy to charge, and the Aztecs had learned to make good use of long lances to combat cavalry. The towers had to be abandoned. Slowly the column turned and trudged back towards the palace. It was cut and thrust every step of the way. As if to save something from the wreck, Cortés led a dash at the Great Temple, from which vantage-point the Aztecs had been able to pour down missiles and command the whole façade of the palace. He got right to the top, set the Aztec images in the sanctuary ablaze, but was then forced to retire. His little group was lucky to regain the palace without heavier loss. As it was, that day a further sixteen Spaniards were killed and another hundred wounded.

The Aztec grip on the palace and its occupants was seemingly unbreakable. It appeared only a question of time before the last line of defence, the muskets and cannon, ran out of powder and the Aztecs broke in. Furthermore, the garrison was at odds with itself. The Narváez contingent hurled abuse at Cortés, says Díaz, 'cursing him, cursing this country, and cursing Diego Velázquez, who had tricked them into leaving Cuba. They were quite crazy and uncontrolled'.

Cortés determined to make one final attempt to negotiate, to talk himself out of trouble as he had talked himself out of it so many times in the past. Next day he went on to the palace balcony—or what remained of it—and, protected by the shields of his guards, tried to parley with the Aztec leaders. They gave him a hearing, but told him that he and his companions must make up their minds either to die in battle or be taken prisoner and sacrificed. Nothing could have made it clearer to Cortés that he and his fellow Spaniards had long ago lost their magical authority of *teules* or gods. At the end of his tether, he played a last card. He had Moctezuma brought up to the roof. He stood beside him as the former Emperor began to talk to his own people (Plate 10). Perhaps Moctezuma could persuade them when he had failed. Moctezuma was addressing the murmuring, restless ocean of warriors below when something he said provoked them to a roar of contempt and anger. A host of spears, arrows and slingstones was hurled at the little knot of figures on the parapet. The Spanish escort were taken by surprise and were slow to raise their shields. Moctezuma was hit and fatally wounded by three slingstones.

He was carried down from the roof and taken back to his apartments. He was carefully tended, and lingered on for three days; but on the third day he died. It is part of the *leyenda negra* that the Spaniards murdered him. The Indian historian Ixtlilxóchitl, baptized as Fernando de Alva, wrote that Moctezuma was wounded by a blow on the head, dagger-thrusts and a sword-stroke through the loins. Fray Diego Durán had it from his Indian informants that 'the king was found dead with a chain round his ankles and five wounds in the chest, surrounded by many chiefs and notables, who had been prisoners, and who were all stabbed to death before the Spaniards left the palace'. Sahagún was told after the Conquest that the bodies of Moctezuma and the ruler were thrown from the palace windows four days after the battle in the sacred precinct. Nor was the Spanish case improved by the pious refusal of the generally fair-minded Torquemada to accept one version rather than another, but to leave the matter to the judgment of God.

It is easy to understand that the defeated Aztecs, overflowing with feelings of hatred, would have attributed this atrocity to the Spaniards; they cannot be blamed for believing it. The Spaniards committed many pointless acts of cruelty during the Conquest: but it is difficult to credit Cortés, weary and freshly wounded though he was, with such a piece of insane malice. He was angry with Moctezuma, but he needed him as his only important intermediary; and even if Moctezuma had failed to sway his people by means of the speech from the rooftop, Cortés meant to remove the king with him as a hostage. Far from killing his prisoners, we know that Cortés took with him other Aztec dignitaries in the imminent retreat. Moctezuma still had value. His people had deposed him: but they had repeatedly demanded that his person be returned. Cortés knew that the slaying of the former king would infuriate his opponents to a pitch not far from madness. As Díaz observed: 'Because of Moctezuma's death they never let us alone: we stared death in the face.' Besides, if the Spaniards had murdered him in a fit of spite, would they not have hurled his body into the street there and then, instead of removing him to his apartments and tending him for the next three days?

The facts suggest that the account given by Cortés to the Emperor Charles in his Second Despatch, an account which was later endorsed and amplified by Díaz, patently an honest and truthful man, ought to be taken at its face value. Gómara too speaks with the voice of reason when he writes: 'So Moctezuma was killed by his own vassals, who would rather have torn out their eyes than have done so. They did not see him because a Spaniard was covering him with a shield to protect him from the hail of stones; nor did they really believe he was there, in spite of the signs and shouts of the Spaniards. Cortés told them immediately of the king's wound and how dangerous it was, and though some believed him, others did not, and the battle continued. To prove to them that the king had died of a blow from an Aztec stone, Cortés had the body carried out by two

Aztec prisoners, who told their fellow-countrymen the truth. Even then the Aztecs would not abandon the war, as many Spaniards thought they might, but fought even more fiercely. Weeping bitterly, they withdrew to bury their king at Chapultepec.' Díaz concludes: 'Cortés and all the captains and soldiers wept for him, and there was no one among us who knew him and had dealings with him who did not mourn him as if he were our father.' They were all particularly grieved in that, although he had accepted and received instruction in the Christian religion, there had been no time, amid all the hubbub and confusion, to baptize him into the Holy Faith.

*   *   *

Cortés had captured a priest during his raid on the Great Temple. He sent this man, who was a person of importance, to the Aztec leaders, freeing a number of other prisoners at the same time to show his good faith. He instructed the priest to tell Cuitláhuac, the new Emperor, that he would relinquish all his gold and other booty if the Aztecs would permit the Spaniards to withdraw from the city within eight days. This was a blind, as he was making plans to leave Tenochtitlán immediately, in the dead of night. Night had favoured him in the clash with Narváez; perhaps it would help him in his present extremity.

Since the bridges on the causeways had been dismantled, he ordered his carpenters to hammer together a portable bridge that he could take with him. He deputed a hundred and fifty Spaniards and four hundred Tlaxcalans to transport it from one gap in the causeway to the next. Sandoval and Ordaz would lead the vanguard; Cortés, Alonso de Ávila and Cristóbal de Olid would command the middle of the column; there would be two squads of picked skirmishers under Francisco de Saucedo and Francisco de Lugo; and Alvarado and Velázquez de León would take charge of the rear. Tucked into a secure place in the front of the column were the cannon, protected by a second mixed force of Spaniards and Tlaxcalans; and positioned towards the rear was the Narváez battalion, which had become more of an embarrassment than an asset; while a special contingent was delegated to guard the hostages, La Malinche and other friendly civilians. Near the head of the column went the King's representatives, bearing the all-important Royal Fifth, encircled by a platoon of eighty Tlaxcalans. The danger was so pressing, the whole arrangement so makeshift, that the bulk of the gold and treasure had to be left behind. Matters must have reached an unprecedented pass for the Spaniards to surrender the wealth they had come so far and made so many sacrifices to maintain. Cortés had the boxes of bullion and jewels brought down and

8

stacked in the hall. Then he told the royal notaries: 'Bear witness that I can do no more with these riches. There are seven hundred thousand pesos' worth. I shall give it over to any soldiers who care to take it. Otherwise we shall lose it to those dogs.' Needless to say, Narváez' men weighed themselves down with as many valuables as they could carry. The veterans like Díaz, on the other hand, were wise enough not to burden themselves with more than their armour and their weapons, on the sound old principle that he who travels lightest is the one who travels fastest and farthest.

The doors were quietly opened and the huge column, trying to maintain the strictest silence, crept out of the palace just before midnight. They crossed the sacred precinct, and marched westwards down the causeway that led to Tlacopán, or modern Tacuba. A light rain was falling. Since the three great causeways began at the sacred precinct, it was not necessary to traverse a maze of minor thoroughfares. The Tlacopán causeway was chosen because it would take the column out of the city, across the lake, and on to dry land as rapidly as possible. At first all went well. The column reached the first breach in the causeway, the makeshift pontoon was dropped into place, and the vanguard and most of the files in the centre passed over. Then a shrill whistle sounded somewhere in the blackness, and suddenly the night was alive with tens of thousands of shouting Aztecs. The enemy had been lying in wait for them.

The column now lost all semblance of discipline. The vanguard and those who had crossed the breach had no choice except to continue to fight their way forward towards Tlacopán. Fleets of canoes were landing wave after wave of Aztecs in the vicinity of the breach, where the temporary bridge had already been torn down. The column was a severed snake. A few men of the rearguard managed to struggle across the gap, aided by Cortés and a party from the vanguard who went back to lend assistance. Alvarado got over by making a tremendous jump on his horse from one side of the gap to the other; it has entered into Mexican legend as Alvarado's Leap. Eighty men of Nárvaez' company were killed or captured at that spot, most of them impeded by the treasure they had insisted on taking. The hostages, including sons and daughters of Moctezuma, were slaughtered in the mad mêlée. Some of the stragglers managed to return to the palace of Axayácatl, whence they were eventually routed out and sacrificed on the Great Temple.

The survivors struggled on down the causeway, beset on both sides by strings of canoes whose occupants showered them with stones and darts. They halted in the main square of Tlacopán and tried to re-form, still under ceaseless attack from an adversary that never ceased to press home the advantage.

Cortés took stock. Alvarado reported to him the losses of the rearguard. Many brave captains were slain, including Francisco de Saucedo and Francisco de Morla. Worst of all, Alvarado had seen the body of Velázquez de León lying among the broken timbers of the ruined bridge.

Bernal Díaz relates that 'when Cortés and the other captains saw that no more soldiers were coming down the causeway, tears sprang to their eyes'. In accounts of the Conquest, this night of rain and blood, when Cortés reached the nadir of his fortunes, is called by the traditional name of *La Noche Triste*, the Night of Sorrow. Today, in that city where so much of the Aztec past lies directly beneath one's feet, exciting the imagination even though the monuments themselves are dust, one can still follow the footsteps of the Spaniards as they trod their *via dolorosa*. Starting from the Plaza de la Constitución, one can walk along the line of the Tlacopán causeway as represented by the Avenida Hidalgo, the Puente Alvarado (location of the famous Leap) and the Calzado Mexico-Tacuba. At a point in the last-named thoroughfare, where it widens out into the little Callejón Noche Triste, a few streets beyond the Colegio Militar, stands the *arból de la noche triste*. This is a splendid cypress, of majestic girth and height, and manifestly several centuries old, which spreads its thick and scraggy branches over the little patch of dusty green that surrounds it. On the benches below its vast scabbed trunk sit old men, lovers, young mothers and *criadas* with children. A pretty, peaceful scene. Yet it was here, according to legend, that Cortés halted on that catastrophic night of July 1, 1520, letting the tears pour down his cheeks as he stood in the rain, and heard the tidings of the defeat of his army and the deaths of his friends.

3

¡ Honor al que trae cautiva la extraña bandera!
¡ Honor al herido y honor a los fieles
soldados que muerte encontraron por mano extranjera!
¡ Clarines! ¡ Laureles!

Honour to him who bears the foreign banner he captured!
Honour to the wounded and honour to the faithful
soldiers who met death at the hands of the stranger!
Trumpets! Laurels!

                                        Rubén Darío: Marcha triunfal

KEATS was wrong when, in his sonnet, he spoke of Cortés as silent upon a peak in Darien. He was confusing Cortés with Balboa. But he was not at all mistaken when he paid tribute to Cortés as 'stout'. A man who was capable of suffering, surviving, and finally surmounting the events of the Night of Sorrow possessed more than his share of what Winston Churchill called intestinal fortitude.

Nor had his time of testing ended in the plaza at Tlacopán. His troops were penned there by the enemy during the whole of the following day, and by nightfall no less than another hundred and fifty Spaniards, two thousand Indian allies, and nearly fifty horses had been added to the death-roll. As Cortés reported in his forthcoming despatch: 'No horse could run, no horseman lift his arms, no infantryman place one foot in front of the other.' There was no help for it but to make another attempt, as at Tenochtitlán, to steal away under cover of night.

This they did, leaving their camp-fires burning in the plaza to try to mislead the enemy. They encountered a little better fortune than on the previous night, for this time they went creeping along till dawn before the enemy roused up and gave the general alarm. Perhaps this was because they were now unencumbered by baggage, had practically no horses, and were far fewer in number—and those few were mainly Cortés' original veterans. At dawn, they were again engulfed by the now familiar clouds of Aztecs, and by the time the merciful night dropped once more they had managed to cover only a meagre seven or eight miles.

At first they marched aimlessly, their sole idea to escape the merciless and unending torrent of blows that fell upon them. Then they picked up an Indian who said he was a Tlaxcalan, and who offered to lead them to safety. Willy-nilly, Cortés had to trust him. To reach Tlaxcala, where they hoped they would at last find refuge, they were forced to make a wide detour to avoid the shores of the great lake and the hostile Aztec townships. They staggered on across rough country, wounded, footsore, sleepless, hungry. Looping around, three days later the men of the little shattered column sought shelter behind the walls of the town of Otumba. Many of them limped into it on the crutches that Cortés had ordered them to use, in order to spare the handful of horses and leave the few troops still unwounded free to continue the running-battle. In three days, since leaving Tlacopán, they had traversed only forty miles; there was a long fifty miles' route ahead of them before they reached Tlaxcala. In the last day's fighting five Spaniards and five horses had been killed. The latter at least was not an unmixed evil, since it gave the refugees some meat to sustain them.

When they crawled out of Otumba the next morning, they had hobbled no more than three painful miles before what seemed to them to be the entire Aztec army suddenly hove into view above the rocky skyline of the surrounding plateau. The Spaniards swayed to a halt; they were encircled. This time it seemed impossible that they could escape. 'So many Indians attacked us,' wrote Cortés of the first charge of that glittering horde, 'that we could not see the ground about us. Their onslaught on all sides was so violent that we could not distinguish each other for being so pressed and entangled with them. Certainly we believed that to be our last day, so great was the force of the Indians and so feeble our resistance, for we were already exhausted and almost all of us were wounded and fainting from hunger.'

He himself had received two wounds in the head from sling-stones the previous day, and was swathed in bandages. Nevertheless he fought on that famous day of the battle of Otumba with wonderful courage. Accompanied by Gonzalo de Sandoval, Cristóbal de Olid, Gonzalo de Domínguez and Juan de Salamanca, he rode everywhere about the field, instructing his men to concentrate their efforts on trying to cut down any Aztec whose particularly gorgeous plumage singled him out as one of the enemy leaders. As his confinement of Moctezuma showed, he had divined that the most effective way to throw a semi-barbarous people into confusion was to deprive it of its chieftains. It was certainly this tactic, in the day-long struggle, that ultimately decided the issue in favour of the Spaniards and enabled them, as Cortés put it, 'with all our weakness to break their great pride and haughtiness'. Díaz describes the culminating action thus: 'It was a desperate battle, and a fearful sight to behold. We moved through the midst of them at close quarters, slashing and thrusting with our swords. And the dogs fought back furiously, dealing us wounds and death with their lances and their two-handed blades. And by God's grace, Cortés came to the place where the Aztec commander-in-chief marched with his banner displayed, in rich golden armour and high silver plumes, followed by his great band of warriors. And Cortés said: "Now, gentlemen, let us cut our way through them, and leave none of them without a wound!" And commending themselves to God, they charged, and Cortés, riding straight for the Aztec commander, made him drop his banner, and Juan de Salamanca dealt him a lance-thrust and snatched his rich plume, which he afterwards gave to Cortés, saying it was his by right. And when the Aztec chief and many other leaders were killed, it pleased the Lord that their attack should slacken. Then our horsemen followed them, and we felt neither hunger nor thirst. It was as if we had suffered no disaster and undergone no hardships, and our allies the Tlaxcalans became like very lions. And we all gave great thanks to God for our escape from this mighty host: for there had never been seen throughout the Indies so many troops assembled for any battle.'

*   *   *

It was therefore in slightly better order than they could have anticipated that they entered Tlaxcala. They did not return as all-conquering heroes, but they had inflicted a major defeat on the enemy that had restored some measure of their confidence in themselves and repaired their sagging reputation in the eyes of their allies. If they no longer enjoyed their original status as gods, at least they had retained some of their god-like attributes. Velázquez de León and several of the other captains had fallen, but Cortés, Alvarado, Sandoval and the others had surmounted impossible dangers and must have seemed virtually indestructible.

No sooner were they at Tlaxcala, where they found to their infinite relief that the Tlaxcalans were still determined to stand by them, than Cortés gave fresh evidence of his mettle. Disregarding plans from all sides, he refused to retire to Villa Rica, which at that stage would have been the easy and obvious step to take. Instead he decided to remain in the field. He knew that it was essential to maintain contact with the enemy and recover the initiative as quickly as possible. Had he allowed his men to regain the shelter of Cempoala, they might have suffered a moral and physical collapse and sunk into a lethargy from which he would never have been able to revive them. He wanted to keep them keyed up; not for a moment were they to be allowed to assume that the campaign had been abandoned. They would return to Tenochtitlán.

He gave them three weeks to lick their wounds. Strangely enough, he seemed to be actually elated by the fact that his numbers had shrunk. In place of the comparatively large army, sixteen hundred strong, who had accompanied him to the Valley, he was now reduced to a mere four hundred and forty infantrymen, twelve crossbowmen, seven musketeers, and a score of horsemen. He was worse off than he had been at the very beginning. But the men who had survived were the bravest and the best—Ironsides, all of them. It is impossible to overestimate the regard which the members of that little army felt for one another. They had been tried in the fire and had come through. They were a band of brothers. 'The human heart,' said Marshal Saxe, 'is fundamental in all matters pertaining to war': and the legionaries of Cortés possessed that essential quality of heart. As the Romans would have put it, they were few, but they were eagles. They had taken the heaviest blows the enemy could aim at them: and now the Aztecs would learn what it meant to injure the self-esteem of Spaniards. Every outstanding feat of courage and endurance increases the stature of mankind, confirming it in the exalted idea it should have of itself. Cortés was about to display courage and endurance of that order.

His situation would nonetheless have been utterly untenable, and a withdrawal to Villa Rica have been inevitable, if the Tlaxcalans had proved fickle. As time progressed, however, it quickly became apparent that he could count on the firm support not only of the Tlaxcalans but of all the other non-Aztec peoples within a radius of several hundred miles of Tenochtitlán. The Aztecs were not beloved: and, though they had succeeded in reducing the Spaniards to the level of mortal men, the Spaniards in turn had shown that the Aztecs themselves were very far from invincible. The coming of the Spaniards, coupled with Cortés' promise to rid them from Aztec tyranny, had brought hope to the Tlaxcalans and their fellow sufferers. They were willing to support him in the next and no doubt final round in the struggle for Tenochtitlán. He had started a civil war, and the flames he had kindled were not to be easily quenched. The vassals of the Aztecs had in any case reached a stage from which there could be no going back. Having dared to raise their hand against their masters, they could guess what their fate would be if the Aztecs drove out the Spaniards and reasserted their former rule. The Aztecs were not renowned for their forgiving nature.

Cortés began to build up his forces, systematically training the Indian contingents that poured into Tlaxcala in the Spanish methods of warfare. He took the survivors of the Narváez contingent and drilled them too, ignoring their plea to be allowed to depart to Villa Rica. He also received additional reinforcements from an unexpected quarter. Diego Velázquez had not yet received news of the defeat of Narváez, and under the impression that the latter must have disposed of Cortés had sent off another two ships containing fresh supplies. Their contents were gratefully commandeered by Cortés. A further three ships also arrived from Jamaica, whose Governor, Francisco de Garay, following up a report from Pineda and Camargo, who had touched the northern coast of Mexico in 1520, believed that promising developments might be set afoot on the mainland. The Jamaican ships had been ordered to keep clear of the area under the jurisdiction of the Governor of Cuba. They sailed far up the Mexican coast and made landfall a full two hundred and fifty miles north of Villa Rica, on the Pánuco river where Tampico now stands. The crew of the first ship failed to establish a viable settlement, and the survivors crawled down the coast to Villa Rica in such a moribund state that Cortés' men christened them *panzaverdetes*, Green Bellies. Most of them died. The second and third ships, however, sailed promptly to join Cortés when their crews found the Pánuco settlement had been abandoned. They contained ninety-three excellent fighting men, as we can tell from their nicknames of *lomos recios*, Strongbacks, and *albardillas*, Pack-saddles. They also brought seventeen horses. Rather than return to Jamaica empty-handed, they cheerfully threw in their lot with Cortés, and their arrival represented a very valuable and unexpected windfall. He was now up to his original strength of about six hundred infantrymen, and had thirty horsemen. He would now proceed to show that what a man can do once, he can do again.

While he was busy at Tlaxcala, organizing his Indian auxiliaries and superintending the bringing up of supplies from the coast, he sent an expeditionary force under Cristóbal de Olid back to the lake, with instructions to attack the Aztec community of the town of Tepeyac. This town lay on the northern portion of the lake, commanding the entrance to the northern causeway of Tenochtitlán. The shrine of the mother-goddess Tonantzin stood there, a site now occupied by the shrine of the Virgin of Guadalupe; and the line of the ancient causeway as it debouched into the sacred precinct and the Great Temple is now represented by the Avenida de la República de Argentina and its continuation, the Calzada Guadalupe, as they strike north from the Zócalo. The choice of Tepeyac as a target was governed by several factors. To some extent it was a feint to conceal the direction of the final advance; but it was also rich country and accessible to the Tlaxcalans, and in addition the Tepeyacs had killed or captured for sacrifice sixteen Spaniards during the retreat of the Night of Sorrows. The Spaniards had an account to settle.

After three weeks at Tlaxcala, Cortés had moved his headquarters to a village closer to Tenochtitlán, on the borders of Tepeyac territory, which he re-named Segura de la Frontera. It cannot now be identified with any certainty, though according to some modern authorities it was the town of Tepeyac itself. He founded there a Spanish town in due style, with the same ceremonies as at Villa Rica de Vera Cruz, and probably for the same reason. During the month of October he was busy writing his Second Despatch, which covered the entire period from the first march to Tenochtitlán from Cempoala, fourteen months before, to the aftermath of the battle of Otumba. Although fifteen months had passed since he had sent off his First Despatch from Villa Rica in the hands of Portocarrero and Montejo, he had not yet received any intimation that it had reached the Emperor, let alone any reply, any instructions, or any confirmation in the high offices to which he had elected himself. He could not await the royal answer indefinitely: it was time to submit a fresh report, a fresh justification. To prevent its bearer from being arrested by the agents of

Bishop Fonseca, the man had, like Portocarrero and Montejo before him, to be given the protection of an official title and position as a dignitary of a Spanish township. However, although it was dated October 30, 1520, the despatch was not sent until the following March 5, because, as Cortés later explained, he was short of ships. It reached Spain in the autumn of 1521 by the hand of Alonzo de Mendoza. Mendoza, like Cortés, Portocarrero and Montejo, was a native of Medellín, and therefore a man more to be trusted than most in those mistrustful times.

By the time the Second Despatch reached Spain, the war was over. But the Emperor and his court were not to know that: to them, the despatch stopped abruptly on a note of high drama as Cortés prepared to make his second assault. Recounting the atrocious condition of his men after Otumba, Cortés related how he himself had 'lost two fingers of my left hand', but refused to retreat to Villa Rica. 'Remembering that Fortune is always on the side of the brave, and that we were Christians, I confided in the very great mercy of God, who would never permit us to perish. This great and noble country must not be lost. The war must be continued. Disregarding all difficulty and danger, I said that I would not abandon my cause, for that would be disgraceful to me, dangerous to my followers, and disloyal to Your Majesty. I determined to return against the enemy from all possible points and take the offensive against them in every way I could.' Not surprisingly, these stirring words made a deep impression in Spain, and the Emperor resolved to share the excitement of the story and impress the daring of Spanish arms on the remainder of Europe. In November 1522 it was published at Seville, and quickly reprinted in France, Germany, England and Italy. The men of those days recognized and applauded an epic when they saw one.

Cortés, with cool presumption, described himself in the despatch as Captain-General of the new territories. He also took the considerable liberty of designating those territories by a name of his own devising. 'There is so much similarity,' he told the Emperor, 'between this country and Spain, that it seemed to me the most suitable name for it would be *New Spain of the Ocean Sea*, and thus in the name of Your Majesty I have christened it.'

One of the passages in the despatch had touched on a new and interesting topic. The expeditions which he and his allies were sending into Aztec territory returned with substantial hauls of prisoners. These he made slaves, explaining to the Emperor that he did so because they were cannibals, and because the tactic would strike terror into the Aztecs. It is true that some practical step had to be taken to house and feed these great numbers of captives, and to save them from being put to the sword by

8*

their captors. Assigning them either to their fellow Indians or to individual Spaniards fulfilled both contingencies. It is also true that slavery was a widespread practice among the Aztecs themselves. However, it was a sad day for Mexico and for Spanish America when Cortés finally bowed to necessity and introduced what was to become the *encomienda* system.

From the outright slavery now sanctioned were to grow the *encomiendas* of the post-Conquest era. The system was a method of tying the Indian to the land, and not one that Cortés liked. It had already been established by Diego Colón in Hispaniola, when Cortés landed there as a raw settler, and had been further developed by his patron Nicolás de Ovando. In the islands the system had been known by the frank name of *repartimiento*, or 'allotment'; in Mexico it took the milder name of *encomienda*, or 'charge', to 'give it a coat of varnish', as Las Casas drily observed. Cortés himself had watched it being put into practice by Diego Velázquez after the conquest of Cuba. In the islands, it consisted of making a census of the population and parcelling them up in blocks of a hundred, keeping village populations as much together as possible, then making each block available to a Spanish settler. It began in Mexico on the same scale, but in that larger territory the individual blocks grew in a matter of a few years to five hundred then to ever more substantial units.

Cortés had possessed an *encomienda* of his own in Cuba. It was not possible for a settler to exist in the Indies without becoming an *encomendero*. How else was he to work his new land? The Spaniards who crossed to the New World were not only few in number but were aristocrats, petty aristocrats, or professional adventurers; and the Spanish peasant was preoccupied with tilling his own soil, to which he was in any case fettered by means of the *mayorazgo*. If the settler's lands were not worked by the Indians, they would not be worked at all. The *encomienda* system also helped to re-establish order and social cohesion after conquest. The Indians took to the bush after the coming of the Spaniards, and had to be enticed back to their villages and re-settled in order that the economic life of the islands could be carried on. Unfortunately, many of the early Spanish settlers, apart from being innately ignorant, cruel and conscienceless, were not interested in working the land but only in tearing from it whatever treasure it would yield. Those were gold-rush days. To dig in the mines and pan the rivers the early Spaniards turned their indentured Indians into chain-gangs, heedless of the fact that by doing so they were destroying their own source of labour.

The government at home had always been sensitive about these developments. The peasant in Spain had never been a slave, in the sense that the North American negro was to become a slave; within wide limits, he could own property, choose his profession and his place of residence, and enjoyed free access to all courts of justice. The Spanish government did not wish to make the Indian the personal chattel of his master and create a race of helots. 'Since Almighty God has made the Indians free,' the Emperor wrote later in his instructions to Cortés, 'their freedom cannot be taken from them.' It was a matter of Christian conscience; in particular, a Catholic king, responsible before God for the liberty and welfare of his subjects, did not wish to have such black matter on his soul. It was not a new-found dogma of the Enlightenment that men were born free: it was an ancient and fundamental tenet of the Catholic religion. By and large, slavery in the modern world, after the excesses of the Reconquest in Iberia, during which prisoners on both sides were enslaved as a matter of course, was to be a joint product of Islam, of Mohammedan Africa, and of Protestant Northern Europe and North America.

The Castilian government had given partial approval to Ovando's innovations in 1503, and in 1509 had confirmed its earlier sanction by a regular decree. Two years later the official view was codified in the Laws of Burgos, in which the rights of settlers and Indians were systematically set forth. The *encomiendas* were sanctioned, for otherwise the colonizing of the New World could not be pursued: but the Indians in the *encomiendas* were to be regarded as belonging to the crown, not to individual Spaniards, and officials of the crown would be solely responsible for running the system. An Indian would work for his Spanish master for nine months of the year, and in return the latter would pay him, house him, clothe him, and be accountable for his education and spiritual welfare. One-third of the male labour-force would be set aside for work in the mines and rivers, under a system specifically called the *repartimiento*, which resembled the compulsory *mita* of the Incas or the *corvée* of the French *ancien régime*; but the conditions under which he worked were to be strictly regulated and his basic freedom safeguarded. The Spanish government was treading with particular care at this stage because in 1511 the Dominicans in the Indies had embarked on the first round of their bitter battle against the Spanish settlers on behalf of the Indian. It was a battle which was to continue for two centuries, but it was at no time more fierce than in its first two decades, which was the time when Cortés was in the Indies. The Dominicans whipped and scourged the conscience of the government and the court, although the conscience of Bishop Fonseca was covered with a tough integument, and since he was primarily concerned with extracting gold from the New World he provided the Dominicans with an inflexible opposition.

The Dominicans not only disputed the right of the settlers to become *encomenderos*: they disputed their right to hold land there in the first place. They were fanatically anti-colonist in their bias. The royal and official conscience was thus doubly tender: were the *encomiendos* compounding an original crime of the illegal seizure of native territory? It is often assumed, particularly in our own century, that the formation of the Spanish colonial empire was brought about in an altogether heedless, mindless and bluntly rapacious manner. Such was not the case; the debate concerning whether the wars in the Indies were just or unjust was conducted from the beginning with extreme, not to say excessive vigour. On one side were two great Dominican divines, the mild and academic Francisco de Vitoria, who challenged the Ostiensian thesis in a famous series of lectures delivered at Salamanca in 1539, and 'the Apostle of the Indies', Bartolomé de las Casas, whom we have already briefly mentioned in these pages. Born in Seville in 1474, like Cortés he had studied law at Salamanca, although unlike Cortés he had completed his studies. His father had sailed to the New World with Christopher Columbus, and he himself went out there with Nicolás de Ovando. He took part with Diego Velázquez, Cortés and the others in the expedition to Cuba; and shortly thereafter, becoming the first Catholic priest consecrated in the New World, he denounced Velázquez' treatment of the natives and returned to Spain to plead their cause. He was sympathetically received by the great Cardinal Cisneros, and later worked with the jurist Juan López de Palacios Rubios in framing the New Laws for the Indies, promulgated by the Emperor Charles in 1542. Sent back to the New World as official protector of the Indians, he refused the influential see of Cuzco in Peru and chose instead to spend many years of arduous and obscure missionary work in Guatemala and Nicaragua, and in writing his vast, ill-organized but comprehensive *Historia general de las Indias*. His later and more intemperate work, *De la destrucción de las Indias*, formed the basis for the *leyenda negra* which was to hang like a curse over all Spanish colonizing efforts. Eventually named Bishop of Chiapas in Mexico by the Emperor, at the end of his remarkable and selfless life he journeyed home to die in Madrid in 1566.

Opposed to this passionate and devoted man, in addition to the pragmatic Fonseca, was the theorist Juan Ginés de Sepúlveda. Brilliant and incisive, a native of that most ironic and rigorous of all cities, Córdoba, and a product of the universities of Alcalá and Bologna, he was official historian and chaplain to the Emperor. He propounded what now would be called a hard or hawkish line concerning the Indies in a forceful work entitled *Democratus secundus o de justus belli causi apud indios*; and his dispute with Las Casas became so acrimonious, roused so much partisan emotion, and touched on such deep issues, that in 1550 the Emperor summoned a special theological congress at Valladolid to hear the issues debated. Here Las Casas and his friend Melchor Cano openly accused Sepúlveda of heresy, and although he fought back energetically his writings were afterwards condemned. His *Apologia*, published in 1550, did not help him, and he died in obscurity.

Cortés, who had been an associate of Las Casas, must have been very well aware of these ideological issues, which were the subject of incessant controversy on the very highest level. It would not have been in the nature of a man with such a sense of diplomacy, and with such a demonstrable personal piety, to have ignored them. He had already shown his appreciation of the delicate feelings of his superiors in these spiritual matters by the scrupulous way in which, during the previous fifteen months, he had caused the *requerimiento* to be read to the enemy before each of his battles. After the crown of Castile had decided that its right to rule in the Indies had been established by Pope Alexander VI's bull *Inter Caetera* of 1493, and also by the old thesis of Cardinal Hostiense or Ostiensis that the Pope of Rome possessed temporal dominion over all the world, given to him by Christ and St. Peter, it nonetheless reinforced its judgment by means of the quaint device of the *requerimiento*. This was a formal declaration, to be carried by the captain of every expedition, that was required to be read solemnly three times to the enemy before engaging in combat. It called upon the leader of the other side to give allegiance to Christ and the Emperor, warning him of the consequences of a refusal. The original document, in the form of a message from the King of Castile to the Indians, had been drawn up in 1512 by Las Casas's colleague Palacios Rubios, at the request of the Council of the Indies, and was first used by Pedrarias Dávila on his expedition to Tierra Firme. Cortés enacted this legalistic pantomime with invariable gravity, addressing the hostile ranks in front of him through the mouth of his two priests or the royal notary, with La Malinche translating phrase by phrase. Of course, the enemy could not hear a word of it above the preliminary din of battle; and in any case the readers of the message were placed far to the rear in order to protect them from the missiles that were already flying; but the proprieties had been duly observed. The *requerimiento* actually survived until 1543, when it was replaced by a *cartamensaje* addressed by the Emperor to the 'kings and *señores*' of the New World, aimed now at persuading rather than compelling them to accept his 'mild, Christian and perfect method of government'.

Even his most unshakeable detractors could not claim that Cortés was in favour of slavery, or of the systems of *encomienda* and *repartimiento*; he is on record as having expressed vehement disapproval. His Third

Despatch, written eighteen months later, ends with a fine passage in which he sets forth his reasons for the steps he was forced to take in this regard. It deserves to be quoted at length. 'In one of my letters,' it runs, 'I told Your Majesty that the natives of these parts were much more capable than those of Hispaniola and Cuba, and appeared to be quite intelligent and reasonable. Therefore I felt it would be wrong to compel them to serve the Spaniards as those of the islands do, although without some assistance the conquerors and settlers of these parts would be unable to maintain themselves. In order not to force the Indians to help the Spaniards, and to compensate the Spaniards for this, I thought Your Majesty might order that they receive assistance from the incomes here which belong to Your Majesty. In view of the many and continual outlays of Your Majesty, we ought rather to augment your rents by all possible means, rather than to be the occasion of further expense. However, we have spent a long time in the wars which has caused us much debt and difficulty. Furthermore we know there will be a delay until Your Majesty has made a decision in this case, and that Your Majesty is importuned on all sides by your officials and all the Spaniards here, which I could not possibly avoid. In view of all these considerations, I found myself almost forced to place the chiefs and natives of these parts among the Spaniards, to recompense them for the service they have rendered to Your Majesty. Until I receive other orders or this action is confirmed, these chiefs and natives continue to serve and to give each Spaniard to whom they are allotted what is necessary for his subsistence. I took this step with the approval of intelligent persons who have had great experience in this country. There was nothing else I could do, not only for the maintenance of the Spaniards, but to assure good treatment for the Indians.'

Later still, in March 1524, when he had been confirmed by the Emperor as Governor and Captain-General of New Spain, he issued his *ordenanzas* on the subject, simultaneously discussing them in detail with the Emperor. The latter had, by this date, specifically forbidden the granting of *encomiendas*, as his advisers had declared that they infringed the liberty of the Indians. Cortés now admitted that he had disregarded the royal instructions on this point, for to disband the *encomiendas* would result in the economic collapse and the loss to the Emperor of the whole of New Spain. But he pointed out that he had tried hard to temper the system so as to protect the Indians in every way possible: indeed, he asserted on quite reasonable grounds that the vast majority of Indians actually preferred the *encomienda* system to the condition of slavery in which they had existed before the coming of the Spaniards; the new masters were more tolerable than the old. The *ordenanzas* placed strong restrictions on

the Spaniard who owned an *encomienda*. The latter had to agree to stay
in New Spain for at least eight years after receiving his *encomienda*; he
had to plant a thousand vines for each hundred Indians he possessed; and
to prevent him keeping an Indian harem he had to bring over his wife from
Spain within eighteen months or get married within the same period.
Cortés, in fact, was to prove himself an enlightened ruler, and it was a
pity for Mexico, then and afterwards, that the Emperor replaced him with
less able and less experienced nominees. However that may be, it is fair
to say that he never recovered, in the royal estimation, from his action
at Segura de la Frontera in the autumn of 1520, when he decreed slavery
for the Aztec prisoners of Tepeyac and other provinces without first
obtaining royal sanction. The young Emperor, according to the standards
of the age, was a liberal and a humanitarian; he did not want the peasants
of the New World to suffer the conditions which the peasants of the Old
World were only just beginning to shed; as a prince of the Habsburg
Empire at the close of its mediaeval phase, he knew something about the
evils of peasant servitude at first-hand. So, as a product of Medellín and of
Baracoa, did Cortés. The Emperor and his servant had much in common;
but by his act of insubordination Cortés had forfeited the royal trust.

Yet how could he have done otherwise? Thanks to Fonseca's intrigues,
and to the royal dilatoriness, he had received neither instructions nor any
word of encouragement from Spain in answer to his First Despatch. The
Aztecs had deprived him of Moctezuma's treasure; also, by means of a
daring raid, they had managed to recover the stock of gold which he had
accumulated at Villa Rica. His army had endured unbelievable hardships
and was near-mutinous from lack of pay; unless he soon produced some
kind of tangible reward, an earnest of something more substantial to
follow, portions of it might decamp. His Indian allies too demanded
material benefits. In any case, war to them had always been primarily and
basically a naked economic exercise, in which the taking and giving of slaves
was an integral part. Cortés was caught between the sword and the wall.
The only commodity he had available was prisoners; he had to use them.

Cortés has been blamed, as for so much else, for initiating the system
of peonage which was to become the bane of the New World. Undoubtedly that system sprang from the institution of the *encomienda*: but
instead of finding Cortés unequivocally guilty it is only fair to look at the
facts, from the scrutiny of which a certain number of mitigating circumstances emerge. One might, for example, compare Cortés' actions in this
respect with those which the heartless Pedrarias Dávila was currently
carrying out as Governor of Darien. On the other hand, it would be
ridiculous to represent Cortés as a man overflowing with the milk of

human kindness: he was a hard man in a hard situation. If he disliked the *encomienda* system, as much as anything else it was because of the wasteful and inefficient manner in which he had seen it applied in Hispaniola and Cuba. He was—or rather, should have been given the chance to become— one of history's great administrators; he was *Fundador* as well as *Conquistador*. It is really very extraordinary that this man, who three months before had undergone almost total defeat, and who was now preparing for a new campaign, should at that moment have been looking forward to the problems he would have to meet when he finally assumed the government of the country. He was not merely bold and crafty: he was long-sighted and sagacious.

Nevertheless, it is possible to detect what might be called a growing callousness in his nature. If we look at the portraits which were afterwards made of him, we are struck by his harsh and haggard expression (Plate 1). The experiences of the previous year and a half, and of the years immediately ahead, had left their mark on that ravaged face. He was not now the devil-may-care young adventurer who had sailed from Cuba. When a man has fought a dozen pitched battles, been wounded in the head, lost the use of two fingers, been baked and frozen by the climate, marched many hundred miles, witnessed the deaths of many of his friends and of half his army, put down a couple of mutinies, and captured and executed Emperors—it changes his character. Cortés had shed his youth and had matured into a man of enormous strength and stature. He had faced a massive challenge and had proved equal to it: but in doing so he had had to sacrifice any softness or gaiety of attitude which he had formerly possessed. In the career of Cortés we are watching a man grow: and if he was to surmount the responsibilities that confronted him he had to grow into a man of steel. There was no other way. What had begun as a fairly light-hearted expedition to found a small colony, of the size of Darien or Pánuco, had turned into an undertaking of colossal scale and complexity. In part this was due to his innate eagerness and ambition, but partly to pure chance. How could he have guessed, when he landed at Cozumel, that he would stumble not on a narrow isthmus populated by half-naked savages, but on a vast country and on the seemingly illimitable Empire of the Aztecs? To meet this giant test it was necessary for him to transform himself into a giant: and one feels that, had this one man been unable to effect such a transformation within himself, the history of the Americas and of Europe would have been different from what it was. '*History is made by men.*' But not by weak or too-amiable ones.

*   *   *

By the middle of December he was ready to make his move. He returned from his outpost at Segura de la Frontera to Tlaxcala, visiting Cholula en route. The Cholulans now appeared to be willing to forgive the massacre of the previous year, and to be eager to join the other vassals of the Aztecs in the war of liberation.

At Tlaxcala he had been preparing a brand new weapon for use against Tenochtitlán: he had been building a fleet. The four brigantines he had constructed during his first occupation of the city, and in which Moctezuma had delighted to sail around the lake, had been destroyed during the Night of Sorrows. He was replacing them with a squadron of no less than thirteen vessels, stout enough to carry cannon and to ferry sizeable platoons of soldiers from one landing-place to another. His carpenters—those unsung heroes of the Conquest—were working night and day to have the ships ready in time. They were using timber and pitch from the local pine-forests, and the sails and gear were those that had been stripped out of Cortés' original fleet and been brought up from Villa Rica. Who but Cortés would have conceived and carried out the manufacture of a navy, at an inland town, fifty miles away from the water on which they were to be launched?

He called back his flying columns from the surrounding countryside. Sandoval returned from the coast; Olid had acted with a certain amount of indecision but, significantly, had been rescued and redeemed by the vigour of his Tlaxcalan auxiliaries. All the Indian contingents, now at least a hundred thousand strong, including ten thousand Tlaxcalans, were clamouring for Cortés to lead them in the great culminating final attack on the Aztecs. It was largely because of their enthusiasm for the cause and their eagerness to fight that in the past five months Cortés had managed to cut a huge swathe out of the Aztec Empire, penetrating even as far as the heart of the Mixtec country.

On December 27, he reviewed his Spaniards. The men fit and ready to march comprised five hundred and forty infantrymen, including eighty crossbowmen and musketeers, whom he parcelled out into nine companies of sixty men apiece. He possessed forty cavalrymen, whom he divided into four groups of ten. They were regaled with one of his customary exhortations, in his most fervent vein, and then he caused to be read out to them a list of six articles of war which he had drawn up. Neither he nor his men needed any prophet to tell them what dire and bloody events lay ahead: and once more he was trying to impress on them that they should try to conduct themselves like members of a professional army, not like unbridled freebooters. The articles warned them that no one might blaspheme the Holy Name of God; that no Spaniard might quarrel with another

Spaniard; that no one might wager his arms or his horse; that no one might rape a woman; that no Spaniard might injure an Indian, or rob him, or sack an Indian town without express permission; and that no one might insult a friendly Indian warrior or exchange the Indian *tamemes* or carriers as gifts. The six rules tell us a great deal about Cortés' army and the kind of warfare in which it participated.

He led the combined Spanish-Indian forces out of Tlaxcala the following day, December 28, 1520. It was the Feast of St. John, or Holy Innocents' Day. The marching files made a splendid spectacle. The reverses of the summer were behind them; their leader had restored their morale and self-esteem; they stepped out rapidly and in high spirits. That day they covered nine miles, most of it climbing the steep ascent to the high pass that would bring them down to the Valley of Mexico. After a cold night at a towering altitude, next morning they brushed aside the barriers of tree trunks with which the Aztecs had attempted to block the road and saw spread out before them, as they had seen over a year before, the broad valley with the great lake and the huge white city at its heart.

Following almost the same route that he had taken on that first occasion, Cortés reached Texcoco at noon on December 31. In view of the ancient and unshakeable ties between Tenochtitlán and Texcoco, he expected to receive a hostile reception. Instead, he found it deserted, its ruler and chieftains having already fled to Tenochtitlán. He therefore decided to halt at Texcoco and occupy it, since it was strategically sited to command the entire eastern aspect of the lake. He strengthened its defences and made it his headquarters for the next four months, during the period when he was systematically preparing to lay final siege to Tenochtitlán.

It was not his plan to attack the capital immediately. He meant to move around the shores of the lake, cutting off the Aztecs inside the city from their supplies and from their allies in the provinces beyond. He also wanted to await the arrival of his brigantines from Tlaxcala.

He spent a week taking stock at Texcoco, then embarked on what was to be the first move in the mobile war that was meant to erode the strength of the Aztecs and tighten his grip on the city. He led out a sizeable striking-force of two hundred and fifty Spaniards and two thousand natives and struck at the Aztec town of Iztapalapa, which stood on the southern isthmus of the lake, at the foot of one of the causeways of the capital. He had been accorded a friendly welcome there in the original advance on Tenochtitlán: but now he was made to fight. More, the townsfolk opened one of the dykes in a surprise attempt to drown the Spanish-Indian army, an attempt in which they very nearly succeeded. After a battle fought chest-high in the water, the town was taken. Retribution followed. 'More than six thousand men, women and children perished,' Cortés wrote, 'for our Indian allies had only one idea—to kill right and left.'

After Iztapalapa, it was the turn of the equally important town of Chalco. Cortés sent out Sandoval on a sortie which resulted in its submission, and which also permanently secured the highroad leading to Tlaxcala and Villa Rica. Sandoval further cheered his chief by reporting that he had made contact with the shipwrights, whose thirteen brigantines were on their way to Texcoco, carried piecemeal on the backs of eight thousand *tamemes* and proudly escorted by twenty thousand Tlaxcalan warriors under the command of Cortés' old friend Chichimecatecle. Cortés had now officially appointed Sandoval his *alquacil mayor*, or chief of staff. After the cruel fiasco of the Great Temple massacre, Alvarado had evidently been judged unfit to hold the highest post after Cortés. Sandoval was only twenty-three, but he had earned the right to be considered Cortés' deputy by his brilliant performances in a number of assignments in which dash and tact had been called for in equal proportions.

With a strong garrison to hold Texcoco, and with Sandoval operating from Chalco, Cortés made an expedition round the extreme north of the lake and down the west side as far as Tlacopán. He took some of the Aztec satellite-towns on the lakeshore by storm, others by parley. He passed through Acolmán, the regions of Xaltocán and Zumpango, and drove south on the far side of the lake through Cuahtitlán, Tenayuca and Atzcapotzalco to Tlacopán (Tacuba), the town where six months earlier he wept in the rain beneath the cypress-tree. There was no weeping now. In spite of constant skirmishing, he was in control again. The Spanish nucleus of his army received constant dribbles of reinforcement from the coast, where, among other small benefits, another ship had put in at Villa Rica with a further forty soldiers and eight horses.

He spent six days at Tlacopán, sounding out the defences of nearby Tenochtitlán. The Aztecs in the city were full of fight. They tried to lure the Spaniards along the causeways with insolent shouts of '*Come on in and enjoy yourselves!*' The main reason for their assurance was that in place of the passive Moctezuma they had now acquired a new young leader of outstanding energy. Cuitláhuac, Moctezuma's successor, survived only for a few short months before he was carried off by the smallpox brought into the country by Narváez' negro; indeed, the part which the epidemic played in weakening Aztec resistance must not be underestimated. Cuitláhuac's place was taken by his nephew, Cuauhtémoc, another son-in-law of Moctezuma. Cuauhtémoc, 'The Eagle That Falls', was about twenty-five years old at this time, and later impressed Bernal Díaz as being 'very much of a gentleman, for an Indian, and very valiant'. The resistance which he was now about to offer to the Spaniards saved the honour and self-respect of later generations of Mexicans; and whereas Moctezuma is everywhere execrated, Cuauhtémoc is a popular hero. His gilded statue stands on top of a towering column in the Paseo de la Reforma, Mexico City's handsome main boulevard, and scores of different coloured portraits of him are everywhere on sale and are pinned up in Mexican homes beside those of Zapata and Father Hidalgo.

His accession explained why the Aztecs now taunted the Spaniards with cries of: 'Do you think you've still got Moctezuma to deal with?'; and why Cortés reported that: 'When our men called out to them that they would starve to death, because we were keeping them penned in, they retorted that they needed no food because they would eat both us and the Tlaxcalans.' Cortés was not discouraged. As always, he tried to limit the potential area of destruction by effecting a peaceful negotiation. 'I have always tried, Most Sovereign Lord,' he assured the Emperor, 'to win the people of Tenochtitlán to our friendship by every means I could. On the one hand, I did not wish them to provoke their own ruin; on the other, I wanted to rest from the hardships of all the past wars. Most important of all, however, I felt this would serve Your Majesty best. Whenever I could lay hold of anyone from the city, I would send him back to it to urge the inhabitants to come to terms of peace. I prayed them to tell their lords that, although I had every reason to wage war, I did not wish to fight them but to be friends with them as we had been before. To assure them still more, and to win them back to the service of Your Majesty, I sent them word that I knew that the principal persons who had been responsible for the last war were dead; that the past was the past, and that they ought not to provoke the overthrow of their lands and cities, for this would distress me greatly.' Cuauhtémoc, to his credit, was deaf to these appeals. There is a time to talk and there is a time to fight. One way or another the Spaniards were determined to seize his country: he would not yield it to them without a struggle.

Cortés was working up to the final investment of the city. He was still not quite ready. He returned to Texcoco and, having made his sweep to the north, embarked on a corresponding sweep to the south. He took Sandoval from Chalco, where the latter had been fighting hard and had earned a respite, placed him in charge at Texcoco, and himself went to Chalco to subdue the towns of the lower Valley. One by one they went down before him, but only after spirited resistance. Setting out on April 5, he went through Huaxtepec, Yautepec and Xiutepec. At Yautepec there was a sharp action, but he pressed on to his goal, the important town of Cuauhnahuac, later to be renamed Cuernavaca, where he would afterwards build himself a palace. Anyone familiar with that rocky, thorny, precipitous valley must be impressed by the almost casual way in which he refers to his perambulations around it. As it was, he had a hard time taking Cuernavaca, which was sited between two deep ravines and fancied itself impregnable: but take it he did, and his Tlaxcalan allies duly sacked it. He then marched back up the tortuous valley to Xochimilco, arriving there on the 15th and immediately plunging into another series of battles. Xochimilco was on the lake, and the enemy war-canoes descended on the Spaniards in swarms. The fighting continued for three days, and at one stage Cortés was nearly captured when his horse collapsed from fatigue. He was saved from being sacrificed to Huitzilopochtli, the ultimate fate of four other Spaniards taken on that particular day, by the bravery of a Tlaxcalan warrior and a young Spaniard called Cristóbal de Olea. As it was, Olea had received three cuts from an Aztec sword and Cortés himself had suffered a wound in the head by the time Andrés de Tapia and Cristóbal de Olid came up with the cavalry to complete the rescue.

There was nothing fanciful or theoretical about the prospect which faced a man taken prisoner by the Aztecs. When the Spaniards entered Texcoco, at the beginning of their present advance, they found hanging up in the temple the flayed skins of several of their comrades, as well as the hides of five horses, all beautifully stretched, dried and tanned.

*   *   *

Cuauhtémoc had done his best to take advantage of his opportunity to trap the Spaniards and Tlaxcalans at Xochimilco. He had strained every nerve to surround and overwhelm them. In the end the Spanish-Tlaxcalan army prevailed: but they were shaken. The Aztecs were performing like men who expected to win. For Cortés, Xochimilco represented an unexpected reverse. He dared not lead his men back to the safety of Texcoco by the shorter, southern road that led through Chalco; the situation there was not sufficiently stable. Instead he would have to take them home right round the north of the lake, on the route through Tlacopán, Tenayuca, Atzcapotzalco and Cuahtitlán. He hurried off towards Tlacopán more like a general retreating after a drubbing than one who has just gained a string of victories. He continued to lose more Spaniards in constant ambuscades, and was particularly disconcerted when two of his young pages were snatched away by Aztec raiders to be sacrificed on the altar-stone. When he arrived in Tlacopán, that town of tears, he 'almost had tears in his eyes', as Díaz tells us. To add to the gloom of the retreat, it started to rain as they were about to leave Tlacopán—that unremitting, oppressive

Mexican rain that soaks into one's very soul. They took what shelter they could from the downpour, but were afraid to linger more than two hours in case Cuauhtémoc pressed home the attack and sent his armies across the causeway to surround them. They slogged on through the mud for four days, wet and weary, feeling safe from pursuit and annihilation only when Sandoval came up from Texcoco to meet them at Acolmán, a day's march from base.

Even when he reached Texcoco there was no immediate respite for Cortés. The officers of the Narváez contingent had taken advantage of his absence to get up yet another attempt at mutiny. He acted promptly, seized the ringleaders and hanged one of them. After the fatigues and anxieties of the past ten days, he must have been tempted to hang the lot: but with that superhuman forbearance, which was so seldom discomposed, he contented himself with making a token example. Although he had in his pocket a paper which the condemned man had given him, containing the names of all the men involved, he coolly announced that the latter had swallowed it when he was arrested. Nevertheless it was at that point in the Conquest that, on his friends' advice, he recruited a personal bodyguard of six men, commanded by a captain from Zamora. This indication of an estrangement from his men strikes a melancholy little note. It betokens once again the changing character of the Conquest and of Cortés himself; the old carefree buccaneering days were over, the era of empire-building had begun.

As usual, the Spaniards displayed their remarkable recuperative powers. The feeling of despondency was temporary; it wore off as quickly as the change in the weather. Sandoval had brought news of fresh reinforcements from the coast, and within a few days of the army's re-arrival at Texcoco there was a general rise in spirits with the launching of the thirteen ships. Under Sandoval's direction, eight thousand Indians had been labouring for fifty days to dig a canal, twelve foot wide and twelve foot deep, all firmly revetted, to float the brigantines into the lake from the site over a mile distant where they had been assembled. The fleet took to the Lake of Texcoco on April 28, and immediately Cortés held a review of his troops. On calling the roll he found that he had available for the coming siege of Tenochtitlán a force of nearly ninety horsemen, over seven hundred infantry, almost a hundred and twenty crossbowmen and musketeers, three heavy iron guns, and fifteen small bronze field pieces. This powerful Spanish nucleus was supplemented by the Indian contingents, drawn principally from Tlaxcala, Huejotzingo, Chalco, and a few from Cholula. They were all hand-picked warriors, nearly a hundred thousand strong, and had been well-trained in Cortés' methods. Díaz writes of them: 'When Cortés heard that Xicotenga and his brothers and captains were approaching, he went out a mile to receive them, and greeted and embraced them all. They marched in fine order, all very brilliant, beneath their great devices, each company separately with its banners streaming, and the white bird, like an eagle with wings outstretched, that is their badge. Marching in good order, in their feathered head-dresses, they whistled, shouted, and cried: "Long live our lord the Emperor!" and "Castile! Castile!" and "Tlaxcala! Tlaxcala!" They took more than three hours entering Texcoco.' The Spaniards too were put through their paces. There were drills and manœuvres, and the troops were issued with the new stores of gunpowder, lances, arrowheads and crossbow-bolts which Cortés had been diligently amassing ever since their original entrance into Texcoco.

Early in May he paraded them again and told off the Spanish contingent into three divisions. To Sandoval he gave twenty-four horsemen, a hundred and fifty foot-soldiers, and thirty thousand Indians; to Alvarado, thirty horsemen, a hundred and fifty foot-soldiers, and twenty-five thousand Tlaxcalans; and to Olid, thirty horsemen, a hundred and sixty foot-soldiers, and twenty thousand Indians. For his brigantines, he had three hundred Spanish sailors available, so that each ship had a crew of at least twenty-five men. From the numbers involved—and the Ibero-Indian army was substantially smaller than that of the Aztecs—it is easy to appreciate that this was no petty bush-war fought out at the back-of-beyond. Anything up to a half million troops were about to grapple with each other. The prize was one of the most populous cities in the world at that time.

The divisions of Alvarado and Olid moved out on May 10. They followed the northerly path around the lake and took up their assigned stations on the west bank. Alvarado halted at Tlacopán; Olid went on a further twelve miles to Coyoacán. Both towns commanded the end of a main causeway, and both were deserted. The Aztec inhabitants had carried out a scorched-earth policy, removing or destroying anything that might be of service to the enemy before withdrawing into the capital. The two Spanish commanders found that Cuauhtémoc had hacked holes in the causeways or erected barricades at intervals along them. The Aztecs were digging themselves in for a long siege, preparing to sit out the Ibero-Indian onslaught, confident that the enemy would tire or find himself in difficulties before they themselves did. But it was their opponents who got in the first blow. Acting on orders from Cortés, Olid sent out a small raiding-party to cut the great aqueduct at Chapultepec, thus robbing the city of its principal supply of fresh water. 'A very politic stratagem,' as

Cortés reflected in his next despatch, with a touch of complacency.

He himself remained at Texcoco with three hundred men and the thirteen brigantines. He sent off Sandoval and the third division southward round the lake to recapture Iztapalapa, at the end of one of the two branches of the great southern causeway; then he embarked with his own men on the boats and set off across the lake.

He landed near Iztapalapa, captured an enemy outpost, then reembarked and at once became embroiled in a major and protracted seabattle. The entire tussle for the city, on both sides, was to possess an amphibious character. Cortés had guessed correctly when he stated in his Third Despatch, and in the memoirs he later dictated to Gómara, that 'the brigantines held the key to the whole war'. The city in the water could not have been effectively attacked, much less subdued, by means of dry-land operations alone. This first engagement was significant in that it immediately proved the efficacy of the little Spanish flotilla and established its supremacy over the Aztec war-canoes. With the help of a following wind, the brigantines went tacking through and through the frail craft of the enemy, and, with cannon, musket and crossbow, pounded them and their occupants to pieces. The Aztec canoes ran in disorder for the quays of Tenochtitlán, with Cortés in hot pursuit. 'We destroyed an infinite number of canoes and killed and drowned many of the enemy,' he wrote later. He added that it was 'the greatest sight to be seen in the world', for people were not so reticent in those days in expressing a frank satisfaction in the pleasurable aspects of warfare, nor in ascribing a similar satisfaction to the Almighty: 'And so it pleased God to give us the best and greatest victory which we could have asked or desired.'

Cortés now moved to bottle up his enemy by blocking the five landward exits of the three great causeways, the southern and western of which forked into two branches. He sent Sandoval north to Tepeyac to control the end of the northern causeway, and while Alvarado sat on the western exits at Tlacopán and Chapultepec, he himself lent Olid a hand with the Coyoacán and Iztapalapa exits in the south. Of course, as soon as his troops fought their way as far as the forks of the western and southern causeways, the number of exits would be reduced to three. The struggle for the city was the struggle to advance along the causeways—three narrow defiles or passages, flanked by water, where every day attackers and defenders congregated to engage each other in fanatical combat in the most cramped and restricted conditions imaginable. The Ibero–Indian spearhead attempted to bore its way a yard at a time along each causeway, while on both sides they were given close support by the Spanish brigantines. Cortés divided his flotilla among his divisions for this purpose, giving Sandoval two ships, Alvarado four, and keeping the remainder in the south with himself and Olid.

Day after day the murderous battles on the causeways continued (Plate 11). It was evident from the start that Cuauhtémoc meant to resist to the death. Moreover, he too had put the time of preparation to good use, and his warriors appeared to have an inexhaustible supply of missiles of every description. The causeways were knee-deep in the rocks, stones, darts, spears and arrows with which they bombarded their attackers. They constructed formidable barricades which had to be taken one by one, and a barricade that had been overrun during the day usually had to be yielded up during the night, when the Aztecs returned in greater strength than ever. As effective as the barricades were the gaps and holes which the defenders tore in the solid material of the causeways—destroying, in their determination to resist to the end, the labour of centuries, the very structures on which the existence of their city depended. They filled the gaps and holes with sharpened stakes that inflicted fearful wounds, sometimes planting the stakes below water-level, even digging down into the lake-bed beneath the breaches to make it impossible for the enemy to wade across the gap. They also placed rows of stakes in the water on each side of the causeways to rip out the bottoms of the brigantines, or at least to prevent them from operating as closely and effectively to the causeways as they wished. The Spaniards and their allies had to clamber across the breaches under fire, then fill them with rubble and wooden beams to provide a safe footing for the troops behind them. To make matters worse, the cavalry were unable to function under such circumstances, where there was no room to manœuvre. On occasion four or five well-armoured horses and their riders were placed at the head of the column and used like *chars blindés* to cut a path for the following infantry. Cortés was so afraid that horses would be lost in this uncertain tactic that it could only be employed sparingly.

Thus the struggle went on, day after day, night after night. The aim of the Ibero-Indians was to penetrate into the city, where their three divisions would finally coalesce in the great market square of Tlaltelolco, two miles north of the centre of the city and at the foot of the northern causeway. The aim of the Aztecs was to stop them. Nor was the Aztec cause by any means doomed from the start. Although the city was so closely invested by land, the Aztec canoes continuously ferried in supplies from all around the lake. As for the Spanish flotilla, it had been divided up, and was incapable of intercepting so many small craft or seriously incommoding them. Conversely, the Spaniards and the enormous mass of Indian allies who accompanied them were existing in hostile country and on a starving shore. They were reduced to a scanty diet of tortillas, cherries, and the fruits of the prickly-pear, eked out with a few vegetables. The attackers also had to endure the hard summer rains from which, unlike their enemies, who could shelter in their houses in the city, they had no protection. Lastly, many of the Aztec towns on the lake-shore were still unsubdued, and harassed the rear and communications of the opposing army as it inched its way along the causeways.

After three weeks of bloody and more or less inconclusive warfare of this type, it looked, as Díaz says, as if the besiegers had become the besieged. 'It was as if,' he wrote, 'we were the ones in the trap, and the enemy were in possession of the shore, the countryside and the lake. We warned Cortés that we might be falling into the same devilish trouble as when we first retreated from Tenochtitlán. He listened to our opinions, but only ordered that next day we were to advance again from all three positions with the greatest possible strength.' He knew that there was no going back, that the climax had been reached. The contest was about to be resolved once and for all, in favour of himself or Cuauhtémoc. The one who weakened would be the one who lost. Victory would go to whoever could endure the struggle one minute longer than the other.

Cortés had certainly been weakened. Sandoval rode around the lines with his arm in a sling and his head swathed in bloody rags; Alvarado had sustained a wound on the head, though no wound except a mortal one would ever hold that staunch scrapper in check. He gained so much more ground than his companions that Cortés, visiting his camp, was astonished at his progress, and the admiration that Cortés felt went far towards effecting a rapprochement between him and his awkward subordinate.

There came a day when it appeared that the Ibero–Indian army had actually been routed, and that the Aztecs had won. The rout began when Cortés, at the head of his men, found it necessary to retire down the causeway after an unsuccessful attack. At first they gave ground in good order, but under unrelenting pressure from the Aztecs they broke and ran. Díaz gives a graphic picture of what happened next. 'On seeing them thus scramble back in disorder,' he wrote, 'Cortés tried to hearten them with cries of: "Stop, stop, gentlemen! Stand firm! What do you mean by turning your backs?" But he could not halt them. And then, at that gap in the causeway which they had neglected to fill, on that little, narrow, broken causeway, the Mexicans, aided by their canoes, defeated Cortés, wounding him in the leg, taking sixty-six of his soldiers alive, and killing eight horses. Six or seven Mexican captains had already seized our Captain, but the Lord was pleased to help him and give him strength to defend himself, although wounded. Then, in the nick of time, that very valiant soldier Cristóbal de Olea came up to him and, seeing Cortés held by so many Indians, promptly killed four of them with thrusts of his sword; and another brave soldier called Lerma helped him (Plate 9). Such was the personal bravery of these two men that the Indian captains let Cortés go. But in defending him for the second time Olea lost his life and Lerma was almost killed. Then many other soldiers rushed up and, although badly wounded, grasped Cortés and pulled him out of his dangerous position in the mud. The quartermaster Cristóbal de Olid also ran forward, and they seized Cortés by the arms to drag him out of the mud and water, and brought him a horse, on which he escaped from death. At that same moment his steward Cristóbal de Guzmán arrived with another horse. Meanwhile the Mexican warriors went on fighting very bravely and successfully from the rooftops, inflicting great damage on us and capturing Cristóbal de Guzmán, whom they carried alive to Cuauhtémoc; and they continued to pursue Cortés and his men until they had driven them back to camp. Even after that disaster, when they reached their quarters the Mexicans continued to harry them, shouting and yelling abuse and calling them cowards.'

Díaz himself learned of these events only afterwards, at second hand, for he was a member of Alvarado's division on the Tlacopán causeway. As Cortés wrote in his Third Despatch, when giving the Emperor details of his hair-breadth escape, what had occurred was 'a rout, in which the enemy killed thirty-five to forty Spaniards and more than one thousand of our Indian allies. A cannon was lost, also many muskets and crossbows'. We can imagine the feelings of Alvarado and Díaz when a yelling mob of Aztecs pitched four severed Spanish heads along the causeway and shouted that two of them were the heads of Cortés and Sandoval, and that this was the fate that was about to be meted out to every other Spaniard and Tlaxcalan. Simultaneously, other heads were hurled at Sandoval on the neighbouring causeway, with the claim that they were those of Cortés, Olid and Alvarado; while still others, purporting to be those of Alvarado and Sandoval, were cast down at the heels of Cortés' confused column. This was cunning tactics at such a moment, when among the alarms of that hectic day it was impossible for one Spanish commander to form an accurate estimate of what was happening to the others. The Ibero-Indians came very close to a general panic. Had it occurred, the result could only have been complete disaster. At length, by throwing in the remaining horsemen and artillerymen, and using desperate measures to ram the brigantines through the breakwaters erected by the Aztecs, the position was retrieved, but only at a cost of more men killed and forty captured, and the loss of a brigantine.

To round off a miserable episode, the nerves of the Ibero-Indians were further excoriated when many of them were compelled to witness from afar the ritual sacrifice of their captured comrades. As Cortés wrote: 'Immediately after this victory, the defenders of the city, in order to frighten Gonzalo de Sandoval and Pedro de Alvarado, brought all the live and dead Spaniards they had taken into the main square. There they stripped them and dragged them to the top of the temples and opened their breasts, taking out the hearts and offering them to their idols. The Spaniards with Pedro de Alvarado could see the naked white bodies from where they were fighting, and recognized them. They were saddened and dismayed, and retreated into their camp.' Díaz gives his own trenchant eye-witness account, from his vantage-point with Alvarado: 'Facing the enemy, and never turning our backs, we gradually retired, forming a kind of dam to hold up their advance. Some of our crossbowmen and musketeers shot while others were loading, the horsemen made charges, and Pedro Moreno loaded and fired his cannon. Yet despite the number of Mexicans that were swept away by his shot we could not keep them at bay. On the contrary, they continued to pursue us, in the belief that they would carry us off that night to be sacrificed. However, when we had retired almost to our quarters, across a great opening full of water, their arrows, darts, and stones could no longer reach us. Sandoval, Francisco de Lugo, and Andrés de Tapia were standing with Pedro de Alvarado, each one telling his story and discussing Cortés' orders, when the dismal drum of Huitzilopochtli sounded again, accompanied by conches, horns, and trumpet-like instruments. It was a terrifying sound, and when we looked at the tall temple from which it came we saw our comrades who had been captured in Cortés' defeat being dragged up the steps to be sacrificed. When they had hauled them up to a small platform in front of the shrine where they kept their accursed idols we saw them put plumes on the heads of many of them; and then they made them dance with a sort of fan in front of Huitzilopochtli. Then after they had danced the priests laid them down on their backs on some narrow stones of sacrifice and, cutting open their chests, drew out their palpitating hearts which they offered to the idols before them. Then they kicked the bodies down the steps, and the Indian butchers who were waiting below cut off their arms and legs and flayed their faces, which they afterwards prepared like glove leather, with their beards on, and kept for their drunken festivals. Then they ate their flesh with a sauce of peppers and tomatoes. They sacrificed all our men in this way, eating their legs and arms, offering their hearts and blood to their idols, and throwing their trunks and entrails to the lions and tigers and serpents and snakes that they kept in the wild-beast houses.

'On seeing these atrocities, all of us in our camp said to one another: "Thank God they did not carry me off to be sacrificed!" Though we were not far off we could do nothing to help, and could only pray God to guard us from such a death. Then at the very moment of the sacrifice, great bands of Mexicans suddenly fell upon us and kept us busy on all sides. We could find no way of holding them. "Look!" they shouted, "that is the way you will all die, as our gods have many times promised us," and the threats they shouted at our Tlaxcalan allies were so cruel and so frightening that they lost their spirit. The Mexicans threw them roasted legs of Indians and the arms of our soldiers with cries of: "Eat the flesh of these *Teules* and of your brothers, for we are glutted with it. You can stuff yourselves on our leavings. Now see these houses you have pulled down. We shall make you build them again, much finer, with white stone and fine masonry. So go on helping the *Teules*. You will see them all sacrificed." Cuauhtémoc also did something more after his victory. He sent the hands and feet of our soldiers, and the skin of their faces, and the heads of the horses that had been killed, to all the towns of our allies and friends and their relations, with the message that as more than half of us were dead and he would soon finish off the rest, they had better break their alliance with us and come to Tenochtitlán, because if they did not desert us quickly he would come and destroy them.'

The Aztec argument was hard to resist. Cortés' allies did indeed begin to drop away from him. They left his camp in their thousands and returned to their villages, leaving him with only a few hundreds to help him maintain his perilous position on the causeways. Even the mass of the Tlaxcalans deserted him—all except his staunch old comrades in arms, Xicotenga and Chichimecatecle. This remarkable pair not only stood by him: they fought with increased vigour. When the Spaniards themselves began to flag, the two Tlaxcalan leaders reproached them and went on hacking and hammering their way down the choked causeways on their own account. It should also be added that Ixtlixóchitl, the *cacique* of Texcoco, also held firm at this time, and that this unexpected fidelity to the Spanish cause on the part of the ruler of one of the principal cities of the Aztec confederation produced a strong impression on friend and foe alike.

The example of the chiefs of Tlaxcala and Texcoco, coupled with Cortés' own undiminished resolution, slowly rallied his Indian allies and put new heart in his tired and hungry Spaniards. After a three-day lull he gathered his strength for a fresh advance. Mercifully, it was successful, and carried his forces off the causeways and among the streets and houses of the island itself. However, Alvarado again exceeded, or rather disregarded, his orders, taking his troops over a treacherous gap in the causeway without securing his retreat. In the ensuing *mêlée* many Spaniards and Indians were killed, and four captured Spaniards were dragged away to be sacrificed.

The campaign had been continuing without respite for three weeks, and Cortés saw that he could no longer afford to delay his grand attack. His overtures of peace had been repeatedly rejected; he could not leave his troops exposed in the streets to the fire poured down on them by the enemy from every roof. He had to make a quick end to the matter, and he believed that could be done by capturing the principal square, the geographical and spiritual centre of the Aztec capital and Aztec state. He put Juan de Alderete in charge of a special task-force which was to lead the way, consisting of seventy Spaniards, several thousand Indians, and a few horses. He ordered a simultaneous assault from the water by seven brigantines and three hundred war-canoes. Then, with Alvarado and Sandoval, he set out after Alderete with a high heart—only to meet yet another rebuff. Alderete could make little impression on the Aztec defenders, and had to fall back. Cortés himself rode off a makeshift bridge into the water, was seized by Aztecs and for the second time in the siege only rescued after two of his friends had been killed while extricating him. He suffered a further loss of nearly forty Spaniards, and yielded up a cannon and many muskets and crossbows.

It was at this stage that he took his decision to destroy Tenochtitlán. It was not a decision taken from pique or vengefulness: it was a case of hard military necessity. In future he would not permit any of his captains to advance a single yard until every obstruction—every pit, barricade, wall, parapet or roof that could give shelter to the enemy was filled in or levelled with the ground. The Aztecs were proving such experts at house-to-house fighting that it was foolish to sap his resources by playing them at their own game. Henceforward his advance would be slow, but it would be thorough. By grinding forward across the plain of rubble which he had created, there would now be no call to surrender at night a barrier or block of buildings it had taken him all day to capture (see Plate 11).

The preliminary fighting around the main square occupied another week. The stench of unburied bodies lying in the streets or floating in the canals, the rain, the rubbish, the blood and misery, rendered the scene sordid and gruesome in the extreme. However, if the Spaniards were nearing their last gasp, so were their adversaries. Food was scarce and pestilence was raging. The anonymous author of the Manuscript of

Tlaltelolco in the Bibliothèque Nationale in Paris, writing less than twenty years after the events of which he was evidently an eye-witness, described the plight of the defenders. 'This was how it was with us. This was the sad and miserable fate with which we were tormented. The streets were littered with bloody darts and the carcasses of horses. The houses were roofless, their walls smeared with blood and spattered with brains. Worms swarmed everywhere, the water was dyed scarlet and tasted of salt. We knocked down our adobe buildings to afford us protection. All we had left was a skeleton city. Our shields had been our safeguard—now they were shattered. We ate pies made of thrushes, reeds, bits of adobe, lizards, rats, earth, worms. We ate half-baked meat, snatching it off the fire before it was cooked. We took the captives to Cuauhtémoc, and their breasts were opened, Cuauhtémoc doing the work himself.' One wonders whether, under these circumstances, cannibalism was not more widespread than previously.

The Aztecs were manifesting not merely a determination to resist, but a determination to perish. Welcoming death, they were intent on suicide. Cortés was disconcerted by this un-Western, un-Christian urge to embrace mass extinction. He lost no opportunity to send messages to them by the mouths of distinguished prisoners. In the Manuscript of Tlaltelolco he is represented as asking plaintively: 'Why won't they negotiate? What are they thinking about? Is Cuauhtémoc a young idiot? Have they no pity for their own women and children and old folk?' Repeatedly he protested, as Gómara later put it, that he was 'reluctant to destroy such a beautiful city', and in his Third Despatch he wrote: 'The people of the city were so stubborn and displayed such a resolve to die that I did not know what means to use to relieve our dangers and hardships, and to avoid utterly destroying them and their capital, which was the loveliest thing in the world.' Above everything, he sought an interview with Cuauhtémoc. Several lesser intermediaries presented themselves; but it was only an Aztec ruse to gain time, and he knew that in dealing with a society like that of the Aztecs it was useless to negotiate with anyone except the head and leader of the people. Cuauhtémoc absolutely refused to meet him.

He was left with no alternative but to continue the slaughter. He was now in possession of over two-thirds of the city. The causeways had been repaired and re-paved, and it was possible to ride from one Spanish camp to another on the central island, without following a circuitous route back along the causeways and around the shore. The enemy forces, together with the surviving citizens of the capital itself and the refugees from the lakeside towns, were all crammed into the main square and the area around it. The summits of the great temples rose above this packed and pitiful mass of humanity. The Spaniards, says Gómara, 'saw a great deal of gnawed bark and roots, and men who were so emaciated that the Spaniards were filled with pity for them. Cortés proposed another truce, but they, although their bodies were starved, were strong of heart, and told him he would get nothing here, because they would burn whatever was left, or throw it into the water, and if a single one of them survived he would die fighting'.

And so, after three months of siege-warfare, and a final four-day lull, Cortés gave the order for the last attack. The first day a whole district fell, and a number of Aztecs assessed at the staggering total of twelve thousand were slain, owing as Gómara says 'to the cruelty of our Indian allies, who would spare the life of no Aztec no matter how hard we tried to dissuade them from it'. He goes on: 'The Aztecs were now so crowded that there was hardly room for them to stand in the remaining houses, and the streets were so covered with dead bodies that one had to walk over corpses. Cortés wanted to find out how much of the city had yet to be taken, so he mounted a tower, looked, and estimated it to be about an eighth. The next day he again attacked the remnant, but ordered his troops to kill only those who resisted. The Aztecs, bewailing their evil fortune, begged the Spaniards to kill them and have done with it, and certain Aztec gentlemen urgently summoned Cortés, who hurried to them in the hope that they might be seeking an arrangement. He stood at the edge of a breach, and they called out to him: "Ah, Captain Cortés, since you are a child of the Sun, why do you not persuade him to finish us? O Sun, who can make the circuit of the earth in the short space of a day and a night, kill us now and relieve us of this long and dreadful penance, for we desire to rest with Quetzalcóatl, who awaits us." Then they wept and invoked their gods with loud cries. Cortés answered with whatever came to his mind, but could not persuade them. Our Spaniards were struck with pity.'

The next morning Cortés called a halt to the fighting and tried again. This time he received the impression that Cuauhtémoc would actually come to speak with him. Gómara states that he therefore 'went back to his camp very happy, thinking that the two of them would reach agreement'. On the day following he ordered a dais to be erected, and as royal a banquet as his own scanty resources would provide to be set out; but the only Aztecs who arrived to sample the feast were five of the king's courtiers. After feeding them, he sent them back to their master with the message that he would wait a further two hours. Finally, at sunset, they returned to say that the king would speak with Cortés the following day. Unfortunately, the next day's proceedings merely repeated what had gone before. A deputation arrived, without Cuauhtémoc; it was given another two hours' grace, and then returned with an empty and temporizing reply.

Cortés saw that protracted delay was pointless and dangerous. His Spaniards were impatient to get the business over, and his Indian allies were baying for blood and could be restrained no longer. He placed himself at the head of the troops on land and ordered Alvarado to take charge of the fleet. A further massacre then took place, which cost the Aztecs another hecatomb. Atrocious and heart-rending spectacles were enacted. But now let us—as is fitting—allow Prescott to paint the epic canvas of those last and most terrible scenes. He portrays with a heightened pen the death-throes of the Aztec nation, as it battled to its end among the towering temples that a few months before had been the emblems of its pride and power.

As Cortés advanced, Prescott writes, he found the Aztecs prepared to receive him. 'Their most able-bodied warriors were thrown into the van, covering their feeble and crippled comrades. Women were seen occasionally mingled in the ranks, and, as well as children, thronged the *azoteas*, where, with famine-stricken visages, and haggard eyes, they scowled defiance and hatred on their invaders.

'As the Spaniards advanced, the Mexicans set up a fierce war-cry, and sent off clouds of arrows with their accustomed spirit, while the women and boys rained down darts and stones from their elevated position on the terraces. But the missiles were sent by hands too feeble to do much damage; and, when the squadrons closed, the loss of strength became still more sensible in the Aztecs. Their blows fell feebly and with doubtful aim, though some, it is true, of stronger constitution, or gathering strength from despair, maintained to the last a desperate fight.

'The arquebusiers now poured in a deadly fire. The brigantines replied by successive volleys, in the opposite quarter. The besieged, hemmed in, like deer surrounded by the huntsmen, were brought down on every side. The carnage was horrible. The ground was heaped up with slain, until the maddened combatants were obliged to climb over the human mounds to get at one another. The miry soil was saturated with blood, which ran off like water, and dyed the canals themselves with crimson. All was uproar and terrible confusion. The hideous yells of the barbarians; the oaths and execrations of the Spaniards; the cries of the wounded; the shrieks of women and children; the heavy blows of the Conquerors: the death-struggle of their victims; the rapid, reverberating echoes of musketry; the hissing of innumerable missiles; the crash and crackling of blazing buildings, crushing hundreds in their ruins; the blinding volumes of dust and sulphurous smoke shrouding all in their gloomy canopy,—

made a scene appalling even to the soldiers of Cortés, steeled as they were by many a rough passage of war, and by long familiarity with blood and violence. "The piteous cries of the women and children, in particular," says the general, "were enough to break one's heart." He commanded that they should be spared, and that all, who asked it, should receive quarter. He particularly urged this on the confederates, and placed men among them to restrain their violence. But he had set an engine in motion too terrible to be controlled. It were as easy to curb the hurricane in its fury, as the passions of an infuriated horde of savages. "Never did I see so pitiless a race," he exclaims, "or anything wearing the form of man so destitute of humanity." They made no distinction of sex or age, and in this hour of vengeance seemed to be requiting the hoarded wrongs of a century. At length, sated with slaughter, the Spanish commander sounded a retreat. It was full time, if, according to his own statement,—we may hope it is an exaggeration,—forty thousand souls had perished! Yet their fate was to be envied, in comparison with that of those who survived.

'Through the long night which followed, no movement was perceptible in the Aztec quarter. No light was seen there, no sound was heard, save the low moaning of some wounded or dying wretch, writhing in his agony. All was dark and silent,—the darkness of the grave. The last blow seemed to have completely stunned them. They had parted with hope, and sat in sullen despair, like men waiting in silence the stroke of the executioner. Yet, for all this, they showed no disposition to submit. Every new injury had sunk deeper into their souls, and filled them with a deeper hatred of their enemy. Fortune, friends, kindred, home,—all were gone. They were content to throw away life itself, now that they had nothing more to live for.'

It seems inconceivable, but even that day's terror did not break the will of the Aztecs to resist. Their resolve to die was unimpaired. They had been a nation willing to submit everything, for good or ill, to the arbitration of the sword. The high powers whom they had served had decreed that they must perish as they had lived. Another race had been appointed to execute the divine duty of feeding the sun. The gods had turned down their thumbs and, like the professional gladiators they were, they accepted their fate. They were a fierce people and they remained fierce to the end. They did not betray themselves or betray posterity. They died uncomplaining.

One last short, sharp action and—mercifully—it was over. Prescott takes up the sad burden of the story. 'It was the memorable 13th of August, 1521, the day of St. Hypolito,' he continues, 'that Cortés led his warlike array for the last time across the black and blasted environs which lay around the Indian capital. On entering the Aztec precincts, he paused, willing to afford its wretched inmates one more chance of escape, before striking the fatal blow. He obtained an interview with some of the principal chiefs, and expostulated with them on the conduct of their prince. "He surely will not," said the general, "see you all perish, when he can so easily save you." He then urged them to prevail on Cuauhtémoc to hold a conference with him, repeating the assurances of his personal safety.

'The messengers went on their mission, and soon returned with the *cihuacoatl* at their head, a magistrate of high authority among the Mexicans. He said, with a melancholy air, in which his own disappointment was visible, that Cuauhtémoc was ready to die where he was, but would hold no interview with the Spanish commander; adding, in a tone of resignation, "it is for you to work your pleasure." "Go, then," replied the stern Conqueror, "and prepare your countrymen for death. Their hour is come."

'He still postponed the assault for several hours. But the impatience of his troops at this delay was heightened by the rumour, that Cuauhtémoc and his nobles were preparing to escape with their effects in the *piraguas* and canoes which were moored on the margin of the lake. Convinced of the fruitlessness and impolicy of further procrastination, Cortés made his final dispositions for the attack, and took his own station on an *azotea*, which commanded the theatre of operations.'

*   *   *

And so it ended. All that remained was the capture of Cuauhtémoc. The young king had fled from the city in a fast canoe, with the intention of reaching the eastern shore and continuing the war from whatever lakeside towns would remain faithful to the Aztec cause. He was overtaken by a friend of Sandoval, García Holguín, in a launch, and at his own request taken straight to Cortés. The latter, hearing of his approach, made elaborate preparations to receive him, and on his appearance, as Díaz records, 'embraced him joyfully, treating him and his thirty courtiers with a great show of affection'. Then came the painful matter of capitulation. ' "Lord Malinche," said Cuauhtémoc, "I have assuredly done my duty in defence of my city and my vassals, and I can do no more. I am brought by force as a prisoner into your presence and beneath your power. Take the dagger that you have in your belt, and strike me dead immediately." He sobbed as he spoke and the tears fell from his eyes, and the other great lords whom he brought with him wept also. Cortés answered him very kindly through our interpreters that he admired him greatly for having had the bravery to defend his city, and did not blame him at all. On the contrary, he thought rather well than ill of him for having done so. What he wished, however, was that he had sued for peace on his own accord when his defeat was certain, and had thus prevented so many of his people from losing their lives. But now all this had happened, there was no help for it. Nothing could be mended.'

Prescott writes: 'It was the hour of vespers when Cuauhtémoc surrendered. The evening set in dark, and the rain began to fall. During the night, a tremendous tempest, such as the Spaniards had rarely witnessed, and such as is known only within the tropics, burst over the Mexican Valley. The thunder, reverberating from the rocky amphitheatre of hills, bellowed over the waste of waters, and shook the *teocallis* and crazy tenements of Tenochtitlán—the few that yet survived—to their foundations. The lightning seemed to cleave asunder the vault of heaven, as its vivid flashes wrapped the whole scene in a ghastly glare for a moment, to be again swallowed up in darkness. The war of elements was in unison with the fortunes of the ruined city. It seemed as if the deities of Anahuac, scared from their ancient abodes, were borne along shrieking and howling in the blast, as they abandoned the fallen capital to its fate.'

Despite the storm, however, the Spaniards felt the satisfaction and relief that comes to a victorious army when its labours are ended. Díaz concludes the matter with his usual original and graphic touch when he tells us: 'It rained and thundered that evening, and the lightning flashed, and up to midnight heavier rain fell than usual. After Cuauhtémoc's capture all we soldiers became as deaf as if all the bells in a belfry had been ringing and had then suddenly stopped. I say this because, during the whole ninety-three days of our siege of the capital, Aztec captains were yelling and shouting night and day, mustering the bands of warriors who were to fight on the causeway, and calling to the men in the canoes who were to attack the launches and struggle with us on the bridges and build barricades, or to those who were driving in piles, and deepening and widening the channels and bridges, and building breastworks, or to those who were making javelins and arrows, or to the women shaping rounded stones for their slings. Then there was the unceasing sound of their accursed drums and trumpets, and their melancholy kettledrums in the shrines and on their temple towers. Both day and night the din was so great that we could hardly hear one another speak. But after Cuauhtémoc's capture, all the shouting and the other noises ceased, which is why I have made the comparison with a belfry.'

*   *   *

What passed through the mind of the Conqueror, as he stood at nightfall in the centre of the ruined city and surveyed the carnage?

He was experiencing both a triumph and a tragedy. He had fought one of the great campaigns of history. He had earned himself the immortality dear to the soul of a man of the Renaissance. Yet the manner of his triumph had left behind a wounded name. In his own mind he felt himself to be justified. He had conducted himself according to the standards of a Christian, a gentleman of Castile, and a servant of the Emperor; indeed, he had observed those standards more scrupulously than anyone could reasonably have expected. And yet—what sensible man would not have been appalled by the price he had been made to pay for all that fame and glory? His despatches, and Gómara's biography, show us that his conscience troubled him.

He had set out with a score of ships and a handful of men towards an unknown shore. His intention, like that of Balboa, had been to found a modest colony and amass a modest fortune. Even in his broadest imaginings he had not envisaged the discovery of a vast kingdom, its monuments certainly as imposing as those of Europe, ruled by an Emperor more wealthy, more powerful and more feared than his own. He had suddenly been confronted with an unexpected and monumental task, for which he was wretchedly provided. He had been required, with puny and contemptible means, to surmount a whole cordillera of setbacks and obstacles, to overthrow that Emperor and conquer that kingdom. It was a challenge to his courage, his manhood, his intelligence, his pride as a Spaniard and as an individual. And he had won through. He had begun as a small-time freebooter and captain of a band of mercenaries—and two years later, when he was still only thirty-six, had emerged as a general of great armies, the manipulator of grand diplomatic strategies, the occupant of the most enormous proconsular power in the world. He was the ruler of a territory larger than that of his imperial master: and he had seized that territory by his own exertions, by means of his own will, strength, brains, courage and endurance.

Everything he had done was justified. He had attempted to act, according to his lights, with justice and with a reasonable moderation. He had brought light to the heathen. He had introduced the civilization of Spain and Europe to a backward and barbarous continent. He had put his own mark and that of the imperial *raza* on a huge segment of the globe. He had placed his brand on Time itself.

And yet, what else did he feel on that stormy August night, in that stinking square, with the wounds in his head and hand aching, as he attempted to envisage the gigantic measure of what he had brought into existence and what he had destroyed? That day a vast and ancient order-ing of human life had largely passed away, and a vast new ordering of human life had taken its place. The thought was exciting—and melan-choly. Perhaps that was the symbolic moment when the profound melancholy of Spain and the ineradicable melancholy of Mexico fused together to constitute one of the basic traits of the new breed of men that was henceforward to arise.

Thus ended the world of the Aztecs, signalling the end of the great aboriginal world of the Americas. If Cortés had failed to reach his goal our world would have been different. But reach it he did. On that night of agony, death, and rain, the world of Spain was superimposed on the world of Mexico. The far-ranging community of Spanish-America was born.

PART FOUR

AFTERMATH

As long as the world breathes life, as long as the globe
turns, as long as the invigorating wave nourishes an illusion,
as long as there is a lively passion, a noble task, an impossible
quest, an impossible feat, a hidden America to find, *Spain shall live!*

I

¡ Cuán diversas sendas
se suelen seguir
en el repartir
las honras y haciendas!
á unos da encomiendas,
á otros sambenitos:
cuando pitos flautas
cuando flautas pitos.

By what different ways men arrive at
honours and estates! Some get
encomiendas, some get the shrouds
of penitents. Whistles instead of flutes!
Flutes instead of whistles!

Don Luis de Góngora:
Romances cortos y letrillas

'THEY were not,' writes J. H. Parry of the *conquistadores* in his *Age of Reconnaissance*, 'the stuff of which bureaucrats are made'; and in his *Spanish Seaborne Empire* he elaborates further: 'The rule of the *conquistadores* was quarrelsome and brief. They had gone to America at their own expense, endured great hardships, risked their lives and (such as they were) their fortunes, without much practical help from the government at home; and the government never fully trusted them. Most of the leaders died violent deaths. Among those who survived the hardships, the campaigns and the knives of jealous rivals, very few were permanently entrusted with administrative power. Obviously they were not men of a kind likely to settle down as obedient bureaucrats; and it was natural that the Crown should supplant them—once their conquests were secure—with men of its own choice: officials, lawyers, ecclesiastics. Their followers and successors, however—the second and third ranks of the conquest, a wave of emigration representative of almost every class and group in Spain, except the highest nobility—settled in considerable numbers in the lands they had conquered, and created their own characteristic society, highly resistant to bureaucratic regulation. This society—turbulent,

9*

aristocratic, loosely organized and jealous—was to set an enduring stamp upon the whole story of Spanish America.'

For the moment, Cortés' usefulness was by no means over. And although —and largely by his own fault, as we shall see—he was not destined to be the *administrator* of New Spain, the vigorous qualities that had enabled him to conquer it now enabled him to become its *fundador*.

The first months after the fall of the Aztec Empire were inevitably attended by dislocation and chaos, although the disorganization was greatly lessened by the natural discipline and cohesiveness that have always marked village-life in Mexico. Cortés sent out numerous flying columns to troubled areas, himself leading one to the vicinity of Pánuco, where he wanted to find out what had attracted Francisco de Garay's attention to that particular point on the coast, and whether there might be a possibility of discovering a good harbour and founding a new town. Sandoval accompanied him, remaining to put down with a heavy hand a mutiny among the relics of Garay's settlers and general disaffection in the surrounding countryside. He executed no less than four hundred native *caciques*.

With his innate tirelessness and constructive imagination, Cortés began the rebuilding of what we must now call Mexico City. The bodies were carted away and buried, the rubble cleared, the houses levelled, and the great new city which he intended to become the most imposing in the New World was laid out on the familiar Spanish plan. While he was waiting for his own palace in the central plaza to be completed, he established temporary residence in the palace of the former lord of Coyoacán, the town at the end of the southern causeway which had been his head-quarters during the earlier part of the siege. The palace, pretty in appearance and attractively sited, became his favourite place of residence, closer to his heart than the somewhat foursquare and barrack-like palace that nine years later he began building for himself at Cuernavaca, two days' march away to the south. It was in this period that the worst excesses of gold-hunting occurred. The Spaniards were eager to discover what had happened to the loot they had been forced to leave behind in the palace of Axayácatl on the Night of Sorrow; they were also curious as to whether or not the Aztecs had recovered any of the treasure dumped near the Tlacopán causeway during that same retreat. They suspected that Moctezuma had not handed over the whole of the royal accumulations of gold and jewels. Cortés, desperate for money to pay his followers, ordered Cuauhtémoc and the prince of Tlacopán to be put to the question. Apologists for Cortés, particularly Torquemada, have argued that the man really responsible for this brutal incident was Alderete, the royal notary and the officer in Cortés' entourage entrusted with the collection of the Royal Fifth. Alderete, not to be confused with the Juan de Alderete who had saved Cortés' life, was an old crony of Velázquez and Fonseca, and is said to have insisted that Cortés would be derelict in his duty to the Emperor if he neglected any means of laying hands on the wealth of the Aztecs. However, Cortés was in command, and must assume responsibility for the torture of the two young men that now occurred. They were pinioned and their feet were burned. At one stage the prince of Tlacopán cried out to Cuauhtémoc in fear and pain, receiving from the latter the celebrated, laconic reply: '*And me? Do you think I'm lying here on a bed of roses? . . .*' According to Torquemada, 'Cortés, disgusted, then gave a forthright order to stop the proceedings, declaring that it was barbaric and degrading to treat a King in such a way'.

Cortés had reaffirmed Cuauhtémoc as lord of the small fief of Tenochtitlán, but the torture episode shows that he was merely a king of straw. There was now no longer any need to pretend that the Spaniards were working in conjunction with the Indians; after the fall of the city the relationship was that of victor and vanquished. The real king of Mexico was Cortés—and though he was never to be crowned, as it were, by being appointed Viceroy, in the eyes of the Indians he stayed king to the end. No other Spaniard ever received such obedience and adulation; he remained the one authentic *teule* or god. We should remember this natural and unassailable ascendancy when we contemplate his later bouts of self-pity and the lamentations of his admirers on his behalf. He had his compensations—though for such a titanic figure, and after such an achievement, anything less than complete authority, absolute and unquestioned power, appeared to be an affront and a betrayal.

He began to live like a king. He had always been attached to high living and free-spending, even when he was the mayor of a backwoods village in Hispaniola; now, as ruler of Mexico, he had ample opportunity to indulge his tastes. As Gómara says, 'He always spent lavishly, on war, women, friends and caprices.' The trouble was that, although he had already collected his own agreed fifth and remitted a further fifth to the Emperor, neither the torture of Cuauhtémoc nor other shifts, such as stripping Aztec captains of their nose-plugs, lip-plugs, earrings and other personal ornaments, sufficed to scrape up a respectable sum to divide among the rest of his men. The poor wretched infantrymen received fifty pesos each, the horsemen sixty. It was not surprising that all of them—his original followers, as well as the Narváez and Garay factions—were thoroughly angry and disillusioned. He never lost his ability to exercise command over them, or to urge them on to further feats of arms; nor had he ever sought to be a popular or beloved captain, only one who was obeyed. But in antagonizing his men in this way he was sacrificing an advantage that might have stood him in good stead in the years ahead. Nightly the white walls of the palace at Coyoacán were covered with obscenities, scrawled in charcoal and couched in choice Castilian, and daily he sallied forth to erase them or write sarcastic rejoinders of his own. Finally the criticisms became so vehement and uncouth that he had to call a stop to them, on penalty of severe punishment—thus tacitly yielding his opponents the game. With his luxurious establishment and his palace-guard he had ceased to be *primus inter pares*, and was moving in the direction of self-confessed autocrat.

In those first troubled months he ruled solely by force of personality, ignoring the mounting tide of envy, fear and dislike. He was still Captain-General of New Spain of the Ocean Sea simply by virtue of the fact that he said he was. For fourteen months after the Aztec capitulation, until October 1522, he received no word from the Emperor to confirm him in the offices to which he had appointed himself when founding Villa Rica over two years before. He now had to fend off an attempt by Fonseca and Velázquez to unseat him by sending a nobody called Cristóbal de Tapia, furnished with letters signed in the name of the Emperor, to assume the governorship of New Spain. Fortunately the Emperor had not placed his personal signature on the letters; he was absent from Spain, occupied with the little matter of the Reformation. The Ninety-Five Theses had been posted at Wittenberg in 1517, and his confrontation with Luther at Worms had taken place in 1521. Cortés realized that the visit of Tapia was another manœuvre of Fonseca in his guise as head of the Council of the Indies. In his usual manner, he greeted Tapia with a great parade of legalistic showmanship, showered him with gifts, and sent him back to Velázquez in Cuba. At the same time he despatched to Spain an instalment of the Royal Fifth, consisting of 45,000 gold pesos and a mass of beautiful objects of art, in the care of Antonio de Quiñones and Alonso de Ávila. Unfortunately, the consignment was captured at sea by Jean Florin, a French buccaneer; Quiñones was killed, Ávila captured, and the treasure delivered up to the Emperor's arch-enemy, Francis I. However, when the Emperor had arrived back in Spain, and had an opportunity to consult advisers, he duly issued letters patent to Cortés appointing him Governor, Captain-General and Chief Justice of the great country in which no Spanish monarch would ever set foot, and of which no Spanish monarch ever seems to have been able to form an accurate impression.

The Emperor Charles, and his son Philip II, were totally absorbed in the affairs of Europe, which were in all conscience serious enough to monopolize their attention. If the Emperor, now and later, appeared cold towards Cortés, it was because his mind was continually occupied elsewhere. This may argue, perhaps, a certain lack of imagination; but it is not hard to understand. The Emperor liked and respected Cortés, and when he took the trouble to deal with him in person he handled that unique character, now becoming increasingly haughty and prickly, with tact and sympathy. He understood Cortés better than Cortés understood him. Unfortunately, the Emperor had little time to devote to the troubles of individual subjects, even a subject as deserving as Cortés. Obtaining an interview with the present Queen of England or President of the United States is easy compared with the difficulties of obtaining one with Charles V, for which a petitioner might wait ten years. Ironically, the two great men had much in common. They were both a blend of romantic and realist, man of action and man of intellect; both began life with the chivalrous assumptions of the old mediaeval world and found it difficult to adjust themselves to the colder and more complex realities of the new world that was being born; and for both of them the resplendent early years were succeeded by years of discouragement and decline.

For almost exactly two years, between October 15, 1522, when he received his appointment from the Emperor, to October 12, 1524, when he set out on his expedition to Honduras, Cortés was at the peak of his pride and power. True, the Emperor had accompanied the official patent with a number of officials from Spain whom Cortés, left to himself, would not have chosen as his own subordinates; but at this stage his relations with them were equable. He pacified the country, sent out numerous expeditions, and introduced the enlightened method of government which were formally enshrined in the famous *ordenanzas* that he issued in March 1524. The Emperor's confirmation of his offices signified his final victory over Diego Velázquez. The Emperor had legitimized his disobedience and sedition. Both Velázquez and Fonseca were in fact to die soon—though not before Velázquez, as we shall see, aimed one last blow at Cortés that would finally, if posthumously, bring him a measure of revenge.

In the meantime, Cortés rid himself, as he thought, of two minor nuisances. After some prompting by Fonseca and the Council of the Indies, he released Narváez from gaol in Villa Rica and had him brought to Coyoacán. Bernal Díaz relates how that luckless warrior, lacking the eye that had been knocked out at Cempoala, was so impressed by the great state in which Cortés lived that he dropped to his knees and attempted to cover Cortés' hands with kisses; but Cortés, pained, gently lifted him up, behaving towards him with kindness and generosity. He presented him with two thousand gold pesos and allowed him to leave peacefully for Spain. Needless to say, his magnanimous gesture did not earn him Narváez' gratitude. Narváez was not without friends at court, even after the deaths of Velázquez and Fonseca. He was quickly recruited by the anti-Cortés party, which was dedicated to securing the prizes of the Conquest for itself; and during the crucial years when Cortés was seeking to stabilize his position Narváez was among those busily undermining his reputation in the mother-country. That the latter still retained a good deal of influence can be judged by the fact that in 1528 he was named, much to the disgust of Cortés, who by that time had been reduced to coveting such a position for himself, *adelantado* of Florida. Intending to follow up the exploratory voyages of Ponce de León in 1513 and 1521, he landed on the west coast of Florida with five hundred men, including a hundred horsemen, meaning to press westwards on a march of discovery and annexation. In November 1528 the whole company, except for eighty survivors, was lost mysteriously and without trace, perhaps by shipwreck, perhaps at the hands of Indians, perhaps by misadventure in the matted bayous of Florida. Narváez was unlucky to the end. The eighty survivors, who had become separated from the main body, were led by the treasurer of the expedition, Alvar Núñez Cabeza de Vaca. In a few weeks the eighty had been reduced by sickness to four—Cabeza de Vaca, two other Spaniards, and a Negro. They remained on the mainland and on the islands of the Gulf coast for seven years, leading the lives of the most primitive of savages. Cabeza de Vaca estimated that during the course of their wanderings they covered six thousand miles. By the time they were found by a Spanish raiding party they had reached the upper regions of New Spain. One appreciates the mettle of the Spaniards of that era when one adds that Cabeza de Vaca, undeterred by his experiences in North America, undertook in 1542 to lead two hundred men through the jungles of Brazil into Paraguay. He survived for one year as Governor of Paraguay until he was deposed by Martín Irala, another *conquistador*. He was shut up in a mud hut for eight months before being sent back to Spain in irons. When one contemplates the fate of a good two-thirds of Cortes' colleagues, one cannot but conclude that, for all his complaints, in his later years the Captain-General was exceedingly fortunate.

Cortés treated his other remaining rival in the Indies, Francisco de Garay, with similar magnanimity. Garay, unsuccessful in his colonizing missions at Pánuco, journeyed to Coyoacán to consult Cortés and to come to an agreement with his princely rival. The two men agreed that Garay would surrender all his claims in the neighbourhood of Pánuco in exchange for rights in the land in the region to the north, at the Río de las Palmas (the Río Grande). The treaty was to be celebrated in regal style with week-long festivities, and sealed by the marriage of Garay's son to Doña Pizarro, a daughter whom Cortés had fathered on an Indian woman in his Cuban days and given his mother's name. On the eve of the celebrations, Garay died. His death was sudden and unexpected, and as he had eaten his Christmas dinner in Cortés' palace three days before it was put about that Cortés had poisoned him. It was becoming a standard calumny. Three months earlier it had been whispered that the exalted Governor had poisoned his wife. Doña Catalina had never enjoyed nor returned his affections; she nonetheless felt a perfectly natural desire to secure what compensation she could by sharing her husband's good fortune. She took ship from Cuba in July 1522, and landed at Coatzacoalcos. Díaz relates that the tidings of her arrival did not rouse enthusiasm in the breast of her spouse; but with his usual good manners and amiability he bade Sandoval, who was in the area, to meet her and bring her in state to Coyoacán, where he received her graciously. However, the mood of reconcilation was short-lived. Doña Catalina proved exacting, and was not disposed to overlook her husband's current *fredaines*. One evening, two months after her arrival, she had a violent and embarrassing quarrel with her husband at the dinner-table and withdrew to her own quarters. A little later her maids, hearing Cortés' voice, entered her bedroom and found her lying dead in his arms. Her necklace was broken and the skin on her neck was marked by several dark spots or bruises. Had Cortés poisoned her, or strangled her? We shall never know the truth of that Othello-like scene. Life had become cheap in Mexico in the previous two years; Cortés had either witnessed or ordered the deaths of many thousands of people in that time; he wielded arbitrary power. The age was in any case a vehement one. One would like to assume that he was not guilty of her death; but he was at a stage in his life when his temper tended to be explosive, and Doña Catalina was certainly a trying woman.

Needless to say, his enemies would not let such an opportunity pass. Seven years after the event, an official commission was still keeping it alive. The commission was unable—or afraid—to indict Cortés with murder, but its deliberations did nothing to dissipate the cloud of hatred and innuendo with which he was surrounded, and which in a few years was to drive him back to Spain. The whisper was that he had rid himself of Doña Catalina because he was now obsessed with social pretensions, and wished at some future date to make a splendid marriage with a great house. Probably she died of pestilence, as Cortés' own mother did about this time, soon after landing at Villa Rica and before she could be reunited with her famous son. Death by pestilence would account for the mark or rash on Doña Catalina's throat.

He was already beginning to experience trouble with the quadrumvirate whom the Emperor had sent from Spain to form his entourage. They had prevented him subtracting his own agreed fifth from the wealth that was accruing from taxes, tithes and the mining of gold and silver, and in his Fourth Despatch, dated October 15, 1524, he spoke bitterly to the Emperor about his financial plight. He wrote that he had been forced to subtract sixty-two thousand pesos from the royal revenues and to borrow more than thirty thousand pesos on his own account. 'I am quite wasted and exhausted,' he declared, 'by all I have done and spent in the expeditions I have fitted out and in providing ammunition and artillery in this city, and in many other expenses that occur daily.' Nevertheless, having heard that his previous consignment of treasure was in the hands of the French, and in order to whet the imperial appetite, he accompanied his despatch with the sum of sixty thousand pesos, 'which I imagine Your Sacred Majesty might need on account of the wars and other things'. He also told the Emperor that 'I am positive that, God willing, I shall discover for Your Majesty more kingdoms and dominions than all those discovered up till now, and that, with His guidance, my projects will succeed and Your Highness will become the Sovereign of the World'.

*   *   *

In truth, the rage to conquer still burned in him with an undiminished vigour. He had proved himself a clear-sighted and judicious administrator, the promoter of wise edicts: but that force which had seized him in youth and impelled him from Salamanca to Seville, Seville to Santo Domingo, Santo Domingo to Baracoa, Baracoa to Tenochtitlán, was not disposed to let go of him even after the rigours of the Conquest. He possessed the passion of the great discoverers—Columbus, Cabot, Vasco de Gama, Cabral—the passion that at this moment was driving Magellan and del Cano to make their three-year circumnavigation of the globe, steering further and further across the seemingly limitless ocean. It was not for nothing that he had added the four words '*of the Ocean Sea*' to the name which he had given New Spain. His imagination was by no means land-bound. In particular, he was infatuated with the notion of being the first man to discover that route to the Indies which had been the ambition of Columbus. Those were the fabled 'kingdoms and dominions' of which he had spoken to the Emperor. It seems extraordinary that he could envisage a more shining realm than that he had already been vouchsafed by the realm of Moctezuma and Cuauhtémoc: but such was the case. His capacity for wonder and appetite for adventure were unimpaired. It was this appetite which now drew him on towards his own personal downfall.

As soon as the Conquest was completed, he began to turn his attention to that passage across the Americas, that link between the Atlantic and the Pacific, which had preoccupied Columbus, Balboa and so many other Spaniards of his day and which, if found, would mean so much to his country. With fifty thousand gold pesos of his own money he fitted out two separate expeditions, and planned a third. The first expedition would march to the coast of the Gulf of Mexico, the second to the Pacific coast. There, they would take ship and follow both the northern and southern coastlines in an easterly direction. The northern expedition was to sail in the direction of Las Hibueras (Honduras), the southern expedition in the direction of Tehuantepec (Guatemala). 'If the strait exists,' Cortés told the Emperor, 'it cannot escape both those who go by the North Sea and those who go by the South Sea. On one side or the other we cannot fail to discover the secret.' In case the strait was not located towards the east, but towards the west, Cortés planned to send another expedition to the Gulf coast that would proceed in the direction opposite to that followed by the Hibueras expedition. This would trace the coastline from Pánuco northwards to Florida. It will be recalled that the men of that time still believed, with Columbus, that Florida was an island; and for some years to come they would believe that Lower California was an island too. Between those islands there must certainly exist, they thought, a stretch of water representing the coveted strait. Perhaps they confused it with vague stories that might have reached them of the broad waters of the Río Grande or the Mississippi. In any case, once it had been located it would, as Cortés put it, 'open out a good passage from the Spice Islands to New Spain at least two-thirds shorter than the present route, besides being much safer. And if the strait does not exist, then it will be useful that this should be known, so that other means may be discovered by which Your Caesarian Majesty may draw profits from the Spice Islands and other countries bordering on them'. He was thus reiterating Columbus' old dream of finding the westward route to the Indies. The Portuguese, by using the eastward route, had already beaten the Spaniards in the race for the Indies: but to some extent Cortés' optimism would be vindicated. Even as he was writing his Fourth Despatch, Magellan, unknown to anyone in Mexico, had reached the Philippines in March 1520, claimed them for Spain, and named them the St. Lazarus Islands. There, a month later, he was killed on the island of Cebu, off Mindanão. He was barely four hundred miles from the Moluccas, the true Spice Islands. In the upshot, the Portuguese eventually annexed the Moluccas, as Spain had annexed the Philippines. The administration of the Philippines was entrusted to the Viceroyalty of New Spain: so the Spaniards had their Asiatic dependency in the region of the Spice Islands after all, even though a despatch sent from Manila to Mexico City required more than a year to receive a reply. Columbus and Cortés were justified.

Cortés placed Pedro de Alvarado in charge of the southerly expedition, which began its journey on December 6, 1523. Alvarado was provided with nearly two hundred horsemen, three hundred infantrymen, and four cannon. In charge of the northerly expedition, equipped in a similarly lavish manner, was Cristóbal de Olid. It set out on January 11, 1524. At this time Cortés was engaged in manufacturing his own cannon as rapidly as possible, little realizing that he was thereby enabling his enemies to start a rumour that he was trying to create a private army and set himself up as independent Emperor of New Spain.

During the course of 1524, apart from the cares of office and their accompanying financial complexities, his fortunes appeared to be set fair. The future was bright. Then, in the late summer, he received tidings that shocked him and completely upset his normal balanced judgment. Cristóbal de Olid had mutinied, and was attempting to establish a separate little kingdom of his own. In itself, the matter was of small significance; it scarcely constituted an important crisis. Olid, a light-hearted, devil-may-care young man of thirty-six, was tucked away in an obscure corner of Central America with an army too inconsiderable to undertake a serious revolt. Cortés could have taken his time in coping with what was actually a minor nuisance. He could have used his arts of persuasion with Olid; he could have sent another captain to deal with him; he could even have ignored him. But for the first time—and it proved fatal—his good sense deserted him. He reacted to the news in a strangely exaggerated manner. He determined not only to gather a punitive force without delay, but to lead it to Las Hibueras in person. It is ironic to reflect that, had chance prompted him to put Alvarado in command of the northern expedition and Olid in command of the southern expedition, the necessity to commit himself to such a mistaken course of action might never have arisen. In all probability he would have finished his days in glory, not merely as the Governor but as the Viceroy of the country he had conquered.

In leaving Coyoacán at such a time, he was giving his opponents the opportunity they had been seeking. He should have remained at the centre of affairs, maintaining a firm and unequivocal control. However, it is easy to possess hindsight, and one can understand his probable reasons for taking the step he did. In the first place, there was obviously the wound of a personal betrayal. Olid had been one of that band of brothers who had fought beside him all the way from Cozumel to Tlaltelolco. Besides, Olid's betrayal was deeply unsettling. If he was unable to trust Olid, who had only just returned from an extremely important mission in Michoacán, whom could he trust? If he sent another captain to cope with Olid, what guarantee had he that the man would not desert him in his turn? Furthermore, it transpired that Olid had received encouragement from no less a person than Diego Velázquez, with whom he had taken part six years earlier in the conquest of Cuba. Though he himself had mutinied against Velázquez, Cortés was unreasonably aroused by mutiny on the part of others. It was a case of poacher turned gamekeeper. Velázquez had recently incensed him by a refusal to allow horses—the prerequisite of conquest—to be exported from Cuba, and it was observed that the mere mention of Velázquez' name seemed to madden him. He spoke wildly of arresting Velázquez and executing him. There was also the distinct possibility that Olid and Velázquez would join forces with the insatiable Pedrarias Dávila, the Governor of Darien. Pedrarias was already probing northward in the direction of Honduras and Guatemala, and had penetrated Nicaragua and eastern Honduras. The whole as-yet-undelimited territory would belong to the Governor who could seize it first: and as Guatemala in particular was reported to be rich in gold, Cortés could not afford to let a rival wrest it away.

In addition to these practical reasons, he must also have possessed subjective ones. Underrating the animosity felt towards him in the capital, and tired of what he took to be petty squabbles, no doubt he could not resist the call to exploration and adventure. In place of the perplexities and responsibilities of governing, he could slip back into the comfortable and familiar role of general of a small expeditionary army. And who knows, he might even secure for himself the glory of discovering the strait which he had sent Olid to look for?

He dated his Fourth Despatch from Tenochtitlán on October 15, 1524. In fact he had left Coyoacán and taken the road for Yucatán and Honduras three days earlier. Prudently, he decided to keep his troubles to himself; he told the Emperor nothing of the challenge to his authority. He sent two envoys, Gil González Dávila and Francisco de las Casas, ahead of him by sea, with instructions to take Olid into custody; but he was not sanguine of their success, and in fact Olid disarmed them as soon as they reached Triunfo de la Cruz, the town he had founded in Honduras six months previously. Cortés himself, as though revelling in the prospect of facing and surmounting the same kind of difficulties that had confronted him in his campaign against the Aztecs, chose to follow overland. Again, it was an uncharacteristic and wrong-headed decision, even though it was prompted by a mistaken notion of the geography of the region, through which an easily negotiable waterway was erroneously supposed to run. Cortés had seen the wilderness of Yucatán at first-hand, at Cozumel, and when sailing along the coast towards San Juan de Ulúa; he knew the dangers and distances involved. It seems fair to assert that, in a significant degree, during the months since the conquest his judgment of men and affairs had somehow deteriorated.

The first days of the march were in the nature of a triumphal progress. As Madariaga puts it: 'He travelled in state, with the luxury and even the extravagance of a Renaissance prince; his household comprised a steward, two toast-masters, a butler, a pastrycook, a larder-master, a man in charge of his gold and silver services, a chamberlain, a doctor, a surgeon, many pages, including two spear-pages, eight grooms, two falconers, five musicians, two jugglers, and three muleteers.' With him went the constant Sandoval, and at his side, as always, was La Malinche. After revisiting, like an uncrowned queen of Mexico, the scenes of her girlhood and early misery, she then went on to make the long march to Hibueras with the same unflinching spirit with which she had made the march to Tenochtitlán.

All went well on the three hundred and fifty-mile journey eastward to Coatzalcoalcos and the newly-founded Spanish settlement of Espíritu Santo, which was to be the jumping-off point for the trek inland. It was then that the troubles of the army began. The march across Yucatán by Cortés, his hundred horsemen and a hundred and fifty infantrymen, is one of the greatest feats of endurance in history. It has been vividly described by Bernal Díaz, who took part in it, and twice by Cortés himself, once through the agency of Gómara and once in the monumental Fifth Despatch. The latter, dictated on his eventual and miraculous return to Mexico City, was lost until the nineteenth century, when it was accidentally discovered in the Imperial Chancery at Vienna during a search for the First Despatch. The three accounts deepen the sense of awe which one feels for the will-power of this exceptional man. He took his troops, accompanied by a thousand Indians, through swamps, over rivers, across ravines, deserts and almost impenetrable jungle. They traversed mountain ranges; they sailed down oily and treacherous waterways on rafts; they splashed across stagnant, stinking lagoons. Several times they were lost, and were saved only by what Cortés considered to be divine intervention. They were ignorant of direction and distances between the wretched villages, or for how long the ordeal could be expected to last. They knew continuous hunger and thirst, and were plagued by flies and mosquitoes.

Most of the horses perished and many of the Spaniards. Often they seemed to have reached a situation where it was impossible to advance a step further, and were only prevented from turning back by their leader's iron refusal to bow to impossible odds. They zig-zagged from one village to another, scrounging supplies, scrambling around over an endless series of natural obstacles, sometimes pausing to rest among the ruins of the ancient temples of the Mayas. Always there were bridges to build, either temporary affairs of planks or vines, or elaborate structures that were so substantial they survived for centuries and entered into Mexican folk-lore. Once the army reached what appeared to be a complete impasse, which could be surmounted only by a bridge of monumental proportions. Gómara's account of what now took place can be quoted at length, because it may stand as a representative example of the difficulties that Cortés confronted and by incredible exertions overcame.

'From Huatecpán, Cortés set out for the province of Acalán, taking a trail made by the merchants, who, according to them, were almost the only persons to travel from town to town. He crossed a river by canoe; a horse was drowned and several loads of baggage were lost. He marched three days over some very rough mountains, where the army suffered acutely from fatigue, and then came to an estuary five hundred paces wide, which put our army in the direst straits, for they had no boats and could not touch bottom. Their situation was so bad that they tearfully begged God's mercy, because it seemed impossible to get across except by flying, and to turn back, as most of them wanted to do, was to perish, for the floods caused by the heavy rains had washed out the bridges they had built. In a canoe with two Spanish sailors, Cortés took soundings of the whole bay and estuary, and everywhere they found four fathoms of water. They strung pikes together and sampled the bottom, which was covered with two more fathoms of mud and slime, making the total depth six fathoms, so building a bridge seemed to be out of the question. Cortés, nevertheless, determined to try it. He asked the Mexican lords to have their Indians fell trees, fashion long beams, and drag them to the bank for building a bridge by which to escape. They did so, and the Spaniards, mounted on rafts and their three canoes, sank the beams one by one in the mud. Their exertion and irritation were so great that they cursed the bridge and even their captain, grumbling loudly at the man who, with his great cleverness and knowledge, had got them into a spot from which he could not extricate them. They said the bridge would never be finished, and even if it should be they would themselves be finished; that, therefore, they should retreat before their provisions were exhausted, for in any case they would turn back before reaching Honduras. Cortés had never been more perplexed, but, in order to keep the peace, he did not oppose them, but begged them to allow him five days only, and promised that if he had not built the bridge by the end of that time, he would turn back. They replied that they would wait, even if they had to eat stones. Thereupon Cortés told the Indians to consider the necessity they were all faced with, because they had either to get across or perish. He inspired them to work by telling them that just beyond the estuary was Acalán, a land full of friends, where the ships were waiting with a store of provisions and refreshments. He also promised them great rewards back in Mexico if they built the bridge.

'All of them, especially their lords, agreed. They formed themselves into squads: some to gather roots, herbs, and fruits in the forest; others, to fell trees; others, to trim them; others, to drag them; still others, to sink them in the estuary. Cortés was the master architect of the work and put such diligence into it, and they such hard work, that within six days the bridge was completed, and on the seventh the whole army and the horses crossed—a thing that seemed impossible without the help of God. The Spaniards were greatly astonished, and even did their share, for, although they grumble, they work well. The task was performed in common, and the cleverness of the Indians was amazing. As many as a thousand beams were used in it, eight fathoms long and five or six spans thick, and many smaller ones to surface it. For lack of nails, because they had only horseshoe nails and wooden pegs, they lashed it together with vines.

'The universal rejoicing at having crossed the estuary in safety was not, however, of long duration, because they immediately came to a frightful morass, though not a wide one, in which the horses, without their saddles, sank to their ears, and the more they struggled the deeper they sank, until there seemed to be no hope of saving them. Bundles of twigs and grass were inserted under their breasts and bellies to bolster them up, but did not suffice. While they were in this state a channel opened and they swam across, but were so exhausted they could not stand. The Spaniards thanked Our Lord for His great mercy, for without horses they were lost indeed.'

*   *   *

It is against this background that one has to set the most famous—or rather notorious—episode of the march. Cortés was informed that Cuauhtémoc, the lords of the towns of Texcoco and Tlacopán, and another influential nobleman, all of whom he had brought with him as hostages, were actively planning to stir up an Indian revolt. He heard the evidence, then ordered Cuauhtémoc and the lord of Tlacopán to be hanged. The sentence was carried out. It was unfortunate for Cuauhtémoc that the conspiracy had been discovered at an unlucky moment, when Cortés was harassed by the seemingly insurmountable problem of getting his forces across the forty-mile wide lake of Petén Itzá, in the neighbourhood of the famous Mayan sites of Tikal and Uaxactun, with their splendid temples. This was no time to have lent additional stress to the burdens borne by that cold, ferocious, and by now possibly slightly demented man. The Indian chroniclers declare that Cortés, wishing to be rid of the difficulties posed by Cuauhtémoc's presence, executed him on a trumped-up charge. Díaz states that: 'It was thought wrong and unjust by all of us.' However that may be, as Prescott says of Cuauhtémoc: 'No one can refuse his admiration to that intrepid spirit. He was young, and his public career was not long; but it was glorious.' It is from the day of his death that Prescott dates the true extinction of the Aztec nation, the moment when it finally found itself 'broken in spirit and without a head'. Cortés might have had exactly this eventuality in mind.

By the time he made contact with the remnants of Gil Gonzáles Dávila's company, and reached the coast of Hibueras, he himself had paid a terrible price, physically and psychologically, for his arrogant exploit. He was exhausted and ill; he had aged visibly; his nerve was shaken and he was given to bouts of weeping. He assumed the black habit of a Dominican monk and his thoughts lingered on death and the Last Judgment. Ironically, the entire venture had turned out to be pointless, for it did not even achieve the purpose of terminating Olid's rebellion. While Cortés was splashing through quagmires and hewing his way through the forests, that had already been done. Gil González Dávila and Francisco de las Casas had managed to turn on Olid and cut his throat. A long year of toil and travail had all been in vain. Cortés made desultory attempts to explore the coastline of the Gulf of Honduras and the nearby portions of Guatemala; but for six more months, sick and disheartened, he remained in the port of Las Honduras (now a sizeable town called Puerto Cortés) trying to rest and regain his strength. He had taken himself off into the wilderness, undermined his political position, sapped his personal resources, at the very moment when his rivals in Mexico City had declared him officially dead, confiscated his houses and estates, and seized, tortured, and sentenced to death the steward whom he had left in charge of his affairs.

* * *

He took ship from Las Honduras on April 25, 1526, and reached Villa Rica on May 24, after an enforced delay in Cuba because of storms in the Caribbean. The whole population of New Spain, Indians and Spanish alike, had been nervous and apprehensive during his absence; the old order had foundered, and he was the sole rock on which the future could be built. During his fifteen-day progress from the coast to the capital, on the now-familiar road that led through Cempoala and faithful Tlaxcala, he was received as if he was indeed Quetzalcóatl returning to his people. Gómara writes: 'Indians came to greet him from eighty leagues away, bringing presents and offering their services. They showed the greatest joy at his return; they swept the roads and scattered flowers before him, so beloved was he; and his entrance into Mexico City was the occasion for the greatest outburst of jubilation you can imagine. All the Spaniards sallied forth in military array, while the Indians flocked to see him as if he had been Moctezuma himself. They filled the streets to overflowing; they showed their joy by the beating of drums and the blowing of conches, trumpets, and many fifes; and all that day and night they surged through the streets making bonfires and illuminations. Cortés was greatly moved to see the happiness of the Indians, the triumph they offered him, and the peace and quiet of the city. He went straightway to the convent of San Francisco, there to rest and give thanks to God, who had brought him through so many perils to this repose and security.'

His desire for rest and seclusion was indicative of his state of mind. 'I remained six days with the monks,' he told the Emperor in his Fifth Despatch, 'to give an account of my sins to God.' It was on the fourth day that he received an unexpected and disagreeable piece of news from Villa Rica. Luis Ponce de León, a representative of the Emperor, had landed in New Spain. Cortés was ordered to surrender to Ponce de León his office of Chief Justice, which would be assumed by the latter, who was also enjoined to institute an inquiry into the unedifying quarrels which had racked the Emperor's new dominion while its Captain-General had been pursuing a trumpery mutineer in distant Yucatán. Two years earlier, Cortés might have been expected to react to the arrival of the newcomer in the lively way he had treated the would-be incursions into his preserve of Velázquez, Narváez, Tapia and Garay. True, Ponce de León was a representative of the Emperor: but this would only have called forth from the Cortés of old a more than usually dazzling exhibition of guile. But the inner blaze had been dampened by the experiences in Hibueras and the frustrating months that preceded them. Had he wished to, he was in an excellent position to assert himself. Upon his return, the distressing condition of the country had immediately begun to right itself. The council of inept and greedy men who had failed to govern the country in his absence, and who had flouted him and disgraced themselves, at once came to heel like the contemptible crew they were. Even the totally scabrous Nuño de Guzmán, who had got himself appointed Governor of Pánuco in Cortés' absence, and who in Cortés' decline would shortly emerge as the head and scourge of New Spain, had gone tactfully to ground. Cortés could have taken control and laid about him with a strong arm, as he was accustomed to do. But the virtue had gone out of him. Something in him had broken, and was never completely to be mended. He would still be capable of intermittent flashes of energy and enterprise: but a man who had extended himself so prodigally in the earlier portion of his life could scarcely hope to extend himself so massively and successfully in the second. A man only possesses just so much vitality and will-power. The *conquistadores* were not the kind of men who had studied the art of pacing themselves.

Meekly, he submitted himself to Ponce de León and the coming inquiry. All might still have been well had Ponce de León, an able and experienced diplomat, been spared to take control and establish firm government. However, within three weeks the Emperor's commissioner was dead. He died of some contagious ailment which he and his companions had brought over in their ship; thirty other Spaniards died too. This did not prevent Cortés' enemies, promptly resurgent, from reviving the legend, which grew stronger with every accidental death, of Cortés acting the role of poisoner. At this stage, as Captain-General, Cortés could have reassumed the duties of Chief Justice, as his friends urged him to do, and put his detractors finally to rout. Instead, curiously lethargic and diffident, he allowed Nuño de Guzmán and the rest to insert into the post, as a stop-gap, a crony of theirs called Marcos de Aguilar. Aguilar was a rascally, toothless, pox-ridden old attorney whose sole form of nourishment was to suck milk from a wet-nurse's breast. Not surprisingly, within two months the interim Chief Justice had also faded away, another of Cortés' putative victims, leaving the condition of the government of New Spain more chaotic than ever.

Enervated and distracted, Cortés thus passed two miserable years after his return from Hibueras. Quite simply, he had lost the initiative which hitherto he had managed to retain in all his undertakings; with matters in New Spain in the state they were, he had also lost—rightly—the confidence of the Emperor and the royal advisers in Valladollid. And with his increasing weakness, as always happens, his former good luck deserted him. It is the ineluctable rule of history that fortune should favour the strong; when men and countries are no longer strong and lucky, they must yield their place to those that are. The Fifth Despatch which he sent to the Emperor, dated from Mexico City on September 3, 1526, ends with a section, running to many pages, in which he itemizes and attempts to answer the complaints, accusations and scandals alleged against him. He writes simply and with dignity: but it makes sorry reading when one compares it with the fire and *élan* of the earlier despatches. 'I have defended myself until now and have not yielded,' he declared, 'though I can see that there do in reality exist such evils. But I wished Your Majesty to be convinced of my purity and fidelity in your royal service, which is the only thing I care about, because if you think otherwise of me, all other good things in this world are nothing to me, and I would rather die. I hope that neither God, nor Your Majesty out of respect to Him, will allow invidious and corrupt tongues to deprive me of what I prize most. I neither desire nor ask of Your Majesty any other reward in payment of my services than this. God grant that I shall not live without it.'

In these circumstances, his ability to put his nominally ascendant position to effective use was limited. At the end of 1527 his enemies in the council, headed by Alonso de Estrada, whom the Emperor had appointed Chief Justice to succeed Marcos de Aguilar, felt bold enough to forbid him, as the result of a brawl in which some of his retainers were involved, to set foot in Mexico City. He was banished to his own palace at Coyoacán—'such a scandalous act,' says Gómara, 'that the capital was on the verge of bloodshed that day, and even of ruin. Cortés, however, met the situation by leaving the city to begin his exile. If he had the spirit of a tyrant, as he was accused of having, what better opportunity could he have had than the one now presented to him? Nor was this the only occasion, for there were many others when he could have raised the country in rebellion. But he refused to do so and, I believe, never harboured such a thought.'

The only statesmanlike venture of these two barren years was the expedition which he sent to the Spice Islands. The expedition had been suggested to him by the Emperor, who wished to discover what had happened to a ship in Magellan's fleet that was rumoured to be stranded somewhere in the Moluccas. An expedition in 1525 to locate its survivors had failed. The Moluccas were deemed to fall within the purview of the Portuguese, according to Pope Alexander VI's original Line of Demarcation of 1493; but the Spice Islands ought by the same token to belong to Spain, and it was sensible to assert this right. In the autumn of 1527 Cortés sent off three ships from the Pacific harbour of Zihuatanejo, a hundred miles north-west of Acapulco. Two of the ships were lost soon after sailing, but the third, the flagship, commanded by Alvaro de

Saavedra Cerón, a relative of Cortés, reached the Spice Islands. Saavedra made a remarkable voyage, explored Mindanão, and actually found the last survivor of the missing vessel that had accompanied Magellan. He began the long voyage home in May 1528, but died on the way during October and was buried at sea. By this time eighteen of the original crew of fifty remained, and these eighteen were captured by the Portuguese and imprisoned for two years in Molucca. Eight finally survived to see New Spain once more.

Cortés' expedition could hardly be rated a success. As with so many of his other endeavours of this kind, his judgment was sound, but the profits were to be reaped by other men.

*　　*　　*

The boredom and dissatisfaction Cortés felt were so extreme that he had considered leading the expedition to the Spice Islands himself. As Gómara puts it, rather pathetically, 'at that moment he had no war on his hands, nor anything else to do'. However, during 1527 he so far recovered his spirits that he roused himself sufficiently to decide to return to Spain to intercede with the Emperor. He felt that, if the Emperor would give him back the Chief Justiceship—perhaps even grant him the exalted office of Viceroy—he could re-establish his favour with the Crown and put the increasingly sordid politics of New Spain on a sound new footing.

On March 17, 1528, while the fate of the Spice Islands fleet was still unknown, he and his retinue weighed anchor in two ships at Villa Rica and set course for Spain. He was full of hope and enthusiasm. As Gómara says: 'He had made up his mind to go to Castile to despatch his many affairs, which were important to himself, the Emperor, and New Spain. I shall speak of a few of them. One was to find a wife, for he had children and was getting old; another was to appear before the King in person and give him a full account of the vast territory and the many peoples he had conquered and partly converted, and inform him by word of mouth of the quarrelling and dissension among the Spaniards in Mexico, for he suspected that the King had not heard the truth; another was to demand of him rewards commensurate with his merits and services, and a title that would set him above the others. He had, moreover, a number of profitable suggestions for the government of New Spain which he had thought out and written down, and which he wished to present to the King.'

He had an overriding desire at this time to meet the Emperor face to face. He yearned to lay his trophies at his sovereign's feet; he felt that the young monarch would give him approval and recognition, and side with him against his detractors. At the end of the Fifth Despatch he had already written: 'My desire to kiss the Royal feet of Your Sacred Majesty and to be promoted to serve in Your Royal Presence is beyond all expression.' He also, in the same place, had somewhat querulously spoken of 'being obliged to return to Spain and ask people for God's sake to give me food'. To judge from the pomp and ceremony with which he eventually landed in Spain, towards the close of 1528, his circumstances were not quite so pitiable as he represented.

Before he left Coyoacán, he was careful, this time, to make an inventory of all his personal goods. They were valued at 200,000 gold pesos. He took to Spain with him a further 20,000 pesos in fine gold, 10,000 pesos in base gold, 1,500 marks of silver, and a selection of fine jewels. He was accompanied by Sandoval, Andrés de Tapia, a son of Moctezuma and a number of other Indian noblemen, and a colourful and exotic entourage. The latter included acrobats, dwarfs, albinos and other oddities, together with a menagerie of wild animals. As gifts for the Emperor and the court he brought a rich collection of quetzal-plume headdresses, feather-cloaks, fans, shields, toilet articles and other assorted artifacts. It is therefore not easy to credit the protestations of personal poverty which had now become habitual with him, and which were no doubt intended to turn aside the innuendoes of his critics about his wealth and ambitions.

Gómara wrote that 'at that time Cortés was the most famous man of our nation'; and a little later that 'the whole kingdom was agog with his fame and the news of his coming, and everyone wanted to see him'. This we can believe. The reception accorded to this man who had been the first to set eyes on magical new kingdoms can only be compared with that given in our own day to the astronauts who first walked on the moon. It was a marvellous homecoming for a man who had sailed from Spain twenty-four years earlier with nothing but a few castellanos given him by his parents.

He was not received by the Emperor at once, for the court was in the process of making one of its complex ceremonial shifts from Castile to Aragon. He intended his *entrada* into court circles to be as spectacular as possible, and was content to mark time for a few weeks, confer with the members of his own faction in Spain, and recover from the fatigues of the crossing. At forty-three, and after the labours of the past quarter of a century, his powers of recuperation were not what they were. His health was undermined, and he was ailing. Again he sought refuge, as after his return from Hibueras, in the arms of the church. He went into retreat. He established himself and his suite in the Franciscan monastery of La

Rábida, near Huelva, and waited until the time was propitious to make his way to court. La Rábida, on its pretty hill, was a famous intellectual community, and had sheltered and given a hearing to Columbus in the early years of obscurity. It was a restful atmosphere in which Cortés could recuperate. In any case, a shadow had been thrown over the earlier part of his arrival in his native country by an event that had happened a few days after landing. Gonzalo de Sandoval, the gallant, the peerless, the Marshal Murat of the Conquest, his leader's right arm and bosom comrade, fell ill of a fever and died very suddenly and unexpectedly. Cortés had witnessed the deaths of many of his friends. The vocation of *conquistador* was not one in which undue grief was called for in such circumstances. But the passing of Sandoval, the youth from Medellín, the most capable, steadfast and reliable of all his captains must have cut him to the heart. The dead man was only twenty-eight.

The loss of his principal lieutenant was another of the pieces of ill-luck to which he was increasingly prone: and while he was at La Rábida he also committed one more of the diplomatic errors to which he had become susceptible. Using his elderly but long-headed father as a go-between, he had become betrothed to Doña Juana de Zúñiga, the daughter of Don Carlos Arrellano, Count of Aguilar, and niece of his chief patron, the powerful Duke of Béjar. It was a first-class match. Doña Juana was amiable and beautiful, and her family ranked among the most ancient and illustrious in Spain. Unfortunately, it happened that two other ladies were enjoying the hospitality of La Rábida at the same time as Cortés. They were Doña María de Mendoza and her younger sister Doña Francisca de Mendoza. The Mendozas were even more eminent and influential than the Arellanos. Doña María was the wife of the most important man, after the Emperor, in all Spain. This was the chief secretary of state, Francisco de los Cobos. Cobos had recently supplanted the grand chancellor, Gattinara, as the Emperor's most trusted adviser. He was in direct personal command of the day-to-day government of Castile, Portugal, Italy and the Indies. He held high office under the Emperor for over thirty years, and eventually, when his royal master left Spain and remained abroad for fourteen years, he would become one of the three rulers of Spain, in the capacity of chief counsellor to the Emperor's young son.

It was understandable that Cortés should seek to enlist the support of the Mendozas; indeed, in the months ahead the two great ladies would be numbered among his most enthusiastic partisans. But he overreached himself. The details of the scandal are not clear, but it seems likely that the old itch that caused him so much trouble in his earlier days was as wakeful as ever. He appears to have been taken with the attractions of young Doña Francisca and to have aroused in her certain expectations. These, in the end, he could not or would not fulfil. Willingly or unwillingly, he kept his word and married Doña Juana de Zúñiga. However, to play fast and loose with the wives and daughters of Indian chieftains or Spanish emigrants was one thing; to touch the honour of a noblewoman of the imperial household was another. He had blundered, and had alienated the faction of Francisco de Cobos, which then and during the rest of his lifetime would be the dominant force in Spanish politics. He also enhanced the reputation for untrustworthiness and undependability which his opponents had succeeded in foisting on him, and which he could not shake off.

The Emperor welcomed his *conquistador* with the graciousness of a great prince. He even went so far, when Cortés fell sick, as to pay a personal call at the patient's lodgings, an altogether unheard-of mark of favour. He had already bestowed on Cortés the title of 'Don' and the right to bear a shield of arms. In its quarters were displayed the double-headed Habsburg eagle, the three crowns of the defeated Aztec confederacy, a lion rampant, and the water-girt city of Tenochtitlán. Surrounding the shield was a chain with a padlock into which were interwoven the seven heads of the rulers of the seven Indian states that Cortés had subdued. Now, on July 28, 1529, the Emperor confirmed him in his office of Captain-General of New Spain and also dubbed him Marqués del Valle de Oaxaca. With the marquisate went a grant of land which comprised at least thirty thousand square miles, with the right to levy personal taxes and tribute among the fifty large towns and villages and the million or more inhabitants that they contained. Although Cortés took his title from the valley of Oaxaca, over two hundred miles south-east of Mexico City, his lands also included large tracts in the neighbourhood of Villa Rica on the north coast and Colima and Tehuantepec on the south. He was also made overlord of towns with such familiar names as Coyoacán, Cuernavaca, Tlacopán, Tepeyac, Jalapa and Toluca.

The Emperor had not only raised him to the ranks of the nobility—which the boy at Medellín or the poor student at Salamanca could hardly have dreamed of—but had made Cortés the wealthiest and most extensive landowner in New Spain. It would scarcely have been just to accuse the Emperor of being niggardly. But for Cortés it was not enough. He was offered the mantle of a knight of the order of Santiago. He refused, on the ground that he merited the grade not of knight but of commander. He may have been right; but surely it was a strangely petulant gesture. The Emperor may well have been taken aback: and in any case, it may not have been the Emperor's fault that Cortés was not nominated for a higher rank. Although Ferdinand and Isabella had gone some way towards bringing the military orders to heel, their Grand Masters still jealously retained many of their prerogatives. Altogether, during this first return to Spain, Cortés acted, as he had acted for four or five years past, like a man who had lost his touch.

He yearned above everything for the Viceroyalty of the country he had conquered. New Spain was not to have a Viceroy until 1535, the first in the New World, but the man on whom that status was bestowed would become virtually the Emperor's coeval on the other side of the globe, and to be acknowledged as the Emperor's surrogate was the sole status which Cortés now thought worthy of him. With every year that passed the realization of the true immensity of his achievement and the measure of his deserts continued to grow. The Emperor did not respond to his insinuations or outright importunity. Not only had Cortés affronted the Cobos faction, but the Emperor himself could sense defects in the character of Cortés that suggested that he might not be fit for supreme responsibility. The fact was that Cortés had already given of his best energies; he had endangered his own conquest by his thoughtless expedition to Hibueras; and his personality was so powerful that it aroused excessive love or excessive hate in all those who came into contact with him. He had lost the temperate and judicious qualities which he had once possessed, and which would be absolutely necessary in the Emperor's Viceroy.

Nevertheless the Emperor, with remarkable insight, divined how he might soothe Cortés' ruffled feelings while still making use of the phenomenal talents of the finest soldier Spain had produced since Gonzalo de Córdoba. He saw that the craving for adventure still burned in Cortés, even after the hardships and dangers of the past ten years. Cortés had been enraged by the permission which had been given to Narváez to explore Florida; when he had heard the news, at Las Honduras, he had shut himself up and taken to his bed. Now, in the very year when Cortés was at court, the Emperor appointed Francisco Pizarro, who was in Spain and had not even begun the serious conquest of Peru, to be Peru's first Governor and Captain-General. Pizarro had already been driving towards his goal for six years, refusing to be discouraged, and had such blazing faith in his ultimate success that he had imparted it to the Emperor and his advisers. It is piquant to think of the two lions from Extremadura meeting and comparing notes in Toledo at this time, as they must have done. They also got on well, in spite of their rivalry, since nine years later we find Cortés sending to Pizarro from New Spain a valuable cargo of arms and supplies.

The patents given to Narváez and Pizarro had aroused in Cortés all the natural competitiveness of the *conquistador*. The Emperor, understanding this, and seeing how it might be turned to his advantage, made a formal agreement with Cortés whereby the latter would undertake the exploration of the South Sea coast of Mexico and North America, in the direction of the as-yet-unnamed California. Cortés was blocked first by Pedrarias Dávila, now by Pizarro, from extending his bailiwick in the direction of Central and South America, although he had pushed his claim as far as Honduras and Guatemala; but the land to the north and north-west remained open for whoever had the enterprise to snap it up. There, furthermore, was said to lie the realm of Cíbola, an empire more incredible than the empire of Moctezuma, the palaces and houses of whose seven cities were made of pure gold. When the savage Pizarro had taken Cuzco and Cajamarca, and the treasure of the Emperor Atahualpa was found to exceed the treasure of Moctezuma, the existence of Cíbola became less a fairy-story than a probability, and the urge to conquer it correspondingly urgent. In receiving from the Emperor the instruments relating to the exploration of the South Sea, with the right to retain one twelfth of whatever wealth and territories he took for himself, Cortés really believed that he had acquired a licence to seek out and overrun a kingdom that would probably turn out to be more extensive than that of the Aztecs.

It was in this mingled mood of disappointment and renewed hope that he set foot again on Mexican soil in the summer of 1530. During the next ten years he was to devote his principal energies to the prosecution of the South Sea project. For the most part he had no other choice, since during the whole decade, in spite of his nominal offices, he was to be relentlessly frozen out of political affairs. If the Emperor had shown a certain prescience where Cortés was concerned, he showed none at all when he allowed the ruffianly Nuño de Guzmán to be appointed President of the newly-established Audiencia of New Spain in 1529. Nuño seized all the possessions of the still-absent Cortés and sold them at public auction, then had the Captain-General publicly proscribed as a traitor and criminal. Pedro de Alvarado, who had recently been in Spain, where he had made a great impression because of his handsome person and the passionate loyalty with which he supported Cortés, was arrested and thrown in prison. By the time Cortés arrived, Nuño's course was already run. The Emperor sent orders to remove him, whereupon he retired with a gang of gaolbirds and cut-throats first to Pánuco, then to the country north-west of the city of Guadalajara, which he named and founded and made the capital of the province of New Galicia. By 1537 his brutality had become so renowned that he was rounded up, put in irons, and shipped to Spain to answer for his crimes.

The President and members of the second Audiencia, who entered upon their duties in 1531, were intelligent and honest men. They attempted to effect both a public and private rapprochement with Cortés, but in his tetchy mood he had become difficult to deal with. They invited him to return to Mexico City and establish residence there; instead he retreated to Cuernavaca, where he laid the first stone of the cathedral in 1529, and next year began to build himself a palace. He still hoped that his friends in Spain would prevail, that the Emperor would relent and name him Viceroy—in which event the palace at Cuernavaca would become a suitable and semi-regal abode. It was a heavy building, its chilly halls and high, dark rooms symmetrically and unimaginatively laid out. Today it gives the impression of a gloomy fortress, and its atmosphere is not rendered more joyous by the fact that the Emperor Maximilian established a residence there and the building contains sad and dusty associations of his luckless reign. Its most pleasant feature is the wide loggia on the second floor, overlooking the city square, and with a fine view of the distant shining peaks of the volcanoes of Popocatépetl and Ixtaccíhuatl. To Cortés, standing on his balcony, the twin peaks were reminders of the ardent and exciting days when he had passed between them on the march to Tenochtitlán. Those days were gone, and the little band of captains and comrades were discredited, or dead, or scattered. Today the loggia at the rear of the palace is decorated with the fierce, flamboyant frescoes of Diego Rivera (Plate 12), incisive and eloquent but coarsely propagandistic, striving to reduce Cortés, history and the Mexican people to the threadbare dimension of Marxist dogma.

To solace him, he had Doña Juana. He loved her, and she not only looked after the children of his first marriage and some of his illegitimate brood (of whom five were acknowledged) but bore him three daughters and a son. He improved his estate, grew sugar and cotton, planted vines, established a silk industry, and imported horses, cattle and Merino sheep. In these activities he vindicated the claim of Sánchez-Barba to be considered not merely as a *conquistador* but a *fundador*. Nevertheless these peaceful pursuits could not be expected to satisfy his ever-restless spirit. As early as October 1530, three months after his return from Spain, he had laid down at Tehuantepec and Acapulco the keels of four ships with which he intended to prosecute the exploration of the South Sea. In May 1532, a scant eighteen months later, the first two ships had set out. They met with ill fortune. One of them disappeared, the other had to put back to Acapulco. The second pair of ships was despatched. They too

10

crawled back to port, the crews having mutinied and murdered their commander.

He decided that it was high time to take charge himself. If the kingdom of Cíbola were to be found, he could not afford these expensive setbacks. He ordered three more ships to be built at Tehuantepec, and in the spring of 1535 assembled at Cuernavaca a force of three hundred Spanish infantry and a hundred and thirty horsemen. When all was ready, he ordered the ships to sail northwards to the port of Chametla, thirty-five miles south of modern Mazatlán, and led his small army overland to the rendezvous, a march through wild country for a distance of between 550 and 600 miles. Clearly the old vigour had not by any means died down. Chametla was in New Galicia, where Nuño de Guzmán was nearing the end of his un-savoury career; and after settling a score or two with Nuño, Cortés left Andrés de Tapia in charge of the bulk of the men and set sail with his three ships in the direction of Cíbola. He reached the southern tip of the seven hundred and fifty mile-long isthmus of Baja California, and the hopes of the members of the expedition grew high. He then sent back his three ships to fetch over Andrés de Tapia with the rest of the troops: and from that moment disaster was piled upon disaster. Two of the ships, containing the greater part of the supplies, failed to make the return journey. Cortés and his party were stranded in the wilderness of Baja California, waiting in vain for relief. He took the lone ship which had made the crossing, located the two missing vessels, and made a trip to the town of Culiacán on the mainland to purchase, at exorbitant prices, food and water for his starving men. He had to pay thirty gold pesos for every calf and ten gold pesos for every pig. Altogether he voyaged three times across the Gulf of California, which deserves to be known by the name which it bore in former times: the Sea of Cortés. His travails were not over. He still had no transport to extricate his men, who were soon reduced once more to eating roots, berries, shellfish and seaweed. Again one of his ships was lost. Mercifully, he received news that a ship had arrived at Chametla from Tehuantepec and was looking for him. Once more he sailed from Baja California to New Galicia to make contact with it. To his joy, he encountered two other well-found ships in addition, which his wife had commandeered and sent in search of him. He also recovered his own lost ship. Quickly, he sent relief to the troops in Baja California, re-embarked them, and brought them back to New Galicia. The expedition had been a failure, but at least, thanks to the courage and tenacity of its leader, it had ended reasonably well. With his little armada of six ships in all he was able to make a safe return voyage to Acapulco.

From the captain of one of the rescue-ships he learned that a Viceroy had landed in Mexico. The Emperor had finally made his choice, and had not chosen Cortés. Don Antonio de Mendoza attempted, as the members of the second Audiencia had done, to treat the great Captain-General in a kindly and considerate manner. For his part, Cortés tried to put a good face on it and to reciprocate Don Antonio's good intentions: but not many months had passed before the two men were caught up in a series of the bitter legalistic wrangles which were habitual among Spaniards of the epoch. The disputes about Cortés' right to do as he willed with the vast estates which the Emperor had granted him might have been taken as a matter of course. Unfortunately, their relationship was speedily bedevilled by a running disagreement about who was to take charge of an ambitious new expedition to Cíbola which the Viceroy had conceived. Far being discouraged by the recent *débâcle*, Cortés continued to pursue the exploration and conquest of Cíbola with unabated enthusiasm. In a letter to the Emperor in February 1537, he announced that he had prepared a further six ships for another attempt, and that another four were nearing completion. In September 1538, he informed the Council of the Indies that a fleet of nine ships was only prevented from sailing by the lack of experienced pilots, but that his agents were scouring Spain to find suitable men. In May 1539, he ordered three ships to sail north from Acapulco under the command of Francisco de Ulloa, an experienced seaman who had been with him on his own foray towards the north. Ulloa made a memorable journey. Following Cortés' instruction, he used Culiacán as his base, then made his way along the entire east coast of the Gulf of California, reached the end of that land-locked sea, thus establishing that Baja California was not an island, and started south again. Hugging the west coast of the Gulf, he rounded Cape St. Lucas, where Cortes' forlorn little group had been marooned four years before, and cruised for several hundred miles up the Pacific coastline before finally turning for home.

Cortés, therefore, could fairly claim to have been engaged in active and continued steps to prosecute the exploration of the north. If the Viceroy was organizing an army for that purpose, Cortés surely had an unshakeable right to be put in charge of it. He had good grounds for arguing, particularly in view of the sketchy geographical knowledge of the area, that the writ which he had received from the royal hand covered any such enterprise. He fought to uphold his own authority as tenaciously as Diego de Velázquez had once fought to uphold his. The old *hombre de frontera* was still seeking one last frontier. Gómara says that: 'Cortés and Don Antonio de Mendoza quarrelled bitterly over the expedition to Cíbola, each claiming it as his own by the Emperor's order: Don Antonio as Viceroy, Cortés as Captain-General. They exchanged such words that they were never reconciled, although they were once close friends. As a result they wrote a thousand complaints about each other, which damaged and diminished them both.'

To command the expedition, Mendoza had already selected one of the young men who had accompanied him to New Spain. To Cortés, now in his mid-fifties, and forgetful of how young he was himself when he embarked on the Conquest, the twenty-nine-year-old Vázquez de Coronado would have seemed an upstart and a whippersnapper. In fact Coronado, who had come to the New World in the same obscure and penniless condition as the older man, had speedily and deservedly made his mark. Mendoza had sent him as Governor to New Galicia, to clean up the mess made by Nuño de Guzmán. In this capacity he had acted with such wisdom and forbearance that Mendoza had given him a seat on the council of the newly-rising Mexico City. The Viceroy had chosen his man well. Nevertheless Cortés was enraged, making a special journey from Cuernavaca to the capital to confront the no doubt embarrassed young general in person and suggest that, at the very least, they should share the leadership of the expedition. Coronado could only refer the angry and battle-scarred old veteran to the Viceroy, who returned him a dusty answer. Coronado's army left for the far north in February 1540. It consisted of a hundred infantrymen, musketeers and crossbowmen, six cannon, a thousand Indians, six hundred pack animals, and no less than two hundred and thirty horsemen with a thousand horses in reserve.

The Captain-General was not present to wish godspeed to this fair array, which marched forth with as shining expectations as those of the army which Cortés himself had led to Mexico City almost exactly twenty years before. Sick at heart, feeling that he had suffered a crowning humiliation, Cortés had already, one month earlier, set sail from Villa Rica to Spain, once more to carry his grievances to the Emperor. He would live another seven years, but he would not return again to the New World, where he had figured as the greatest of the *conquistadores* and where he had passed thirty-four years of his life.

*　　*　　*

He had not planned to spend longer in Spain than the time it would take to present his various petitions to the Emperor. Unfortunately, he arrived at a bad moment. The Emperor had recently lost his young wife, the Empress Elizabeth, whom he had deeply loved and on whom he had depended. In any event, when Cortés was still on the high seas the

Emperor was already on the road to Flanders, to cope with a rebellion in Ghent, his own birthplace. When Cortés eventually reached Madrid, he therefore discovered that he would have to put his case not to the Emperor, but to Francisco de los Cobos and the Council of the Indies.

He was treated with immense deference. A delegation awaited him outside the gates of Madrid to welcome him to the city with appropriate ceremony. At the sessions of the Council he was accorded the respect due to a personage of his rank and attainments. Nonetheless it soon became clear that the Council was toying with him. It must therefore have been with the liveliest feelings of relief and pleasure that he learned, after twelve full months of kicking his heels in idleness and frustration, that the Emperor was travelling south once more, and that there might be a good chance of obtaining an interview with him.

However, it transpired that the Emperor was not returning to Madrid or to Spain, but was journeying through Italy in order to meet the Pope and then to embark for Algiers. He meant to strike a blow against the Bey of Algiers, Kheirredin Barbarossa, the most renowned of the Barbary pirates and the servant of the Sultan, Suleiman the Magnificent. The Emperor was the legitimate champion of Christendom against the colossal power of the Turk: but, like Cortés, he tended to throw himself into romantic expeditions in order to try to regain the prestige he had lost elsewhere, or to forget in action and adventure the grey realities of his actual situation. The war in the Mediterranean was the last chapter in the glorious and chivalric saga of the Reconquest. It was therefore fitting that the Emperor and Cortés should have taken part in it together.

The Emperor had scored a resounding success in 1535, when he had led an army in person to Tunis, stormed and captured it, seized over eighty Moorish galleys, and caused Barbarossa to take refuge in Algiers. A quarter of a century before, Cardinal Ximenes, on behalf of King Ferdinand, had taken Tunis and placed a Spanish garrison there; but thereafter the Spanish position in the Mediterranean had deteriorated. Tunis had fallen once more into Moorish hands. The Emperor now planned to deal with Algiers and with Barbarossa once and for all. He assembled a fleet of a hundred and fifty ships under Andrea Doria, and landed on the coast of North Africa with an army of seven thousand Spaniards, six thousand Germans and five thousand Italians. He intended to repeat the glamorous victory of Tunis all over again.

It was at this stage that a contingent of Spanish volunteers, including Cortés and two of his sons, arrived in Africa to join him. Cortés no doubt expected to find an opportunity to confer with the Emperor about his own problems. It was also very likely that, experienced and fearless warrior that he was, he would perform deeds of valour in the coming campaign which would put the Emperor in his debt. He had brought his two sons of fighting-age with him so that they too could earn themselves a place in the royal regard. In the upshot, the fiasco that now occurred was merely the continuation of his previous disappointments. A tremendous storm destroyed the bulk of the fleet, and in any case the Emperor had reached Algiers too late in the year to undertake any serious operations. The attack on Algiers was half-hearted and badly co-ordinated, and the Emperor was compelled to give the order to re-embark and raise the siege in order to avoid a complete *débâcle*. Cortés had not even been invited to take part in the deliberations of the Council of War. He was old and crippled by wounds; he was a back-number; doubtless other members of the Council of War were jealous of him. He was like those British generals of the Indian Army who, in the early nineteenth century, had commanded huge armies and undertaken vast campaigns, but whose capabilities were not called upon in the Crimea and elsewhere because they were thought to be slightly uncouth and their social position was uncertain. They were the only soldiers who had seen action, but they were passed over in favour of amateurs because their sunburned faces looked out of place in the clubs of Pall Mall and the corridors of Whitehall. It is said that Cortés sent an appeal to the Emperor in which he begged to be placed in command of a small force, with which he promised to take Algiers. The Council of War not only ignored him, but apparently laughed at him. The Emperor would have been wise to have heeded his plea. The Algiers fiasco would rank as one of the outstanding reverses of his reign. A modest gamble involving a handful of men would have cost him little. There was good reason to suppose that a general who had captured Tenochtitlán with a few hundred troops might well be able to do the same at Algiers with an equivalent number. Cortés might possibly have retrieved something from the wreck.

Perhaps the Emperor himself was not above feeling a tinge of jealousy where his great captain was concerned. It is hard for a king to contemplate the success of a subordinate in a venture in which he himself has failed. Certainly the Emperor was growing tired of Cortés and the endless querulous remonstrances which the latter directed at him. Cortés had made the error, always fatal in court circles, of becoming a bore. He took to following the Emperor about, showering the royal secretaries with complaints concerning Viceroy Mendoza and petitions for a pension of monumental and impossible proportions. No doubt the secretaries, on royal instructions, had long ceased to forward them to their imperial addressee. Paul Horgan, in his *Conquistadors in North American History*, recounts a touching and curious story which, though it cannot possibly be true, indicates in a symbolic way the mood of resentment and despair into which the old man had lapsed. 'One day in the street—so the story went—he saw the royal carriage approaching, and in desperation he threw himself upon it, clinging to its straps and calling to its occupant. "Who is this man?" asked Charles V. "I am the man," cried Cortés, "who brought to Your Majesty more kingdoms than your father left you towns!" The coach swept on. Cortés was swallowed up by the street crowds.'

*   *   *

In this sad and pathetic manner Cortés passed his remaining years. It is true that, owing to his open-handed and profligate habits, he was at the end in somewhat straitened circumstances. His will, which he dictated on October 12, 1547, lists a series of bequests that seem relatively modest for a man who in happier years had been one of the world's greatest magnates. The bequests were all of a family nature, and he took care to provide for his illegitimate children as carefully as for his legitimate ones. He was still rich in land, but he was hard up for cash. The expenses of litigation had denuded his store of gold, already depleted before he left New Spain by the cost of his successive expeditions in search of Cíbola. Like King Lear, he also insisted in keeping up an elaborate and costly household in accordance with what he considered his personal dignity.

At the end, when his health was giving way, he felt a longing to die in Mexico. He set out for Andalucia, intending to sail to Villa Rica. He was too weak to begin the voyage, and on December 2, 1547, he gave up the ghost in the village of Castilleja de la Cuesta, near Seville, at the age of sixty-three.

Date obolum Belisario. In this way died the man of whom F. A. Kirkpatrick remarks in his *Spanish Conquistadores*, that 'to some, whose view is not focused upon European courts and camps, he stands out as the greatest Spaniard of a great age'.

He had given specific instructions in his will that his body was to be interred in the Hospital de Jesús Nazareno in Mexico City. The Hospital, which he had founded and endowed in 1527, and which is the oldest hospital in the Americas, stands three blocks south of the Zócalo, where, in anticipation of the viceroyalty that was never to be his, he had begun to build his principal palace. The palace itself, as he conceived and executed it, was damaged by riots in 1562, and totally destroyed by more severe disturbances in 1692. For some years his body remained in Andalucia, in the family vault of the Dukes of Medina Sidonia; but afterwards his bones were taken to Mexico, as he had stipulated, and placed in a vault in the Chapel Niño Jesús behind the Hospital de Jesús.

What happened later is described by J. Patrick McHenry, who adds a comment on the subsequent reputation of Cortés. He writes: 'After Mexico achieved her independence in 1821, a campaign was started to discredit the name of Cortés. Neophyte politicians professed their patriotism by urging vandals to deface or destroy anything that honoured the great Spanish general. During the riots of 1828 his tomb was ransacked, but found empty. Descendants of Cortés had rescued his funeral urn the night before and kept it in a family vault until the rioting had ended. In 1840, William Prescott, writing his celebrated *History of the Conquest of Mexico*, deplored the fact that not one single statue or monument to one of the most amazing men in history could be found anywhere in the Mexican republic. To this day, nothing to commemorate him exists; indeed, during the twenties and thirties of this century, he was most strongly vilified when Mexico's world famous painters (Rivera, Orozco, and Siquieros) covered the walls of public buildings with murals depicting Cortés as a kind of moronic monster branding and flogging docile Indians. As paintings, they are undeniably decorative; as history, they are malicious distortions of fact. They give no credit to his indomitable courage, his genius in organizing and carrying out a campaign, his great generalship (which Prescott compared to that of Caesar and Alexander the Great), his humanitarian acts of founding hospitals (some of which still exist), and of forming a government based on coexistence with the Indians, not in extinguishing them (as Pizarro did in the conquest of Peru) or in driving them like animals from Christian colonies (as the Puritans did in New England). The words of Antony might well have been applied to Cortés instead of Caesar when he said: *The evil that men do lives after them: The good is oft interred with their bones. . . .*'

Cortés has entered into legend in Mexico. The strangest stories are circulated about him, even by educated and sophisticated Mexicans. One is told that he was a hunchback, a cripple, a *brujo* or wizard, a member of the fanatical sect of *penitentes*, who before their suppression in both Mexico and New Mexico used to crucify one of their own number on Good Friday. No story about him is too wild to be believed. It is therefore very curious, when one considers the gigantic imprint he made on the life of Mexico, that he should have left behind almost no physical evidence of his passage. There is the barrack-like palace at Cuernavaca, and the mere site of another palace in Mexico City; the Hospital de Jesús Nazareno; the cypress of the Noche Triste; two portraits in the room perfunctorily devoted to the Conquest in the Castle of Chapultepec; a house at Coyoacán, now the local police station, which is pointed out as being that of Cortés,

ut which was built by his descendants; and a tablet outside the town of
Texcoco to mark the spot where he launched his fleet on the lake. The
Lake of Texcoco itself was drained little by little during the course of
our centuries, largely at the beginning of the present century by a firm
of British engineers. Nor, although he had made the initial decision to
rebuild it, does Mexico City show the imprint of Cortés. The real founder
of the city, the man who first laid it out in its modern form, was Juan de
Padilla, Conde de Revillagigedo, who became Viceroy in 1789.

One is equally at a loss to discover traces of Cortés in Spain. There is
almost nothing. All that remains is a long stone bench, once a door-lintel,
in the Plaza de Cortés at Medellín, bearing the illegible remains of an
inscription. Near the bench the town council has set up a solitary stone
escutcheon, on which is painted: '*Escudo de Hernán Cortés*', 'Shield of
Hernán Cortés'. On the reverse side of the escutcheon the words: '*Aquí
stuvo la habitación donde nació Hernán Cortés en 1484*', 'Here stood the
house in which Hernán Cortés was born in 1484'. Both the door-lintel
and the escutcheon are dubious, to say the least. Medellín itself is a
cramped little town with much the same atmosphere it possessed when
Cortés was a boy there. Above it, on the hill, are the remains of the still-
imposing castle. The parish church and the whitewashed houses still bear
the scars of the Civil War, when a column of General Franco's army
passed through Medellín on its way to join up with the forces of General
Mola and was bombed by a squadron led by Commandant André Malraux
of the Loyalist airforce, in a raid which Malraux has vividly described in
L'Espoir. Below the town is a wide sweep of the Guadiana, with its shingle
bars and rushy islands, and beyond it and all around are the arid wastes of
Extremadura. The hills are dotted sparsely with ilex trees, and in the
distance beckon the dusty sierras. The whole of the career of Cortés
would appear to have been nothing more than a dream, were it not for the
statue that dominates the plaza that bears his name (Plate 13). Cortés
stands alert and proud, his gaze directed eastwards towards the New
World. In his right hand he holds a baton, in his left a banner surmounted
by a cross. He stands on a tumbled pile of masonry from an Aztec temple,
with his left foot resting on the head of an Aztec idol. On the four sides of
the plinth are shields bearing the words: *Mejico*, *Tlascala*, *Otumba*, and
Tabasco.

The real memorials of Cortés are not to be sought in a few broken bits
of stone and metal. They exist in the cities he established and in the
nation, a blend of the races and traditions of two continents, of which he
was *El Fundador*. He has no statue or imposing relic in Mexico. His spirit
haunts it everywhere.

10*

*Lands and kingdoms are won or lost as
chance dictates: and what was praised
when it led to conquest is condemned
when it leads to loss.*

Machiavelli: *Letter to Piero Soderini*

IT DOES not lie within the province of this book to offer an account of the post-Conquest history of Mexico, let alone of Latin America. Nevertheless a brief discussion of the character of the Spanish Empire which the *conquistadores* founded, and of whom Cortés was the prime exemplar, might not be out of place. The Viceroy of New Spain came, after all, to administer an area many times greater than that of his master at home; and at its height the Spanish Empire occupied a land mass eight times larger than that of Europe. At one time, between 1580 and 1640, when the kings of Spain were also the kings of Portugal, it also embraced the huge demi-continent of Brazil.

Cortés had completed the conquest of Mexico, from the moment of setting sail from Cuba to the surrender of Cuauhtémoc, within the space of twenty-two months. The other *conquistadores* accomplished their missions with similar celerity. Pizarro, sailing from Panama with a hundred and eighty men and twenty-seven horses at the end of 1530, had effectively completed the conquest of Peru by January 1535, when he founded Lima, notwithstanding the bloody battles that marked the six years that followed. The founding of the other great capitals of Spanish South America, all laid out on the familiar ground-plan which Cortés had employed at Villa Rica de Vera Cruz and his other Mexican towns, and which had been introduced into the New World from metropolitan Spain, took place within a few years of each other in the 1530s and 1540s. Quito in Ecuador was founded a year before Lima; Asunción in Paraguay in 1537; Bogotá in Columbia in 1538; Santiago de Chile in 1541; Sucre and La Paz in Bolivia in 1538 and 1548; and Buenos Aires initially in 1536, although the early attempts to settle there were unsuccessful and a permanent city was not established until 1580.

There is no space here to chronicle the careers of individual members of the tempestuous generation of *conquistadores*. Their deaths were usually in keeping with their lives—sudden and sanguinary. Of Cortés' own captains, Pedro de Alvarado, Diego de Ordaz and Francisco de Montejo went on to achieve notable feats which deserve our passing notice. Montejo, as has been mentioned, became the conqueror of Yucatán, where he somehow contrived to die in his bed, a rich and respected Governor, in the handsome palace which can still be seen in Mérida. Diego de Ordaz became an explorer in South America, and in 1530 led an ambitious expedition of four vessels and five hundred men first to the Amazon, then to the Orinoco. For a year he was swallowed up in the jungles of Brazil. On emerging, he became embroiled in a political quarrel, was arrested by the Audiencia of Santo Domingo, and shipped back to Spain. He died on the journey, possibly as a result of poison.

Pedro de Alvarado continued to show the outstanding if equivocal qualities that had marked him throughout the Conquest. We have seen that Cortés had sent him, in December 1523, on an *entrada* into Guatemala, as one prong of a thrust to find a waterway across the Isthmus of Tehuantepec, the other prong being the army of Cristóbal de Olid. The inhabitants of Guatemala, who were of Mayan stock, proved very accomplished and determined fighters, and Alvarado had to wage a vigorous campaign, taking a leaf out of Cortés' book and succeeding largely by setting the two principal tribes, the Calchiquels and the Quiches, against one another and afterwards subjugating both. He then moved onward into what is now San Salvador, clashing with the men of Pedrarias Dávila in the process, but resolving the dispute by means of the diplomatic skills that he did not lack when he chose to use them. After a triumphant return to Spain in 1527, where he was made *adelantado* of Guatemala and a knight of Santiago, he spent seven years chafing at the tasks of administering his newly-won fief. Like Cortés, however, he hungered for a life of action and adventure, and in 1534 began to organize an expedition to explore the South Seas. On hearing rumours of immense conquests by Pizarro and Almagro in Peru, he changed his plans, and sailed instead with a large force of five hundred Spaniards, two hundred and twenty-seven horses and two thousand Guatemalan slaves for the coast of modern Ecuador. His aim was to carve out a kingdom for himself before Pizarro and Almagro were ready to turn their attention northward from their pre-occupations in the south. Luck ran against him, and when he finally staggered with what remained of his men on to the plateau of Quito, he found that his rivals had forestalled him. Belalcazar, one of Pizarro's captains, had already subdued the country, and on the news of Alvarado's arrival Almagro hastened from Peru to help Belalcazar to expel him.

Alvarado possessed numerical superiority to his opponents; but on reflection, and in view of the unsoundness of his legal position, he prudently offered to cede his pretensions in the area. He sold his ships, guns and equipment to Almagro, paid a courtesy visit to Pizarro, and then returned to Guatemala. He paid a second visit to Spain, where he was received in as flattering a manner as before, and was authorized to make a second effort to cross the South Seas and discover fresh lands to the west. Again he organized a formidable force—only to allow himself once more to be diverted by tales of the fabulous wealth to be found elsewhere. This time he gave ear to the stories trickling down from Mexico City about the Seven Cities of Cíbola, in the distant north.

In February 1540, Francisco Vázquez de Coronado had mustered at Compostela, in New Galicia, that ample army for the exploration of Cíbola that Cortés had wanted to command and had not been allowed to. Coronado had since vanished beyond the northern deserts into the unknown lands beyond: and once again Alvarado was fired with the notion of cutting out Coronado, as he had tried to cut out Pizarro and Almagro, in order to seize a luscious chunk of territory for himself. Antonio de Mendoza, the Viceroy of New Spain, readily granted him permission to mount the proposed expedition, for Mendoza was the driving spirit behind Coronado and took a close interest in the exploration of Cíbola. Mendoza was an able and energetic man, who after serving for fifteen years as Viceroy of New Spain would go to Lima in 1551 as Viceroy of Peru. His task would be to restore order after the civil war in which Gonzalo Pizarro had lopped off the head of the previous Viceroy with his own hand, only to be defeated and beheaded in turn by the priest-general Pedro de la Gasca. Only an outstanding man would have been sent to take charge in Peru at such a time. Perhaps Cortés was unfortunate in that the first Viceroy of New Spain was as shrewd, polite and immovable as he was himself. However that may be, before he allowed Alvarado to proceed towards Cíbola, Mendoza requested him to land at New Galicia on his way north to put down an Indian revolt that had broken out there. The province had been restless ever since the depredations of Nuño de Guzmán, now in gaol in Spain, despite the capable exertions of Francisco Vázquez de Coronado, its previous governor. Now the Chichimecs, those ancestors of the Aztecs, or at least their first cousins, had risen against the Spaniards and were terrorizing the citizens of Guadalajara. Alvarado complied with the Viceroy's summons. There was much hard fighting. After an attack on an enemy strongpoint, from which the Chichimecs rolled down an avalanche of boulders on the Spaniards, Alvarado, when he had thrust home one last reckless cavalry charge, was compelled to retreat. By sheer chance, he was thrown off his mount and pinned beneath it. He died eleven days later of his injuries. It was left to Antonio de Mendoza to proceed in person to quash what became known as the Mistón rebellion, after the place where he gained his final victory over the insurgents. Thus ended the charmed life of Pedro de Alvarado, one of the most brilliant members of a brilliant breed—and, unfortunately, one of the most inflexible. He perished while at the height of his powers, when great successes still lay ahead of him. Such were the hazards of his profession. He had lived by luck, and was ready to accept the rub of the green.

He would not have enjoyed any success in his search for Cíbola, even had he reached it. No Spaniard, however intrepid, was ever to enjoy success in that direction. There was no success to be had. Coronado was away for over two years, and made one of the greatest land explorations known to history. He led his army through northern Mexico, across the Sonoran desert, crossed into Arizona south of Tucson, and struck north-east until he came at last to the pueblos in the valley of upper New Mexico. The seven cities of gold, which were supposed to have been founded by seven Portuguese bishops fleeing from Iberia at the time of the Moorish invasion in the eighth century, turned out to be the modest little adobe pueblos that one can visit today, standing in the same place where they have stood for many centuries, the oldest inhabited sites in North America. There one can see the annual dances described by D. H. Lawrence (his ashes are buried within sight of the largest of them, on the Kiowa Ranch above Taos) and by Ruth Benedict in her classic *Patterns of Culture*. Apart from these poor and pretty mud villages, there was nothing. Coronado's army went into winter quarters, while one of his lieutenants, López de Cárdenas, took a scouting party and became the first Westerner to see the Colorado River and the Grand Canyon. The present writer has driven for many weeks and for many thousands of miles in New Mexico, Arizona and Colorado, and has traced, where they are known, the routes of the principal *conquistadores* through the American South-West: and it seems truly unbelievable that a handful of horsemen could have committed themselves for years at a time to those vast and empty distances. They were men who lived by harder imperatives than ours.

Coronado was filled with the unquenchable optimism that sustained every *conquistador*. He would yet find another Peru, another Tenochtitlán. It was inconceivable that a great kingdom did not lie concealed in one or other of those endless plains and valleys. One had only to keep up one's courage and press onwards. A wandering Indian arrived in camp with marvellous stories of a kingdom called 'Gran Quivira', situated just beyond the horizon. Through it ran a river six miles wide, and the very rowlocks on the canoe of the king who ruled it were made of pure gold. When spring came, Coronado left the main body of his men on the Río Grande and pushed ahead with thirty-six horsemen and six infantrymen. In the autumn he returned. He had found nothing. Undismayed, he put his men into winter quarters for a second time and planned to fare forth again in the spring. But two days after Christmas he suffered, like Alvarado, a riding accident that finished his career. He was engaged in an impromptu race with one of his young lieutenants when his horse threw him and kicked him on the head. He was almost totally incapacitated, and in April 1542 his troops turned reluctantly for home, carrying him on a litter. He lingered on in Mexico City for another twelve years, feeble-minded and more dead than alive. When he died there in 1554 this most gallant young man was still only forty-four.

In later years other expeditions were made in an attempt to find Quivira and extend the boundaries of New Spain. In 1596 Juan de Oñate, one of the wealthiest men in the New World, whose wife was both a granddaughter of Cortés and a granddaughter of Moctezuma, persuaded Philip II to appoint him Governor of New Mexico. He set out in 1598 on the same path as Coronado to hew out a kingdom for himself. He passed through El Paso del Norte and travelled up the valley of the Río Grande. He established small settlements which managed to put down tenuous roots and which, though not prosperous in his own time, formed the basis of the tolerably thriving Spanish community that existed in upper New Mexico in the following century. He despatched a handful of troops under his nephew Vicente de Zaldívar into the western fastnesses, where, on November 8, Zaldívar attacked and captured the hill-top pueblo of Ácoma. Ácoma, the most striking and inaccessible of all the pueblos, stands on the summit of a four-hundred-foot-high mesa. Its people are strong, forceful and direct. To examine the cliff up which Zaldívar led his men is to increase, if that were possible, one's respect for the courage of the *conquistadores*. Zaldívar captured the pueblo, where in later times the resident priest erected a huge mud-brick church, his parishioners carrying up every bit of the materials by hand. Oñate himself took another column to the west, in the direction of Zuñi pueblo. On a steep scarp of rock in the wilderness, guarding the only pool of water for miles around, he carved his name with the point of his dagger. Today one can drive the lonely road between Zuñi and Inscription Rock to see his signature, cut with many proud flourishes in an elegant script. There too are the names of other explorers, Spanish, British and American, including those of members of nineteenth-century wagon-trains moving westwards to California.

Oñate remained in New Mexico for ten years, leaving in 1609 as a consequence of unjust accusations that had been levelled against him in Mexico City and in Spain. It took him the remaining twenty years of his life to clear his reputation and emerge from the clouds of disgrace, dying in Spain confirmed in the possession of the Governorship of the country he was never to see again. It was left to his successor in New Mexico, Pedro de Peralta, to found the royal city of Santa Fé in 1610. It underwent many vicissitudes. It was burned to the ground in the successful pueblo rising of 1680, when all the Spanish settlers in New Mexico fled to the shelter of El Paso, which had been founded in 1659. It was not re-captured and re-founded until 1694, when Governor Diego José de Vargas reimposed Spanish rule. For his pains, Vargas was secretly replaced by a scoundrelly place-seeker called Pedro Rodríguez Cubero, who shut him up in solitary confinement for four years in a miserable hole at one end of the small but beautiful palace of the governors in Santa Fé. When news finally reached Madrid of this outrageous act, Vargas was immediately released, made a marquess, and restored to the governorship. In his case, therefore, amends were made with what for those days was commendable speed. Vargas was a truly noble and magnanimous man— and if one were permitted to name one's favourite *conquistador*, the present writer would name, after Cortés, the man who was almost the last representative of the breed, Don Diego José de Vargas Zapata Luján Ponce de León y Contreras. His story is well told in *Great River*, Paul Horgan's study of the Río Grande.

In time, the Spaniards extended their dominions northwards along the Río Grande (or Río Bravo, as the Mexicans call it) and westwards as far as Washington and Oregon. One can visit the Franciscan mission churches of California, established in the eighteenth or early nineteenth centuries, or the great mission church of San Xavier del Bac near Tucson, in the parish of the legendary Father Kino. But the Spanish settlement in the north was always thin, and the churches had to be closely associated in most cases with a nearby *presidio* or military outpost. Life in the north remained hard until modern times, as one can gather from Willa Cather's *Death Comes for the Archbishop*, a fictionalized account of the career of the first Archbishop of Santa Fé. This fine and original book paints an unforgettable picture of the pioneering years in New Mexico, and is compulsory reading for all who are interested in the area. One of its most vivid chapters is devoted to the pueblo at Ácoma. Although the northern province was without economic importance to New Spain, and the links with it remained tenuous, nonetheless the Spaniards achieved the astonishing feat of establishing a *Camino real* or Royal Road fifteen hundred miles long, starting in the Zócalo of Mexico City and ending in the *plaza* of Santa Fé. One can still ride great stretches of the Royal Road, and to do so is to realize once more that the men who built the Spanish Empire were men who were dismayed by nothing.

*   *   *

There is a school of thought which holds that the Aztec Empire did not fall because of any inherent weakness—because it was overripe, or because, like the German Third Reich, it deserved to. Some writers of this school are Mexicans, attempting, as it were, to represent their civilization not as a morbid perversion of pre-Columbian culture but as its peak and flower. However, a distinguished British archaeologist, Glyn Daniel, has recently written in his *The First Civilizations* that the Aztec, Mayan and Incan civilizations were 'brutally destroyed'; and another non-Mexican authority who holds to this view is Jacques Soustelle, not a man to disagree with lightly and one who, as Governor-General of Algeria during the Algerian War, has witnessed a violent and terrible historical tragedy at first-hand. In his *Daily Life of the Aztecs* he writes: 'The Aztecs had not reached their zenith; their rising star had scarcely passed the first degree of its course. Nothing had even begun to weaken their upward impetus before the advent of the Europeans stopped it dead.' And Mlle Séjourné is able to pay tribute to the spiritual qualities of Aztec philosophy and poetry even while maintaining that what provoked their defeat was their neighbours' 'resentment of their excessive rapacity, and of the hateful way in which they distorted a deeply revered religious tradition'. But though she deplores their 'cruel state philosophy', she adds that: 'We may perhaps idly imagine that, with inspired mysticism as a basis, and with the elementary determinism and unbridled will towards material conquest of the Chichimecas superseded, the Meso-American people might, thanks to their prodigious creative power, have succeeded in forging a synthesis of human and divine such as that which Greece was once able to offer to the West.'

This seems to be a rather large 'if', in view of the fact that the Aztec Empire was one of the largest, most highly-developed and rigid military states the world has known. Such states do not evolve peacefully, in the way Jacques Soustelle seems to envisage; their decline is as sudden and bloody as their rise. When they are swept away, almost nothing remains of them; the bigger the military monolith, the more finely-ground the subsequent dust. The world at large, and particularly those peoples having any association with them, seem to want to put them completely out of mind, and therefore grind them up exceedingly small. Whether or not one wishes to assert that Cortés murdered Aztec civilization, it is a fact that it disappeared almost simultaneously with the fall of Tenochtitlán, as though he had waved a magic wand. The Náhuatl and other Mexican peoples saw that their own gods had not only abandoned them but had been defeated, and thereby proved to be inferior to the gods of the victors. The Mexicans thereupon dropped their own ethical and religious system and adopted that of the Spaniards. In our own time we have seen something of the sort happen in 1945, when after their defeat by the Anglo-Americans the Germans and Japanese relinquished, overnight and without argument, their previous system and embraced the political and economic forms of their conquerors. Of course, like the Germans and Japanese, the Mexican peoples could not then, and have not still, changed many of the forms of thought which were habitual to them, and which had grown up during three millennia in the pre-Cortesian epoch. But though the forms of thought did not change, the content changed completely. The Spaniards perforce retained the Mexican mould, but into it they poured their own pungent and idiosyncratic essences. The situation is perhaps comparable to that of the Welsh or Scots after their conquest by the English. The modern Welshman or Scotsman still feels the tug of an old, lost way of life; he still feels in a dim but insistent way that the basic shape of his personality is not English: but nonetheless he has to admit that, after the loss of the ancient frame of existence, and even the loss of the language itself, history has condemned him to live to all intents and purposes as an Englishman. He may not like it, and is forced to grapple with every kind of psychological and cultural strain: but the fact of conquest and its aftermath are real and undeniable. To a Welshman, such as the present writer, the sullenness and sense of puzzlement, the identity-problem of the modern Mexican is not hard to grasp.

* * *

The Spaniards very thoroughly destroyed the ancient life-style of the Mexicans. They then very thoroughly introduced a life-style of their own. Mexico was the first and most systematically colonized of all the Spanish overseas possessions. In South America, and in what is now North America, they had to wrestle with geographical problems which they never overcame. Even with modern communications, the states of South America are still not winning the battle with their geography. Mexico, however, was easily accessible from Hispaniola and Cuba, which had long been settled. For the most part, the fertile and populous portion of the colony was readily reached from Mexico City, the seat of government. In contrast with most of the other colonies, the prosperous and productive region of the country was relatively compact. It is also noteworthy that, after the Conquest had occurred, the Mexicans quickly settled down to a peaceful life under their new masters. Incidents like the Mistón rebellion were comparatively few; the Mexican Republic, since its inception in 1821, has known more numerous and serious Indian revolts than the Spaniards did. If the Spaniards had feared that the Mexicans, because of their bloodthirsty religious rites, might prove hard to subdue, there was no need for anxiety. The Mexicans immediately became strangely docile and tractable. It was as though they were actually glad to give up an ancient way of life that had become exhausted and oppressive, and wished to try that of their conquerors. We must not forget that Cortés was quite genuinely hailed as the deliverer of Mexico.

On the other hand, the Spaniards were helped in the work of organizing their great new colony by an entirely fortuitous factor. If we accept the commonly-agreed figure of twenty-five million for the pre-Cortesian population of Mexico, we can see that it would have been virtually impossible for a handful of Spanish emigrants to have dominated and governed so numerous a people. But scarcely had they established themselves in Mexico when nature stepped in to help them. Epidemics began to reduce the native population on a scale which it is difficult for us to visualize. We have already seen that an epidemic was probably responsible for extinguishing some of the high cultures of Mexico, including perhaps the Mayan, at the close of the Classic or Golden Age. Now, after the Conquest, whole tribes disappeared, like the tribes of North American Indians that were wiped out by pestilence in the 1830s and 1840s, and whose once famous names are now only names in the history-books. Smallpox and pthisis accounted for millions of deaths, and malaria for millions more. Malaria was not endemic to Mexico, but once it was introduced local insects became its carriers and spread it throughout the country. One can imagine what the incidence of malaria must have been in the densely-populated marshlands around Mexico City and the marsh-areas of the northern and southern coasts.

There were two great epidemics in Mexico in the half-century following the Conquest, those of 1545-6 and 1576-9. They were only the peaks of a continuous process. We know from reports prepared for Philip II when he was heir to the throne, and later when he was king, that in 1538 the population of New Spain was in the region of 6,300,000, and that in 1580 it had sunk to a mere 1,900,000. In the space of sixty years, then, it had declined from 25,000,000 to approximately 2,000,000, or at the rate of

350,000 to 400,000 a year—7,000 or 8,000 people a week. A dreadful statistic. For some of these deaths the Spaniards must bear the blame, and there may also have been subjective factors at work, such as a paralysis of the Indian will-to-live because of despair, bewilderment and social disruption. But nature must have been the chief agent of annihilation. To the Spaniards, after all, the inhabitants of Mexico were a priceless natural resource: they had not conquered the country only to watch it founder through lack of hands to till its fields and toil in its mines.

The Spaniards would have had to have been totally cynical and incompetent to have connived at the depletion of the population on such an awesome scale. They were neither the one nor the other. They were simply without medical means to arrest it, just as the civic authorities of the Mexican Republic were without means to halt the terrible cholera epidemic of 1833, when Mexico City resembled London during the Great Plague. The Spaniards themselves suffered proportionately from the wastage of disease. We have seen how the forces of Cortés were regularly decimated by sickness: and we can judge from the number of persons whom he was accused of poisoning that the life-expectancy of a Spaniard in Mexico was short. The medical advances of the twentieth century tend to make the Westerner forget how brief was the average life-span of even a member of Western society until a generation or two ago, and how brief it is today in most of the countries of Africa, Asia, and Central and South America.

It is against this sombre background that one must view the workings of the Spanish colonial administration, whose task was rendered progressively easier by the steady diminution of the population. For over a century after the collapse of Spanish rule, it was customary to decry the entire Spanish colonial effort. Indeed, in our own time there are plenty of ignorant politicians and journalists who make a life's work of disparaging almost everything Spanish or Portuguese. Such is the pernicious legacy of the *leyenda negra*. However, as a French aphorist remarked, it is no great tragedy not to be popular with all sorts of people. Among historians, on the other hand, there has been a movement towards a re-evaluation of the aims and achievements of the Spanish Empire which has entailed an admiration for the speed and thoroughness of the way it was established and the consistency with which it was afterwards maintained. To view it as purely corrupt, lethargic and inefficient is to give too much credence to various kinds of propaganda. Nor should one make the mistake of taking its last and most deranged phase as representative of the whole. Such retrospective condemnation is often the fate of empires that have gone into decline.

In fact the Spanish Empire, given the scale of the problems involved, was organized quickly and proved to be a very capable instrument. Its great merit was its essential simplicity. Its fundamental concept, which gave it its character and shape, was strong, clear and easy to grasp. It was arranged in an orderly pyramid of power, at the apex of which presided the king. Bearing in mind the fact that it was founded at what was virtually the close of the Spanish Middle Ages, and that the Emperor Charles has been called the last medieval monarch, it was constructed on the unambiguous medieval concept of hierarchy. The rigidity of its structure was redeemed, of course, by the restless, individualistic, often irreverent spirit of the Renaissance. The Spanish Empire, by the circumstances of its birth, was thus a curious amalgam of the conservative and the adventurous, like the Spaniards themselves, whose own modern character was being formed at that epoch. We must also remember that the Spanish Empire was the first of the great world-empires in point of time, with a complexion utterly different from that of the later, utilitarian empires of the Dutch, the British or the American.

At the head of the entire edifice was the ruler of Spain, who issued personal directives concerning all sorts of matters, directives that in the main were blindly and instantly obeyed. The Spanish Empire was regarded by the Spanish king as almost a piece of personal property. To assist him, he had his Council of the Indies, and in the colonial territories themselves he appointed, in the early days, Governors or *adelantedos* ('advance agents'), a title later used for the chiefs of provinces which had become grouped together into larger unities. By the end of the sixteenth century the Empire consisted of four Viceroyalties—New Spain, New Granada, Peru and La Plata—to each of which were depended various Captaincies-General, Presidencias and Audiencias. Each separate province, under its appointed head, possessed its own *audiencia*, a cabinet and supreme court, usually with a separate committee on Indian affairs. The members of the *audiencia* were called *oidores*—'listeners'—and although not all of them were active in the judiciary it was their corporate duty to hear complaints, offer advice, and generally regulate the day-to-day affairs of state. Other functionaries with well-defined titles and duties existed in every town. Spanish society was by nature urban, and when they went to the New World the Spaniards clung to their urban habits. The towns were the nuclei of the Empire and, as the administrative hierarchy of every town was identical, the system presented a uniform and consistent appearance throughout its vast area. The members of the *cabildo* or town council were known as the *regidores*, and from among themselves they named the mayor (*alcalde*), the town constable (*alguacil mayor*), and the other officers, including a treasurer, a town clerk, an inspector of weights and measures, a surveyor, a commissioner of public works, a pageant-master, and an officer whose special task it was to collaborate with the other towns in the neighbourhood and carry petitions to the authorities in the capital. In the larger towns, the king maintained his own personal representatives to collect the Royal Fifth and protect his prerogatives. It was inevitable that the *cabildos* should be dominated exclusively by wealthy settlers, and run largely to protect or enlarge their interests. To redress the balance, in the third quarter of the sixteenth century the crown set up a very active and enlightened *juzgado general de Indios*. This was a special court that worked in association with each *audiencia* to safeguard the rights of the Indians and investigate their grievances. Without justice, as St. Augustine remarked, kingdoms are but great robbery, and according to their lights the Spaniards sought to deal justly with men who, like themselves, were free subjects of the king and whose souls were as precious in the eyes of God as their own.

Inevitably, men being what they are, there were inequalities and injustices in the system; there was muddle, cruelty and corruption. On the whole, however, it worked well enough—better, in many respects, than in Spain itself. There, the system had grown up piecemeal over the centuries, and each of the highly individual provinces clung jealously to its immemorial rights. In Mexico and throughout the New World, Spanish government was introduced in a rapid and straightforward way: and paradoxically enough, the king was often obeyed more promptly and cheerfully abroad than he was at home. The colonists had a vested interest in order and discipline.

The system was additionally effective because it was such a clear-cut replacement for the system operated by the Aztecs. The Aztec upper-class had been suddenly sliced away and immediately replaced, without any hiatus, by an upper-class provided by Europe. As Ralph Beals puts it, in a contribution to *The Heritage of Conquest*: 'It was the dominant classes which suffered most in the Conquest, and in large measure the small number of Spanish succeeded in controlling the situation in the early post-Conquest period by virtue of the fact that they simply replaced the dominant classes. I doubt very much if the average *macehual* on the central plateau was any worse off under the Spanish or that his way of life was materially changed. For the average man I suggest the major difference for many years was simply a change of masters or the replacement of a discredited official or public official by another with the prestige of success.'

The religious institutions which the Spaniards introduced into Mexico shared the same general character as the political institutions. The church, as presented to the defeated peoples, was on the whole simple and centralized. Again, it owed its loyalty directly to the king. By means of clever manœuvring, aided by several pieces of luck, the kings of Spain managed to wrest from the Papacy absolute and unprecedented control of the colonial church. In fact the king enjoyed greater control over the church overseas than he did over the church in Spain. He appointed the dignitaries of the Mexican church personally and dismissed them at will. Its members had virtually no opportunity of direct appeal to Rome: and indeed, would not have wished for it. The church in Mexico was an exclusively Spanish and nationalist institution, and even Las Casas and his adherents confined their fierce disputes to the circle of their own countrymen; there was no need to bring in outsiders. Las Casas had confidence in the desire and ability of the king of Spain, who was not merely a Christian monarch but the leader of Christendom, to act wisely and justly. He could also take comfort from the fact that the church was always well represented on the Council of the Indies—not always by worldly priests like Fonseca—and ultimately came to dominate it.

During the half-century after the Conquest, the church and the administration were bitterly and continually at odds. This was the era of Las Casas and the great Dominican protest. It must not be thought, however, that these disagreements continued indefinitely. When churchmen and settlers had more or less agreed on their respective spheres of activity, they settled down into a reasonably harmonious relationship. It was in the interest of neither to tear the country apart. As early as 1542 we find the Mexican church co-operating wholeheartedly with the settlers to contest the provisions in the New Laws of the Indies which would have meant the abolition of the *encomienda* system. The church had come to appreciate not only that there was a case to be made for the system, but that its abolition would mean the collapse of Spanish rule in Mexico, and with it the collapse of the church. But at no time were the representatives of the Mexican church to become the supine yes-men of the settlers and politicians. Although the church, like secular society and like metropolitan Spain itself, lost much of its fire and missionary zeal towards the close of the sixteenth century, with the passing of the generation of *conquistadores*, it still produced men of energy and integrity. It was, after all, a priest who, though not meaning to be disrespectful to the king of Spain or to his religious superiors, eventually began the movement that would lead to Mexican independence. And when the banner fell from the hand of Father Miguel Hidalgo, it was promptly retrieved by his friend and pupil, Father José María Morelos. Hidalgo uttered the famous *grito de Dolores*, which the President of Mexico still utters annually from the balcony of the National Palace, on September 15, 1810; and on September 8, 1813, Morelos convoked the congress at Chilpancingo which declared that Mexico was no longer the property of Spain. Mexico owes its independence to two priests.

Hidalgo and Morelos were reviving the ardent spirit that characterized the Mexican church at the opening of the colonial period. Except that they sought souls and not gold, the first generation of priests to enter Mexico were *conquistadores*. Cortés himself had sent a request to the Spanish crown to send holy men to Mexico to begin the task of spreading the faith, and the first mission, comprising twelve Franciscan friars, reached San Juan de Ulúa in May 1524. Cortés sent a special escort to meet them and bring them to the capital, to which they walked barefoot from the coast. Crowds flocked to see them, marvelling at their humility and meekness, and at their poverty-stricken appearance. When they reached Mexico City they were greeted by Cortés, who had brought with him a splendid retinue that included Cuauhtémoc. The Captain-General kneeled down in the dust to kiss the hem of their garment, a gesture in which piety and calculation were mingled, for as Díaz remarks: 'When Cuauhtémoc and the other Aztec noblemen saw Cortés kneeling, they were amazed. The friars looked careworn and thin, in threadbare gowns, not riding horses but with bare feet—and here was Cortés, whom the Aztecs regarded as almost a god, bending the knee before them.' He had impressed on the spectators the importance of the newcomers, who were the forerunners of other groups of friars who arrived later, the Dominicans in 1524 and the Augustinians in 1533.

For over fifty years the three mendicant orders were granted exclusive rights in the New World, and by the end of the century they had established nearly three hundred churches in Mexico alone. The first bishops were also mendicants, including the first Archbishop of Mexico, the Franciscan Juan de Zumárraga, who was inducted in 1527. However, J. H. Parry warns us not to be deceived by their unpretentious appearance and origins. 'The men who led the spiritual conquest of the Indians,' he writes in *The Spanish Seaborne Empire*, 'were not simple friars; they were picked men, daring religious radicals representing both the authority and the intellectual ferment of Church reform in Spain; many of them had training and experience highly relevant to the task which faced them. They were, moreover, a spiritual army whose commanders stood close to the throne; royal support gave them, in their extravagant humility, a masterful authority. Their mission was planned with the discipline and detailed attention of a military campaign.'

Martial it was, and in its initial phase it was destructive. Juan de Zumárraga asserted that within five years of arriving in Mexico City he had destroyed five hundred temples and twenty thousand idols in his diocese alone. As noted earlier, Zumárraga is also often blamed for destroying priceless native codices; but there is reason to believe that many of these disappeared in the anarchic conditions of the nineteenth century; for example, in the bonfires lit in the streets of Mexico City when Juárez's army ran amok there in the terrible winter of 1861. Nonetheless, the friars did their work even more thoroughly than the Copts, equally pious and misguided zealots who defaced the holy places of ancient Egypt. The old order was to be swept away completely, so that the new order could be built the more thoroughly upon its ruins. As in the field of politics, the previous structure was comprehensively demolished and another structure purposefully substituted in its place. Only when the work of destruction was more or less completed could the next phase, the phase of rebuilding, commence. Zumárraga introduced the first printing-press to the New World in 1534, and a chain of mission schools was organized, for the conduct of which it became as necessary for the preceptors to learn Náhuatl as for the pupils to learn Spanish. At Texcoco a language-school for Spanish priests was set up, and a chain of hospitals was established, notable among them the famous Hospital de Santa Fé near Mexico City, founded by Vasco de Quiroga, an *oidor* of the second *audiencia* who later took holy orders and became Bishop of Michoacán. It was thanks to these cultural exchanges that certain Spanish missionaries, particularly Father Toribio Motolinía, one of the original twelve Franciscan friars, and Father Bernardino de Sahagún, were inspired to regret the destruction which had been wrought and seek to gather memorials of the old Mexican way of life before the memory of it passed utterly away. Similarly, Mexicans who had been baptized, taken Spanish names and learned the Spanish tongue, like Ixtlilxóchitl (Don Fernando de Alva), took the opportunity to commit to paper memorials of their own.

As in civil matters, the Mexican Indians adapted themselves to the new order without resistance. They were baptized in their tens of thousands. The very zeal with which the newcomers dismantled the temples and smashed the idols only added to the impressiveness of the new creed. The friars preached the new doctrines with an enthusiasm that surpassed that of the practitioners of the old. They themselves believed that the new Indian Church was a return to the spirit of the primitive Apostolic Church of Christ's time. And the message which they brought was one of hope and consolation. Love had arrived to drive out fear. There were no more sacrifices; no more ripping out of hearts to provide

the blood to sustain a sick and sinister universe. If men still died of pestilence and ill-usage, at least the old dark pessimism had been banished.
Nevertheless, it has often been pointed out that the Christian religion
would never have evoked such a deep response in Mexican breasts unless
it possessed some affinity with the religion it superseded. Doubtless in
many respects this affinity was superficial; the Indians clung with such
desperation to the Cross because they had nothing else to cling to. On
the other hand, there were certain pre-Cortésian rituals with enough
resemblance to baptism, communion, confession and absolution to enable
them to be related on a subjective level to their counterparts in Christianity. The two religions also shared a general interest in the ideas of
suffering and redemption. The lurid martyrdoms of the saints would
appeal to a people who had practised elaborate forms of human sacrifice,
and who had been bidden by their priests to lash themselves with thorns
and drive cactus-spines through their cheeks and tongues. The passion and
crucifixion of Christ, a powerful example of the tortured, dying, all-
redeeming god, a divine scapegoat, would possess a natural appeal for the
Mexican Indian. There were parallels between the careers of Christ and
Quetzalcóatl, spiritual leaders who had been rejected but who had
promised to return in glory, which would not be lost on the Indian mind.
Nor would the parallel between the Virgin Mary and the various protective goddesses whom they had previously worshipped. A further rich
confusion in the Indian mind was represented by Cortés, a culture-
bringer like Quetzalcóatl, who had been accorded semi-divine status. In
the pueblos of New Mexico on Christmas Day one can still see dances in
which figures representing Christ, the Universal Church, Moctezuma,
Cortés and La Malinche all perform together in an amiable religious
syncretism.

A final comment on the religion and the social order which the Spaniards imposed on Mexico may be left to Octavio Paz, one of the most
discerning and compassionate of modern Mexican poets and philosophers.
As a product of the two great cultures, he possessed a special authority,
and in his incomparable *Labyrinth of Solitude* he writes: 'The rapidity
with which the Spanish state re-created its new possessions in the image
and likeness of the metropolis—despite the ambitions of its military commanders, the infidelities of its judges, and rivalries of every kind—is as
amazing as the solidity of the social edifice it constructed. Colonial society
was an order built to endure. That is, it was a society designed in con-
formity with judicial, economic and religious principles that were fully
coherent among themselves and that established a vital and harmonious
relationship between the parts and the whole. It was a self-sufficient

world, closed to the exterior but open to the other world. It is very easy to laugh at the religious pretensions of colonial society. It is still easier to denounce them as empty forms intended to cover up the abuses of the conquistadors or to justify them to themselves and their victims. To a certain extent this is true, but it is no less true that these other-worldly aspirations were more than a simple addition: they were part of a living faith which, like the roots of a tree, sustained other cultural and economic forms. Catholicism was the centre of colonial society because it was the true fountain of life, nourishing the activities, the passions, the virtues and even the sins of both lords and servants, functionaries and priests, merchants and soldiers. Thanks to religion the colonial order was not a mere superimposition of new historical forms but a living organism. The fate of the Indians would have been very different if it had not been for the Church. I am not thinking only of its struggle to improve their living conditions and to organize them in a more just and Christian manner, but also of the opportunity that baptism offered them to form a part of one social order and one religion. This possibility of belonging to a living order, even if it was at the bottom of a social pyramid, was cruelly denied to the Indians by the Protestants of New England. It is often forgotten that to belong to the Catholic faith meant that one found a place in the cosmos. The flight of their gods and the death of their leaders had left the natives in a solitude so complete that it is difficult for a modern man to imagine it. Catholicism re-established their ties with the world and the other world. It gave them back a sense of their place on earth; it nurtured their hopes and justified their lives and deaths. Their personal existence became part of a greater order. It was not out of simple devotion or servility that the Indians called the missionaries *tatas* (dads) and the virgin of Guadalupe *madre* (mother). The difference between colonial Mexico and the English colonies was immense. New Spain committed many horrors, but at least it did not commit the gravest of all: that of denying a place, even at the foot of the social scale, to the people who composed it. There were classes, castes and slaves, but there were no pariahs, no persons lacking a fixed social condition and a legal, moral and religious status. Its differences from the world of modern totalitarian societies was equally decisive.'

And Octavio Paz concludes his exposition with a splendid passage: 'I am not attempting to justify colonial society. In the strictest sense, no society can be justified while one or another form of oppression subsists in it. I want to understand it as a living and therefore contradictory whole. In the same way, I refuse to regard the human sacrifices of the Aztecs as an isolated expression of cruelty without relation to the rest of that civilization. Their tearing out of hearts and their monumental pyramids, their sculpture and their ritual cannibalism, their poetry and their "war of flowers", their theocracy and their great myths, are all an indissoluble one. To deny this would be as infantile as to deny Gothic art or Provençal poetry in the name of the medieval serfs, or to deny Aeschylus because there were slaves in Athens. History has the cruel reality of a nightmare, and the grandeur of man consists in his making beautiful and lasting works of the real substance of that nightmare. Or, to put it another way, it consists in transforming the nightmare into vision; in freeing ourselves from the shapeless horror of reality—if only for an instant—by means of creation.'

* * *

If, as Paz suggests, the spiritual difference between colonial Mexico and the English colonies was immense, so was the economic difference. The English colonies were utilitarian and mercantile in character; the Spanish, founded earlier, were close in time and ethos to the medieval and Renaissance world, the world of idealism and faith. When one studies the economic history of Spain and her colonies, one is conscious that the end of Spanish economic activity was not the down-to-earth commercialism and materialism of the English. The treasure which the rulers of Spain obtained from the New World was not devoted wholly to practical and materialistic ends: it was obtained so that those rulers could organize armadas to combat the heretic English or the infidel Turk, or armies to fight the Protestant forces of the Reformation. They were bound in the service of what they took to be a higher power.

The Spanish colonial empire appears in retrospect to be less efficient than the English because at the date when it was founded the principles of business and trading were still relatively primitive. The very quixoticism and idealism of the Spaniards of that age militated against hardheaded business efficiency. The Spaniards were engaged in a quest for souls to bring to God. The Spanish colonial empire was not, in the final analysis, operated on a simple cash basis, as the differing quality of life in North and South America still testifies.

The basic pattern of economic life in colonial Mexico was the *encomienda* system. As we have seen, the Emperor Charles was unhappy with *encomiendas*, although Cortés had persuaded him not to abolish them. The New Laws of 1542 specifically did away with them. However, the system was reluctantly reprieved, on practical grounds, although *encomiendas* were not henceforth to be permanent or hereditary but merely leased from the crown for a fixed term of years. The hereditary estates which the

Emperor had granted in perpetuity to Cortés and his heirs were the only ones exempted from this decree. Nonetheless, during the 1550s the system was gradually and stealthily replaced by the inherently much more obnoxious *repartimientos* or work-gangs, not only because the colonists wished to avoid a system that had incurred official disapproval but because they needed work-gangs for the mining operations which constituted their main economic activity. Ninety per cent of the cargoes that left Mexico for Spain during the three centuries of the colonial era consisted of precious metals. There was some export of such materials as indigo, cochineal and hides, but after the first decade the bulk of each cargo, in volume and value, was overwhelmingly represented by ingots of silver. In exchange for its silver, Mexico received from Spain the machinery needed to mine it, machinery for textile mills and sugar refineries, and the luxury articles which could only be obtained from Europe, together with the foodstuffs on which the colonists subsisted. Spaniards would not eat Mexican tortillas and tamales, and remained faithful to their original diet. Similarly, there was little call in Europe for the maize and chile products of the New World.

Thanks to a burst of energy in the 1530s, New Spain became the first of the Spanish colonies to show a profit. Because of the unsettled situation in Europe in the 1550s, there followed a decline in silver shipments, but in the 1560s trade began to revive and, in spite of temporary setbacks, continued on a rising scale for another seventy years. One of the setbacks was caused by the depredations of Hawkins and Drake, another by the defeat of the first Armada, that of 1588, to which Philip II had committed ships of the *Carrera de Indias*, and which went down with the rest. The treasure of the Indies financed the fleets and armies of the Counter-Reformation, although the individual contribution of New Spain towards that end fluctuated between wide extremes. In the early 1570s, the silver-mines of Guanajuato, Taxco, San Luis Potosí, Zacatecas, Querétaro and other places were yielding two-thirds of the total sum; a decade later the amount had fallen to one-third, owing to the 1576 epidemic and to the fact that the unbelievably prolific silver-mine of Potosí, in upper Bolivia, had begun to pour out its inexhaustible stream of silver. Discovered in 1545, by the mid 1570s Potosí was annually producing more silver than all the mines of New Spain combined. The mining experts who had been hired from Protestant Saxony carried the new technique of amalgamation by means of mercury from Mexico to Bolivia, and the stream of Potosí was transformed into a torrent.

It was the bullion of Mexico, Peru and Bolivia that underpinned Spain's supreme position in the world. In 1560 Spanish imports of bullion had risen to 10 million pesos a year; by 1600 the figure had soared to 35 million pesos. Philip II, who had engineered an extraordinarily swift recovery from the annihilation of his Armadas of 1588 and 1596, fully appreciated the importance of the American treasure-shipments. He devised an admirably efficient schedule for the sailings of his rebuilt *Carrera de Indias* from Veracruz, Acapulco, Callao, Nombre de Dios and Havana. The ships of the fleet were well-founded, well-officered, and consisted of sturdy galleons escorted by the *Armada de la Guardia de las Indias*. The escort vessels were the light, speedy, well-armed *zabras*, whose task it was to seek out the enemy and destroy him. The administration and colonists of New Spain were required to match the efficiency of their king. For the bi-annual sailings of the silver fleet, the prescribed amount of bullion had to be ready. We may suppose that many of the methods by which it was procured were none too tender. On the other hand, there is reliable evidence that the mines of Mexico were not operated with the well-known ruthlessness of the mines in South America. Indeed, it might be said that the colonial society of Mexico always tended to show a somewhat more settled, humane and responsible character than colonial society elsewhere.

If the treasure of the Indies became the foundation of Spanish power, it also helped to destroy that power. Thanks to New World silver, Spain became enormously wealthy: but the influx of silver caused continuous price-rises that eventually produced an inflation of unmanageable proportions. Financial theory was in its infancy, and the relationship between inflation and the increased supply of money was noted only by one or two obscure theorists. Between 1500 and 1600 prices in Spain quadrupled, while real wages fell by almost half. Moreover, the bulk of the specie did not profit Spain herself, but found its way into the coffers of Spain's creditors, the Welsers, the Fuggers, and other foreign usurers, or into the pockets of her greedy and ungrateful Austrian cousins. The money was devoured by Spain's imperial and religious dreams. The beggarly Knight of the Woeful Countenance was a true representative of Spain's situation at the opening of the seventeenth century. On the other hand, it is worth pointing out that, even with steadily improving techniques of mining, during three centuries Spain did little more than literally scratch the surface of the mineral deposits of the Americas. In a much shorter span of time, in the late nineteenth and early twentieth centuries, the entre-preneurs of France, England and the United States grubbed out a vaster quantity of precious metals than the Spaniards had ever done. The Spanish colonial government had carefully vested all subsoil rights throughout Mexico in the state, but in 1880 President Manuel González, a creature of Porfirio Díaz, rescinded this wise provision. The result was that foreign business interests saw their opportunity, rushed into the country, and in the next twenty years extracted more minerals from Mexican soil than had been extracted during the previous four centuries. Díaz himself, in his venal way, saw fit to compound González's monumental blunder. By 1904, when 9,500,000 of Mexico's 10,000,000 people owned no land, and two-thirds of the country was owned by 3,000 families, three-quarters of Mexico's mines and one-half of her oil-fields were owned by seven American companies. During the dictatorship of Díaz, 125 million acres of land, a quarter of the area of Mexico, were sold outright to foreign oil and mining interests.

In general terms, the economic fortunes of colonial Mexico may be said to have followed those of the mother-country with whom she was so closely tied. Thus she prospered, in spite of uneasy undertones, in the sixteenth century, stagnated in the seventeenth, and was making an excellent recovery in the eighteenth when events in Europe and the Americas terminated Spain's last pretensions to be considered a major power. The final burst of prosperity which the Spanish Empire enjoyed between 1770 and 1800 was due to the Habsburg king Charles III (1759–88) who, building on a base provided by his sensible half-brother Ferdinand VI (1746–59), managed to introduce widespread reforms within Spain herself and throughout her possessions. Assisted by a number of able viceroys, particularly Bucareli and Revillagidedo, both of whom have streets named after them in Mexico City, and by such gifted ministers as José Campillo and José de Galvez, the founder of Galveston, these kings appeared to be creating the climate for a promising future. Such St. Martin's Summers are not unusual in history, and we may instance the hopeful appearance which imperial Russia was beginning to present at the turn of our own century, when the unfortunate Peter Stolypin was prime minister.

This tri-partite view of colonial economic history is open to criticism, and some authorities choose to ignore the decades of late flowering and represent the course of events in two parts, an ascent followed by a decline. Ralph Beals puts the matter thus: 'In the Early Colonial period in Mexico a number of things occurred. One was the continuation of the class society with a great deal of intermarriage with the Indian population at the upper levels. The Spanish interest in mining together with the shortage of population caused by the devastating epidemics meant that the Indians in many cases prospered. As late as the latter seventeenth century and in some cases the early eighteenth century there is good documentary evidence that the Mexican Indians were more prosperous than they have been at any time since. There is also good evidence that in the early post-Conquest period there was rapid and often eager acculturation. For many Indians the period was one of hope and progress rather than the traditional picture of enslavement and degradation. The facts upon which the traditional picture was created undoubtedly existed, but it makes a great difference whether one looks at these facts from the standpoint of a modern free democratic society or from the standpoint of a pre-Conquest *macehual* or a subject people to the Aztec.' Mr. Beals continues: 'The Early Colonial period, then, is the period in which most of the medieval characteristics of the content of contemporary Indian cultures was absorbed. The Second Colonial period, corresponding roughly with the disestablishment of the missions, coincided with a radical change in both Spanish colonial society and a reflex change in the Indian cultures. The Spanish economy turned more and more to the development of plantation economics, whether in the production of sugar or the development of cattle raising. The economic position of the Indian (and incidentally of the Mestizo class) took a sharp turn for the worse. Moreover, except in the regions of the *encomienda*, the disestablishment of the missions brought about a virtual cessation of intercommunication as a result of the church policy of preventing the Indians from learning Spanish wherever the church had complete control. As a result the Indian was almost completely isolated linguistically. A function of this deteriorating economic situation, the development of a caste society, and the increasing isolation, resulted in severe disillusion, a sharp rejection of European culture, and a more or less conscious effort to revive the native cultures, an effort doomed to failure after the lapse of several generations. Perhaps the most important aspect of these observations is the explanation for the origin of the strong rejection patterns which in many cases persist to the present, at least in some aspects of culture.'

Mr. Beals has here succinctly indicated the reasons why the Indian, the largest and humblest component of colonial society, was feeling an increasing disenchantment as the eighteenth century progressed. Left to himself, however, the Indian would never have challenged the power of Spain, even when Spain was exhausted and enfeebled from her long, lonely, noble, foredoomed struggles, and her power was everywhere crumbling. The Indian was passive and long-suffering: and in any case it was not a function of his cultural ethos to produce the kind of aggressive, individualistic leaders who promote revolutions and wars of independence. In all the turmoil of the Republic during the nineteenth century, the only outstanding leader who was an Indian was Benito Juárez, a full-blooded Zapotec from Oaxaca—though in his brutal power and massive integrity he was, admittedly, worth a hundred of his non-Indian political con-temporaries. The real opposition to metropolitan Spain, in Mexico as in the rest of the Spanish Empire, was furnished by two categories of person who had not existed in Mexico or in the world two centuries before. These were the *criollos*, or Creoles, and the *mestizos*, sometimes called the *ladinos*. The *criollos* were of pure Spanish descent on both sides, but born in the colonies and domiciled there; they were the true 'colonials'. The *mestizos*, on the other hand, were half-castes, people sired by Spanish fathers on Indian mothers; the word is from the verb *mezclar*, to mix. Thus Spain created these two human categories, and in turn the *criollos* and *mestizos* eventually cast out Spain, in that classic 'rejection pattern' which is the mark and badge of the modern Mexican race.

It took nearly three hundred years for *criollos* and *mestizos* to become sufficiently numerous to exert themselves. When that moment arrived Spain herself was far too weak to be able to combat or contain them. At the end of the eighteenth century, the population of Mexico had so far recovered from the ravages of pestilence as to comprise about 6,000,000 people. The Indians numbered about 3,500,000, or more than half, but the *criollo* community had now risen to 1,000,000 and the *mestizo* to 1,500,000. The purely Spanish community in Mexico numbered only about 50,000. However, although it was minuscule in comparison with the others, the members of the Spanish community, known as *peninsulares* from their home in the Iberian peninsula, still occupied almost every important official position throughout the whole of Mexico. The sale or bestowal of offices remained a perquisite of the Spanish crown. Spain, through the *peninsulares*, still adhered to its old high-handed methods in circumstances that called for a more flexible and sensitive approach; the concept of centralization, which had once been the essential strength of colonial administration, was now its weakness. The *criollos* naturally resented being confined to unimportant posts by the *peninsulares*, bureaucrats with a very imperfect knowledge of the country. However, at least the *criollos* enjoyed the compensation of wealth, for they formed, under the *peninsulares*, the large land-owning upper class. The *mestizos* were in much worse case, for their social position was highly equivocal. They were acknowledged neither by Spaniards nor by Indians, and existed in a cultural, economic and legal limbo, like the Cape Coloureds in modern South Africa. The powers-that-be had neither found nor looked for any way of fitting them into the existing social structure. These frustrated non-persons formed, by 1800, approximately one-fifth of the population, and were therefore a potent breeding-ground for discontent.

Although the *criollos* were humiliated by their subsidary role, in the main they represented an ultra-conservative force, devoted to the *status quo*, loyal in spite of their grievances to throne and church. If they disliked the arrogance and pretensions of the *peninsulares*, they feared much more the growing rancour of the *mestizos* and Indians. Nonetheless, towards the close of the eighteenth century a significant number of *criollos* had become radically disaffected, and were willing to try to seize power for themselves. Their disaffection was the result of a combination of factors, some material and practical, others emotional. On the material level they were angry at being excluded from the Spanish spoils system; and they were as resentful as Canadians, Australians and New Zealanders once were at being patronized by the imperial representatives and regarded as uncivilized boors. In particular, *criollos* in the army were treated—or fancied they were treated, which was the same thing—in a supercilious fashion by their senior officers, who were, almost without exception, Spaniards. Moreover, an increasing number of rich *criollos*, like the Venezuelans Miranda and Bolívar, began to travel to Europe for education or pleasure. Arrived there, they were surprised to find that at that time the much-vaunted mother-country looked distinctly shabby and backward in comparison with England or France. This surprised and shocked them, and awoke in them a desire to cut adrift from the foundering Spanish ship of state. For political reasons, high society in London and Paris also flattered and fêted them, which put dangerous thoughts in their heads and made it increasingly difficult for them to readjust to an inferior position on their return to Mexico. While abroad, they also absorbed the ideas of the Enlightenment, while the works of such writers as Hobbes, Locke, Voltaire, Rousseau, Franklin, Payne, and even the bitterly anti-Spanish Abbé Raynal, began to circulate freely inside Mexico, giving rise to a rash of fashionable debating-societies like those that flourished in Europe in the 1770's and 1780's.

Among the emotional and subjective reasons which contributed to the the break with Spain, we may cite the growing need of *criollos* and *mestizos* alike to create roots for themselves. They belonged neither to Spain nor to Mexico; they were caught in a painful social and psychological dilemma. They tried to solve it, as Ralph Beals put it, by 'an effort to revive the native cultures', an effort which has been studied at some length by J. M. Phelan in his *Neo-Aztecism in the Eighteenth Century and the Genesis of Mexican Nationalism*. Mr. Phelan points out that, in spite of the fact that the *criollos* had no racial affinity with the colonial Indians or their Aztec ancestors, they came nonetheless to adopt the Aztec world of pre-Conquest times as the 'classical antiquity' of Mexico. 'They felt the need for an American past, one totally disconnected from the Europe they had come from. The American past that began with Cortés was too brief in duration and too European in content to satisfy their need to identify themselves with a historical tradition indigenously American.' The business of manufacturing such a past began as early as Torquemada's *Monarquía indiana* of 1615, and was later continued in Valbuena's epic poem *Grandeza mexicana*, and the historical works of Sigüenza y Góngora, Veytia and Clavigero. The gods of the Aztecs were identified with the gods of Greece and Rome, the Aztec rulers with the Roman emperors. As the determination to rehabilitate the pre-Conquest era grew, the desire to belittle the Spanish era increased. By the time the two leading publicists for Mexican independence, Servando Teresa de Mier and Carlos María de Bustamente, were writing in the early 1800s, the image of Spain had become that of a brutal and deceitful usurper that had held Mexico in thrall for three centuries. As a culmination of this process of romantic nationalism, the inaugural address of Father Morelos, himself a *mestizo*, to the Congress of Chilpancingo, the foundation document of Mexican independence, was, as Mr. Phelan says, 'saturated with neo-Aztecism'.

There is no space here to chronicle the wars of independence that broke out in Central and South America in the decade 1810–20. In South America, the outstanding names were those of Bolívar, Miranda, Páez, San Martín, and Bernardo O'Higgins, the amiable bastard Irishman who had risen to the rank of Viceroy of Peru. In Mexico, the generation of liberators included Father Hidalgo, Father Morelos, Vicente Guerrero, and the young *mestizo* soldier Augustín de Iturbide, whose rebel army entered Mexico City in triumph on September 27, 1821, after promulgating the *Plan de Iguala* and negotiating with the last of the viceroys, Don Juan O'Dónoju, the peaceful withdrawal of the Spanish forces. Ironically, the last Spanish stronghold in Mexico was San Juan de Ulúa, the fortress established by Cortés at the outset of the Conquest. The thirty-seven-year-old Iturbide was crowned Emperor of Mexico in the cathedral of Mexico City in July 1822, abdicated in March 1823, and like Father Hidalgo and Father Morelos before him was executed by firing-squad in July 1824. The bloody and tragic procession of events that was to characterize the history of Mexico throughout the coming century had begun. The terrors of that pitiless time are summed up by a sentence in Joseph Conrad's Latin-American novel *Nostromo* where, in describing the later history of his 'Republic of Costaguana', he remarks that 'the continuous political changes, the constant "saving of the country", seemed like a puerile and bloodthirsty game of murder and rapine played with terrible earnestness by depraved children'. Later, in this novel devoted to the fortunes of a silver-mine very like those of Mexico or Bolivia, he speaks of the atmosphere of political outrage in which 'friends and relatives were ruined, imprisoned, killed in the battles of senseless civil wars, barbarously executed in ferocious proscriptions, as though the government of the country had been a struggle of lust between bands of absurd devils let loose upon the land with sabres and uniforms and grandiloquent phrases. And on all those lips was a weary desire for peace, the dread of officialdom with its nightmarish parody of administration without law, without security, without justice'.

In comparison with such lamentable and sanguinary figures as Santa Anna, Paredez, Tejada, Lerdo, Corral (who sold the Yaqui Indians of Sonora to the planters of Quintana Róo for 75 cents a head), Orozco, Mondragón, Villa, Carranza, Obregón, Huerta, Calles—to select just a few names at random—the viceroys of New Spain and even the majority of the *conquistadores* appear to be models of temperance and sagacity. The colonial era must have seemed a Golden Age to the poor souls condemned to endure the nightmare that followed it. Alvarado's massacre in Mexico City was neither the first nor the last example of its type. To take instances from the modern period alone, two hundred corpses were left on the stones outside the National Palace after the night of May 24, 1911; five hundred more were killed there on February 9, 1913; there were violent and ugly demonstrations in 1958; and police and rioters were enthusiastically shooting each other at Tlaltelolco on the eve of the Olympic Games in 1968. The list of atrocities perpetrated in Mexico from the time of the fall of Iturbide to the arrest and deportation of Calles would fill many pages. However, it is not for a twentieth-century European to criticize the misdeeds of nineteenth- or twentieth-century Mexicans. In fact, Europe was in large part responsible for the original state of anarchy and the misery that ensued. By reserving every important post for *peninsulares*, and neglecting to train native cadres, Spain left Mexico without experienced men to run the government when she withdrew. In our own time we have witnessed the havoc which the precipitate withdrawal of the imperial power causes in such circumstances. In the past quarter of a century the British, French, Dutch and Belgians have delivered up large sections of Africa, Asia and South-East Asia to a similar condition of misrule. It is inevitable that, when a centralized and paternalistic mode of government is overthrown, power should fall into the hands of ignorant and callous demagogues. Such men are difficult to get rid of—though in the end, mercifully, they usually exterminate each other.

The expulsion of Spain, brought about as much by her own impotence as the exertions of the colonists, was the signal not only for the break-up of the Spanish Empire but for the dismemberment of the Viceroyalties. The Audiencia of Guatemala, which comprised the small modern Central American republics, split away from New Spain in 1821 to become, in 1823, the Republic of Central America. After six years of fighting, which reached a climax with William Travis's defence of the Alamo at San Antonio and Sam Houston's victory at San Jacinto, Texas became a sovereign Republic in 1836. The Oregon Territory, claimed after 1818 by Russia, Britain and the United States, dropped into the lap of the latter in 1846; and two years later the United States, after defeating Mexico and sending an army under General Winfield Scott to occupy Mexico City, coerced the Mexican government into parting with California, Nevada, Utah, Arizona, half Colorado and half New Mexico for a derisory $15 million by the terms of the Treaty of Guadalupe Hidalgo of 1848. For a further $10 million, in 1853, the Gadsden Treaty rounded off America's real-estate holdings in the South-West by purchasing the remaining portions of Arizona and New Mexico and establishing the Río Grande as the common boundary from El Paso to the Gulf. Nor were these huge physical losses the only ones which the United States inflicted on the distracted young Republic, torn by the permanent civil strife engendered by endless 'plans' and *pronunciamentos*. Aided by vain and corrupt generals and politicos, and by a succession of dishonest American ambassadors, the United States practised relentless economic imperialism within Mexico itself. Britain and France were not slow to follow suit, and were equally willing to wage armed intervention in defence of their business interests. The Mexican adventure of Napoleon III, in which he was originally abetted by the English, occupied five years, between 1862 and 1867; the British supported the Mayas throughout the nineteenth century in their successive bids to set up an independent Republic of Yucatán; and the Americans mounted a second war against Mexico in 1914. In April of that year Woodrow Wilson sent eighty warships into the Gulf of Mexico and ordered his marines ashore at Veracruz. The fighting claimed a hundred American and a thousand Mexican dead and wounded.

It was only after Lázaro Cárdenas became president in 1934, and rid the country of the squalid Calles in 1936, that Mexico began to regain some semblance of the order and stability she had possessed under Spanish rule. Cárdenas took a firm grip of the Partido Revolucionario Institucional (PRI) which had been established in 1929, and which ever since that time has held power in Mexico. Cárdenas, the son of peasant parents, was a dictator, but also a man of rare will and vision. In March 1938 he expropriated the American oil companies, a step which, though it cost Mexico an almost crippling sum in compensation (the United States in such circumstances always demands—and gets—its pound of flesh), nevertheless restored to his country much of its pride in itself. The successors to Cárdenas—Camacho, Alemán, Cortines, López Mateos— continued to build on the firm foundation which Cárdenas provided. The PRI, like the Salazar and Franco regimes in Iberia, has given Mexico a spell of peace and relative prosperity unprecedented in modern times. Yet it would serve no purpose to blind oneself to the fact that, beneath the usual liberal garnishings (words cost nothing), the PRN rules with an iron hand. Its opponents are hounded by the secret and not-so-secret police; ballot-boxes are mysteriously lost; bodies are found in the desert. In fact the outlook of the PRI is not 'progressive', as it claims to be, but pragmatic and conservative: and in the present circumstances, remembering the dreadful record of the 'socialists' of previous years, such a form of government may make good sense for a country as volatile and innately self-destructive as Mexico.

*   *   *

What legacy has Spain bequeathed to the Americas? Her influence is incontestable, though difficult to define.

By chance, the *conquistadores* had encountered, throughout the New World in general and Mexico in particular, a race of people which in its habitat and physical appearance bore a close resemblance to their own. Except for Indians of the remotest and most dark-skinned breed, the conformation of the Mexicans agreed on the whole well enough with that of the Spanish newcomer. Miscegenation was rendered easy and natural, from the early days when the native *caciques* offered their daughters to Cortés and his captains as a matter of course. Similarly, the Spaniards felt at home in Mexico from the moment they set foot there. The contrast between the arid cordilleras and the lush valleys reminded them of the contrasts that existed in their own country, where harsh Extremadura lay cheek-by-jowl with green and fertile Andalucia. Thus accident and nature had already provided a basis for unforced exchanges between the two cultures.

As in British India, the first decades were the time when such exchanges flowed most freely, before the imperial power became pompous and aloof. The creation of the *mestizo* class began early; and, having started the creation of a new breed of men, the Spaniards also saw to it, through the operation of their immigration laws, that the breed would remain remarkably homogeneous. The Spanish ban on foreign immigration into their colonies was very strict and severely applied. During the colonial period it was highly unusual to find any non-Spaniard domiciled in, or even being permitted to work in, a Spanish possession. In part this policy was dictated by a desire to preserve an economic monopoly for the mother-country; but it was reinforced by the social exclusiveness of the Spaniards, always a reserved and xenophobic nation. It also, as an important side-effect, resulted in the true breeding of the Mexican-Iberian sub-race which was coming into existence. The dilutions came later, and were never so important in Mexico as in South America, where the original *mestizo* breed was to be significantly modified by the influx of immigrants from England, Germany and Italy in the late nineteenth-century.

The heyday of the *conquistador* was short. We can date it almost precisely, if we wish, from the time when the son of Christopher Columbus arrived in the Indies in 1509 to become the resident Governor of Hispaniola, to the issuing of the *Ordenanzas sobre descubrimientos* of 1573, which specifically forbade any more armed *entradas*, except in very exceptional cases, and made the missionaries and not the military responsible for pacifying the frontier areas. In a little over sixty years the *conquistadores* had begun their great task and been adjudged to have finished it. We have seen that Cortés, considered a hero in the 1520s, in the 1540s was treated as a nuisance and an embarrassment.

Nevertheless, brief though its moment of glory was, the generation of the *conquistadores* was a vivid and memorable one—more memorable than the generations of quill-drivers that followed them. It would have been remarkable if they had failed to leave a deep impression on the minds and hearts of the peoples they subdued. They bestowed on the countries they conquered the ideals and standards they themselves had inherited from their part-medieval, part-Renaissance background. To the medieval notion of hierarchy, of unswerving service to God and king, was added the individualistic passion of the Renaissance. Thus the tradition of the *caudillo* or strong leader vies with an absolute and immoderate love of liberty in the breasts of Latin Americans. The latter have imbibed to the full the fanaticism of the Spaniards, a fanaticism which was at its peak at the opening of the *siglo de oro*, when the *conquistadores* sailed forth to seek their fortunes. Nor must we overlook the influence of the friars of the early post-Conquest period, those ardent men whom we have termed spiritual *conquistadores*. Like their secular counterparts, and Spaniards in general, they were a blend of the practical and the visionary. Vasco de Quiroga, founder of schools and hospitals, also attempted to establish on the shores of Lake Pátzcuaro an ideal community based on the *Utopia* of Sir Thomas More, a book that also exerted an influence on Archbishop Zumárraga. Latin America is, *par excellence*, the place where dream and reality are dramatically juxtaposed, where visions of Utopia and the City of God alternate or exist side by side with the *rurales* and the *ley fuga*. As the late Irene Nicholson remarks in *The Liberators*, the last of her stimulating works on Latin America, one of the springs of the revolt against Spain was the burning desire for 'a new kind of society established on earth'. And just as the politics of Latin America reflect the quixotry of the *conquistadores*, so too the Church in Latin America resembles the Church of Spain more closely than the Church of Italy. Extremes of religious conservatism and radicalism exist simultaneously; the hierarchy strives to exercise its traditional authority while dissident young priests become leaders in the social struggle, or seek to re-establish an order reminiscent of that of the early Mexican missions or the Jesuit missions in Paraguay. If history, as Octavio Paz asserts, consists in 'transforming the cruel reality of nightmare into vision', then this notion of history as epiphany is peculiarly precious to Spaniards and Latin Americans.

The attitudes of the Reconquest and the *siglo de oro* imparted to Spanish life its peculiar flavour. In turn, the Spaniards bequeathed those attitudes to their colonial empire. The posture of the *conquistador* in his suit of armour is the posture of the *matador* in his *traje de luces*—and where else but in Spain, Mexico or South America can a twentieth-century spectator watch a man despatch his opponent with a sword? The bravura of the Spaniard, the search for the most striking and virile pose, is also characteristic of Latin America. What the Mexicans call *machismo*—from the word *macho*, meaning male, masculine, manly—is a conception that Mexico must have imbibed from Spain. Like Don Juanism, the cult of *machismo* can be, at its worst, excessively tiresome and silly; but one imagines that the *machismo* of a Pedro de Alvarado must have been undeniably impressive.

No doubt the ethos which the *conquistadores* and their successors introduced into the New World was invigorating. But its engrafting upon the native stock also gave rise to distressing symptoms. It is difficult for the exaltation of the *hidalgo* or priest to coexist peacefully with the mournful stoicism of the Mexican Indian. The Mexican may, at times, embrace and endorse the Spanish element in his make-up, but he knows that it is a borrowed characteristic. It is a foreign body which, after four centuries, his organism is still trying to expel. It is the more irksome because it is the symbol of the conqueror, of the Mexican's own historic defeat. As Madariaga puts it, in a graphic phrase, 'Every day, within the soul of every Mexican, Moctezuma dies and Cuauhtémoc is hanged, and every day the white man conquers and humiliates the Indian.' This internal tension is responsible for producing those painful 'rejection patterns' of which Ralph Beals spoke, and which quickly become apparent during any conversation with a Mexican. Mexicans tend to suffer from a form of cultural schizophrenia; one day it suits them to think and act like Spaniards, the next day like their Mexican ancestors. In Mexico, the subject of Spain is still a good one to avoid.

The tension within the soul of the Mexican was not only the product of his uneasy relationship with the Spaniard; there was also the tension created by the antipathy between Indian and *mestizo*. The *mestizo*, like his Spanish father, was a town-dweller; the Indian was an agriculturalist. The *mestizo* or *ladino* was thus ground between the upper millstone of *peninsular* and *criollo* and the lower millstone of the Indian, and was therefore forced to live by his wits. *Ladino* means sharp, cunning or crafty. The *mestizo* became the merchant, money-lender and middle-man. Even after the Liberation, the tensions between the various castes did not miraculously disappear, as the liberators had hoped, but were perpetuated, and in the decades to come were actually intensified.

The modern Mexican, in his more irritable moments, tends to blame all his country's woes on what he contemptuously calls the *gachupines*, the 'men with the spurs'. But it is obviously unfair to hold the Spaniards responsible for all the ills of Mexico. Their mark was deep and indelible, but all the fury and vigour of *conquistador* or priest could hardly have eradicated traditions and habits that had existed for three thousand years. From the time of the Olmecs to the time of the Aztecs, the Mexicans had evolved a way of life that was unique and distinctive. It could not be swept away in a mere three centuries, simply because the thin layer of a dominant class had been eliminated. Native Mexico is tenacious. As Graham Greene puts it, in *The Lawless Roads*, Mexico is 'a state of mind'. Anyone who has visited Spain and Mexico will agree that the differences in life-style between them are as notable as the similarities. In Spain the spirit of the people is lofty and assured; they have their roots in an aristocratic and imperial past whose presence is everywhere evident. In Mexico, on the other hand, one feels what D. H. Lawrence calls, in *The Plumed Serpent*, 'the dark undertone, the black, serpent-like fatality'. Everywhere there is the sensation of the 'old, heavy, resistant Indian blood', the 'passive negation of the Indian, like a weight of obsidian'. It is a country with 'two moods, of natural, soft, sensuous flow, and of heavy resentment and hate, alternating inside every man like shadow and shine on a cloudy day, in swift, unavoidable succession'.

If the Spaniards brought confusion to the Mexican personality, one feels that they were only adding to a confusion that already existed. We have produced evidence to show that, on the eve of Cortés' landing,

Mexico was a disturbed and divided country, psychologically as well as politically, and that this disturbance was an important factor in enabling the Spaniards to conquer it. The Mexicans, more than any other Latin American people, are still waging these ancient mental battles. Spaniard and Indian still contend with each other in the Mexican soul. The Mexicans do not possess the mongrel cheerfulness of the Chilians or Argentinians. They are, as they always were, a people apart.

Nonetheless, one might perhaps detect that there has been a certain softening of the old attitudes. With the improvement in education and living-standards that has resulted from the recent decades of firm government, there has come a new mood of relaxation and cautious optimism. The instinctive pessimism of the average Mexican has undergone a definite mellowing, slight but unprecedented. It is easier, in this more expansive frame of mind, to accept the Spanish heritage or to resurrect the pre-Columbian past, recognizing their virtues while making allowance for their vices. 'Neo-Aztecism' is now triumphant, but not in a strident or exaggerated way. The head of Cuauhtémoc figures, among other things, on the label of one of Mexico's excellent beers, while the head of the Eagle Knight is the device of Aeronaves de Mexico. The old, negative hatred of the *gachupín*, so wasteful of psychic energy, has also been reduced by the natural weakening of the bonds between the two countries which has been brought about by distance and by the passage of time. Just as the bonds between Britain and Australia, Canada and South Africa have grown more tenuous, so have those between Spain and the countries of her former empire. In any case, Spain as the symbol of exploiter and oppressor has long been superseded by that of America, which for a century has inflicted appalling economic damage on its neighbours to the south. This condition of economic helotry is now in turn being corrected, and when the political dust has settled the relationship between North America and Latin America will be immeasurably more healthy. Far from accepting hand-outs from the United States, Mexico now makes her own loans and gifts to other Latin American countries, and has organized her own Latin American Peace Corps. At the same time, and because she is able to make gestures of this kind, her relationship with the United States is more natural and dignified than at any time for more than a century.

Official relations between Mexico and Spain have been non-existent since the Spanish Civil War. At the time of writing, the two countries do not possess diplomatic representation with one another. One hopes that this unconstructive situation will not persist indefinitely. There is no point, in present circumstances, in keeping old wounds open and perpetuating obsolete grudges. The situation of Mexico, like that of Spain and the other European countries, is precarious. Apart from the possibility of a devastating war, the seeming economic prosperity of large portions of the globe is relative and dubious. In the case of Mexico, poverty is real and extensive, as anyone knows who has visited the country or read such studies as Oscar Lewis's *The Children of Sanchez*, an account of daily life in the *barrios* of Mexico City. Mexico's present comparative affluence—or, rather, lack of the most grinding evidences of poverty—is threatened, as elsewhere, by a frightening surge in population. One wonders whether the Catholic Church, to which the suffering people of Mexico have clung so long and with such devotion, is helping its charges by refusing to countenance family limitation. Circumstances are worsening so rapidly that bold measures will soon be called for. The Mexican population, 13 million in 1900, 25 million in 1950, has swelled to an estimated 50 million in 1970. The population of Mexico City and the Distrito Federal, 2 million in 1940, is currently estimated at 9 million. How long can such increases continue unchecked? Reduction or at least control of the steeply rising birthrate is essential. Economic models have shown that, with smaller populations, countries like Mexico would have fewer mouths to feed, fewer jobs to find, better opportunities for personal and state savings, greater use of resources for economic development, and less need to spend a high proportion of gross national product in maintaining the current *per capita* income. True, there are signs of hope. 75 per cent of the Mexican population in 1980 will be under 35 years of age. One would expect so young a population to be able to work energetically in order to provide for itself. Similarly, the prospect of mass world starvation has lost some of its terror with the introduction of new farming techniques, new fertilizers, and new high-yielding food-grains. Economists tend to believe that the potential for economic growth exceeds, fortunately, the potential for population growth. Nevertheless, if a certain amount of slack remains, the problem of global overcrowding is bound to cause concern—nowhere with more gravity than in Mexico, where according to World Bank estimates the 1968 GNP *per capita* was only U.S. $300–$600.

*　　*　　*

If Mexico and other Latin American countries no longer feel an overwhelming physical and spiritual kinship with Spain, such a kinship nonetheless exists, and is a part of Latin America's blood and bone.

At the beginning of our century, the Nicaraguan-born Rubén Darío cherished a vision of the future destiny of *la raza*. It was like the vision

Rudyard Kipling had of the destiny of the British Empire. History has extinguished such Pan-Hispanic and Anglo-Saxon enthusiasms—but the visions were noble, for all that.

The sense of what it means to be the child of Hernán Cortés and of La Malinche has never been so well expressed as in Darío's celebrated ode to Theodore Roosevelt. It breathes the fervour, poetry, and otherworldliness of the Spanish-American soul.

> Los Estados Unidos son potentes y grandes.
> Cuando ellos se estremecen hay un hondo temblor
> Que pasa por las vértebras enormes de los Andes.
>
> Mas la América nuestra, que tenía poetas
> Desde los viejos tiempos de Netzahualcoyotl,
> Que ha guardado las huellas de los pies del gran Baco,
> Que el alfabeto pánico en un tiempo aprendió;
> Que consultó los astros, que conoció la Atlántida,
> Cuyo nombre nos llega resonando en Platón,
> Que desde los remotos momentos de su vida
> Vive de luz, de fuego, de perfume, de amor;
> La América del grande Moctezuma, del Inca,
> La América fragante de Cristóbal Colón,
> La América católica, la América española,
> La América en que dijo el noble Guatemoc:
> "Yo no estoy en un lecho de rosas", esa América
> Que tiembla de huracanes y que vive de amor;
> Hombres de ojos sajones y alma bárbara, vive.
> Y sueña. Y ama, y vibra; y es la hija del Sol.
> Tened cuidado. ¡ Vive la América española!
> Hay mil cachorros sueltos del León español.
> Se necesitaría, Roosevelt, ser, por Dios mismo,
> El Riflero terrible y el fuerte Cazador,
> Para poder tenernos en vuestras férreas garras.
>
> Y, pues contáis con todo, falta una cosa: ¡Dios!

'The United States is great and potent. When it trembles, a deep shudder passes down the enormous spine of the Andes. But our own America, which has had its poets since the ancient times of Netzahualcoyotl; which preserved the footsteps of the great Bacchus and once learned the Punic alphabet; which consulted the stars and knew Atlantis, whose name has come ringing down to us in Plato; which from its earliest moments has lived in light, in fire, in perfume, and in love—the America of Moctezuma and The Inca, the fragrant America of Christopher Columbus, Catholic America, Spanish America, the America in which noble Cuauhtémoc said: "*I am not on a bed of roses*"—our America that shivers with hurricanes and shudders with love. O men with Saxon eyes and barbarous souls, our America lives! dreams! loves! shakes itself! Our America, the daughter of the sun! So take care! Long live Spanish America! A thousand cubs of the Spanish Lion are roaming abroad—and you will have to become, Roosevelt, by the will of God, the terrible Rifleman and mighty Hunter before you can catch us in your iron claws. And although you believe you have everything, one thing you lack—*God!*"

BIBLIOGRAPHY

BIBLIOGRAPHY

Lond.=London; M.C.=Mexico City; N.Y.=New York.

ALTAMIRA, M. *A History of Spain* (N.Y. 1949)

ANON. *Art of the Aztec Empire* (University of Kansas, Lawrence, 1957)

ANONYMOUS CONQUEROR *Narrative of Some Things of New Spain and the Great City of Temestitán* (N.Y., Cortés Society, 1917)

ATKINSON, William C. *A History of Spain and Portugal* (Lond. 1960)

BABGLON, Jean, *Hernán Cortés* (Madrid, 1944)

BALLESTEROS, A. (*ed.*) *Historia de América y de los pueblos americanos* (Barcelona, 1940–)

BARLOW R. H. *The Extent of the Empire of the Culhua Mexica* (Berkeley, Cal., 1949)

BERNAL, Ignacio *Tenochtitlán en una Isla* (M.C., 1959)

BERNAL, Ignacio (*ed.*) 3000 *Years of Art and Life in Mexico* (N.Y., N.D.)

BERNAL, Ignacio and SOUSTELLE, Jacques *Mexico: Pre-Hispanic Paintings* (UNESCO World Art Series, No. 10)

BLOCH, Marc *The Historian's Craft* (N.Y., 1953)

BRADEN, C. S. *Religious Aspects of the Conquest of Mexico* (Duke University, Durham, 1930)

BRENAN, Gerald, *The Spanish Labyrinth* (Cambridge, 1943).

BRENAN, Gerald *The Literature of the Spanish People* (Cambridge, 1951)

BURLAND, C. A. *Art and Life in Ancient Mexico* (Oxford, 1947)

BURLAND, C. A. *Magic Books of Mexico* (Lond., 1962)

CASAS, Bartolomé de las *Historia de las Indias* (*ed.* G. de Reparez) (Madrid, 1929)

CASO, Alfonso *La Religión de los Aztecas* (M.C., 1936)

CASO, Alfonso *El Pueblo del Sol* (M.C., 1936); *The Aztecs, People of the Sun* (Norman, Oklahoma, 1958)

CASTRO, A. *España en su historia, Cristianos, Moros y Judíos* (Buenos Aires, 1948)

CASTRO LEAD, A. (*ed*). *Twenty Centuries of Mexican Art* (M.C., 1940)

CERVANTES de Salazar *Crónica de la Nueva España* (Madrid, 1914)

CODEX MENDOZA (*ed.* J. Cooper Clark) (Lond., 1938)

CODEX VINDOBONENSIS (*ed.* Lehmann and Smital) (Vienna, 1929)

COE, Michael D. *Mexico* (London, 1962)

COLECCIÓN DE DOCUMENTOS *para la historia de México* (*ed.* J. G. Izcabalceta) M.C., 1858)

COLLIER, John *Indians of the Americas* (N.Y., 1947)

COLLIS, Maurice *Cortés and Montezuma* (Lond., 1954)

COOK, P. *Guide to Mexican Flora* (M.C., 1964)

COOK, S. F. and W. BORAH *The Indian Population of Central Mexico* (Berkeley, Cal., 1960)

CORTÉS, Hernán *Cartas y Documentos* (*ed.* M. H. Sánchez-Barba) (M.C., 1963)

CORTÉS, Hernán *Letters* (*trans.* F. A. McNutt) (N.Y., 1908)

CORTÉS, Hernán *Dispatches* (*ed.* I. R. Blacker and H.M. Rosen) (N.Y., 1962)

COVARRUBIAS, Miguel *Indian Art of Mexico and Central America* (N.Y., 1957)

CUEVAS, M. *Historia de la Iglesia en México* (M.C., 1921)

DAVIES, R. Trevor *The Golden Century of Spain*, 1501–1621 (Lond., 1954)

DÍAZ del Castillo, Bernal *True History of the Conquest of New Spain* (*ed.* and *trans.* A. P. Maudsley, Hakluyt Society, London., 1908) *trans.* J. M. Cohen, Lond., 1963)

DARÍO, Rubén *Selected Poems* (*trans.* Lysander Kemp, *prologue* by Octavio Paz) (University of Texas, Austin, 1965)

DICCIONARIO DE HISTORIA DE ESPAÑA (Madrid, 1952)

DICCIONARIO PORRÚA (M.C., 1966)

DURÁN, Fr. Diego (*Historia de las Indias* M.C., 1951)

ELLIOTT, J. H. *Imperial Spain*, 1469–1716 (Lond., 1963)

FOSTER, G. M. *Culture and Conquest: America's Spanish Heritage* (Chicago, 1960)

FRAZER, Sir James *The Golden Bough* (Lond., 1911–)

GARIBAY, Angel *Historia de la Literatura náhuatl* (M.C., 1953)

GIBSON, C. *Tlaxcala in the Sixteenth Century* (New Haven, Conn., 1952)

GIBSON, C. *The Aztecs under Spanish Rule* (Stanford, Cal., 1964)

GÓMARA, Francisco López de *Cortés: The Life of the Conqueror by his Secretary*, *trans.* and *ed.* L. B. Simpson (Berkeley, Cal., 1965)

GREENE, Graham *The Lawless Roads* (Lond., 1939)

HAGEN, Victor von *Sun Kingdom of the Aztecs* (Lond., 1960)

HAMILTON, E. J. *American Treasure and the Price Rise in Spain*, 1501–1650 (Cambridge, Mass., 1934)

HANDBOOK OF LATIN AMERICAN STUDIES (Harvard, 1936–50; Florida, 1951–)

HELPS, Sir Arthur *The Spanish Conquest in America* (Lond., 1855: N.Y. 1966)

HORGAN, Paul *Great River: The Rio Grande in American History* (N.Y., 1954)

HORGAN, Paul *Conquerors in North American History* (N.Y., 1963)

HUMBOLDT, A. *Vues des Cordillères et Monuments des Peuples Indigènes de l'Amérique* (Paris, 1810)

IXTLILXÓCHITL (Don Fernando de Alva) *Obras historicas* (*ed.* A. Chavero) (M.C., 1912); (*ed.* Douglass K. Ballentine, Texas Western Press, El Paso, 1969)

KELLY, J. W. *Pedro de Alvarado* (Princeton, 1932)

KIRKPATRICK, F. A. *The Spanish Conquistadores* (Lond., 1934; N.Y. 1946)

KROEBER, A. L. *Anthropology* (N.Y., 1948)

KUBLER, George *The Art and Architecture of Ancient America* (Lond., 1962)

LAS CASAS, Bartolomé *see* CASAS

LAWRENCE, D. H. *The Plumed Serpent* (N.Y., 1926)

LEON-PORTILLO, Miguel *El Reverso de la Conquista, Relaciones Aztecas, Mayas y Incas* (M.C., 1964)

LÉVY-BRUHL, Lucien *Primitives and the Supernatural* (N.Y., 1935)

LINTON, Ralph *The Tree of Culture* (N.Y., 1956)

LÓPEZ de Gómara *see* GÓMARA

LYNCH, John *Spain under the Habsburgs* (Oxford, 1964)

McHENRY, J. Patrick *A Short History of Mexico* (N.Y., 1962)

McNUTT, F. A. *Fernando Cortés and the Conquest of Mexico* (N.Y., 1907)

MADARIAGA, Salvador de *The Rise and Fall of the Spanish American Empire* (Lond., 1947)

MADARIAGA, Salvador de *Spain, A Modern History* (N.Y., 1958)

MADARIAGA, Salvador de *Hernán Cortés: Conqueror of Mexico* (University of Miami, 1962)

MARQUINA, Ignacio *Arquitectura Prehispánica* (M.C., 1951)

MARTIN, M. R. and LOVETT, G. H. *An Encyclopaedia of Latin American History* (N.Y., 1956)

MENÉNDEZ PIDAL, R. *The Cid and His Spain* (Lond., 1934)

MENÉNDEZ PIDAL, R. *Historia de España* (Madrid, 1935–)

MERRIMAN, R. B. *The Rise of the Spanish Empire in the Old World and the New* (N.Y., 1918–25)

MOTOLINÍA (Fr. Toribio de Benevente) *Historia de las Indias de la Nueva España* (*ed.* D. Sánchez García, Barcelona, 1914) (*trans.* F. H. Steck, Washington, D.C., 1951)

338   BIBLIOGRAPHY

OBREGÓN, Luis González *Cuauhtémoc* (M.C., 1955)
D'OLWER, Luis Nicolau *Fray Bernardino de Sahagún* (M.C. 1952)
ORTEGA y Gasset, José *Man and Crisis* (N.Y., 1958)
OVIEDO y Valdéz, G. F. *Historia general y natural de las Indias* (Madrid, 1851)

PARKES, Henry B. *History of Mexico* (N.Y. 1938: 1950: Lond. 1962)
PARRY, J. H. *The Spanish Theory of Empire in the Sixteenth Century* (Cambridge, 1940)
PARRY, J. H. *The Age of Reconnaissance* (N.Y., 1963)
PARRY, J. H. *The Spanish Seaborne Empire* (London. and N.Y., 1966)
PAZ, Octavio *The Labyrinth of Solitude* (*trans.* Lysander Kemp) (Lond., 1967)
PENDLE, George *A History of Latin America* (Lond., 1963)
PEREYRA, Carlos *Hernán Cortés* (Madrid, 1931: M.C., 1946)
PETERSON, Frederick *Ancient Mexico* (N.Y., 1959)
PHELAN, John Leddy *Neo-Aztecism in the Eighteenth Century and the Rise of Mexican Nationalism*, in *Culture and History, Essays in Honor of Paul Radin* (N.Y. 1960)
PRESCOTT, W. H. *History of the Conquest of Mexico* (N.Y. 1843; many later editions)
PRITCHETT, V. S. *The Spanish Temper* (Lond. 1954)

RICARD, R. *La conquète spirituelle du Mexique* (Paris, 1933)

SAHAGÚN, Fr. Bernardino de *Historia general de las cosas de Nueva España* (ed. W. Jiménez Moreno, M.C., 1938) (*ed.* Angel Garibay, M.C., 1956) (*trans.* and *ed.* Anderson and Dibble, Santa Fe, New Mexico, 1950–)
SALAZAR *see* CERVANTES de Salazar
SÁNCHEZ ALONSO, B. *Fuentes de la historia española y hispano-americana* (Madrid, 1952)
SÉJOURNÉ, Laurette *Burning Water: Thought and Religion in Ancient Mexico* (N.Y., 1957)
SIMPSON, L. B. *The Encomienda in New Spain* (Berkeley, Cal., 1950)
SIMPSON, L. B. *Many Mexicos* (Berkeley, Cal., 1959)
SOUSTELLE, Jacques *La pensée cosmologique des anciens Mexicains* (Paris, 1940)
SOUSTELLE, Jacques *La Vie quotidienne des Aztèques* (Paris, 1955; London., 1961)

TAX, Sol (*ed.*) *Heritage of Conquest: The Ethnology of Middle America* (Free Press, Glencoe, Ill., 1952)
TERRY, T. Philip *Guide to Mexico* (*rev.* James Norman, N.Y., 1965)
THOMPSON, J. Eric *Mexico Before Cortés* (N.Y., 1933)

TLAXCALA, El Lienzo de (M.C., 1892)

TOYNBEE, Arnold *A Study of History*, Vol. XII (*Reconsiderations*) (O.U.P., 1961)

TOYNBEE, Arnold *Change and Habit* (O.U.P., 1966)

VAILLANT, George C. *Aztecs of Mexico* (N.Y., 1944, 1962; Lond., 1965)

VASCONCELOS, José *Breve Historia de Mexico* (M.C., 1944)

VASCONCELOS, José *Hernán Cortés, Creador de la Nacionalidad* (M.C., 1944).

VICENS VIVES, J. (*ed.*) *Historia social y economica de España y América* (Barcelona, 1957-)

WAGNER, H. R. *The Rise of Fernando Cortés* (Berkeley, Cal., Cortes Society, 1944)

WOLF, Eric R. *Sons of the Shaking Earth* (Chicago, 1959)

WRIGHT, L. A. *The Early History of Cuba*, 1492–1586 (N.Y., 1916)

ACKNOWLEDGMENTS

Acknowledgments are due to the following for permission to quote passages from published books: George Allen & Unwin Ltd for Ortega y Gasset's *Man and Crisis* and for Frederick Peterson's *Ancient Mexico*; Basil Blackwell for John Lynch's *Spain under the Habsburgs*; Cambridge University Press for Gerald Brenan's *The Literature of the Spanish People;* Chatto & Windus Ltd. for V. S. Pritchett's *The Spanish Temper*; Doubleday & Company Inc. for J. P. McHenry's *A Short History of Mexico*; the Free Press, Glencoe, Illinois for *The Heritage of Conquest*, edited by Sol Tax; Dutton & Company Inc. for Lucien Lévy-Bruhl's *Primitives and the Supernatural*; Grosset & Dunlap Inc. for Irwin C. Blacker and Harry M. Rosen's *Conquest: Dispatches of Cortéz from the New World;* Grove Press Inc. for Octavio Paz's *The Labyrinth of Solitude*; Harcourt, Brace & World Inc. for A. L. Kroeber's *Anthropology*; The Hogarth Press Ltd., Sigmund Freud Copyrights Ltd and the Institute of Psycho-Analysis for *Why War?* in Volume XXII of the Standard Edition of the Complete Psychological Works of Sigmund Freud, revised and edited by James Strachey; Hutchinson Publishing Group Ltd. for J. H. Parry's *The Spanish Seaborne Empire*; Macmillan & Co. Ltd. for Sir James Frazer's *The Golden Bough* and for Thomas Hardy's *The Convergence of the Twain* from *Selected Poems of Thomas Hardy* by permission of the Hardy Estate (the latter in conjunction with the Macmillan Company of Canada); William Morris Agency Inc. for James Michener's *Iberia;* Oxford University Press for A. J. Toynbee's *A Study of History*; Penguin Books Ltd. for William C. Atkinson's *A History of Spain and Portugal* and for J. M. Cohen's translation of Diaz's *The Conquest of New Spain*; Thames & Hudson Ltd. for M. D. Coe's *Mexico* and for Laurette Séjourné's *Burning Water*; University of California Press for Leslie Bird Simpson's translation of *Cortés: The Life of the Conqueror by His Secretary*; University of Texas Press for Ruben Dario's *Selected Poems*; A. P. Watt Ltd., the author and The Bodley Head Ltd. for Salvador de Madariaga's *Hernán Cortés*; and George Weidenfeld & Nicolson Ltd. for Jacques Soustelle's *The Daily Life of the Aztecs.*

INDEX

Index

FINE WORKS OF NON-FICTION AVAILABLE IN QUALITY PAPERBACK EDITIONS FROM CARROLL & GRAF

- [ ] Anderson, Nancy/WORK WITH PASSION $8.95
- [ ] Arlett, Robert/THE PIZZA GOURMET $10.95
- [ ] Asprey, Robert/THE PANTHER'S FEAST $9.95
- [ ] Bedford, Sybille/ALDOUS HUXLEY $14.95
- [ ] Berton, Pierre/KLONDIKE FEVER $10.95
- [ ] Blake, Robert/DISRAELI $14.50
- [ ] Blanch, Lesley/PIERRE LOTI $10.95
- [ ] Blanch, Lesley/THE WILDER SHORES OF LOVE $8.95
- [ ] Buchan, John/PILGRIM'S WAY $10.95
- [ ] Carr, John Dickson/THE LIFE OF SIR ARTHUR CONAN DOYLE $8.95
- [ ] Carr, Virginia Spencer/THE LONELY HUNTER: A BIOGRAPHY OF CARSON McCULLERS $12.95
- [ ] Conot, Robert/JUSTICE AT NUREMBURG $11.95
- [ ] Cooper, Duff/OLD MEN FORGET $10.95
- [ ] Cooper, Lady Diana/AUTOBIOGRAPHY $12.95
- [ ] Edwards, Anne/SONYA: THE LIFE OF COUNTESS TOLSTOY $8.95
- [ ] Elkington, John/THE GENE FACTORY $8.95
- [ ] Farson, Negley/THE WAY OF A TRANSGRESSOR $9.95
- [ ] Gill, Brendan/HERE AT THE NEW YORKER $12.95
- [ ] Goldin, Stephen & Sky, Kathleen/THE BUSINESS OF BEING A WRITER $8.95
- [ ] Haycraft, Howard (ed.)/THE ART OF THE MYSTERY STORY $9.95
- [ ] Harris, A./SEXUAL EXERCISES FOR WOMEN $8.95
- [ ] Hook, Sidney/OUT OF STEP $14.95
- [ ] Keating, H. R. F./CRIME & MYSTERY: THE 100 BEST BOOKS $7.95
- [ ] Lansing, Alfred/ENDURANCE: SHACKLETON'S INCREDIBLE VOYAGE $8.95
- [ ] Leech, Margaret/REVEILLE IN WASHINGTON $11.95

☐ Lifton, David S./BEST EVIDENCE $10.95
☐ McCarthy, Barry/MALE SEXUAL AWARENESS $9.95
☐ McCarthy, Barry & Emily/SEXUAL AWARENESS $9.95
☐ Mizener, Arthur/THE SADDEST STORY: A
 BIOGRAPHY OF FORD MADOX FORD $12.95
☐ Moorehead, Alan/THE RUSSIAN REVOLUTION $10.95
☐ Mullins, Edwin/THE PAINTED WITCH Cloth $25.00
☐ Munthe, Axel/THE STORY OF SAN MICHELE $8.95
☐ O'Casey, Sean/AUTOBIOGRAPHIES I $10.95
☐ O'Casey, Sean/AUTOBIOGRAPHIES II $10.95
☐ Poncins, Gontran de/KABLOONA $9.95
☐ Pringle, David/SCIENCE FICTION: THE 100 BEST
 NOVELS $7.95
☐ Proust, Marcel/ON ART AND LITERATURE $8.95
☐ Richelson, Hildy & Stan/INCOME WITHOUT
 TAXES $9.95
☐ Roy, Jules/THE BATTLE OF DIENBIENPHU $8.95
☐ Russel, Robert A./WINNING THE FUTURE Cloth $16.95
☐ Salisbury, Harrison/A JOURNEY OF OUR TIMES $10.95
☐ Scott, Evelyn/ESCAPADE $9.95
☐ Sloan, Allan/THREE PLUS ONE EQUALS
 BILLIONS $8.95
☐ Taylor, Telford/MUNICH $17.95
☐ Werth, Alexander/RUSSIA AT WAR: 1941–1945 $15.95
☐ Wilmot, Chester/STRUGGLE FOR EUROPE $12.95
☐ Wilson, Colin/THE MAMMOTH BOOK OF TRUE
 CRIME $8.95
☐ Zuckmayer, Carl/A PART OF MYSELF $9.95

Available from fine bookstores everywhere or use this coupon for ordering:

Caroll & Graf Publishers, Inc., 260 Fifth Avenue, N.Y., N.Y. 10001

Please send me the books I have checked above. I am enclosing
$_____ (please add $1.75 per title to cover postage and
handling.) Send check or money order—no cash or C.O.D.'s please.
N.Y. residents please add 8¼% sales tax.

Mr/Mrs/Miss _____

Address _____

City _____ State/Zip _____
Please allow four to six weeks for delivery.